APPLIED CRIMINAL PSYCHOLOGY

ABOUT THE EDITOR

Richard N. Kocsis, Ph.D., is a forensic psychologist in private practice. He is the author/coauthor of close to 90 scholarly publications (articles, book chapters, etc.) on the topics of criminal profiling, serial violent offenders, and their investigation. He has served as an expert consultant to law enforcement, emergency, and prosecution agencies as well as to law firms. In addition to his clinical and forensic work, he has held various academic positions in the areas of forensic psychology and criminology. In 2000, he was awarded the Australian Museum's prestigious *Eureka* prize for critical thinking in recognition of his scientific research in the area of criminal profiling.

APPLIED CRIMINAL PSYCHOLOGY

A Guide to Forensic Behavioral Sciences

Edited by

RICHARD N. KOCSIS, PH.D.

CHARLES C THOMAS • PUBLISHER, LTD.
Springfield • Illinois • U.S.A.

Published and Distributed Throughout the World by

CHARLES C THOMAS • PUBLISHER, LTD.
2600 South First Street
Springfield, Illinois 62704

©2009 by CHARLES C THOMAS • PUBLISHER, LTD.

ISBN 978-0-398-07842-3 (hard)
ISBN 978-0-398-07843-0 (paper)

Library of Congress Catalog Card Number: 2008035459

Printed in the United States of America
LAH-R-3

Library of Congress Cataloging-in-Publication Data

Applied criminal psychology : a guide to forensic behavioral sciences
/ edited by Richard N. Kocsis
    p. cm.
Includes bibliographical references and index.
ISBN 978-0-398-07842-3 (hard) -- ISBN 978-0-398-07843-0 (paper)
1. Criminal psychology. I. Kocsis, Richard N
HV6080.A69 2009
364.0--dc22

                                        2008035459

Anyukám,
Ebben az életben mindenemet neked köszönhetem

CONTRIBUTORS

Justin S. Albrechtsen

Justin S. Albrechtsen is a Ph.D. candidate in the Legal Psychology Doctoral Program at the University of Texas at El Paso. He is currently investigating the underlying cognitive processes involved in detecting deception and in the study of alibis, including their production and assessment in a legal context.

Coral Dando

Doctor Coral Dando, BSc (Hons), Ph.D., is a Research Associate at the University of Leicester, United Kingdom and is currently conducting research aimed at assisting the process of investigating criminal and terrorist activity. She is also a tutor at London South Bank University, teaching Investigative Forensic Psychology. Prior to commencing an academic career, Coral served as a Police Officer with the Metropolitan Police Service London where her primary duties involved conducting investigative interviews with both the victims and the perpetrators of serious sexual offences. Coral has both a first degree and a Ph.D. in Psychology. Her Ph.D. research falls into the domain of Forensic and Investigative Psychology but draws on the theoretical aspects of memory and cognition with an applied focus.

Pär Anders Granhag

Pär Anders Granhag is Professor of Psychology at Göteborg University. He has conducted research within legal psychology for more than 15 years and has published more than 130 scientific reports and several books. His main research topics are eyewitness testimony, deception detection, and issues pertaining to investigative psychology. He is on the editorial board of the following scientific journals: *Applied Cognitive Psychology*; *Psychology, Crime & Law*; *Legal & Criminological Psychology*; and *Journal of Investigative Psychology & Offender Profiling*. Since 2000 he has been the head of the research unit for Criminal, Legal, and Investigative Psychology (CLIP), which is situated at the Department of Psychology, Göteborg University.

James S. Herndon

Doctor James S. Herndon has been a police psychologist for more than twenty years. He served as the Staff Psychologist for the Orange County (Florida) Sheriff's Office from 1992 to 2002. In that capacity, he was a member of the Crisis Negotiation Team and responded to more than 100 calls involving barricaded subjects and hostage situations. Prior to that, he was the Executive Director of Police Psychological Services of Hampton Roads, Inc. in Virginia, and in that capacity provided assistance to 14 law enforcement agencies, including crisis intervention advice and training. He has been trained by the FBI and other law enforcement organizations in the techniques of Crisis Negotiation. He is a past president of the Council of Police Psychological Services (COPPS), as well as a past president of the Society for Police and Criminal Psychology (SPCP). He holds a Diplomate in police psychology from SPCP and is the Chair of the Diplomate Committee. He serves on the editorial board of the Journal of Police and Criminal Psychology. Additionally, he holds Diplomate status from the American College of Forensic Examiners. He currently consults with law enforcement agencies on organizational and operational issues and serves as an adjunct professor at four colleges and universities in Florida. His Ph.D. is in industrial/organizational psychology from Old Dominion University, and his Ed.D. is in counseling psychology from the University of Sarasota.

Allyson J. Horgan

Allyson J. Horgan is a Ph.D. candidate in the Legal Psychology Doctoral Program at the University of Texas at El Paso. Her research interests include false confessions, interrogation techniques, and the evaluation of alibis.

Andreas (Andros) Kapardis

Andreas (Andros) Kapardis is Professor of Legal Psychology and Acting Chairman of the Department of Law, University of Cyprus. He has a Ph.D. in Criminology from Cambridge University and for a number of years taught in the Law and Legal Studies Department of La Trobe University. He also teaches forensic psychology at the Cyprus Police Academy. Since 1995, he has also been teaching as a part of the Masters in Criminology program at Cambridge University. His research interests center around criminology, penology, and legal psychology. He has published extensively internationally, and his books include *Psychology and Law* (2nd edition, Cambridge University Press, 2003); *Sentencing by English Magistrates as a Human Process* (1985); *They Wrought Mayhem: an Insight into Mass Murder* (River Seine Press, Melbourne, 1989); *Sentencing in Cyprus* (Sakkoulas Press, Athens, 2003); *Economic Crimes in Cyprus* (Sakkoulas Press, 2001) and *Society, Crime and Criminal Justice in Cyprus in the First Years of British Rule* (Sakkoulas Press, 2001).

Cara Laney

Cara Laney is a lecturer of Forensic Psychology at the University of Leicester in the United Kingdom. She received her Ph.D. in Psychology and Social Behavior from the University of California, Irvine in 2006. She has conducted research in various aspects of memory, including false memory, and the interaction between emotion and memory.

Elizabeth F. Loftus

Elizabeth F. Loftus is Distinguished Professor at the University of California - Irvine. She holds faculty positions both in Criminology, Law & Society and in Psychology and Social Behavior. She is also Professor of Law. She received her Ph.D. in Psychology from Stanford University. Since then, she has published 20 books and more than 400 scientific articles. Loftus' research for the last 30 years has focused on the malleability of human memory. She has been recognized for this research with five honorary doctorates and election to the National Academy of Sciences, the American Philosophical Society, and the Royal Society of Edinburgh. She is past president of the Association for Psychological Science, the Western Psychological Association, and the American Psychology-Law Society.

Christian A. Meissner

Christian A. Meissner is Associate Professor of Psychology & Criminal Justice at the University of Texas at El Paso. He holds a Ph.D. in Cognitive & Behavioral Science from Florida State University (2001) and conducts empirical studies on the psychological processes underlying investigative interviews, including issues surrounding eyewitness recall and identification, deception detection, and interrogations and confessions. He has published more than 35 peer-reviewed journal articles and book chapters, and he has been funded by both the National Science Foundation and the U.S. Department of Defense. Because of his research, Dr. Meissner has also served as a consultant and expert witness on issues of eyewitness misidentification and false confession in numerous state and federal courts in the United States.

Rebecca Milne

Doctor Rebecca Milne, BSc (Hons), Ph.D. in Criminal Psychology & Criminal Science is a Principal Lecturer at the Institute of Criminal Justice Studies at the University of Portsmouth. She is the course leader of the FdA Investigation and Evidence, a distance learning degree program specifically for investigators. A chartered forensic psychologist and scientist and Associate Fellow of the British Psychological Society, she is an Associate Editor of the *International Journal of Police Science and Management* and is the academic lead member of the Association of Chief Police Officers' Investigative Interviewing Strategic Steering Group. She has worked closely with the police and other criminal justice organizations (in the United Kingdom and abroad) through training of the enhanced cognitive interview, and witness interview advising and also in the interviewing of vulnerable groups (Tier 3 and 5) and providing case advice. Recently Rebecca was part of a writing team that developed the Achieving Best Evidence Document (Home Office, 2007), and national guidance regarding how best to interview vulnerable and intimidated witnesses and victims and she co-organized the Second International Conference on Investigative Interviewing that took place in Portsmouth in July 2006.

Alan Newman

Alan Newman, M.D., is an Associate Professor of Clinical Psychiatry at Georgetown University Medical School, where he is Director of Residency Training and Codirector of the Fellowship in Forensic Psychiatry. He is the Medical Director of the inpatient psychiatry service at Georgetown University Hospital. He is the former director of the Fellowship in Forensic Neuropsychiatry at Tulane University. He is board certified in Psychiatry and Forensic Psychiatry. Dr. Newman attended medical school and residency at the University of Arkansas, where he was elected to Alpha Omega Alpha. Dr. Newman was a 1996 Rappeport Fellow of the American Academy of Psychiatry and the Law and the 1997 Daniel X. Freedman Congressional Fellow, where he served on the Health Staff of the U.S. Senate Committee on Labor and Human Resources. He completed his Fellowship in Forensic Neuropsychiatry at Tulane University in 1998. He is the former chair of a 1999 Insanity Defense reform taskforce in Arkansas, which led to substantial legislative changes in how criminal responsibility and trial competency evaluations are administered in Arkansas. Dr. Newman lectures extensively on forensic issues and has published articles and book chapters on a variety of forensic psychiatry topics, including cyberstalking, the misuse of hypnosis by police, admissibility of hypnotically refreshed testimony, and the treatment of stalking victims. Dr. Newman is a member of the Executive Council of the American Academy of Psychiatry and the Law. He is the former president of the Southern Chapter of American Academy of Psychiatry and the Law.

George B. Palermo

Dr. George B. Palermo graduated from the University of Bologna Medical School, Bologna, Italy, and was trained in general medicine and psychiatry in the United States. He is a Diplomate of the American Board of Psychiatry and Neurology in Psychiatry and a Fellow of the American Board of Forensic Examiners and a Diplomate of Forensic Medicine. In 2004 he received a Master of Science Degree in Criminology from the University of Rome, La Sapienza. He is presently Clinical Professor of Psychiatry at the University of Nevada Medical School and at the Medical College of Wisconsin and Professor Adjunct of Criminology and Law Studies at Marquette University in Milwaukee, Wisconsin. Dr. Palermo is Editor-in-Chief of the *International Journal of Offender Therapy and Comparative Criminology* and is a member of the Executive Board of the International Academy of Law and Mental Health. In addition, he is on the review boards of various national and international psychiatric and criminology journals. He has published numerous articles and book chapters on forensic psychiatry and criminology as well as several books. Dr. Palermo operates a private practice of forensic psychiatry, with offices in Milwaukee, Wisconsin, and Henderson, Nevada. He was the court-appointed psychiatrist in the case of the serial killer Jeffrey Dahmer and in various other high-profile criminal cases.

Georgia Panayiotou

Georgia Panayiotou is an Assistant Professor in the Psychology Department, University of Cyprus. She holds a Ph.D. in Clinical Psychology from Purdue University and has taught at Mississippi State University. Her research interests are emotional processes in antisocial behavior, anxiety and affective disorders, emotional and cognitive processes in psychopathology, and the psychophysiology of emotion and cognition. She has published extensively in international journals.

Phillip J. Resnick

Dr. Resnick is a Professor of Psychiatry and Director of the Division of Forensic Psychiatry at Case School of Medicine in Cleveland, Ohio. Dr. Resnick has served as a consultant in many high-profile cases, including those of Jeffrey Dahmer; Susan Smith; Timothy McVeigh; Andrea Yates; Scott Peterson; William Kennedy Smith; and Theodore Kaczynski, the Unabomber. Dr. Resnick has served as President of the American Academy of Psychiatry and the Law. He has published more than 130 articles and book chapters.

Charles L. Scott

Charles L. Scott, M.D., is Chief of the Division of Psychiatry and the Law, Forensic Psychiatry Training Director, and Associate Clinical Professor of Psychiatry at the University of California, Davis. He is board certified in general psychiatry, child and adolescent psychiatry, addiction psychiatry, and forensic psychiatry. He is a member of the American Academy of Psychiatry and the Law (AAPL), a national task-force to develop guidelines for the evaluation of criminal responsibility and insanity. Dr. Scott is also the AAPL Forensic Psychiatry Review Course faculty instructor for psychiatry and the death penalty. He has served as a forensic psychiatric consultant to jails, prisons, and maximum security forensic inpatient units and to the National Football League (NFL), providing training on violence risk assessment for NFL counselors. Dr. Scott has published articles and book chapters in the areas of risk assessment of violence and aggression, the death penalty, juvenile violence, and mental health law. He has coauthored book chapters on child psychiatry and the assessment of dangerousness. His research interests include the relationship of substance use to aggression among mentally disordered offenders. He was first editor of *The Handbook of Correctional Mental Health*, from American Psychiatric Publishing, Inc., and was guest editor for the September 2006 edition of the Psychiatric Clinics of North America devoted specifically to forensic psychiatry. Dr. Scott is a member of the California Judicial Action Committee and is a counselor for AAPL. He lectures nationally on the topics of violence risk assessment, juvenile violence, substance use and violence, the assessment of sex offenders, correctional psychiatry, and malpractice issues in mental health. His academic subspecialty is child forensic psychiatry. He is a graduate of Emory University School of Medicine.

Leif A. Strömwall

Leif A. Strömwall is an Associate Professor at the Department of Psychology, Göteborg University, Sweden. He has published on topics such as deception detection in general, police interrogations, verbal correlates of deception, and adults' ability to detect children's lies. He, with collaborators and alone, has received funding for several research grants. He has furthermore developed courses in legal and investigative psychology for graduate and undergraduate students and regularly instructs legal professionals such as prosecutors and police investigators in legal and investigative psychological matters.

John W. Thompson, Jr.

John W. Thompson, Jr., received his medical degree at the University of Texas Medical Branch in Galveston, Texas. He completed psychiatry residency training and a forensic psychiatry fellowship at the University of Florida College of Medicine in Gainesville, Florida. He is board certified in psychiatry with added qualifications in forensic psychiatry and addiction psychiatry. He is presently the Director of Forensic Neuropsychiatry and Vice-Chairman of Adult Psychiatry in the Department of Psychiatry and Neurology at Tulane University School of Medicine in New Orleans. In addition, Dr. Thompson is the Founding Director of the Tulane Fellowship in Forensic Psychiatry and is Clinical Director of Eastern Louisiana Mental Health System, a 500-bed civil and forensic hospital system in Louisiana. Dr. Thompson's major research interests include the fields of competency restoration, gambling, aggression and violent behavior, and the insanity defense.

Hjalmar J. C. van Marle

Hjalmar J. C. van Marle is Professor of Forensic Psychiatry at the Erasmus Medical Center and the School of Law of the Erasmus University in Rotterdam, The Netherlands. He is also the scientific adviser of the Center of Expertise for Forensic Psychiatry in Utrecht and a sworn expert witness. As a forensic psychiatrist, he works in the outpatient clinic Het Dok in Rotterdam.

FOREWORD

I am delighted to welcome this new book on forensic aspects of psychology, psychiatry, and behavioral sciences. The volume is introductory and wide-ranging and provides valuable information about many key forensic issues, including personality disorders, risk assessment, the forensic psychologist as an expert witness, detecting deception, eyewitness memory, cognitive interviewing, forensic hypnosis, false confessions, criminal profiling, and crisis negotiation. These are all topics in which psychologists and other behavioral scientists have made great contributions. The book is international and interdisciplinary in its scope and focus. It should be of great interest to both scholars and practitioners and indeed is highly relevant to forensic practice.

The editor, Richard Kocsis, is well-known, especially for his contributions to criminal profiling. His book Criminal Profiling: Principles and Practice (Humana Press, 2006) contains a valuable compendium of knowledge about profiling and presents his own theory of "Crime Action Profiling." Many of the contributors to this book are also well-known scholars or practitioners. All of them have useful information to impart.

Forensic psychology is a booming subject. Every year, there is a greater appreciation of the contributions of psychology to understanding and working with offenders, victims, and witnesses in prisons, hospitals, courts, and police settings. Conse-quently, the need for trained scholars and practitioners in forensic behavioral sciences grows every year, and their work is increasingly valued by government agencies. In the United Kingdom, the number of psychologists employed by the prison service more than doubled in the early years of this century. This book should be of great interest to students who are planning careers in forensic psychology, criminology, and policing.

In the view of the general public and the mass media, forensic psychology seems to be dominated by criminal profiling. This book shows that criminal profiling, while extremely important, is only one of many topics that are included within forensic behavioral sciences. The real contribution of applied criminal psychology is in applying scientific methods and scientific knowledge to problems involving human behavior and human decision-making. The work of psychologists should contribute greatly in reducing the prevalence of many troubling social problems, including crime and violence. This book is an excellent showcase of the contributions of those who apply criminal psychology methods.

David P. Farrington

Professor of Psychological Criminology,
Cambridge University

PREFACE

The human race has held an almost primordial interest in seeking to fathom the psyche of those within our societies who commit crime. Although scholars from a variety of disciplines have contemplated this issue over the centuries, only recently has a dedicated focus begun to emerge on the issue of crime from the discipline of psychology. Distinct from the care provided by psychiatrists and psychologists to the mentally ill who have perpetrated crimes or the various mental state evaluations of individuals (Melton, Petrila, Poythress & Slobogin, 2007; Rogers & Shuman, 2000) for the purpose of court/legal proceedings,[1] the application of psychology in the context of crime, its perpetration and investigation, is a comparatively recent development. In this sense, much has been developed in the past few decades in terms of our knowledge about the many manifestations of crime.

In contemplating the application of psychology in the context of crime and the criminal justice system, it occurred to me that no one text seemed to encapsulate the spectrum of topics that can be conceptualized as criminal psychology. There seemed to be a range of fine books available on discrete topics such as the reliability of eyewitness memories, the detection of deception, and even hostage negotiation. What appeared to be absent however was a text that cohesively drew together the diverse topics comprising this area of criminal psychology. With this apparent paucity in the scholarly literature, I decided to embark upon the production of the book.

However, in setting out to produce this text on the growing area of criminal psychology I did not want to simply try and offer my summary and interpretation of the existing and quite sophisticated literature. Rather, I wanted to identify what I saw as the key topic areas and enlist the aid of experts in those respective topics to write the best possible overview for the uninitiated reader.

The result is this book, which comprises three core components. The first

---

1. *The Oxford English Dictionary* (1970, p. 438) defines the word forensic as "pertaining to, connected with, or used in courts of law" and is derived from the Latin word *forensis*, which translates as relating to the forum. In ancient Rome, the forum was the legal structure of the civilization analogous to courts encountered in contemporary western common law jurisdictions (Jolowicz & Nicholas, 1972). Thus, the application of a body of disciplinary knowledge using the prefix forensic is typically in reference to the application of such knowledge or expertise in the context of the courts and legal proceedings.

part examines the various forms of mental disorder and their relationship or manifestation in criminal behavior. Additionally, within this section is some discussion on the role and input of both psychologists and psychiatrists in examining that interface. The second part of the book focuses on the key areas of deceit, eyewitness memory and confessions; the third and final part of the book is dedicated to examining the application of psychology in terms of investigating or responding to crime.

Consequently, the opening chapters focus on human psychopathologies and how they manifest themselves in crime. The first chapter examines the not always clear interplay between mental disorder and criminal behavior as well as typical DSM Axis I disorders associated with criminal behavior. Chapter Two then provides an overview of the DSM Axis II or personality disorders and their specific relevance to criminal behavior. In the third chapter, the role and assessment techniques employed by psychologists and psychiatrists and their application in the criminal justice context are discussed. These issues are discussed by reference to Western based case law from various countries, including the United States of America, the United Kingdom, Canada, Australia, and New Zealand. Chapter Four then examines one of the key applications of criminal psychology (excluding traditional forensic psychological evaluations such as competency or insanity) in the assessment of dangerousness, and thus the evaluation of risk in a potentially diverse range of contexts.

The second part of the book is concerned with the detection of deceit in assessing the guilt or otherwise of individuals and in judging the veracity of what suspects and witnesses assert. The reliability of eyewitness memory is explored: how reliable is human memory, for instance, in circumstances of stress, illness, or trauma? The psychology of interviewing witnesses for the purpose of extracting statements is also examined, along with the fallibility of memory and techniques for enhancing memory in the form of cognitive interviewing. This part of the book also discusses the technique of hypnosis, not within the traditional context as a psychotherapeutic tool, however, but in the sense of whether it has application in an investigative context to improve eyewitness memory. Finally, the last chapter of this section deals with another rapidly developing field of study – the phenomenon of false confessions. In investigating crimes, circumstances can be created whereby people falsely confess to crimes. The complexity of the reasons for this phenomenon is discussed in detail.

The third and final part of the book deals with topics related to the application of psychology in the context of responding to and investigating crimes. Thus, the technique of criminal profiling and the capacity to examine exhibited crime behaviors for the purpose of identifying probable characteristics of the likely perpetrator of the crime is explored. Following on from criminal profiling is the perhaps lesser-known technique of psychological autopsy, wherein psychology is applied to the evaluation of equivocal deaths as in the context of coroners' inquiries to ascertain the purpose or motive(s) underlying a suspicious death. Was the death the result of suicide, murder, accident, or some natural cause? The final and concluding chapter to the book examines the topic of crisis negotiation and when individuals such as psychologists, psychiatrists, or law enforcement personnel assume a highly specialized communicative role in attempting to foster a desired outcome in various crisis situations. Examples range from the release of hostages in kidnapping or siege contexts through to communicating with individuals who have barricaded themselves in an area. Negotiation techniques in such situations are intended to encourage a peaceful resolution of a siege situation in place of a forced incursion by law enforcement to extract the individual and thus end the siege.

It has been a great pleasure for me to produce this book and an immense honor to be able to secure the cooperation of such an esteemed collection of scholars for this project. I have learned a great deal in the process, and I only hope that the reader derives the same amount of satisfaction and enjoyment in reading the final text as I have had in gathering together the material.

R.N.K.

REFERENCES

Jolowicz, H.F., and Nicholas, B. (1972). *Historical introduction to the study of Roman law.* Cambridge: Cambridge University Press.

Melton, G.B., Petrila, J., Poythress, N.G., and Slobogin, C. (2007). *Psychological evaluations for the courts: A handbook for mental health professionals and lawyers* (3rd ed.). New York: Guilford Press.

Rogers, R., and Shuman, D.W. (2000). *Conducting insanity evaluations* (2nd ed.). New York: Guilford Press.

CONTENTS

PART C: INVESTIGATING OR RESPONDING TO CRIME

APPLIED CRIMINAL PSYCHOLOGY

Part A
CRIMINAL BEHAVIOR AND MENTAL DISORDER

Chapter One

MENTAL DISORDERS AND CRIMINAL BEHAVIOR

Hjalmar van Marle

In the criminal court, forensic psychiatrists and psychologists are sometimes called upon as expert witnesses to answer questions relating to responsibility for a crime, dangerousness for reoffending (i.e. risk-assessment), and treatment for the prevention of reoffending given the presence of a mental disorder. The main purpose is to describe the connection, if any, between the presence of any mental disorder and the criminal behavior of the accused to enable a judgment to be made about the offender in court.

Forensic psychiatry entails both a medical and psychiatric/psychological assessment of the individual within a legal context. "Forensic" means that accumulated medical and psychological knowledge is interpreted according to the law in an explanation of the individual under examination (Rogers & Shuman, 2005). The results of the person's examination are interpreted in terms of the relevant law so that legal questions can be answered.

Forensic psychiatry has as its paradigm the biopsychosocial model (Engel, 1980), which is an interpretive philosophy and research model of a person as a unity of different levels of functioning – molecular, cellular, biological, psychological, and social – and leads to different forms of psychiatric and psychological treatment. The question of why one person develops one disorder but not another, or no disorder at all, is an important question in medicine. It leads researchers not only toward disease-promoting factors but also to "resilience", the often-unknown factors, that prevent illness. For contemporary psychiatry, it is biological research into neurological (i.e. brain) activity that strives to answer why some people develop a mental disorder but others do not. Personal and social factors should not be underestimated because their impact on criminal behavior is essential and determinative. The effect of psychological and social factors on the functioning of our brain is the central question, because it is the seat of our actions. For forensic psychiatry, a key question is which patient becomes an offender and which offender becomes a patient (van Marle, 1996) and what was first, the proclivity toward crime or the mental disorder (Goethals, Fabri, Buitelaar & van Marle, 2007). There are many disturbed mental patients and a number of offenders, but the forensic behavioral sciences concern themselves with the combination "mad and bad" and "disorder and offense" coming together in one person. Forensic psychiatrists/psychologists judge the person in the totality of these aspects and offer their professional opinion about that person.

Questions typically posed to forensic psychiatrists/psychologists can include the following:

1. Is a mental disorder present now and was it present at the time of the crime?
2. Can a connection between the two be demonstrated?
3. If so, what is the nature of this connection and what is the strength of it?
4. What is the level of responsibility of the offender for the crime?
5. What is the risk for reoffending, and which risk factors are present?
6. Is treatment possible to reduce reoffending? (van Marle, 2007)

The objective of this chapter is to briefly explore the range of mental disorders and their relationship to criminal behavior. Emphasis is placed predominantly on mental disorders, that are frequently observed among criminal offenders, although others are also mentioned.

UNDERSTANDING AND DEFINING MENTAL DISORDER

Disorders are diagnosed by clinicians. Mental health experts agree on a certain number of symptoms and their combination (as syndromes) and their possible interplay with causal factors. These combinations can be labeled as mental "disorder", "disease" or "illness." Mental disorders only exist via the manifestation of symptoms and behaviors. The patient, the person with a disorder, is a unique person who prints his or her unique picture on the phenotype of the disorder, depending on his or her personality and circumstances. People with the same psychiatric disorder can manifest themselves totally differently as patients because of these unique individual differences in the manifestation of the disorder.

For mental health researchers, the ideal disorder for scientific research is one that always has the same cause, a typical course, measurable organic abnormalities, agreed-upon characteristic treatments with a steady prognosis and a known terminal stage, with and without treatment. A holistic perspective is required (Kaplan & Sadock, 1995). Unfortunately, psychiatric/psychological sciences are not currently able to describe mental disorders in this ideal way. This is the reason why the word illness in psychiatry and psychology is replaced by the broader term disorder. Additionally, in mental disorders, there is no such thing as "the cause". Causality depends on many factors, including those of a biological, psychological, or social origin, or a combination of these. As such, vulnerabilities in childhood development and even in pregnancy may be involved as well as situational factors leading directly to the origin of the disorder and more circumstantial factors sustaining the disorder by their persisting influence. Some factors can be influenced by education whereas others relate to the brain's functioning. Treatments exist both in biologically influencing the brain's functions by medication and in psychological therapies.

In forensic psychiatry and psychology one has to be extremely cautious because of the danger that criminal behaviors (abnormalities in a social way) may be labeled as mental disorders. A conflict between a person and public authority can never be held as a mental disorder *per se*. Someone committing an offense, and as such being socially deviant, is not mentally ill until proven so by the existence of a mental disorder.

In mental health assessments the examiner does not avoid using the psychodynamic model: a model that is based on the axiom of psychic forces in the personality that strive together to produce a healthy balance between the person and his environment (adaptation). Central is the connection between this unique individual – his behavior and actions – and the context of the legal system in which he lives. That is, between his personality and his criminal behavior and his capacity as a human being to act responsibly. Why a person committed a crime or why a certain mental disorder has led to a certain impairment can only be understood by looking at the functioning of this personality directly within the context of the crime. At this time we cannot examine specific biological brain functions within any theory of aggression or crime because we cannot identify biological data that discriminate one person from another with respect to certain criminal behavior. For example, to date no brain abnormality or structure can be identified that is commonly inherent to all individuals who commit crimes of arson. Similarly, social theories of crime cannot be applied to individual perpetrators in terms of determining questions about individual responsibility. Accordingly, individual psychiatric/psychological evaluations are resorted to and often involve measuring personality traits by psychological tests that have good validity for the purposes of a court. Mental health questions that a court and mental health practitioners are often interested in understanding include the following:

1. How easily can somebody express himself or herself?
2. Is somebody able to continue and to end his or her actions?
3. How are somebody's standards and values in society compared with those within the society itself?
4. What is the ideal for which we should be striving?
5. How does somebody cope with stress factors?
6. How does somebody have control over his or her impulses and aggression?
7. How well is somebody able to endure uncertainty and misfortune?
8. What is the nature and quality of intimate relationships?
9. What is the capacity to create equilibrium between one's own needs and those of the environment?

The transition from deviancy to a mental disorder depends on the definition adopted from the *Diagnostic and Statistical Manual* (4th ed.) (*DSM-IV*) criterion (American Psychiatric Association [APA], 1994).[1] A mental disorder should imply suffering or impairment for the patient in his or her professional or social functioning.

CLASSIFICATIONS OF MENTAL DISORDER: THE *DSM-IV* AND THE *ICD-10*

Although the *International Classification of Diseases* (10 ed.) (*ICD-10*) section on psychiatric disorders and the *DSM-IV* are comparable and can be translated by codes into each other, in many countries in the western world the *DSM-IV* (APA, 1994)[2] is used more often than the *ICD-10*, probably because most countries are oriented toward North America for their psychiatric/psychological research. Consequently, the different disorders that will be discussed herein come from the *DSM-IV*. The *DSM-IV* is a classification of disease over five axes, and each axis points to a domain of knowledge that deals with the planning of treatment for patients and predicting the outcome. The five axes to the *DSM-IV* are:

- Axis I: Clinical disorders and other problems that can be a reason for mental health care

---

1. The *Diagnostic and Statistical Manual*, 4th edition, edited by the American Psychiatric Association (1994) provides information about the different mental disorders and the criteria necessary for a certain classification in name and code. Comparable to the *DSM-IV* is the *International Classification of Diseases*, 10th edition, (*ICD-10*) edited by the World Health Organization (1992).

2. It should be noted that subsequent to the development of the *DSM-IV* a text revision has also been published that currently represents the most contemporaneous version of the *DSM* (i.e. *DSM-IV-TR*; APA, 2000).

- Axis II: Personality disorders and mental handicap
- Axis III: General somatic health
- Axis IV: Psychosocial and environmental problems
- Axis V: Global assessment of functioning (GAF)

The differing axes of the *DSM-IV* are independent of each other, and most mental health experts would agree that there is no theory *per se* behind the *DSM-IV*; thus it is a largely descriptive lexicon. The five axes are necessary to do justice to the complexity of psychiatric classification. Axis I is the category with the clinically well-known mental disorders.[3] Axis II classifies the personality disorders into categories, with three main clusters: A, B and C. Mental handicaps are also classified here. Axis III classifies the somatic disorders, which are in some way relevant for the mental state of the patient. They can be a condition for the disorder in a biological or psychological way, and these somatic disorders may have implications for a particular treatment regime, for instance, as a contraindication for certain medications. With Axis IV, social problems can be present, such as problems in the individual's primary support network, in social relations, in work or study, with housing or economics, with health care, or in crime-related issues.

With respect to Axis V a global assessment of the individual's personal functioning is performed, and classified from 0 to 100 percent. A value of 100 suggests functioning perfectly in a variety of activities, 70 stands for mild symptoms, 50 for serious symptoms or a serious impairment in social functioning, 10 means a persistent danger for injuries or the life of the patient or others. Zero (0) as a score means inadequate information. Axis V indicates the extent to which the mental disorder impairs the patient's daily life functioning as mentioned in the earlier axes. Consequently, Axis V indicates the severity of the impairment in social functioning. The overall evaluation of an individual is referred to as the status praesens (present state) and shows the combination of all symptoms present across all five axes.

It should be noted that a number of different disorders from the same axis can potentially be diagnosed in a patient. This circumstance, in which different disorders may be present in a person, is known as comorbidity. It is, however, a point of debate as to whether a person can have two separate diagnoses from the same axis. That is, whether a person has two or more different and separate mental disorders instead of one that may in fact account for all the observed symptoms.

---

3. In Axis I, other problems that need immediate attention and are a reason for care are also classified.

COMMON MENTAL DISORDERS IN CRIMINAL BEHAVIOR

In this section the main categories of Axis I mental disorders from the *DSM-IV* will be discussed,[4] Axis II disorders (i.e. personality disorders) are explored separately in the following chapter. In this chapter, particular attention will be given to Axis I disorders including the following[5]:

- disorders usually first diagnosed in infancy, childhood, or adolescence
- cognitive disorders
- substance-related disorders
- schizophrenia and other psychotic disorders
- mood disorders
- anxiety disorders
- somatoform disorders
- factitious disorders
- dissociative disorders
- sexual and gender identity disorders
- eating disorders
- sleeping disorders
- impulse-control disorders not elsewhere classified
- adjustment disorder

Some of these can be associated with criminal behavior.

Disorders Usually First Diagnosed in Infancy, Childhood, or Adolescence

Pervasive developmental disorders are disorders present from childbirth, that continue for the entire life of the person. Possibly one of the most prominent is autism, which is characterized by pathological introversion and the incapacity to communicate adequately with other people as well as the presence of stereotyped behavior patterns. Individuals with autism also have an excessive need for order. That is, a need to know what is happening next, which is referred to as "the need for sameness." Another prominent developmental disorder is Asperger's Syndrome, which is characterized by

---

4. It should be noted that when a particular constellation of symptoms cannot be clearly classified within one of the main diagnostic definitions contained in the DSM, each of the major categories described in the DSM nonetheless includes a miscellaneous category referred to as Not Otherwise Specified (NOS).

5. Mental disorders due to a general medical condition are not discussed in this chapter.

demonstrations of impaired communication and relationships; these patients have a strong daily occupation with one or more stereotyped patterns of interest in an abnormal and restricted way, for instance, collecting. Also within the rubric of developmental disorders are mental handicaps such as mental retardation[6] and borderline intellectual functioning that have a genetic origin or have been caused by difficulties in childbirth. Head injury or trauma can also cause them.

Beyond the pervasive developmental disorders there are three disruptive behavior disorders in childhood of relevance to criminal behavior. These include conduct disorder (CD), oppositional defiant disorder (ODD) and attention-deficit hyperactivity disorder (ADHD). CD is an externalizing disorder, which implies a disorder in social functioning involving behaviors such as lying, stealing, fighting, and burglary. ODD is a mild form of conduct disorder and manifests itself in disobedience, temper tantrums, or negativism, but it does not directly imply criminal behavior. ADHD involves a deficit in attention and involves hyperactivity. Some patients suffer more from symptoms of attention deficit than from hyperactivity; others have it the other way around. ADHD does not lead directly to delinquent or antisocial behavior, but because these individuals with ADHD often have social problems related to their disorder, over time more of them may drift toward antisocial or delinquent behavior because of their social discrimination and exclusion.

Finally, learning disorders and language disorders are also relevant to the considerations of forensic psychiatrists/psychologists as far as they may complicate social development in childhood because these complications may lead to isolation, aggression and antisocial behavior.

Cognitive Disorders

Delirium and dementia are disturbances in cognition and social functioning that typically have an organic basis in the brain itself. Dementia is characterized by dysfunction in memory, especially in terms of disorientation with time, place, and people. These individuals have lost their awareness for time or place or are not able in any way at all to recognize one person from another. There are also problems in information processing, the planning and execution of activities, and recognizing things, together with malfunction in language and impaired motor skills.

Delirium disorders involve a lowering of consciousness with impairment

---

6. Mental retardation means an intelligence quotient of 70 or lower on an individual IQ test.

of memory, anxiety attacks, hallucinations, and agitation. Often delirium has organic causes, such as fever, or it can be induced through the consumption of alcohol or drugs, or both. Withdrawl from substances of abuse is also able to cause delirium.

Substance-Related Disorders

Substance use can lead to medical conditions such as addictions, dependency, or social abuse of soft drugs (e.g. cannabis) and hard drugs or medications, including alcohol and nicotine. Intoxication, withdrawal, delirium and persistent dementia, amnesia, psychotic disturbances, affective disorders, anxiety disorders sleep disorders and sexual dysfunction can all result from substance abuse and some of these may ultimately culminate in differing forms of criminal behavior. Also the wide variety of affects and side-effects produced by different drugs and the criminal activities which a drug user may need to become involved in in order to obtain drugs may result in criminal offenses.

Schizophrenia and Other Psychotic Disorders

Schizophrenia is a disorder that features delusions and hallucinations, along with identity loss and difficulty with interpersonal contact. In addition to these *positive* symptoms, there are also what are known as *negative* symptoms, such as apathy, blunted and/or inappropriate affect, and deficits in speech and thought.[7] Delusions, especially paranoid and grandiose delusions,[8] are more frequent than other forms of delusion. Hallucinations are sensations from perception that are not real but cannot be corrected by the individual. Individuals experiencing hallucinations may hear voices or see certain things that have a special, often delusional, meaning for them. However, hallucinations can also be experienced through other senses such as smell and touch.[9]

Schizophrenia as such is widespread throughout the world, with a prevalence of approximately 1 percent. The form in which schizophrenia manifests itself also depends on the culture in which the individual lives.

For many years there has been debate about the degree of dangerousness (in terms of risk assessment and risk management) of individuals suffering from schizophrenia (Monahan & Steadman, 1994). Some researchers have found that they were more dangerous than ordinary people, whereas others

---

7. Chaotic or catatonic behavior also belongs to the symptoms of schizophrenia.

8. For example, individuals may feel themselves sent by a magical power or messenger to save society.

9. Hallucinations can be ameliorated by the use of antipsychotic medication. The end stage of schizophrenia symptomology is referred to as "residual type" which features negative symptoms and two or more of the symptoms mentioned earlier.

have found the opposite. Selection of effectively different populations in the research is a very common factor, which may account for the differences in research outcomes (i.e. selection bias). Central to committing offenses is also the degree of social pressure and loss of social coherence in the daily lives of these patients, through living in a big city or in poverty (Weiser et al., 2007). The more chaotic the environment around them, the more aggressive and chaotic they are themselves (Cantor-Graae & Selten, 2005). On the other hand, too much intimacy is also harmful to them. Intimate relationships are a burden on them because of the emotional load of attachment and expectations (Gunn & Taylor, 1993).

Many individuals with schizophrenia who are in an adequate equilibrium are not more dangerous than other people are, although their situation is more prone to disruption. The immediate surroundings of patients influence their dangerousness and are probably the only cause, next to vulnerability, of the schizophrenic patient.[10] In addition, individuals with schizophrenia are more prone to abuse drugs and alcohol. Drugs might mitigate their symptoms in a subjective way but lead socially toward unpredictable and chaotic behavior that often lapses into aggression. Because circumstances are very important in terms of improving or worsening their condition, these patients should refrain from using alcohol and drugs and should also be housed in a clean and socially adjusted environment.

Mood Disorders

Mood disorders are disturbances in mood or affect, or both, and are characterized by certain episodes of depressive, hypomanic, or manic moods. Bipolar disorder is diagnosed when alternating mood episodes occur in the same person. With mood disorders, single episodes of depression or mania can be frequent and recurrent.[11]

A major depressive disorder means a substantial depression not due to schizophrenia or a schizoaffective disorder or other psychotic disorders. In less severe forms of depression individuals comprehend reality, but a depressive mood pervades their thoughts. There is mental insight by the patient in the manifestation of the disease. Their thoughts are not psychotic, and they can be partly corrected sometimes. There is often a loss of interest and initiative. As the depression deepens, other symptoms may appear, including suicidal thoughts or tendencies, impairment of vital functions such as loss of

---

10. For instance, chaotic and catatonic behavior as primary symptoms of schizophrenia increase with circumstantial stress. The negative symptoms are mostly a negative sign for the progression of the treatment. The positive symptoms are easier to treat by antipsychotic medication.

11. It is important to distinguish mood disorders, however, from schizoafffective disorder, in which symptoms of depression and symptoms of schizophrenia are combined.

appetite, loss of sleep or irregular sleep, and deterioration of movement and sexuality.[12]

In a manic episode, the mood is elevated and expansive. There is often psychomotor agitation and hyperactivity with no real purpose. There are often disturbances in sleep patterns, with a decreased need for sleep while thoughts and language are disjointed and fast paced. There is poor concentration and easy distraction. These patients are irritable and prone to superficial aggressive outbursts. In the context of criminal behavior these patients are known to experience delusions of grandiosity and may make unwise decisions about financial matters.

Another notable mood disorder is that of dysthymic disorder, which is a less-severe depression than a major depressive disorder. The depressive mood of individuals with dysthymic disorder is not present all day, nor is it present for all days but only most days.[13] Some basic symptoms also exist here, such as deficiencies in concentration or decision making, feelings of helplessness and hopelessness, tiredness, loss of self-esteem, disturbances in sleep patterns, and decreased or increased appetite.[14]

Anxiety Disorders

Anxiety disorders are characterized by abnormal degrees of anxiety[15] and can include panic attacks, specific phobias, as well as more general social phobias. Anxiety disorders of relevance in the context of criminal behavior may include obsessive-compulsive disorder (OCD) and posttraumatic stress disorder (PTSD). Obsessive-compulsive behavior is characterized by persistent thoughts, impulses, or fantasies acting upon the person. They are experienced as not belonging to the patient's own values and thoughts, so they cause distress, anxiety, and self-doubt. The individual tries to suppress or ignore these impulses or fantasies or to neutralize them with other thoughts or engaging in behavioral routines. Resisting the urge for these behaviors

---

12. A good indicator for requiring antidepressant medication is that the patient manifests mood swings within a day, with the patient feeling very depressed in the morning when he or she awakes but feeling better in the evening. The course of the depressive disorder changes, so there are periods of depression and spontaneous recoveries to normal, but sometimes the mood swings are so pronounced that after a period of depression a period of mania follows. In these cases not only is an antidepressant necessary for treatment but so are so-called mood stabilizers, such as lithium carbonate. Often a depressive disorder manifests itself mainly in somatic complaints such as tiredness, pains in the joints or in the back, headache, and not being able to enjoy things in life (anhedonia).

13. Additionally, there is more of a reactive component to dysthymic disorder and thus reactive depressions due to life events that have a negative impact on individuals also belong to dysthymic disorder.

14. For a dysthymic disorder, antidepressants can be of use but a far better treatment is cognitive behavioral therapy.

15. Also by routines or forms of behavior designed to potentially reduce anxiety.

leads to further anxiety and agitation.

PTSD relates to individuals who repeatedly relive and thus again experience a seriously traumatic event in their lives. Classic manifestations of this disorder include individuals involved in major disasters and combat within environments of war.

Somatoform Disorders

Somatoform disorders concern bodily complaints for which no somatic (i.e. organic) origin can be traced, although there are unexplained symptoms, complaints, and impairments. Somatoform disorders do not typically involve a person in criminal activity.

Factitious Disorders

Factitious disorders involve causing or malingering somatic or mental symptoms or complaints to give oneself the role of a patient. This disorder is also known as Munchausen syndrome when an individual harms himself or herself for this reason. Of particular relevance to criminal behavior is Munchausen syndrome by proxy, which commonly involves harming next of kin (typically a son or daughter) for the reason that the perpetrator unconsciously likes to be acknowledged as a supporting and loving family member or parent.

Dissociative Disorders

Dissociation in the context of dissociative disorders involves the separation of a person's consciousness into two or more states. Thus, the individual may be within a certain state of mind that is not perceptible and consciously accessible by the individual. Some of the dissociative disorders that may be associated with criminal behavior include dissociative amnesia, dissociative fugue, depersonalization disorder, and dissociative identity disorder (DID).

Dissociative amnesia is characterized by individuals who cannot remember one or more episodes of personal memory that are typically related to traumatic or stressful events. A notable feature of dissociative amnesia is that the manifested memory loss typically entails some type of important life event to the individual and as such cannot be easily explained by mere forgetfulness.

Dissociative fugue involves individuals who abruptly engage in travel far away from their home or work, with an inability to remember their own past, thus not knowing anymore who they are and from where they come. Depersonalization disorder relates to individuals who experience persistent and/or repetitive experiences of alienation from the world around them such that they are an external observer of their own behavior as in a movie or dream.

Finally, within the dissociative disorders is the rare condition currently known as DID wherein a form of dissociation is believed to occur that gives rise to the presence of two or more discernible identities or states of mind within a single individual.[16] These differing identities are able to influence and regulate the individual's behavior. Additionally, amnesia plays a role in the manifestation of this disorder because one state (i.e. identity) or another of the patient cannot remember the things he or she has done or thought.

Sexual Disorders and Gender Identity Disorders

Sexual disorders and gender identity disorders are only related to criminal behavior in so far as they can be the basis of abnormalities in sexual behavior to the extent that the behavior is regarded as deviant and thus contrary to law. As far as we are currently aware, sexual dysfunctions (with the exception of the paraphilias) do not have any clear significance to criminal behavior.

Paraphilia involves recurrent, intense, sexually arousing fantasies, sexual urges, or behavior that can involve nonhuman objects and suffering or humiliation of oneself or another person, of children, and of other nonconsenting persons. The object of the sexual desire is abnormal and thus is not typically directed at another person but rather at a part of a person or on other objects such as sexually appealing clothing, and so on. Some of the commonly recognized forms of paraphilia are discussed below.[17]

Pedophilia: Where children, usually before puberty, are the objects of sexual desire and sexual behavior. The sexual attraction does not necessarily need to be gender specific and can be manifested toward either boys or girls or both genders. If this behavior arises within a family, it is termed "incest" and should be described as such.

Exhibitionism: Persistent and intense sexual feelings, urges, and deviant behavior to expose one's genitals to unsuspecting strangers.

Fetishism: Persistent intense sexual fantasies, urges, and behavior connected with the fondling of inanimate objects.

Frotteurism: Sexually exciting fantasies, urges, and behavior by touching and rubbing against somebody else without his or her consent.

---

16. This condition was formerly know as multiple personality disorder.

17. Paraphilia not otherwise specified is the classification for all other, typically rare, paraphilias such as necrophilia (i.e. sexual stimulation related to dead people), zoophilia (sexual stimulation related to animals), etc.

Sexual masochism: Sexually arousing fantasies, urges, or behavior involving the act of being humiliated, beaten, or otherwise made to suffer.

Sexual sadism: Sexual excitement derived from the physical or psychological suffering, or both, of a victim.

Transvestic fetishism: Sexual arousal is derived from wearing the clothes of the other gender.

Voyeurism: Sexual arousal is attained from the act of observing an unsuspecting person who is naked, or disrobing, or engaging in a sexual activity.

The fantasies inherent to paraphilias can best be understood through the conceptualization of a sliding scale from normality through to pathology, thus transgressing the social and criminal laws. For example, some behaviors encapsulated within the domain of paraphilia are essentially accepted. One case in point is sadomasochism as an adjunct to regular sexual activity, another is when both partners engaging in the paraphilia have consensual roles. For this reason, a second important criterion in understanding paraphilias is that they should cause significant suffering or impairment in social or professional functioning or in functioning in other important domains of life before diagnosis of such disorders. Accordingly, it is important to note that the involvement of minors is strictly prohibited by the criminal law because they are not able to have an opinion of their own in these matters.

Finally, in the context of the sexual and gender identity disorders, it is therefore important to recognize that rape *per se* is not a mental disorder. It can, however, be the consequence of a paraphilia or compulsive sexual behavior.[18] Sometimes individuals who commit rape may look to justify their crime (i.e. defend their offense) by claiming or feigning a mental disorder and in such circumstances a separate psychiatric/psychological examination is necessary to determine the veracity of such claims and thus the presence of any disorder.

Eating Disorders

Eating disorders such as anorexia and bulimia nervosa do not typically have specific forensic relevance in terms of the manifestation of criminal behavior.

Sleeping Disorders

Sleeping disorders do not typically have specific relevance in terms of criminal behavior; however, they may accompany other disorders and can

---

18. Similarly, sexual addiction is not a medical concept but belongs to the category of compulsive sexual behavior.

often be persistent in nature.

Impulse Control Disorders Not Elsewhere Classified

Impulse control disorders not elsewhere classified represents a discrete category within the *DSM-IV* and is composed of various disorders that share some attributes with other *DSM-IV* disorders (e.g. subrelated disorders such as paraphilias) but are sufficiently different such that they cannot be classified in other *DSM* categories. With respect to the manifestation of criminal behavior some of the relevant disorders in this category include intermittent explosive disorder (recurrent episodes of failure to resist aggressive impulses resulting in damage to persons and property), kleptomania (the irresistible impulse to steal), pyromania (the impulse to frequently light fires), pathological gambling (compulsive and repeat gambling to the extent of losing all money, employment, and even friends) and trichotillomania (pulling out one's hair for relief of tension).

Adjustment Disorder

An adjustment disorder is discerned when an identifiable stressing factor is apparent in the individual's life that thereafter leads to impaired functioning (e.g. deterioration in the individual's relationships in social life, work, etc.). Adjustment disorder is distinguished by the need of a specific stress-causing factor that gives rise to the disorder, and thus with the removal of this stress factor, the adjustment disorder will also disappear.

CONCLUSION

This chapter attempts to provide the reader with a brief outline of the most frequent *DSM-IV* Axis I mental disorders that may manifest themselves in criminal behavior. When these mental disorders are restricted to mental phenomenon only and are not acted upon in the form of crime, there is no transgressing of the criminal law, although it should not be forgotten that these symptoms can be persistent and lead increasingly to impairment and suffering if not diagnosed and treated.

REFERENCES

American Psychiatric Association. (1994). *Diagnostic and Statistical Manual of Mental Disorders*, 4th ed. Washington, DC: American Psychiatric Association.

American Psychiatric Association. (2000). *Diagnostic and Statistical Manual of Mental Disorders,* 4th ed. (text revision). Washington, DC: American Psychiatric Association.

Cantor-Graae, E., and Selten, J.P. (2005). Schizophrenia and migration: a meta-analysis and review. *American Journal of Psychiatry, 162,* 12–24.

Engel, G.L. (1980). The clinical application of the biopsychosocial model. *American Journal of Psychiatry, 137,* 534–544.

Goethals, K.R., Fabri, V.A.S., Buitelaar, J.K., and van Marle, H.J.C. (2007). Temporal relationship between psychotic disorder and criminal offense: Review of the literature and File Review Study. *International Journal of Forensic Mental Health, 6,* 153–168.

Gunn, J., and Taylor, P. (1993). *Forensic Psychiatry, Clinical, Legal & Ethical Issues.* Oxford: Butterworth-Heinemann.

Kaplan, H.I., and Sadock, B.J. (Eds.)(1995). *Comprehensive Textbook of Psychiatry/VI,* Vol. 1. Baltimore: Williams & Wilkins.

Monahan, J., and Steadman, H.J. (1994). *Violence and Mental Disorder.* Chicago: University of Chicago Press.

Rogers, R., and Shuman, D.W. (2005). *Fundamentals of Forensic Practice, Mental Health and Criminal Law.* New York: Springer.

van Marle, H.J.C. (1996). Psychodynamic approaches to assessment: a forensic psychiatric interactional perspective. In C. Cordess & M. Cox (Eds.), *Forensic Psychotherapy, Crime, Psychodynamics and the Offender Patient* (pp. 37-45), London: Jessica Kingsley Publ.

van Marle, H.J.C. (2007) Het strafrechtelijk psychiatrisch gedragskundig onderzoek. In B.C.M. Raes and F.A.M. Bakker (red.), *De psychiatrie in het Nederlands recht.* Deventer: Kluwer, (5e druk).

Weiser, M., van Os, J., Reichenberg, A., Rabinowitz, J., Nahon, D., Kravitz, E., Lubin, G., et al. (2007). Social and cognitive functioning, urbanicity and risk for schizophrenia. *British Journal of Psychiatry, 191,* 320–324.

World Health Organization. (1992). *The ICD-10 Classification of Mental and Behavioural Disorders: Clinical Descriptions and Diagnostic Guidelines.* Geneva: WHO.

Chapter Two

ANTISOCIAL BEHAVIORS AND PERSONALITY DISORDERS

GEORGE B. PALERMO

Personality is the totality of emotional and behavioral traits characterizing an individual's behavior in the daily manifestations of life. It is somewhat predictable due to its relative stability; however, in the long run, and because of the vicissitudes of life, it is an evolving construct. A personality is the outcome of attitudes, interests, and needs that stem from a complex of unconscious and conscious biological factors, psychological drives, and emotions that form the self, unique and distinct from others, with its affectivity and intelligence. These components are in a certain equilibrium that allows social adaptability, self-esteem, and empathy, as well as a sense of responsibility and sensible planning for the self and others, especially for one's family. In order to achieve such a harmonious self, the individual must overcome infantile dependency needs, basic narcissism, and ambivalent attitudes toward the important object relations of the early developmental period (parental figures). That will give him or her interpersonal stability and, in essence, fairly good control of negative emotions.

The development of the personality, and later of character, is greatly determined by the way a young child resolves internal object relations and, in later years, in adolescence and early adulthood, how he or she relates to and incorporates parental models, and those of teachers and of other important people in life encounters. It will also depend on the way the child deals with peers and the influence of peers on the child.

As individuals move into the world, at different stages of maturation they develop feelings, drives, and emotions and will attempt, successfully or not, to repress their instincts. They will become aware of anger, fear, love, humiliation, joy, and disappointment. Such emotions will interplay within the self as they relate to others, at times in a passive or aggressive manner, especially when their personality traits are dysfunctional. However, the person with a normal personality will be able to control his or her negative emotions and get along with others. It is only when the personality traits become exaggerated that the personality may become disjointed and what is termed a personality disorder can be observed. The behavior of persons suffering with a personality disorder is pertinent to the discussion of personality, aggression, and criminal manifestations and often, in the latter instance, in ascertaining criminal responsibility.

OBJECT RELATIONS THEORY

The scholarly studies of object relations theorists, including Kohut (1971), Klein (1935), Mahler (1972), Winnicott (2008), and Kernberg (1992), can be of great benefit in order to better understand the origin of aggression toward others. Kernberg is among the most influential object relations theorists in the United States. Kernberg's theory, influenced by Kohut and Klein and also by Edith Jacobson, places a great deal of emphasis on "the splitting of the ego, and on the elaboration of good and bad self-configuration and object-configuration" (Kaplan, Sadock & Grebb, 1994, p. 256). According to Kaplan, Sadock, and Grebb, the id is seen by Kernberg as made up of self-images, object images, and their affects. In his theory, good and bad self-relationships and object relationships become associated with libido and aggression. It is on the basis of object relations' good and bad dichotomy that an individual's drives are given birth. On that foundation, Kernberg described the borderline personality organization, with its weak ego; primitive defense mechanisms, such as splitting (good-bad) projective identification; and a tendency to revert to primary process thinking. It is clear that his theory addresses the underlying problem of those personality-disordered individuals who, because of a problematic childhood, are prone to aggression against others, seeing in them those early images–bad images–that they have been unable to properly resolve during their early development.

The theory of Kohut (1971) also may be helpful in understanding the pathological personality and criminal behavior. For Kohut, during infancy, the child is afraid of losing coveted relations with his or her mother and, because of that fear, reverts to a grandiose self, to an alter ego, or to an idealization of the mother. The grandiose tendency may turn into exhibitionism and a tendency to idealize others. It is easy to understand how this may bring about disappointment from others because of unreasonable expectations, with all the consequences as far as aggression is concerned.

Winnicott (2008) was the central figure of the British school of object relations theory. His theory of multiple self-organizations included a true self, which develops in the context of a responsive holding environment provided by a good-enough mother. However, according to Winnicott, after traumatic disruptive experiences, a false self emerges that monitors and adapts to the conscious and unconscious needs of the mother and, in so doing, provides a protective exterior behind which the true self is afforded the privacy that it requires to maintain its integrity. Transitional objects, Winnicott wrote, such as a substitute mother, give a soothing sense of security. He viewed impulsive deviant behavior as the way in which a child hopes to recapture a primitive maternal relationship. Fenichel (1945) instead linked impulsive behavior to attempts to master anxiety, guilt, depression, and painful affects by means of actions, distorted aggression, or sexual gratification. All of these theories are helpful in understanding the disturbed aggressive behavior of those personality-disordered offenders who commit most of the antisocial actions in society.

PERSONALITY DISORDERS

Personality disorders are enduring patterns of inner experience and behavior that deviate markedly from the expectations of the individual's culture and are pervasive and inflexible in quality. A personality disorder begins in adolescence or early adulthood and leads to personal distress and social impairment. The character traits, not only inflexible but also maladaptive, are a variant of the normal that has gone beyond the range found in most people. The symptoms are ego-syntonic and alloplastic, capable of adapting and altering the external environment. Individuals diagnosed with a personality disorder are not always disturbed by their symptoms and thus may not complain about them; as a consequence, they do not ask for treatment unless the personality disorder is very severe.

Most criminals are classifiable as suffering from some type of personality disorder. Their criminal behavior has been defined as an intentional act that is committed without defense or excuse in violation of the criminal law and penalized by the law (Tappan, 1947). Basic to that behavior is impulsivity, which can be observed in the severe personality disorders, especially the antisocial personality disorder, the borderline personality disorder, the narcissistic personality disorder, and the paranoid personality disorder. Among the psychoses, the paranoid delusional type is more prone to cause an individual to act out impulsively and suddenly. However, only a minimal percentage of psychotics, whether schizophrenic, bipolar, or delusional paranoids, act out.

Many personality-disordered criminals are very young. Nevertheless, their antisocial behavior is often that of a superpredator. Their "identikit" shows "*radically impulsive, brutally remorseless youngsters,* [who] . . . *do not fear the stigma of arrest, the pain of imprisonment, or the pangs of conscience . . .* [and for whom] *the words 'right' and 'wrong' have no fixed moral meaning*" (Bennett, DiTulio & Walters, 1996, p. 27). These are offenders whose behavior is motivated by a profound disregard for societal rules, who try to manipulate others while both in and out of jail or prison, and who generally display a macho attitude out of fear. They are frequently illiterate, but streetwise. They often abide by a group code of behavior, seemingly despising the social and moral codes shared by their communities. On further scrutiny, they are found to be repeat offenders and chronically irresponsible. Their character analysis reveals hatred toward a nonexistent father and benevolent appraisal of a frequently nongiving mother, an ambivalent image of a good-bad object–an idealization of her–a previously frustrated longing for affection, and a misguided rebellion against authority in general. Many have a poor educational background, a lack of job training, or very scarce employment records. They are often dysfunctional and frequently search for escapism through the nirvana of drugs and alcohol, all of which are important contributory factors in their evolution as criminals.

The prison seems to be the right place for their unsolved emotional conflicts with their mother and father. It is in jail or prison that these young offenders unconsciously behave according to "a pathological, perceptual stance known as 'splitting'" (Hofer, 1988, p. 99). This is a defense mechanism, present in the antisocial personality, usually used, however, in order to feel protected and nurtured despite real evidence to the contrary. As Hofer well-described, the splitting is between "the affection directed toward a fantasized, loving, perfect mother image and the aggression directed toward the fantasized abandoning, all-bad father image" (p. 99). The prison allows the inmates, especially the antisocial recidivist, to obtain, even though in a displaced fashion, a certain amount of the nurturing they crave and the possibility to ventilate their resentment toward the paternal authority figure who let them down, displacing it onto the correctional institution guards.

Although many criminals with a personality disorder belong to a low economic group and are without any basic training for a rewarding job in a competitive society, economic poverty cannot be subscribed to as the only determinant of their offensive behavior. In fact, as Bennett and colleagues wrote, "Among all economic classes, including low income people and the poor, it is the irritable, impulsive, and poorly socialized males who are most likely to commit crimes" (1996, p .42). The question of moral poverty in these individuals should be raised. Is it the basis of their criminal acting out?

Just as the cognitive, intellectual self, with its moral and ethical structure, is important in decision making, so the affective state of an individual, with its variations, may influence human behavior. At times, fluctuations of a person's mood, not clearly pathological but limited to a feeling of sadness or joy, may bring about changes in conduct in relation to the people within his or her usual habitat. Occasionally, when this affective fluctuation becomes greatly exaggerated and not controlled by the powers of objectivity, discrimination, and the anticipation of future consequences, the individual may not be strong enough to hold back the negative instinctual, impulsive drives. Indeed, as can be seen again and again, among the characteristic traits of individuals who commit crimes is an inability to exercise the effective will power necessary to control their behavior when under the influence of strong, instinctual negative emotions or alcohol and drugs.

In addition to the impulsivity found among the major personality characteristics of the criminal are restlessness and hostility. A propensity to rage and destructive violence are characteristic of many of them. That includes the criminal's proneness to rage following humiliation and guilt. Restlessness is a frequent anticipatory sign of rage and violence in many offenders. Frequently, it is during a moment of rage that individuals lose their objective, discriminatory powers and self-control.

A sense of lost power or downright impotence is also often the basis of the antisocial behavior of people with personality disorders. Many of them offend because they feel powerless, overwhelmed by and unable to face up to their duties and social demands. Their frustration brings about their acting out. Their hostility may be directed toward the self—a self that is hated because it is not responsive to what is demanded of it, a self that the offender believes must have no value because no one seems to accept him or her, a self that feels deeply rejected. Other characteristic traits of people with personality disorders who act in a criminal fashion are feelings of rejection, a tendency to self- and outer-destructive behavior, and, especially in the so-called psychopath, a lack of a sense of duty and justice. Obviously, previous experiences in school and the family played an important part in the foregoing.

Many criminals experience fluctuations of self-esteem and, more frequently, exhibit low self-esteem. Not only do they feel inferior, but also their conscience talks to them in derogatory ways, and they frequently pass negative judgments on themselves. A modicum of stable self-esteem is essential in the development of a mature individual within a social context. Good self-esteem can be viewed as a psychological vaccination against the ups and downs of life; it is behind the capacity for resiliency to adversity. At times, they experience sudden reactions—assertive reactions in self-defense—which assume the typical stance of antisocial behavior. Fluctuations of self-esteem in an upward manner may also bring about antisocial behavior in those individuals too proud of themselves, too sure of their capabilities, and inconsiderate of others and of the social consequences of their actions.

The most frequently diagnosed personality disorder in persons committing crimes is the antisocial personality disorder and its exaggerated form psychopathy. Egoism, selfishness, a wish to control, and evilness are frequently present in psychopathic personalities. They show a lack of remorse for their offense and an amoral behavior. Reich (1990) defined psychopathic offenders as impulsive characters. Alexander (1948) called them neurotic characters and classified them as the primary psychopath and the symptomatic psychopath. The primary, or smaller, group is characterized by amoral behavior, lack of conscience, deficient superego, lack of anxiety, possibly violent aggression, and often sadism in their criminal behavior. Others described them just as psychopathic personalities (Abrahamsen, 1952). Psychopaths may also suffer from schizophrenia. Sellin (1972) cited studies showing that the criminal psychopath is more likely than the criminal nonpsychopath to have committed serious violent assaults and property crimes. He reported that psychological studies showed that violent psychopaths exhibit more impulsive tendencies and more aggressivity than the symptomatic psychopath (in Palermo, 2004).

Alexander also stated, as did Freud, that the psychopaths are a group of offenders "who engage in antisocial behavior in order to achieve punishment at the hands of the law . . . [because] they have intense guilt feelings over some deeply buried early life experiences" (Guttmacher, 1972, p. 298). They are often tortured individuals, easily apprehended because of clumsy, stupid crimes. Psychopaths may suffer from paranoia and their ego may be overwhelmed by primitive, aggressive, criminal drives. Arieti (1967) subdivided the psychopathic states into the pseudopsychopathic and the idiopathic, attributing the psychopath's impulsivity and desire for immediate gratification to his attempt to overcome unbearable inner tension due to short-circuited anxiety. He asserted that when the paranoid psychopath is prevented from acting out, for instance by imprisonment or hospitalization, the individual becomes more paranoid. Karpman (cited in Wilson & Hernstein, 1985, p. 206) reported that idiopathic psychopaths are less prone to fear, anxiety, or guilt, whereas secondary psychopaths show symptomatic anxiety, and their behavior is frequently accompanied or motivated by emotional disturbance.

The decisional capacity in offenders diagnosed with a severe personality disorder is generally impaired; even though they apparently seem to function normally, they usually reach a decision too rapidly. Strong unsublimated impulses may be disruptive. Wilson and Hernstein (1985) wrote, "Impulsiveness can be thought of as either the cause or the effect of the poor conditionability of the psychopath" (p. 204) and "without the internal mono-logue, time horizons shrink; behavior becomes more tied to its immediate consequences" (p. 205). In fact, it is the quick decision making that is the expression of the lack of reflection before acting that is usually found in the antisocial personality disorder or psychopath. Self-control is essential for a person's achievements after he or she properly channels impulses without giving vent to unbridled impulsivity.

Impulses were viewed by Nietzsche, for example, as important in a per-son's behavior. He believed that "a man without impulses [interests] could not do the good or create the beautiful any more than a castrated man could beget children" (Kaufmann, 1974, p. 244). Nevertheless, impulses need con-trol, and Nietzsche viewed the man who is in control of his passions as pow-erful, able to organize the chaos, and able to give style to his character. He believed that the passionate person who is able to master his or her passions would also be a good, intuitive, and creative individual. He viewed the man who strives for power over others through bullying and criminal activity as a weak person, deeply frustrated. The man who imposes restraints on him-self is not only "a 'rational' animal, but also a 'moral' animal" (Kaufmann, 1974, p. 213). The two are inseparable. Baruk (cited in DiTullio, 1960) viewed the total lack of moral values, visible in the true psychopathic offender, as "one of the worst calamities that can affect a human being, because of its per-sonal and social consequences" (p. 41). In assessing the characteristic traits of these offenders it can be observed that they often lack self-criticism in regard to their criminal acting out. Kaufmann (1974) stated that their offenses are not only irrational but also intrinsically immoral because their impulsivity under-mines their critical reflection.

In order to appreciate the workings of the mind of those criminals suffer-ing from personality disorders, character and temperament should be con-sidered. The ideas of Boven (cited in DiTullio, 1960) are interesting for the understanding of human behavior. Boven's belief was that individuals tend to overcome their biological selves throughout their lifetime. He viewed character as the result of a struggle among the lower instinctive, vegetative, and attitudinal strata; the egocentric forces of the central stratum; and the higher stratum, which comprises the intelligence and the will power. DiTullio (1960), an Italian psychiatrist, stated that individuals tend to develop their character on the basis of their natural instinctive and affective propensities, aided in their maturation by the environment and education, leading to habit patterns that become an intrinsic part of their daily activities.

Character is the composite of distinctive qualities formed by mental and ethical traits that, stimulated by an individual's emotional sensitivity and habitual mode of reaction, give to each one's personality its dynamism. It is the personality in action, and is due to the temperamental propensity of the individual. It is the outcome of life experiences; togetherness; of give and take; and a conscious or unconscious adaptation of id and ego tendencies to the social dictates or appropriate modes of practical, moral, and ethical behavior when confronted with choices. Absence of character is usually found behind much senseless crime, and the knowledge of the personality traits shared by many nonpsychotic criminals is fundamental for the understanding of the criminal behavior that relegates any person to a jail or prison.

Sheldon (1942), well-known for his biotypology (endo-, meso- or ectomorphic body types), which he considered fixed elements of a personality, stressed the importance of human temperament, which adds a dynamic component to the personality itself. Verdun (cited in DiTullio, 1960) stressed the interaction among environment, constitution, and temperament. His emphasis on the importance of the neurovegetative system and its excitability as the basis of human behavior and human emotions anticipated the present-day neurotransmitter hypothesis in normal and disorderly conduct. Such theories lead one to consider the possible predisposition to criminal behavior of many personality-disordered offenders and to the theory that, during the past fifty years, has attributed such behavior mostly to negative environmental factors, since many offenders seem to be recalcitrant to change, even though attempts have been made to change their environmental conditions. The pendulum of nature versus nurture as the basis of human conduct seems to be more on the side of nature.

Gemelli and Zunini (1949) recognized the importance of personality traits and attitudinal disposition in the formation of character. They believed in the plasticity and variability of character and subscribed to the idea that character is the outcome of an interplay of traits, attitudes, and stimuli in a given moment for a given individual. They believed that, although a person's hereditary or organic personality traits are important, education is basic to the manifestation of human conduct. They posited that an individual without education and lacking a notion of morality cannot be considered a mature being because without them the basic self has not evolved to a level of acceptable adaptation to society. Many present-day offenders drop out of school around the tenth or twelfth grade, often displaying only an elementary school level of knowledge, and they exhibit a distinct lack of a moral sense, seemingly confirming the ideas of Gemelli and Zunini.

As throughout past centuries, the common criminal today lacks a mature personality and his or her behavior is primarily driven by instinctual drives, drives that in the noncriminal are usually sublimated, channeled toward more acceptable behavior. Lack of education, and not of basic intellectual endowment, and the lack of exposure to the sociomoral values shared by the community at large have not allowed the psychological self of the future criminal to acquire that sociocivic sense of responsibility that allows one to live in the human consortium.

In fact, crime can be seen as a psychobiological social phenomenon. Offenders give a clue to their criminal character through the type of offense. This is the reason why crimes have been described as essentially aggressive (e.g. murder, robbery, and rape) or passive-aggressive in nature (e.g. burglary, forgery, arson, etc.) or as essentially related to psychophysiological stress (e.g. sexual crimes, pedophilia, indecencies in public, exhibitionism).

Can one perceive the personality of the offender from his or her crime? Toch (1969) thought that "we should be able to reconstruct the man from a sample of his violent acts" (p. 133), and he formulated a typology of the violence-prone individual, and Bromberg (1965) took into consideration the personality characteristics of the offenders from a psychiatric and psychological point of view. Bromberg listed various types of offenders: the aggressive (antisocial, released by alcohol, or a reaction to feelings of inferiority), the emotionally unstable, the unethical (criminal type), the maladjusted adolescent, and the immature adult type. Among the latter, the egocentric, inadequate, shiftless, suggestible, adynamic, or dull types stand out. Bromberg further proposed the interesting classification of the nomadic type—unattached, schizoid to a degree—and the primitive type, whose behavior is simple and instinctive (1965, p. 86). Among adjusted individuals he included those "adjusted to a low cultural level with its own ideologies and mores" and "those obviously maintaining a relationship to the so-called stable world" (p. 86). His first category of so-called adjusted individuals is quite interesting and is reminiscent of those groups described as belonging to the specific subculture of violence.

Necessary conditions for persons with personality disorders or psychotics to act out lie in the vicissitudes of the life instinct, the fate of affects, and the state of ego-consciousness. Frequently, they are socially isolated, but they may become members of groups in an attempt to overcome their feelings of inadequacy and low self-esteem, as is the case with many young people who join gangs. However, many feel isolated even in the presence of others and have a low capacity for interpersonal interaction. Often, they live in a fantasy world and are reactively depressed. It may be that their depression originated in their infancy, because many of them grew up in a dysfunctional family, with the absence of parents, especially the nurturing mother. These psychologically weak individuals, because they are affected by either severe personality disorders or a psychotic personality disorder, usually untreated, under the effect of an unbearable affect of guilt or humiliation, suffer ego decompensation, and their unconscious repressed pathological complexes surface and lead them to serious antisocial behaviors, even murder.

The major and severe personality disorders involved in crimes are borderline personality disorder, paranoid personality disorder, schizoid personality disorder, antisocial personality disorder, narcissistic personality disorder, sadistic personality disorder, and the schizotypal personality disorder; each of which will now be discussed.

Borderline Personality Disorder

Even though the borderline personality disorder is an integral part of the personality disorder classification, it is questionable whether it is an autonomous entity. The characteristics of this personality disorder, according to Gunderson and Singer in their seminal study (1975), were intense depressive or hostile affectivity, impulsivity, mild to moderate social adaptation, brief psychotic episodes, a tendency to disorganization in unstructured situations, and superficial or very dependent relationships. Persons with borderline personality disorder have a weak ego. Their symptomatology is diverse. They may go through sudden mood changes, such as anger, depression, anhedonia, sense of futility, loneliness, and isolation. Their behavior is marginal and transient, and their interpersonal relationships appear to be good only on the surface. They seem unable to control their impulses due to their sudden psychotic thinking because of internal and external stress. At times, they suffer from transitory and fleeting hallucinations or delusions. Their personality disorder can be summarized as stably unstable.

It is important to realize that the psychotic experiences of the borderline-personality individual are ego-dystonic, because the person does not recognize them as part of the self. Their disorder is reminiscent of what Deutsch (Kaplan et al., 1994) stated regarding the "as if" personality. Indeed, the essential characteristics of borderline personality–disordered individuals are that outwardly they conduct their lives "as if" they were essentially normal and in control of the self. Because they often have acceptable social behavior, and function fairly well in social activities, it is sometimes difficult to make an accurate diagnosis. Their reality testing is quite faulty; they are highly vulnerable to stress and emotionally unbalanced. Their inability to test reality and to contain their impulsivity, which at times motivates their conduct, is a mixture of depressive and delusional symptoms and is difficult to predict. In these persons, a psychotic breakdown may take the form of an acute schizoaffective disorder, a break with reality due to intense feelings of depression. The antisocial acting out of some adolescents at times seems to be the forerunner of a prepsychotic borderline state. It may be akin to a psychofunctional disorder of the mind, almost a necessary transitional period prior to achieving a stability of the personality. During this highly unstable period, one can observe in the adolescent's behavior the intermingling of two worlds: the real and the psychotic.

Kernberg (1992) distinguished three stages in the personality borderline organization. In the first stage, the individual still possesses fairly discreet reality testing, with an absence of delusions or hallucinations, and an ability to differentiate the self from the nonself. The second stage is the identity diffusion syndrome (feelings of emptiness, an inability to react well to others), and the third stage is that in which primitive defense mechanisms are resorted to. These include splitting—in which feelings of ambivalence divide people into good and bad—projective identification, feelings of omnipotence, denial, idealization, and devaluation.

In patients with borderline personality organization, wrote Kernberg, "projective identification weakens the ability to differentiate the self from external objects by producing an interchange of character with the object, so that something internally intolerable now appears to be coming from outside . . . [and] tends to diminish the reality testing" (1992, p. 196).

Paranoid Personality Disorder

The prevalence of the paranoid personality disorder varies from 0.5 percent to 2.5 percent in the general population (Kaplan, et al., 1994). The main characteristics of persons with this disorder are chronic suspiciousness and general mistrust. They displace onto others their own shortcomings and responsibilities. Often hostile, irritable, and angry, they rarely seek treatment on their own, being convinced that there is nothing wrong with them. They are usually forced into treatment by family members or the courts, which they resent, and in situations in which such forced treatment is being sought, they are bright enough and able enough to put on a normal facade. They show pathological jealousy, extreme litigiousness, and, under stress, many become clearly delusional and paranoid. At those times they should be considered not responsible for any antisocial actions, because they are unable to conform to the requirements of the law due to a misperception of the behaviors and intentions of others. In essence, the basic problem with their thinking is that they interpret the actions or demeanors of others as threatening, exploitative, or harmful to themselves. They even mistrust family members, friends, and associates. The mechanism of defense used by them is projection: they project onto others feelings that they harbor but that they are unable or willing to accept—It's not me. It's you! Often, they suffer from ideas of reference and illusions. They are cautious and somewhat distant in their interpersonal relationships. In their professional endeavors, they are efficient, but their expectations of themselves, and especially of others, create interpersonal difficulties. Nevertheless, they claim to be rational and objective, and, as Shakespeare would say, they protest too much in their attempt to prove it. They have a tendency to be grandiose, to have superiority feelings, and to disdain the weak, the sickly, and passive individuals. That may be the precursor of paranoia, a psychotic condition, or of a schizophrenic type of psychosis. It may occur because, having a fragile ego structure, they often react to stress in a catastrophic manner.

Individuals with this type of personality disorder are rigid, tense, and unable to relax. In their daily life they are so cautious and suspicious that they seem to search the environment for clues or criticism from others that they misinterpret as being directed at undermining them. This behavior may be reminiscent of the monomania of Esquirol, the persecutory delirium of La Segue, or the slow cognitive delusional disorder of Kahlbaum and Kraepelin (in DiTullio, 1960). The thinking of persons with this type of a personality disorder is seemingly logical. The conclusions they reach, however, are faulty because of incorrect initial premises, and their cognitive distortions are quite evident when they lose control.

Schizoid Personality Disorder

The schizoid personality disorder shows a lifelong pattern of social withdrawal. Individuals suffering from it are usually introverted and lonely. Their affect is constricted, and they isolate themselves because of the discomfort felt in social interactions. They appear to be cold, aloof, distant, unsociable, unemotional, and uninvolved. They frequently hold lonely noncompetitive jobs and lack an intimate life. They have difficulty in expressing anger. They often involve themselves with astronomy, philosophy, mathematics, and dietary health fads. They are in touch with reality but do a great deal of daydreaming and entertain fantasies of omnipotence. This type of personality disorder is not uncommon, reportedly affecting 7.5 percent of the general population, with a male to female ratio of two to one (Kaplan, et al., 1994).

Even though the schizoid personality disorder is fairly stable, at times those who suffer from it move into a schizophrenic breakdown, from which they usually go into remission. Some scholars believe that this personality disorder is a prodromal phase of schizophrenia.

Antisocial Personality Disorder and Psychopathy

Even though the *Diagnostic and Statistical Manual* (4th ed., text revision) (*DSM-IV-TR*) (American Psychiatric Association [APA], 2002) includes under antisocial personality disorder (ASPD) some of the basic characteristics of the psychopathic personality, the consensus is that a distinction should be made between the two. Most persons with ASPD can be viewed as reactors to social stresses, whereas the psychopaths are "real" actors. The characteristics of the latter, as reported by Hare (1993), who seems to retrace Cleckley's (1955) definitions of the psychopath, are that a psychopath is a self-centered, callous, and remorseless person, profoundly lacking in empathy with an inability to form warm relationships with others, a person who functions without the restraint of a conscious self. The untreatability and the recidivism of the psychopath are well-known. The concept of psychopathy dates back to the time of Lombroso (1889), with his characterization of the so-called born criminal, and Pinel, with his emphasis on the lack of morals in offenders.

Many authors have stressed the etiology of psychopathy, presenting it, for example, as congenital, biological, personal, and environmental (Arrigo & Shipley, 2001). Pinel considered the psychopath to be mentally ill, in need of moral treatment, suffering from a *manie sans delire*. Rush (1812) proposed organic causes for psychopathy, which he considered a disease. Prichard (1835) described it as a disorder of a person's feelings and attitudes, without involvement of higher mental faculties but with a predisposition to behave as a morally insane person. In 1891, Koch, coined the term psychopathic inferior, which he considered to be a hereditary disease with emotional and moral aberrations and abnormal behaviors. Maudsley (1898), as well, considered the psychopath to be suffering from moral imbecility due to cerebral dysfunctions. Von Krafft-Ebing (1922) referred to these persons as savages and believed that they should be kept isolated in mental asylums for their own sake and that of society. Kraepelin (1915) described them as liars and manipulators who employed charm and glibness but were impulsive and remorseless.

It was Cleckley (1955), however, who in his seminal work *The Mask of Sanity* made a distinction between the psychopath who ends up in jail and the one who does not, describing them as grandiose, arrogant, callous, superficial, and manipulative. The latter, he believed, keeps a far better and more consistent appearance of being normal. His distinction between the ordinary criminal and the psychopath still holds true. He believed that the first possessed purposive behavior and his aims are well-understood by the average person, even though not accepted and shared with him. "The criminal, in short, is usually trying to get something we all want, though he uses methods we shun," he wrote (1955, p. 292). Ordinary criminals are consistent and persistent in conniving in order to reach their own ends and are aware of the possible legal consequences of their actions. They are shrewd in their planning and in their attempt to avoid being apprehended.

Cleckley pointed out the recidivistic tendencies of psychopaths in the commission of their crimes. He added that psychopathic conduct "varies in severity from a mild or borderline degree up through a great degree of disability" (1955, p. 279). Many paranoid characters show antisocial behavior as well. He postulated that persons diagnosed with an ASPD or a psychopathic disorder have "a genuine and often a very serious disability" (p. 422). He added that "to say that this is merely queer or perverse or in some borderline state between health and illness does little or nothing to account for the sort of behavior he demonstrates objectively and obviously."

In the psychopaths, we are confronted, as Cleckley says, with a mask of sanity, and "all the outward features of this mask are intact. . . . The thought processes retain their normal aspect under psychiatric investigation and also in technical testing . . . An example of la folie lucid," while their expressions, tone of voice, and general demeanor seem normal, but they fail "altogether when [they are] put into the practice of actual living." Their "failure is so complete and so dramatic that it is difficult to see how such a failure could be achieved by anything less than a downright madman, or by one who is totally or almost totally unable to grasp emotionally the major components of meanings or feelings implicit in the thoughts which he expresses or the experiences [they appear] to go through" (p. 124). Their distorted affectivity, their tragic persistence in their antisocial behavior, their inability to learn from their mistakes bespeaks a profound childish immaturity that causes them to move, without reflection, from thought to action, without appraising and discerning what type of decision they should make and act upon. "Our concept of the psychopath's functioning," says Cleckley, "postulates a selective defect . . . which prevents important components of normal experience from being integrated into the whole human reaction, particularly an elimination or attenuation of those strong effective components that ordinarily arise in major personal and social issues" (1955).

The emotions of a psychopath are just pseudoemotions. They use a pantomime of feelings. They are full of rationalizations, their judgment is poor, and their sense of value is almost nonexistent. Their outward behavior seems to be the outcome of a deeply distorted inner personality, akin to a schizophrenic process, at times largely concealed by good reasoning and their ability to go through life in a quasi-sane manner. After years of socially restricted but apparently not psychotic lives, a few psychopaths commit murder or carry out other tragic misdeeds "for which they show little evidence of remorse or other adequate and understandable reactions" (Cleckley, 1955, p. 437). Generally, the psychopaths' masks are very deceptive. They show no obvious signs of traditional psychotic behavior, yet they manifest a conduct not less serious than that of a schizophrenic. Inwardly, they harbor an "incapacity to react with sufficient seriousness to achieve much more than pseudo-experience or quasi experience" (p. 437). Often they seem to belong to those disorders classically thought of as psychoses, which appear in varying degrees of severity.

Macdonald (1961) described the psychopath as lacking "the capacity to 'feel' with others and devoid of affection, callous and cynical . . . egocentric and immature" (p. 247), adding that "their impulsivity and intolerance of frustration may lead to repeated antisocial acts" (p. 248). However, "antisocial personalities may often be quite successful in whatever their chosen professional activity. They may have paradoxically reached their position of success, power, and wealth by ruthless exploitation of others"(Stoudemire, 1994, p. 186).

Psychopaths are usually of average or above average intelligence, have an apparent lack of guilt and remorse, and do not learn from experience. They show a great deal of "impulsivity as manifested by frequent physical fights and abusive behavior . . . [and] encounters with the law and other authorities are frequent, . . . in repetitive criminal behavior" (Stoudemire, 1994, p. 186).

Alexander and Ross (1952) believed that the presence of unconscious conflicts could be expressed in the symptomatic behavior of the psychopath's irrationality, stereotyped repetitive behavior and self-destructive tendencies. They thought that "the actual crime, . . . is often a substitute for incestuous or patricidal impulses" (p. 133).

Halleck (1967) thought that "the psychopath is an activist, who in his efforts to suit the world to his own needs often finds that it is necessary to violate the law" (p. 109). The same type of behavior, cunning and goal directed, can be observed in the paranoid, with variations in the clinical manifestations along the paranoid spectrum. Other authors (Reichard & Tillman, in Macdonald, 1961) suggested that, when lacking an understandable motive, a murder committed by a psychopath with paranoid tendencies represents "an attempted defense against the outbreak of a schizophrenic psychosis, in which the ego seeks to protect itself from disintegration by discharging unassuageable anger through an act of violence" (p. 115). Often, these psychopaths are sentenced to repeated terms in prison or even life terms.

Arieti (1967) subdivided the psychopathic states into the pseudopsychopathic and the idiopathic. He attributed the psychopath's impulsivity and his desire for immediate gratification to an attempt to overcome unbearable inner tension due to short-circuited anxiety. He "is unable to change, repress, postpone or neutralize his need for hostility," he stated (p. 248), and his acting out may be in the form of murder, rape, seduction in men, or promiscuity and prostitution in women. More important and relevant to this discussion, however, is Arieti's reflection on the paranoid psychopath. While pointing out that psychopathic traits or behavior "generally preceded a definite paranoiac symptomatology, or, in some cases, periods of acting out with no freely expressed delusions alternate with obvious delusional periods," he suggested that, most probably, "when the paranoid psychopath is prevented from acting out, for instance, by imprisonment or hospitalization, he becomes more paranoid" (1967, p. 248).

Narcissistic Personality Disorder

People who suffer from a narcissistic personality disorder show a heightened sense of self-importance and grandiose feelings, considering themselves to be special and deserving of special treatment. They have a sense of entitlement and handle criticism poorly. They are ambitious and wish to be famous, are strongly exhibitionistic, almost demanding admiration. At the same time, they are selfish and exploitative. Their relationships are superficial and they do not show empathy for others. They refuse to obey conventional rules. They are vulnerable to middle-life crises. Their judgment is not objective. They seem to exhibit the so-called "mirror hunger" of Kohut and Wolf (1978). When they are frustrated, their manipulative personalities may explode in a narcissistic rage. They are egocentric, like a child, and when they do not achieve their expectations they fall into a state of inner emptiness.

Various theories of behavior can be considered in the attempt to understand malignant narcissism. Kohut (1971) hypothesized that a narcissistic trauma suffered by the child during the process of individuation prevents him or her from taming the archaic, grandiose, and exhibitionistic self necessary for wholesome development. Originally described by Freud, narcissism was later subdivided by Kohut into primary and secondary narcissism. Primary narcissism is seen as the investment of libidinal energy in the achievement of object love, empathy, and possible creativity; secondary narcissism is the withdrawing of the original psychic libidinal energy from objects back to the ego. This latter mechanism seems to be present in the psychodynamics of serial killers. They are not only pathologically narcissistic but also unrealistically grandiose, and their exaggerated self-importance is very fragile and sensitive to shame. Narcissistic tendencies, part of the grandiose self are often present in the serial killer.

Sadistic Personality Disorder

People suffering with a sadistic personality disorder show a pervasive pattern of cruel, demeaning, and aggressive behavior. They have a tendency to inflict pain on others or to humiliate others. They are fascinated by violence, weapons, injury, and torture. When sexually aroused, they become paraphilic and sexually sadistic.

During the eighteenth century, the erotic and licentious writings of the libertine Marquis de Sade (Pauvert, 1965) shocked the world with their descriptions of cruel sadistic violence and unbound perverted lust. De Sade believed that instincts are the motivating force in life and that pleasure is the most important goal for which one should aim. Years later, in 1869, von Krafft-Ebing coined the term sadism, and the term acquired the meaning of a sexual perversion in which the pervert forced physical or moral suffering on the subject of his or her sexual attraction, deriving sexual pleasure from his or her actions. The infliction of pain seems to be part of the complete mastery of another person. The most radical aim of a sadistic act is to make the person suffer, since there is no greater power over another person than inflicting pain. Nevertheless, it has been hypothesized that rather than to express cruelty in and of itself, the object of sadism is to procure strong emotions (MacCulloch, Snowden, Wood & Mills, 1983).

Brittain's seminal work in 1970 laid the foundation for a possible typology of a sexual sadist, and his description is that which fits some present-day sadistic murderers. He described the sadist as a secretive male individual who is generally nonviolent in everyday life but obsessive, insecure, and narcissistic, a loner with a rich fantasy life. He believed that the sexual sadist creates sadistic scenes in his fantasies that he later acts out in his killings. This type of killer is single, his perversion starts early in life, he exhibits an interest in pornography, and he is excited by cruelty. Brittain's description of the sexual sadistic murderer is reminiscent of the serial killer Jeffrey Dahmer who, a typical charming psychopath, behaved well even on apprehension, but hidden behind his calm and socialized appearance were destructive sexual fantasies of a possible psychotic nature.

Many of the fantasies found in the serial killer, as stated earlier, are sadistic sexual fantasies. Most of these offenders are eventually diagnosed with severe personality disorders. It can be theorized that the behavior of the sadistic, power- and control-driven serial killer reflects the conduct of a curious child in the demolition of his toys. Sexual fantasies, at times violent in type, are also present in juvenile offenders and, when frequent, may degenerate into sadistic sexual fantasies. In such cases they may be the forerunner of homicidal acting out. According to MacCulloch and colleagues (1983), sadistic sexual fantasies have their origins at the time of traumatic episodes, such as sexual or physical abuse during early childhood. It has been theorized that the sadist may suffer from an arrest of psychosexual development, possibly at the anal stage (the anal-sadistic stage), or from a neurotic regression to that level. Fantasies of rape or murder were found in 86 percent of the cases of adults in one study of serial sexual homicide conducted by Prentky and colleagues (1989). Similarly, Warren and colleagues (1996) found evidence of violent fantasies in 80 percent of their cases. The important role of sadistic fantasies, especially repetitive masturbatory fantasies, in these killers was emphasized by MacCulloch and colleagues (1983), and that of daydreaming and compulsive masturbation was reported by Prentky and colleagues(1989), and by others.

Although Freud (1960) first viewed sadistic drives as primary instincts camouflaged by the drive to dominate, he later came to believe that sadism is the excessive outward manifestation of the death instinct. The gratuitous cruelty of sadism is possible because of insufficient control by the basic mechanism of defense.

Schizotypal Personality Disorder

Persons with schizotypal personality disorders are strikingly odd or strange, even to lay persons. They entertain magical thinking, bizarre ideas, ideas of reference, suspiciousness or paranoid ideation, and illusions and may have derealization feelings. The diagnosis is based on their peculiar thinking, their unusual way of communicating with others, and their generally strange behavior. They lack close friends, and their manner of speech frequently needs interpretation. Under stress, they become depressed or may fully decompensate into frank psychotic symptomology of brief duration.

NEUROPSYCHOLOGICAL AND NEUROIMAGING STUDIES

Pertinent to this discussion, scientists and criminologists are presently of the opinion that biopsychological factors may contribute to the understanding of criminal behavior. Redding (2006) wrote that "neuropsychological studies show that the prevalence rate of brain dysfunction among the criminal population is extremely high, with prevalence rates of ninety-four percent among homicide offenders, sixty-one percent habitually aggressive adults, forty-nine to seventy-eight percent among sex offenders, and seventy-six percent among juvenile offenders (by comparison, the prevalence rate in the general population is only three percent)" (p. 57). Most of these offenders belong to the diagnostic category of personality disorders. Diamond (1994), a well-known forensic psychiatrist, writing about people suffering from severe personality disorders stated, "Their appearance of normalcy, their apparent ability to exercise free will, choice, and decision (and somehow invariably choose the wrong instead of the right) is purely a facade, an artifact that conceals the extent they are victims of their own brain pathology" (p. 257). At the same time, and that was fourteen years ago, he ventured

---

1. The following studies seem to offer support for the previous statements: The Vietnam Veteran Head Injury Study examined aggressive behavior in 279 Vietnam War veterans with

the following prediction: "Within ten years, biochemical and physiological tests will be developed that will demonstrate beyond a reasonable doubt that a substantial number of our worst and most vicious criminal offenders are actually the sickest of all" (p. 257).[1] Indeed, Redding (2006) reported that "[i]ndividuals with extensive frontal lobe damage may develop episodic dyscontrol characterized by rage attacks in response to minimal provocation. . . . [T]he dyscontrol may lead to unplanned homicide, assaults, spousal and child abuse, reckless driving. . ." (p. 66).

To detect these dysfunctions, neuropsychologists employ various tests, including the Maze Tests and the Bender-Gestalt test, the Twenty Question Test, and the Tinker toy™ test. These tests elicit dysfunctions of conceptual thinking, reasoning, abstraction, and problem solving. The Wisconsin Card Sorting Test (WCST) and the Halstead Category Test evaluate concept formation, hypothesis testing, problem solving and flexibility of thinking. Block Designs and Puzzles tests check verbal reasoning, interpretation, perceptual reasoning, sequential reasoning, and problem solving. Many of these tests require choices and making a decision.

When people confront a social choice or decision making, they call on the neurocortical system, the evolutionary modern sector of the brain, which, as Damasio (1994) stated, "handles basic biological regulations . . . while up above the neocortex deliberates with wisdom and subtleties" (p. 128). In a study by Raine, Buchsbaum, and LaCasse (1997) performed on the brains of convicted murderers, the positron emissionion tomography (PET) scan found abnormalities in the prefrontal cortex, with an 11 percent reduction in the gray matter of the brain. These and other structural and functional abnormalities, especially in the frontal and temporal brain regions, have been found to be associated with violence, especially in those persons with a severe personality disorder–those most frequently involved in crime. Although these offenders are not clinically psychotic, their neuroimaging brain findings may show similarities to those found in psychotics. Thus, it can be opined that at times their sudden criminal acting out is basically psychotic in nature; that is also supported by underlying structural and functional disruptive activity of their brains. The changes found in persons with

---

frontal lobe lesions with 57 noninjured veterans as controls. It found that the brain-injured veterans were more aggressive; 20 percent became aggressive right after the injury. Fourteen percent were violent (Grafman et al., 1996); The Prison Inmate Study reported that 73 percent of the brain-injured inmates had committed crimes of violence compared to 28 percent of those not injured (Bryant, Scott & Golden, 1984); A study by Raine and colleagues (2001) found that psychopathic and violent offenders had structural/functional abnomalities in frontal lobes. Also, on PET scans less frontal lobe activity was found, along with low-volume prefrontal gray matter and excessive activity of the amygdala and hippocampus.

2. Goldberg (2001) asserted that a new legal construct, such as "the inability to guide one's behavior despite the availability of requisite knowlege," may better serve the individual with a dysfunctional frontal lobe in a court of law (p. 149).

a personality disorder appear to be of the same quality but of somewhat less quantity than those found in schizophrenics. Although knowing the difference between right and wrong, many of these individuals cannot translate their knowledge into effective inhibitions (Goldberg, 2001).[2] This appears to be more evidence that personality disorders may be an early stage of psychotic illness. At the same time, the quality of personality disturbances probably influences the predisposition, manifestation, course and treatment of many Axis I conditions. The previous discussion is important in the assessment of offenders suffering from personality disorders.

NEUROIMAGING IN BORDERLINE PERSONALITY DISORDER

Various investigators have found that the impulsive aggression of persons diagnosed with a borderline personality disorder is most probably the consequence of a disruption of the emotional modulation circuits. These circuits include parts of the brain such as the anterior cingulate cortex (ACC), the orbital frontal cortex (OFC), the ventromedial prefrontal cortex (VMC), and the dorsolateral prefrontal cortex (DLPFC). The ACC and the OFC have extensive connections with the amygdala and it is thought that they are "involved in the evaluation of emotional stimuli, responses to conflict, regulation of emotional responses and play an inhibitory role in regulating the amygdala" (Goodman, Triebwasser, Shah & New, 2007, p. 101). The DLPFC, which integrates cognition with emotion to better control emotions, is neurophysiologically deficient in PET studies on persons with borderline personality disorder, just as in schizophrenia. Also, structural neuroimaging studies of the brains of patients suffering from borderline personaltiy disorder show a significant reduction in volume of the right ACC and of the total frontal lobes, also as in schizophrenia. The finding of a reduced concentration of N-acetylaspartate of almost one-fifth (19%) supports a reduction of neuronal density in the DLPFC. The amygdala and the hippocampus are smaller in volume, as are the left OFC and the right ACC. Because of the magnetic resonance imaging (MRI) and functional magnetic resonance imaging (fMRI) findings, borderline personality disorder also is described as a hyperarousal-dyscontrol syndrome due to the lack of inhibitory control by the frontal lobe and the hyperactivity of the amygdala (Goodman et al., 2007). This is also referred to as a deficiency of the top-down control of negative emotions. In impulsive aggression by borderline personality disorder patients, there is an actual frontal disinhibition, and this finding is important in the assessment of their legal responsibility in alleged criminal acting out. A deficiency of the neurotransmitter serotonin, which controls the homeostasis of the brain, has also been reported in these persons.

Neuroimaging in Schizotypal Personality Disorder

The schizotypal personality disorder has a cognitive-perceptual disturbance similar to that found in schizophrenia. In this personality disorder, the
activities of the prefrontal regions are reduced. On MRI examination, the
lateral ventricles of the brain are sometimes found to have a larger volume
and, when that is so, the schizotypal personality disorder is of greater severity. Other radioimaging findings are a larger right hippocampus and increased pointedness of the caudate nucleus (Goodman et al., 2007), which
may interfere with memory and responsivity.

Neuroimaging in Antisocial Personality Disorder and Psychopathy

Neuroimaging findings in ASPD on MRI show that the prefrontal gray
matter of the brain is diminished in volume (thinning) and the volume of the
amygdala is decreased, especially when the level of psychopathy is high. On
fMRI the activity of the amygdala, which is at the base of the brain, is at
times decreased. Also, the amygdala, the PFC, and the DLPFC show dysfunction. One study found that in "criminal psychopaths, the fMRI showed
decreased activity in the amygdala, hippocampal formation, parahippocam-
pal gyrus, ventral striatum and anterior and posterior cingulated gyrus"
(Goodman et al., 2007, p. 103), all of which are important for normal brain
functioning.

CONCLUSION

The earlier discussion supports the idea that in order to assess the criminal behavior of offenders, most of whom can be classified as suffering from
a personality disorder, a complete investigation needs not only a clinical
assessment but also a thorough appraisal of the underlying function of their
brains by neuroimaging and neuropsychological testing.

REFERENCES

Abrahamsen, D. (1952). *Who Are the Guilty?* New York: Rinehart & Co.
Alexander, F. (1948). *Fundamentals of Psychoanalysis.* New York: W.W. Norton.
Alexander, F., and Ross, H. (1952). *Dynamic Psychiatry.* Chicago: University of Chicago Press.
American Psychiatric Association. (2000). *Diagnostic and Statistical Manual of Mental Disorders*
    (4th ed., text revision). Washington, DC: American Psychiatric Association.
Arieti, S. (1967). *The Intrapsychic Self.* New York: Basic Books.

Arrigo, B., and Shipley, S. (2001). The confusion over psychopathy (I): Historical considerations. *International Journal of Offender Therapy and Comparative Criminology, 45*, 325–344 .

Bennett, W.J., DiIulio, J.J., Jr., and Walters, J.P. (1996). *Body Count.* New York: Simon & Schuster.

Brittain, R.P. (1970). The sadistic murderer. *Medicine, Science and the Law, 10*, 198–207.

Bromberg, W. (1965). *Crime and the Mind: A Psychiatric Analysis of Crime and Punishment.* New York: Macmillan.

Bryant, E.T., Scott, M.L., and Golden. C.J. (1984). Neuropsychological deficits, learning disability, and violent behavior. *Journal of Consulting and Clinical Psychology, 52*, 323–324.

Cleckley, H. (1955). *The Mask of Sanity.* St. Louis, Mosby.

Damasio, A. (1994). *Descartes' Error: Emotion, Reason, and the Human Brain.* New York: Penguin Books.

Diamond, B. (1994). From M'Naghten to Currens, and beyond. In J. M. Quen (Ed.), *The Psychiatrist in the Courtroom: The Selected Papers of Bernard L. Diamond, M.D.* (pp. 249–266). Hillsdale, NJ: The Analytic Press.

DiTullio, B. (1960). *Principî di Criminologia Clinica e Psichiatria Forense* [Principles of Clinical Criminology and Forensic Psychiatry]. Rome, Italy: Istituto di Medicina Sociale.

Fenichel, O. (1945). *The Psychoanalytic Theory of Neurosis.* New York: Norton.

Freud, S. (1960). *The Ego and the Id.* (F. Riviere, Trans.), J. Strachey (Ed.). New York: W. W. Norton & Company.

Gemelli, A., and Zunini, G. (1949). *Introduzione alla Psicologia* [Introduction to Psychology]. Milan, Italy: Vita e Pensiero.

Goldberg, E. (2001). *The Executive Brain: Frontal Lobes and the Civilized Mind.* New York: Oxford University Press.

Goodman, M., Triebwasser, J., Shah S., and New, A.S. (2007). Neuroimaging in personality disorders: Current concepts, findings, and implications. *Psychiatric Annals, 37*, 100–108.

Grafman, J., Schwab, K., Warden, D., Pridgen, A., Brown, H.R., and Salazar, A.M. (1996). Frontal lobe injuries, violence and aggression: A report of the Vietnam head injury study. *Neurology, 46*, 1231–1238.

Gunderson, J.G., and Singer, M. (1975). Defining borderline patients: An overview. *The American Journal of Psychiatry, 132*, 1–10.

Guttmacher, M.S. (1972). The psychiatric approach to crime and correction. In D. Dressler (Ed.), *Readings in Criminology and Penology* (pp. 294–300). Glencoe, IL: The Free Press.

Halleck, S.L. (1967). *Psychiatry and the Dilemma of Crime,* New York: Harper and Row/Hoeber Medical Books.

Hare, R.D. (1993). *Without Conscience: The Disturbing World of the Psychopaths Among Us.* New York: Pocket Books/Simon & Schuster.

Hofer, P. (1988). Prisonization and recidivism: A psychological perspective. *International Journal of Offender Therapy and Comparative Criminology, 32*, 95–106.

Kaplan, H.I., Sadock, B.J., and Grebb, J.A. (1994). *Kaplan and Sadock's Synopsis of Psychiatry: Behavioral Sciences/Clinical Psychiatry* (7th ed.) Baltimore: Williams & Wilkins.

Kaufmann,W. (1974). *Nietzsche* (4th ed.) Princeton: Princeton University Press.

Kernberg, O.F. (1992). *Aggression in Personality Disorders and Perversions.* New Haven: CT Yale University Press.

Klein, M. (1935). A contribution to the psychogenesis of manic-depressive states. *International Journal of Psychoanalysis, 16*, 145–174.

Koch, J. L. (1891). *Die psychopathischen Mindwertigkeite* [The Psychopathic Inferiorities]. Ravensburg, Germany:

Kohut, H. (1971). The psychoanalytic study of the child. Monograph No. 4. In *The Analysis of the Self.* New York: International University Press.

Kraepelin, E. (1915). *Psychiatrie: Ein lehrbuch* [Psychiatry: A Textbook], (8th ed., Vol. 4). Leipzig, Germany: Barth.

Lombroso, C. (1889). *L'uomo delinquente* [The Criminal Man], (4th ed.). Torino, Italy: Bocca.

MacCulloch, M.J., Snowden, P.R., Wood, P.J.W., and Mills, H.E. (1983). Sadistic fantasy, sadistic behaviour, and offending. *British Journal of Psychiatry, 143,* 20–29.

Macdonald, J.M. (1961). *The Murderer and His Victim.* Springfield, IL: Charles C Thomas.

Mahler, M. (1972). A study of the separation-individuation process. *Psychoanalytic Study Child, 26,* 403–424.

Maudsley, H. (1898). *Responsibility in Mental Disease.* New York, D. Appleton and Co..

Palermo, G.B. (2004). *The Faces of Violence* (2nd ed.). Springfield, IL: Charles C Thomas.

Pauvert, J.J. (1965). *Vie du marquis de Sade.* Paris, France: Édition Jean-Jacques Pauvert et Éditions Gallinard.

Pinel, P. ([1901] 1962). *A Treatise on Insanity.* (D. Davis, Trans.). New York: Hafner.

Prentky, R.A., Burgess, A.W., Rokous, F., Lee, A., Hartman, C., Ressler, R., and Douglas, J. (1989). The presumptive role of fantasy in serial sexual homicide. *American Journal of Psychiatry, 146,* 887–891.

Prichard, J. C. (1835). *A Treatise on Insanity and Other Disorders Affecting the Mind.* London: Sherwood, Gilbert, and Piper.

Raine, A., Buchsbaum, M., and LaCasse, L. (1997). Brain abnormalities in murderers indicated by positron emission tomography. *Biological Psychiatry, 42,* 495–508.

Redding, R.E. (2006). The brain disordered defendant: Neuroscience and legal insanity in the twenty-first century. *Villanova Public Law and Legal Theory Working Paper* Series, No. 2006-17 [Online]. Available: http://papers.ssrn.com/sol3/papers.cfm?abstract_id=937349. Accessed March 21, 2008.

Reich, W. [1972] (1990). *Character Analysis* (V. R. Carfagno, Trans.) (3rd, enl. ed.). New York: Noonday Press.

Rush, B. (1812). *Medical Inquiries and Observations Upon the Diseases of the Mind.* Philadelphia: Kimber & Richardson.

Sellin, T. (1972). Crime as violation of conduct norms. In D. Dressler (Ed.), *Readings in Criminology and Penology* (pp. 10–19). Glencoe, IL: The Free Press.

Sheldon, W.H. (with S.S. Stevens). (1942). *The Varieties of Temperament: A Psychology of Constitutional Differences.* New York: Harper & Brothers.

Stoudemire, A. (1994). *Clinical Psychiatry for Medical Students.* New York: Lippincott.

Tappan, P. (1947). Who is the criminal? *American Sociological Review,* 97–102.

Toch, H. (1969). *Violent Men.* New York: Aldine.

von Krafft-Ebing, R. (1922). *Psychopathis Sexualis: With Special Reference to the Antipathic Sexual Instinct. A medico-forensic study.* rev. ed.. F.J. Rebman (trans.) New York, Medical Art Agency.

Warren, J.I., Hazelwood, R.R., and Dietz, P.E. (1996) The sexually sadistic serial killer. *Journal of Forensic Sciences, 41,* 970-974.

Wilson, J. Q., and Herrstein, R.J. (1985). *Crime and Human Nature.* New York: Simon & Schuster.

Winnicott, D. (2008). Accessed May 25, 2008. Available: http://changingminds.org/disciplines/psychoanalysis/theorists/winnicott.htm/.

Chapter Three

THE ROLE OF THE FORENSIC PSYCHOLOGIST

Andreas Kapardis and Georgia Panayiotou

Being admitted by a judge as an expert witness to testify in a trial confers status on a professional and his or her specialist scientific field. This chapter first considers forensic psychologists as expert witnesses in the court and then focuses on their role in the assessment of defendants and the impact of crime on victims. The earliest description of the role of expert evidence in common law courts is to be found in the case of Buckley v. Rice Thomas in 1554 (Freckelton & Selby, 2005).[1] One of the earliest psychologists to testify in a criminal trial was J. Varendonck in Belgium in about 1911 (Bartol & Bartol, 2004), but it was in 1921 that an American psychologist testified as an expert in a courtroom for the first time in 1921.[2] Lawyers' and other professionals' demands for expert evidence by psychologists have increased significantly since the 1980s, reflecting growing recognition that psychologists "have a unique contribution to make to judicial proceedings" (Gudjonsson, 1993). Although the specialization most involved in forensic psychology in practice is clinical psychology, other fields showing increasing involvement of psychologists as experts in English-speaking western common law countries include syndrome evidence, confessions by suspects, battered woman syndrome, victim profile evidence, parental alienation syndrome, eyewitness testimony, and family law.

---

1. Plowd 118 at 124; 75 ER E2 at 191. The first psychologist to testify in the U.S. at a civil trial was Karle Marbe in around 1911.
2. 88 W, Va 479, 107 SE 189 (1921)- cited by Bartol and Bartol (2004) p. 9.

THE ROLE OF THE EXPERT WITNESS IN LAW

The role of witnesses in a civil or criminal trial is to state the facts as they have been directly observed by them. In other words, witnesses do not give their opinions. However, the law makes an exception to this basic rule in the case of an expert when a tribunal of fact decides that a specific issue calls for an expert witness because the particular expertise does not fall within the knowledge and experience of the judge or jury and a witness qualifies as an expert. In some jurisdictions (for example, the United States) an expert witness is allowed to also express an opinion on the ultimate issue, the very question that the tribunal itself has to answer.

The question of whether a witness is an expert is a question of fact for the judge to decide. A particular and special knowledge of a subject that has been acquired through scientific study or experience can qualify a witness as an expert (Cattermole, 1984). Haward (1981) identified four roles for forensic psychologists (using the term forensic in a broad sense) appearing as expert witnesses:[3]

Experimental: informing the court (1) about the state of knowledge relevant to some cognitive process or (2) carrying out an experiment directly relevant to the individual's case before the court.

Clinical: testifying, for example, on their assessment of a client's personality, IQ, neuropsychological functioning, mental state, or behavior.

Actuarial: in a civil case, for example, estimating the probability that a plaintiff claiming damages for a psychological deficit caused by someone's negligence could live on his or her own or be gainfully employed, or both.

Advisory: advising counsel before and during a trial about what questions to ask the other side's witnesses, including their expert witnesses.

Kraus and Sales (2001) used 208 psychology undergraduates as subjects and a Texas death penalty case involving the issue of dangerousness to investigate whether mock jurors are more influenced by clinical opinion expert testimony or actuarial expert testimony. They found that mock jurors weigh clinical expert opinion more heavily than they do actuarial expert testimony. However, because the authors of the study do not report any evidence concerning its external validity, their results should be treated with caution.

Psychologists in the United States have been appearing as experts more frequently and in a larger range of cases than do their counterparts in other western English-speaking common law countries. Regarding the "hired gun" effect idea, a mock-juror study by Cooper and Neuhaus (2000) used 140 jury-

---

3. See Blau (2001) for a thorough text on the psychologist as expert witness in the United States.

eligible residents in New Jersey age 18 to 72 years as subjects, and the legal case used involved the scientific issue of whether a chemical to which the plaintiff had been exposed was the immediate cause of his cancer. It was found that: (1) the experts who are highly paid for their testimony and testify frequently are perceived as "hired guns," and (2) they are neither liked nor believed, especially if the expert testimony adduced is complex and cannot be easily processed.

In western common law countries, expert witnesses testify for the side that has retained them and pays their fees. In contrast to this practice, in continental European jurisdictions expert witnesses are normally appointed by the court to assist the court. Cooper and Hall (2000) found that mock jurors sided with the court-appointed expert in every condition except when the expert favored a corporate defendant. Let us next look at expert testimony by a forensic psychologist in the United States but also, briefly, in England, Australia, New Zealand, and Canada for comparison purposes.

United States of America

As far as the courts' criteria for admitting expert testimony is concerned, in the landmark decision in the case of *Frye v. United States* (1923), the District of Columbia Court of Appeals rejected (1) testimony by a lie-detector expert[4] that the defendant was telling the truth when he denied having committed the alleged offence on the grounds that the scientific theory on which it was based was not generally accepted within the relevant professional community and (2) a request by the defense attorney that the lie-detector expert conduct his test in the jury's presence. The decision in Frye made "general acceptance in the particular [scientific] field" (1923, p. 1014) the standard criterion for admitting expert testimony into courts. The *Federal Rules of Evidence* (FRE) were adopted by Congress in 1975 and included a modified standard for admitting expert testimony, namely that the scientific evidence proffered be relevant and reliable. The FRE and Frye standards continued to be applied by courts in the United States until 1993 when a landmark unanimous decision was handed down by the U.S. Supreme Court in *Daubert v. Merrell Dow Pharmaceuticals* (1993). According to the ruling in Daubert, the test for expert witnesses is "vigorous cross-examination, presentation of contrary evidence, and careful instruction."[5] More specifically, the *Daubert* judgment stated, *inter alia*, that, "the subject of an expert's testimony must be 'scientific . . . knowledge' . . . in order to qualify as 'scientific knowledge,' an inference or assertion must be derived by the scientific method" (p. 2795)

---

4. The expert concerned was William Marston, a pioneer in the use of the polygraph to detect lying.

5. Quoted in Landsman (1995, p. 155).

and "the criterion of the scientific status of a theory is its falsifiability, or refutability, or testability. . . . Another pertinent consideration is whether the theory or technique has been subjected to peer review and publication" (pp. 2796–2797).

The next significant Supreme Court decision was handed down in *General Electric Co. v. Joiner*, (1997). The issue in that case was whether Joiner's exposure over sixteen years to electrical transformer chemicals at work (The Water and Light Department of Thomasville in Georgia) contributed to his lung cancer even though he was a smoker. The trial judge excluded the testimony provided by Joiner's expert witnesses on the grounds that, it "did not rise above 'subjective belief or unsupported speculation.'" In other words, the expert witness in *General Electric Co. v. Joiner* did not show the scientific link between his lung cancer and the exposure to chemicals. The appellate court reversed the trial judge's decision, but the Supreme Court reversed it again, reinstating the trial judge's exclusion, stating that the legal standard for allowing expert testimony to be put to the jury is the same as that which the relevant professional community uses (Gutheil & Stein, 2000).

The question of whether the *Daubert* guidelines apply to all forms of technical or otherwise specialized knowledge, or just scientific knowledge, was addressed by the U.S. Supreme Court in *Kumho Tire Co. v. Patrick Carmichael*, (1999). *Kumho* concerned the expert testimony of an engineer testifying that a defective car tire caused a car accident. *Kumho* clarified that the *Daubert* analysis applies not only to scientific knowledge but also to scientific, technical, and otherwise specialized knowledge. The reader should note in this context that although the threesome of *Daubert, General Electric Co., and Kumho* is the basis for federal courts in the United States deciding whether to admit expert testimony, according to Kassin, Tubb, Hosch, and Memon (2001), a large number of state courts continue to use the *Frye* standard of "general acceptance." What, then, has been the impact of the three cases on judges and attorneys in the United States?

Krafka and colleagues (2002) carried out three questionnaire surveys (one each of federal judges in 1991 and 1998 and another of attorneys in 1999) and found that practices and beliefs changed regarding expert testimony in the wake of Daubert in 1993. More specifically, the clarification of the admissibility criteria has encouraged both judges and attorneys to scrutinize proffered testimony more actively. One third of judges admit expert evidence less frequently than were admitted before *Daubert.* There has been a reduction in the number of trials in which all of the proffered expert testimony has been allowed; judges hold more pretrial *Daubert*-like hearings than in the past. Attorneys increasingly scrutinize the qualifications of the experts they hire as well as file more motions to have the expert of the other side excluded. Finally, attorneys are more involved in preparing their expert's testimony. Krafka and coworkers (2002) also found that the *Daubert* and post-*Daubert* decisions have not affected the problems faced by judges (e.g. partisan experts) and attorneys (e.g. excessive fees charged by experts). Finally, Krafka et al's research suggests that judges limit or exclude expert testimony for the same reasons as in the past, namely for being irrelevant, because the expert witness is not qualified, or because the testimony will not assist the trier of fact (2002, p. 17). The findings of Krafka and colleagues, however, should be treated with caution because of the unrepresentativeness of their self-selected sample of judges.

Daubert, Kumho, and *General Electric Co.* assume that American judges are capable of making judgments about the scientific reliability and validity of proffered scientific evidence. Gatowski and coworkers (2001) surveyed a proportionate stratified random sample of state court judges and found that:

- Many of the judges surveyed did not possess the scientific literacy apparently required by *Daubert* in order to perform the "gate keeping" role defined in *Daubert.*
- Only 5 percent knew the meaning of the term "falsifiability" and only 4 percent knew the meaning of "error rate."
- There was little consensus about the relative importance of the *Daubert* guidelines, and judges emphasized they required more "general acceptance" as an admissibility criterion.
- Most did not apply judicial guidelines in differentiating between "scientific" and "nonscientific" expert evidence.

Gatowki and colleagues' findings are undoubtedly a cause for concern. Interestingly enough, Post-*Kumho* decisions such as *United States v. Plaza* (2002) show a preparedness by courts in the United States to admit expert testimony concerning a technique that may not be based on falsifiable theory but enjoys general acceptance within the community of its practitioners. In other words, American courts do not appear to adhere to a strict application of the *Daubert* criteria for admissibility of expert evidence as had been feared.

England and Wales

Until recently, British courts have been rather unenthusiastic about expert evidence by psychologists (Sheldon & McCleod, 1991). The landmark decision in a provocation case *R v. Turner* (1975) has meant that, unlike in the United States, expert testimony has had to surmount a rather difficult impediment to admissibility, namely the "common knowledge and experience" rule of evidence. This common law principle can be traced to the case of *Folkes v. Chadd* in 1782 in which Lord Mansfield ruled that an expert's opinion is admissible if it provides the court with information that is likely to lie outside the common knowledge and experience of the jury. The gist of the *R. v. Turner* decision is that, until recently, the courts in England and Wales have adhered to the view that they do not need a psychologist's or psychiatrist's expert knowledge when it comes to psychological processes except when mental abnormality is involved.

Examination of English authorities since *R. v. Turner* shows that psychological evidence that is not abnormal or does not directly concern the defendant's state of mind or the issue of intent has generally been excluded. However, there have been a number of encouraging decisions indicating greater readiness to admit psychological evidence (Thornton, 1995). The restrictive interpretation of the rule in *R. v. Turner* was relaxed by the Court of Appeal in the case of *R. v. Sally Loraine Emery* (and another) (1993) that concerned the admissibility of expert testimony about posttraumatic stress disorder (PTSD), learned helplessness, and the battered woman syndrome. The reader should note in this context that defense lawyers most often enlist the services of an expert to testify but in the battered woman syndrome an effort is made to strengthen the argument that their client was acting in self-defense.

According to Colman and Mackay (1995), "The effect of the Emery judgment therefore appears to open the door to psychological evidence in a far wider range than has hitherto been the case" (p. 264). More recently, in *R. v. Bowman* (2006), in addition to reiterating a list of duties owed to the court by an expert witness in a criminal trial as set out primarily[6] in *R. v. Harris* and others (2005), it adopted a less restrictive approach to the whole issue of expert testimony admissibility criteria than the U.S. Supreme Court in *Daubert* and post-*Daubert* decisions. The Court of Appeal emphasized the importance of a court having the benefit of developments in scientific thinking and techniques, even if such knowledge and techniques are still at the stage of hypothesis.

In recent years, courts in England have opened the door to a broader range of cases than would have been possible under the restrictive interpretation of the rule in *R. v. Turner*. The common knowledge rule itself, of course, has not been abandoned but has been interpreted more broadly than in *R. v. Turner*. Other examples in which the *R. v. Turner* rule was relaxed and courts have shown a readiness to admit expert evidence are in relation to psychological profiling evidence (see *Guilfoyle* [2001]) and the psychological vulnerability of particular suspects to confess to a crime during police questioning (Gudjonsson, 2002).

---

6. See also *The Ikarian Reefer* [1993] 2 Loyds Rep. 68. *R. v. Kai-Whitewind* [2005] All ER (D) 14 (May) that was also considered.

Further evidence that courts in England and Wales are readier to admit expert evidence by psychologists on matters that do not fall within abnormal behavior is seen in the fact that well-known forensic psychologists have now testified as experts on a broad range of psycholegal issues in a number of cases (Kapardis, 2003).

Australia, New Zealand, and Canada

Drawing on Freckelton and Selby's (2005) book for this section, expert testimony by mental health professionals in Australian and New Zealand courts has been allowed for example, for sentencing, postaccident impairment, competence to stand trial, criminal responsibility, capacity to work, degree of mental retardation, trauma suffered by victims of crime, behavior of victims, insanity defense, operation of memory, trademark infringement and fraudulent advertising, causation of death as a result of mental state, custodial and access arrangements, and effects of discrimination. Interestingly enough, the existing precedent (*Johnson and Johnson*, unreported Full Court of Family Court of Australia, 7 July 1997) offers but limited support to the parental alienation syndrome (Freckelton & Selby, 2005). Evidence from mental health professionals has been disallowed on the working of memory (*R. v. Fong*, 1981; *R. v. Smith*, 1987); the typical behavior of children after they have been molested (*R. v. B*, 1987), the likelihood of a defendant having made a particular record of interview to the police (*Murphy v. R.*, 1989; Freckelton, 1990), and polygraph evidence (New South Wales District Court in *R. v. Murray*, 1982; *Mallard v. The Queen*, 2003).

In Canada, the Supreme Court's decisions in *R. v. Mohan* (1994) and in *R. v. J-L* (2000) "have opened the door to criminal profiling evidence" (Freckelton & Selby, 2005).[7] Canadian courts have generally admitted expert testimony on a broader range of issues instead of focusing narrowly on mental illness, as has been the approach of courts in England, Australia, and New Zealand. Although the impact of the *Daubert* decision on Canadian courts is difficult to predict, it is interesting to note that in *R. v. Johnston* (1992) (a DNA case) it was held that the *Frye* test was not part of Canadian law and that the criteria for admissibility for novel scientific evidence were relevance and helpfulness to the tribunal of fact, helpfulness to be decided by considering a list of fourteen factors. Canadian courts have disallowed expert evidence on the operation of memory (*R. v. M.*, 1997) and eyewitness identification (*R. v. McCarthy*, 1997).

7. See two recent decisions in Canada in *R. v. Ranger* (2003) 178 CCC (3d) and *R. v. Clark* (2004) 182 CCC (ed) which mean that profiling experts may well be allowed to testify if they confine themselves to explaining to the court what the crime scene shows and how the crime was committed and not why they believe the defendant behaved in a particular way and what attributes the offender is likely to possess (Freckelton & Selby, 2005, p. 454).

THE IMPACT OF EXPERT TESTIMONY BY PSYCHOLOGISTS

Testimony by an expert witness can have a significant effect on the outcome of a trial. The impact of an expert testifying in a real case in court can vary, of course, from the size of damages awarded in a civil suit, and jurors' assessment of a witness's reliability to a jury's verdict in a criminal case and even the freeing of persons wrongly convicted and imprisoned for life. Drawing on Kraus and Sales' (2001) discussion of the literature, researchers have reported that juror decision making is influenced if expert testimony is presented on the following issues:

- The fallibility of eyewitness identifications
- Clinical syndromes (for example, battered wife syndrome, rape trauma syndrome, child sexual abuse syndrome, and depressed memory syndrome)
- Insanity
- Future dangerousness of a defendant

Bornstein (2004) reported that in a personal injury case the expert witness had greater impact on mock jurors' verdict when presenting anecdotal case histories than did experimental data and also that the expert's perceived credibility correlated with the subject's liability judgments. A possible explanation for Bornstein's results may be the fact that mock jurors are more likely to be influenced when the expert explicitly links the research findings to the case at hand (Kovera, Borgida & Gresham, 1996).

Appearing as Experts

Poor evidence by forensic psychologists appearing as experts can be very damaging for psychologists in general, undermining the posititve impact that psychologists can have on developments within the legal system, and can have a disastrous effect on individual cases, causing miscarriages of justice (Gudjonsson, 1993). For Gudjonsson, poor psychological evidence is testimony that does not inform and is misleading or incorrect. Furthermore, the characteristics of such poor evidence are "poor preparation, lack of knowledge and experience, low level of thoroughness, and inappropriate use or misinterpretation of test results" (p. 120).

Advice for forensic psychologists, like other expert witnesses,[8] who wish to avoid the embarrassing and unpleasant experience of seeing their expert testimony being distorted and their professional reputation damaged, includes the following:

---

8. See Freckelton and Selby (2005, p. 873–906) for detailed advice to expert witnesses by two very experienced and highly respected barristers.

- Be very familiar with courtroom procedure, rules of evidence, and ways of presenting psychological data to a bench or a jury, and be aware of the conduct expected of an expert witness (Wardlaw, 1984).
- Have well-prepared reports and other evidence and, if inexperienced, undertake some training in how to best handle lawyers' cross-examination (Carson, 1990; Nijboer, 1995).
- Stick to one's own area of expertise and be explicit and open (Nijboer, 1995).
- American attorney Michael Lee[9] lists the following top five mistakes expert witnesses make: (1) relying only on information provided by the lawyer, (2) forgetting that he or she is an advocate for his or her own opinions and methodology but not for the case itself, (3) putting too much in writing too soon and too casually, (4) being myopic, and (5) sounding too much like an "expert." Regarding cross-examination, Wardlaw (1984) lists a number of rules likely to prove helpful for the witness. These include:
- Answer all questions and do not allow counsel for the other side to put words in your mouth. Do not make guesses and take as much time as you need to reply to questions.
- If under attack, keep calm and avoid getting angry or unreasonably defensive.
- Prepare for the cross-examination by trying to anticipate the questions by imagining that you are the one who is to cross-examine.

As already mentioned, a forensic psychologist who will testify in a court case must have a well-prepared report. Let us next focus on what forensic psychological assessment of crime suspects and defendants as well as victims entails.

THE ROLE OF FORENSIC PSYCHOLOGISTS IN THE ASSESSMENT OF CRIMINAL BEHAVIOR AND ITS IMPACT ON VICTIMS

Psychological assessment is one of the chief activities of clinical, forensic, and other applied psychologists. It involves a systematic and ongoing evaluation of the individual. The decisiveness of psychological expert opinion in these settings accentuates the need for applied psychologists to perform evaluations in an ethical, professional, thorough, and, as best as possible, empirically validated manner.

---

9. Source http://library.findlaw.com/2005/jul/22/186441.html

The clinical or forensic psychologist may be called in to answer a variety of questions within forensic settings in order to aid legal decision makers through providing scientifically based information (Grisso, 1986). Questions posed to the psychologist include competency to stand trial, appropriate disposition, danger to self and others, possibility of malingering and so on. Assessment of a suspect's fitness to stand trial may involve an evaluation of the client's cognitive ability (i.e. ability to understand the proceedings), mental status (state of consciousness, psychiatric symptoms that interfere with comprehension of the situation, sensory and perceptual deficits), and organic deficits or use of substances as well as emotional reactivity to certain events that may interfere with his or her judgment. In the case of victims of crime, the psychologist may be asked to determine the severity of the psychological impact of the crime and the degree of disability this may have caused. In both cases, the psychologist may have to judge, based on empirical evidence, whether the perpetrator or the victim is engaged in malingering (faking bad or faking good) for the purposes of securing a better outcome for himself or herself, a task that can prove challenging if appropriate scientific guidelines are not maintained (Rogers & Cruise, 2000). Thus, the role of the forensic psychologist is multifaceted, and the expert will need to rely on a wide array of tools in order to answer the referral questions.

The Process of Psychological Assessment in Forensic Settings

Psychological assessment involves several methods and stages. It almost always includes a clinical interview, often supplemented by the use of standardized tests, behavioral observations, life records, and less frequently the collection of biological and psychophysiological data. Assessment in forensic settings poses some special challenges. The assessment is often court ordered or requested by lawyers, which means that the individual involved may lack the motivation to be fully cooperative in disclosing personal information or presenting an accurate picture of his or her strengths and weaknesses. Limitations aside, the forensic psychologist continues to be ethically bound to carry out the evaluation in an objective manner, treat the subject with respect, and constantly keep in mind the benefit of the person and society in general (which are at times contradictory).

Assessment of Perpetrators of Violence

One of the primary goals of assessment is diagnosis and classification. Although most people with psychological and organic disorders are not violent and do not commit crimes, for those who do act violently, psychopathological processes or organic problems are often the driving force behind their behavior. Through a thorough assessment the clinician will be in a position to give an enlightened expert opinion to courts, direct the perpetrator to appropriate interventions, and help protect potential future victims.

The purpose of the psychological assessment of perpetrators is usually to (1) gather information about the circumstances of the crime; (2) construct a personality profile of the suspect or criminal in order to evaluate his or her potential for committing the crime, and the circumstance under which he or she could have reacted in the specific manner; (3) determine the probability of future danger to self and others; and (4) suggest the best-fitting rehabilitation setting if the suspect is judged to be responsible for the crime.

The Clinical Interview

As in every psychological assessment, the evaluation of a perpetrator or potentially violent client begins with a thorough clinical interview and history, which can be further informed with the use of archival information from previous psychiatric or police records and interviews with family members, former therapists, and others who know the client in various contexts. The clinical interview, in order to be informative, needs to be carried out in a context of rapport.

Once the ice has been broken, the clinician can proceed with gathering the essential components of the client's history, including the history of the present problem (violent or criminal behavior). Was the violent outbreak an atypical behavior that only occurred once or has there been a history of violent actions that happen under specific conditions or provocations or that escalate in predictable ways? As psychologists are well aware, previous behavior is the best predictor of future behavior, so uncovering a history of violence or criminality is crucial. What is the frequency, target, and precursor of violence? Is there a history of other impulsive or violent behavior such as suicide attempts, use of drugs, dangerous sexual activity, or criminality? Answers to these questions may help predict the likelihood of a future expression of violence as well as point to particular diagnostic hypotheses, such as a brief psychotic episode versus a personality disorder. A developmental, medical, social and family history is also essential. Taking the client's history helps form initial diagnostic hypotheses that will then be evaluated through further testing and more targeted interviews. It also allows the client to tell his or her story and the clinician to demonstrate interest, thus further helping to build rapport. Clinical interviews can then extend to family members, employers, or others who know the client (with the client's consent or with a court order) in order to validate and supplement the information gathered and to better understand the family and social context in which the person routinely functions.

Mental Status Examination

The mental status examination is an essential component of assessment, particularly when competency to stand trial or ability to be aware of the consequences of one's actions at the time the criminal act was committed are in question. Some of the information required in this examination will already be obtained through the history interview; the clinician will be able to see if the client is currently oriented, fully conscious, or blatantly psychotic. Richness of vocabulary, long-term memory, concentration, and organization of thought will also usually be apparent through the interview, although specific questions are included in standardized mental status exams to assess these processes (e.g. Folstein, Folstein, & McHugh, 1975). Many organic disorders manifest with impairments in cognitive and affective processes, consciousness and overt behavior. Patients who are in delirium, caused by intoxication, withdrawal from substances, or another medical condition, may be disoriented, demonstrate perceptual and memory disturbances, and show psychomotor agitation (American Psychiatric Association [APA], 1994). Patients with dementia may also occasionally be violent because of paranoid ideas or increased frustration due to realization of their cognitive deterioration. Most importantly, in the context of the mental status exam, the clinician should determine if the client is under the influence of a psychotropic substance or undergoing withdrawal symptoms, because it is often the case that violence and criminal behavior happen during intoxication or in association with the turmoil caused by withdrawal (Haggard-Grann, Hallqvist, Langstrom & Moller, 2006).

Diagnostic Interviews

Diagnostic interviews usually attempt to identify the presence of symptoms as listed in formal taxonomic systems such as the *Diagnostic and Statistical Manual* (4th ed.; APA, 1994) (*DSM-IV*) or *International Classification of Diseases* (10th ed.) (*ICD-10*). To aid in this process, several structured and semi-structured interviews have been developed that include standardized questions that assess the presence and severity of the criteria required for a diagnosis. Commonly used structured interviews include the SCID, SCID-II (Spitzer, Williams, Gibbon & First, 1992) and ADIS-R/ADIS-IV (DiNardo & Barlow, 1988). The purpose of diagnostic interviews is to verify or rule out hypotheses regarding the presence of certain disorders sometimes associated with violence. Such disorders include schizophrenia, schizophrenia spectrum and other psychotic disorders, mood disorders, personality disorders, disruptive behavior disorders, and mental retardation. Reaching the appropriate diagnosis will help determine the appropriate disposition for the forensic client and suggest specific circumstances under which violence may take place. Arriving at a formal diagnosis is crucial in cases in which a suspect may plead insanity or in which mitigating factors are sought for criminal behavior. Diagnosis is also important when trying to predict how a convicted criminal will cope with confinement and with interactions with others within the correctional or rehabilitation facility.

Among children and adolescents who have engaged in violent or criminal behavior the most common diagnoses are oppositional defiant disorder and conduct disorder (Barkley, 1997). Dissociative identity disorder and other dissociative disorders are rare and intriguing conditions that have sometimes been implicated in criminal behavior, or at least have been called for in the context of insanity pleas (Orne, Dinges & Orne, 1984).

DSM-IV Axis II disorders also need to be assessed since the presence of a personality disorder or mental retardation may also have contributed to criminal behavior etiologically. Although patients with mental retardation or low cognitive ability are not typically violent or aggressive, low IQ may be associated with low tolerance for frustration, poor judgment, and lack of coping and verbal skills for solving problems and resisting provocations. When there is a suspicion that low IQ may be implicated in violence, formal testing with tests like the WAIS-R and evaluation of functional skills is in order.

Assessment of Antisocial Personality Disorder and Psychopathy

People commit crimes or engage in violent behaviors for a multitude of reasons that will need to be uncovered. A group of individuals who are at high risk for repetitively engaging in criminal and violent behavior, who show little remorse for their actions and are therefore poor candidates for rehabilitation, are those described as psychopaths or individuals with antisocial personality disorder (APD) (APA, 1994). Many adults with APD were diagnosed with conduct disorder or oppositional defiant disorder, or both as children (Robins, 1978) and, therefore, show long histories of rule violations and aggression against others.

APD is similar but by no means identical to a diagnostic category that is not listed in the *DSM-IV*, namely psychopathic personality disorder. In an early description Cleckley (1941) described the psychopathic personality as someone who was egocentric; deceitful; shallow; manipulative; and lacking in empathy, guilt, and remorse. This description focuses on personality characteristics rather than overt behavior, highlighting the motivating factors behind criminal acts. As Hare (1993) described psychopaths, they are people who "charm, manipulate and ruthlessly plow their way through life," selfishly disregarding the rights and happiness of others. The psychopath looks out for himself or herself, seems to lack a conscience, and shows little empathy toward the pain of others. More recent versions of the *DSM* (*DSM-III, -IV*) base their diagnostic criteria for APD on much more behavioral and observable terms (Hare, 1983). The rationale for this change is that personality traits are often hard to measure and are unreliable, whereas the presence of overt behaviors is easier for clinicians to agree upon.

In addition, the focus on observable behavior aids in the attempt made in the recent versions of the *DSM* to maintain an atheoretical approach to diagnosis. Thus, APD, as it is recently conceptualized, is not identical to psychopathic personality, and this discrepancy has fueled many debates in the scientific literature. Most psychopaths meet the criteria for APD, but most people with APD are not psychopaths. Many APD individuals do have the ability to feel guilt and loyalty and may demonstrate this through their allegiance to gangs and other groups and subcultures. Similarly, a substantial percentage of people with APD and psychopathy will not demonstrate criminal behavior, or at least will not be "caught" and have contact with the legal system. In fact, many psychopaths function well in society, holding prominent roles in politics or business, putting their egocentric traits in the service of acquiring them high positions of power and personal achievement. According to Hart and Hare (1997), a diagnosis of APD does not have good predictive power for future recidivism, whereas psychopathic offenders are three to four times more likely to reoffend. APD can be diagnosed through structured and unstructured interviews that reflect the criteria of the taxonomic system; psychopathy can be assessed through the use of standardized and well-validated psychometric tests.

The Psychopathy Checklist and its twenty-item revised version (PCL-R) (Hare, 1991) have evolved into the golden standard for the assessment of psychopathy and rely on interviews and archival data. Factor analytic results (Cooke & Michie, 2001) yield a three-factor structure of (1) arrogant and deceitful interpersonal style, (2) deficient affective experience, and (3) impulsive and irresponsible behavioral style. Both the two- and three-factor structures have received empirical validation by showing reliable associations with other personality constructs and actual criminal behavior. For instance, the third factor has shown good predictive validity for frequency and severity of arrest and crimes against property, whereas the second factor predicts violence and crimes against people (Hall, Benning & Patrick, 2004).

A self-report measure of psychopathy is the Psychopathic Personality Inventory (PPI) (Lilienfeld & Andrews 1996), which seeks to overcome the common problems associated with self-report measures in this field that have to do with the potential for dishonest responding and lack of validity scales. The PPI contains eight subscales and four validity scales; factor analytical findings reveal that the same two dominant factors previously found in the

PCL (affective-interpersonal and social deviance) can also be extracted (Patrick, 1995). This evidence supports the view that the two constructs supported by the factors are indeed valid aspects of psychopathic personality.

In addition to trait-specific tests, even more specific variants of psychopathy can be traced in an individual through a thorough assessment that includes widely used global measures of personality such as the Minnesota Multiphasic Personality Inventory-2 (MMPI-2), MPQ and NEO-PI-R (Benning et al., 2005). Furthermore, assessment can be supplemented and information can be extracted through trait-specific tests that may appear less threatening and less likely to be faked by the respondent. These can include measures of traits conceptually associated with the core characteristics of psychopathy such as impulsivity (measured with Barratt Impulsiveness Scale-11 for example; Barratt & Slaughter, 1998), sensation seeking (Sensation Seeking Scale; Zuckerman, 1994), low agreeableness and conscientiousness measured with the NEO-PI-R, and high sensitivity to rewards, low sensitivity to punishment measured with the SPSRQ (Torrubia, Avila, Molto & Caseras, 2001).

Several indexes of the MMPI-2, perhaps the most commonly used measure of personality, can be used to make inferences regarding the presence of psychopathy and APD. Sellbom, Ben-Porath, Lilienfeld, Patrick, and Graham (2005) argue that other MMPI scales can be used to supplement the evidence from Scales 4 and 9. Such relevant MMPI-2 scales include the newly developed Restructured Clinical Scales (4, 9). In fact Sellbom, Ben-Porath, Lilienfeld, Patrick and Graham (2005) found that the optimal predictors of psychopathy were RC4 and RC9 for measurement of social deviance, coupled with low scores on RC7 (anxiety) and RC3 (depression) that tap into the interpersonal-affective characteristics (see also Sellbom, Ben-Porath & Stafford, 2007).

Of special concern is the assessment of psychopathy among juvenile offenders. Several rating scales and self-report measures exist for children and adolescents including the Psychopathy Checklist: Youth Version (Forth, Hart & Hare, 1990), Psychopathic Screening Device (Frick & Hare, 2002), Child Psychopathy Scale (Lynam, 1997), MMPI-A, and others. Evidence exists that all of these measures correlate significantly with other indicators of aggressive behavior and predict at least to some degree recidivism for violent crimes over a short period (Brandt, Kennedy, Patrick & Curtin, 1997). However, it will not be clear if such measures predict future violent behavior in adulthood unless longitudinal studies are carried out.

Finally, another useful tool in the hands of the clinician who assesses for the presence of psychopathy and antisocial traits is psychophysiological assessment. This is not used very frequently because it is time consuming and costly, but as the neurosciences develop and psychology evolves into a health science, the validity of these measures, due to their objectivity and nonreliance on self-report, may make them an attractive addition to the process of assessment. With further research into their validity, psychophysiological indexes such as skin conductance, heart rate, and startle response can become valuable in the assessment of psychopathy because of their ability to tap into basic motivational systems and their relative resilience to faking.

Assessment of Malingering

Both perpetrators of crime and victims may have reasons to fake good or fake bad in the process of assessment. It is important for the forensic psychologist to use every available tool for assessing the possibility of malingering. In this context, observation of the behavior and emotional reactions of the interviewee who is lying, and noticing inconsistencies in stories, erroneous descriptions of symptoms and symptom clusters, and exaggerated symptomatology can be important strategies (Palermo, Perracuti & Palermo, 1996) that can be supplemented with the use of valid psychometric tests.

A standard way of assessing malingering involves the validity scales of psychometric tests, such as the traditional F, K, and L scales of the MMPI-2. A T score of 100 on the F scale of the MMPI-2 has often been used to identify with good success (95–100%) those research subjects who have been asked to fake bad, but there was less predictive accuracy in forensic populations (Austin, 1992; Roman, Tuley, Villanueva & Mitchell, 1990). The F-K index and Obvious-Subtle scales are other frequently used tools that may, however, be less discriminating than is the F scale alone.

LEGAL AND ETHICAL ISSUES IN THE ASSESSMENT OF CRIMINAL AND VIOLENT BEHAVIOR

When dealing with suspects of crime or clients who have demonstrated violent behavior, the clinician is often faced with various ethical challenges. In all cases the clinician's best bet is to follow closely the regulations of the ethical code by which he or she abides and to consult with colleagues and supervisors when in doubt. Peer consultation is also important because the constant contact of a forensic clinician with crime and violence may quickly lead to burnout, which alone can lead to suboptimal professional practice and compromise the services offered to clients.

Assessment of Victims of Violence

The role of the clinician should be guided by similar ethical and professional principles when assessing victims, for which assessment questions are somewhat different. Victims of violent crimes require assessment in forensic settings in order to verify the claim that the crime was committed, evaluate the degree of damage, and propose corrective measures required to remedy the situation. Among persons who have experienced sexual or physical abuse, or both, for instance, common outcomes may include anxiety (panic, generalized anxiety disorder, phobias), depression, low self-esteem, somatization, dissociation, and sexual and relationship problems (Briere & Jordan, 2004). For abused children, the possibility of becoming abusers themselves is also a possible outcome. The most common diagnoses, particularly when the traumatic event was life threatening or outside the range of normal human experience involves PTSD or acute stress disorder (diagnosed within the first month after the event).

PTSD occurs when a person has experienced or witnessed an event that "involved actual or threatened death or serious injury or a threat to the physical integrity of the self or others" (APA, 1994). It includes symptoms of reexperiencing the event, such as intrusive recollections, dreams, or flashbacks; intense psychological distress and physiological reactivity when in contact with stimuli that are reminiscent of the traumatic event; avoidance of stimuli associated with the trauma; and general numbing or restriction of emotional experience that may impair relationships and intimacy. Increased startle response is a strong indicator of PTSD, bringing to the forefront psychophysiological methods of assessment as an important auxiliary to more traditional approaches.

Not all persons who have experienced violence or other major traumatic events develop PTSD, which testifies to the power of human resiliency.

Other taxonomic categories that are used with declining frequency for women victims of violence include the rape trauma syndrome (Burgess & Holstrom, 1974) and battered woman syndrome (Walker, 1984). In part, the reason why these constructs are now in use less, is that they have not showed good discriminant validity, because the symptoms are not specific to the conditions described (i.e. raped and battered women) or even to recent victimization. Rather, the PTSD taxonomy is usually preferred because it is encompassing for many types of trauma and symptoms. It may not represent the full range of psychological problems faced by victims, however. As mentioned earlier many other disorders are instigated by exposure to trauma, and particularly to criminal behavior that is viewed as uncontrollable. A woman who has been victimized may suffer depression as a result of her perceived helplessness (Seligman, 1975) and the loss of her ability to feel safe.

Dissociative disorders are often the outcome of severe and repeated victimization of children in as high as 95 percent of cases (Ross, 1997). Dissociation is one of the symptoms of PTSD, and dissociative disorders, such as dissociative identity disorder, may represent a special case of the same disorder with these symptoms as its dominant manifestation. The multiplicity of symptoms that can arise from trauma necessitates a global assessment on the part of the psychologist.

In addition to assessing current response to trauma, it is important for the clinician to assess various other situational and person-specific characteristics because they modify the response to violence. Many victims of abuse, particularly women, have had a history of childhood physical or sexual abuse (Stermac, Reist, Addison & Millar 2002), and this may magnify the impact of the recent victimization experience. Additionally, the interpretation of the violent event by the victim and his or her reaction to it is important in determining the development and degree of symptomatology because a response that includes terror, dissociation and a sense of helplessness is associated with worse psychological symptoms (Bernat, Ronfeldt, Calhoun & Arias, 1998). Thus, many factors make the response of the victim rather idiosyncratic, calling for personalized assessment and treatment. In the assessment package, broad measures of symptomatology and personality should be included, such as the MMPI-2 and the Symptom Checklist-90 or Brief Symptom Inventory (Derogatis, 1983) to determine the range of symptoms and personality characteristics that may determine prognosis and response to trauma. Symptom-specific measures of PTSD such as the Posttraumatic Stress Diagnostic Scale (Foa, 1995), can then be used, along with structured diagnostic interviews such as the ADIS-IV, to determine the presence of PTSD and other anxiety disorders. At a behavioral level, fear hierarchies of situations and stimuli that provoke anxiety and PTSD symptoms (flashbacks, startle response, numbness) should be constructed using ratings of Subjective Units of Distress (SUDS). These hierarchies can then be used in the context of systematic desensitization, and declining levels of distress can be continually assessed after repeated, graduated exposures. Care must be taken by the clinician when assessing and treating trauma victims.

CONCLUSION

The courts in the United States, Canada, England, Australia, and New Zealand have opened the door to psychologists to testify as expert witnesses. In a number of areas (e.g. psychological research on hypnosis; child abuse witness credibility, unless the syndrome evidence has been framed as a medical condition; and the polygraph), however, the courts have disallowed such evidence (Freckelton & Selby, 2005). Psychologists as expert witnesses in English-speaking common law countries have appeared in cases involving child sexual abuse, child custody cases, the battered woman syndrome, eyewitness testimony, PTSD, profiling, and false confessions.

The significance of the U.S. Supreme Court's important judgments in *General Electric Co. v. Joiner* and *Kumho*, which followed in the wake of the *Daubert* decision in 1993, depend on the ability of American judges to understand and implement crucial concepts in *Daubert*, but empirical evidence points to the contrary for most of the American judiciary. Post-*Kumho* decisions such as *United States v. Plaza* (2002) show a preparedness by courts in the United States to admit expert testimony concerning a technique that may not be based on falsifiable theory but enjoys general acceptance within the community of its practitioners. In other words, American courts do not appear to adhere to a strict application of the *Daubert* criteria for admissibility of expert evidence as had been feared. In England and Wales, further relaxation of the *R. v. Turner* rule is evidenced in the Court of Appeal's admitting in a number of cases expert testimony by forensic psychologists on a defendant's psychological vulnerability (i.e. his or her suggestibility) to make a false confession to the police while in custody. Additional evidence can be found in the same court's decision in *R. v. Bowman* that the court should have the benefit of any development in scientific thinking, including expert testimony about scientific knowledge and techniques that are at the stage of hypothesis. Thus, the courts in England and Wales do not seem to consider "general acceptance" as the main admissibility criterion for expert testimony as do American courts.

The task of the forensic psychologist in assessing both offenders and the impact of their criminal acts on victims, as well as in testifying as an expert in the courtroom, is by no means an easy one and calls for professionalism. The role is multifaceted and the expert needs to rely on a wide array of tools in order to answer the referral questions. Particular difficulties are involved in being asked to assess APD and psychopathy. The task is even more challenging when we bear in mind that the forensic psychologist may well have to judge whether the offender or the victim is engaged in malingering. To meet the challenge successfully in assessing suspects, defendants, and victims, the forensic psychologist simply cannot afford but to be guided by ethical and professional principles.

REFERENCES

Austin, J.S. (1992). The detection of fake-good and fake-bad on the MMPI-2. *Educational and Psychological Measurement, 52,* 669–674.

Barratt, E.S., and Slaughter, L. (1998). Defining, measuring, and predicting impulsive aggression: A heuristic model. *Behavioral Sciences and the Law, 16*, 285–302.

Bartol, C.R., and Bartol, A.M. (2004). *Introduction to Forensic Psychology*. Sage.

Benning, S D., Patrick, C.J., Hicks, B.M., Blonigen, D.M., Hicks, and Iacono, W.G. (2005). Estimating facets of psychopathy from normal personality traits: A step toward community epidemiological investigations. *Assessment, 12*, 3–18.

Bernat, J.A., Ronfeldt, H.M., Calhoun, K.S., and Arias, I. (1998). Prevalence of traumatic events and peritraumatic predictors of posttraumatic stress symptoms in a nonclinical sample of college students. *Journal of Traumatic Stress, 11*, 645–664.

Blau, T. H. (2001). *The Psychologist as Expert Witness* (2nd ed.). Wiley.

Bornstein, B.H. (2004). The impact of different types of expert scientific testimony on mock jurors' liability verdicts. *Psychology, Crime and Law, 10*, 429–446.

Brandt, J.R., Kennedy, W.A., Patrick, C.J., and Curtin, J.J. (1997). Asessment of psychopathy in a population of incarcerated adolescent offenders. *Psychological Assessment, 9*, 429–435.

Briere, J., and Jordan, C.E. (2004). Violence against women: Outcome complexity and implications for treatment. *Journal of Interpersonal Violence, 19*, 1252–1276.

Burgess, A.W., and Holstrom, L.L. (1974). Rape trauma syndrome. *American Journal of Psychiatry 131*, 981–986.

Carson, D. (1990). *Professionals and the Courts: A Handbook for Expert Witnesses*. Birmingham: Venture Press.

Cattermole, G.A. (1984). The psychologist as an expert witness. In M. Nixon (Ed.), *Issues In Psychological Practice* (pp. 121–32). Melbourne: Longman Cheshire.

Cleckley, H. (1941). *The Mask of Sanity*. St. Louis: Mosby.

Colman, A.M., and Mackay, R.D. (1995). Psychological evidence in court: Legal developments in England and the United States. *Psychology, Crime and Law, 1*, 261–268.

Cooke, D.J., and Michie C. (2001): Refining the construct of psychopathy: towards a hierarchical model. *Psychological Assessment, 13*, 171–188.

Cooper, J., and Neuhaus, I.M. (2000). The "hired gun" effect: Assessing the effect of paying, frequency of testifying and credentials on the perception of expert testimony. *Law and Human Behavior, 24*, 149-171.

Cooper, J., and Hall, J. (2000). Reactions of mock jurors to testimony of a court-appointed expert. *Behavioral Sciences and the Law, 18*, 719–729.

Daubert v. Merell Dow Pharmaceuticals 113 S.Ct. 2786 (1993)

Derogatis, L.R. (1983). *The Psychosocial Adjustment to Illness Scale*. Towson, MD: Clinical Psychometric Research.

DiNardo, P.A., and Barlow, D.H. (1988). *Anxiety Disorders Interview Schedule-Revised* (ADIS-R). Albany, NY: Graywind.

Foa, E.B. (1995). *Posttraumatic Stress Diagnostic Scale* (PDS). Minneapolis: National Computer Systems.

Folkes v. Chadd [1782]

Folstein, M.F., Folstein, S.E., and McHugh, P.R. (1975). Mini-mental state. A practical method for grading the cognitive state of patients for the clinician. *Journal of Psychiatric Research, 12*, 189–98.

Forth, A.E., Hart, S.D., and Hare, R.D. (1990). Assessment of psychopathy in male young offenders. Psychological Assessment: *A Journal of Consulting and Clinical Psychology, 2*, 342–344.

Freckelton, I., and Selby, H. (2005). *Expert Evidence: Law, Practice, Procedure and Advocacy* (3rd ed.). Sydney: Lawbook Co.

Frick, P.J., and Hare, R.D. (2002). *The Psychopathy Screening Device*. Toronto: Multi-Health Systems.

Frye v. United States 293 F. 1013 (1923)

Gatowski, S.I., Dobbin, S.A., Richardson, J.T., Ginsbury, G.P., Merlino, M.L., and Dahir, V. (2001). Asking the gatekeepers: A national survey of judges on judging expert evidence in a post-*Daubert* world. *Law and Human Behavior, 25*, 433–458.

General Electric Co. v. Joiner 522 US 136, 118 S.Ct. 512 (1997)

Grisso, T. (1986). *Evaluating competencies: Forensic assessments and instruments.* New York: Plenum Press.

Gudjonsson, G.H (2002). Unreliable confessions and miscarriages of justice in Britain. *International Journal of Police Science and Management, 4*, 332–343.

Gudjonsson, G.H. (1993). The implications of poor psychological evidence in court. *Expert Evidence, 2*, 120–124.

Gutheil, T.G., and Stein, M.D. (2000). Daubert-based gatekeping and psychiatric/psychological testimony in court: Review and proposal. *Journal of Psychiatry and Law, 22*, 235–251.

Haggard-Grann, U. Hallqvist, J., Langstrom, N., and Moller, J. (2006). The role of alcohol and drugs in triggering criminal violence: A case-crossover study. *Addiction, 101*, 100–108.

Hall, J.R., Benning, S.D., and Patrick, C.J. (2004). Criterion-related validity of the three-factor model of psychopathy. *Assessment, 11*, 4–16.

Hare, R.D. (1983). Diagnosis of antisocial personality disorder in two prison populations. *American Journal of Psychiatry, 140*, 887–890.

Hare, R.D. (1991). *The Hare Psychopathy Checklist-Revised.* Toronto, Ontario: Multi-Health Systems.

Hare, R.D. (1993). *Without Conscience: The Disturbing World of the Psychopaths Among Us.* New York: Pocket Books.

Hare, R.D. (1996). Psychopathy and antisocial personality disorder: A case of diagnostic confusion. *Psychiatric Times, 13*, 39–40.

Hart, S.D., and Hare, R.D. (1997) Psychopathy: Assessment and association with criminal conduct. In D.M., Stoff, J., Breiling, and J.D. Maser (Eds.), *Handbook of Antisocial Behavior.* New York: Wiley.

Haward, L.R. C. (1981). Expert opinion based on evidence from forensic hypnosis and lie-detection. In S.M.A. Lloyd-Bostock (Ed.), *Psychology In Legal Contexts: Applications and Limitations* (pp. 107–118). London: Macmillan.

Kapardis, A. (2003). *Psychology and Law* (2nd ed.). Cambridge: University Press.

Kassin, S.M., Tubb, V.A., Hosch, H.M., and Memon, A. (2001). On the "general acceptance" of eyewitness testimony research: A new survey of the experts. *American Psychologist, 56*, 405–416.

Kovera, M., Borgida, E., and Gresham, A. (1996). The impact of child witness preparation and expert testimony on juror decision making. Paper presented at the biennial meeting of the American Psychology-Law Society, Hilton Head, March 1, 1996.

Krafka, C., Dunn, M.A., Johnson, M.T., Cecil, J.S., and Miletich, D. (2002). Judges and attorney experiences, practices, and concerns regarding expert testimony in federal civil trials. *Psychology, Public Policy, and Law, 8*, 309–332.

Kraus, S.J., and Sales, B.D. (2001). The effects of clinical and scientific expert testimony on juror decision making in capital sentencing. *Psychology, Public Policy and Law, 7*, 267–310.

Kumho Tire Co. v. Patrick Carmichael 526 US, 13, 152, 119 S.Ct. 1167, 1176 (1999)

Landsman, S. (1995). Of witches, madmen, and products liability: An historical survey of the use of expert testimony. *Behavioral Sciences and the Law, 13*, 131–157.

Lilienfeld S.O., and Andrews B.P. (1996). Development and preliminary validation of a self-report measure of psychopathic personality traits in non-criminal populations. *Journal of Personality Assessment, 6*, 488–524

Lynam, D.R. (1997). Pursuing the Psychopath: the fledging psychopath in a nomological net. *Journal of Abnormal Psychology, 106*, 425–438.

Mallard v. The Queen [2003] 28 WAR 1; WASC 296

Meloy, J.R. (1990). *Symposium on the psychopath and the death penalty.* Presented at the 21st Annual Meeting of the American Academy of Psychiatry and the Law, San Diego, California.

Murphy v. R [1989] 86 alr 35

Nijboer, H. (1995). Expert evidence. In R. Bull and D. Carson (Eds.), Handbook of Psychology in Legal Contexts (pp. 555–564. Chichester: Wiley.

Orne, M.T., Dinges, D.F., and Orne, E.C. (1984). On the differential diagnosis of multiple personality in the forensic context. *International Journal of Clinical and Experimental Hypnosis, 2*, 118–169.

Palermo, G.B., Perracuti, S., and Palermo, M.T. (1996). Malingering: A challenge for the forensic examiner. *Medicine and Law, 15*, 143–160.

Patrick, C.J. (1995, Fall). Emotion and temperament in psychopathy. *Clinical Science,* 5–8.

R. v. B. [1987] 1 NZLR 362

R. v. Bowman [2006] EWCA Crim 41

R. v. Fong [1981] Qd R 90

R. v. Guilfoyle [2001] 2 Cr. App. Rep. 57

R. v. Harris & Ors [2005] EWCA Crim 1980

R. v. J-L [2000] 2 SCR 600; 148 CCC (3d) 487

R. v. Johnston [1992] 69 CCC 395

R. v. M. (W) [1997] 115 CCC (3d) 233

R. v. McCarthy [1997] 117 CCC (3d) 385

R. v. Mohan [1994] 2 SCR 9; (1994) 89 CCC (3d) 402

R. v. Murray [1982] 7 A Crim. R 48

R. v. Sally Loraine Emery and Another (1993) 14 Cr. App. R. (S.) 394

R. v. Smith [1987] VR 907 at 910-11, (1990) 64 ALJR 588

R. v. Turner [1975] Q.B. 834

Robins, L.N. (1978). Aetiological implications in studies of childhood histories relating to antisocial personality. In R.D., Hare & Schalling (Eds.) *Psychopathic Behavior: Approaches to Research* (pp 255–271). Chichester, England: Wiley.

Rogers, R., and Cruise, K.R. (2000). Malingering and deception among psychopaths. In C.B., Gacono (Ed.). *The Clinical and Forensic Assessment of Psychopathy: A Practitioner's Guide.* Silver Spring, MD: Erlbaum, Lawrence & Associates.

Roman, D.D., Tuley, M.R., Villanueva, M.R., and Mitchell, W.E. (1990). Evaluating MMPI validity in a forensic psychiatric population: Distinguishing between malingering and genuine psychopathology. *Criminal Justice and Behavior, 17*, 186–198.

Ross, C.A. (1997). *Dissociative Identity Disorder: Diagnosis, Clinical Features and Treatment of Multiple Personality.* New York: Wiley.

Seligman, M.E.P. (1975). *Helplessness: On Depression, Development and Death.* San Francisco: W. H. Freeman.

Sellbom, M., Ben-Porath, Y.S., and Stafford, K.S. (2007). A comparison of MMPI-2 measures of psychopathic deviance in a forensic setting. *Psychological Assessment, 19*, 430–436.

Sellbom, M., Ben-Porath, Y.S., Lilienfeld, S.O., Patrick, C.J., and Graham, J.R. (2005). Assessing psychopathic personality traits with the MMPI-2. *Journal of Personality Assessment, 85*, 334–343.

Serin, R.C., & Amos, N.L. (1995). The role of psychopathy in the assessment of dangerousness. *International Journal of Law and Psychiatry, 18*, 231–238.

Sheldon, D.H., and MacLeod, M.D. (1991). From normative to positive data: Expert psychological evidence re-examined. *Criminal Law Review,* 811–820.

Spitzer, R.L., Williams, J.B., Gibbon, M., and First, M.B. (1992). The structured clinical interview for DSM-III-R (SCID). I: History, rationale and description. *Archives of General Psychiatry, 49,* 624–629.

Stermac, L., Reist, D., Addison, M., and Millar, G.M. (2002). Childhood risk factors for women's sexual victimization. *Journal of Interpersonal Violence, 17,* 647–670.

Thornton, P. (1995). The admissibility of expert psychiatric and psychological evidence: Judicial training. *Medicine, Science and the Law, 35,* 143–149.

Torrubia, R., Avila, C., Molto, J., and Caseras, X. (2001). The Sensitivity to Punishment and Sensitivity to Reward Questionnaire (SPSRQ) as a measure of Gray's anxiety and impulsivity dimensions. *Personality and Individual Difference, 31,* 837–862.

United States v. Plaza 188 F. Supp 2d (2002)

Walker, L.E. (1984). *The Battered Woman Syndrome.* New York: Springer.

Wardlaw, G. (1984). The psychologist in court: Some guidelines on the presentation of psychological evidence. In M. Nixon (Ed.), *Issues in Psychological Practice* (pp. 133–143). Melbourne: Longman Cheshire.

Zuckerman, M. (1994). *Behavioral Expressions and Biosocial Bases of Sensation Seeking.* New York: Cambridge University Press.

Chapter Four

RISK ASSESSMENT

CHARLES L. SCOTT AND PHILLIP J. RESNICK

Mental health clinicians are often asked to determine an individual's risk of future violence. Dangerousness assessments are required in a wide variety of situations that include involuntary commitments, emergency psychiatric evaluations, seclusion and restraint release decisions, inpatient care discharges, probation/parole decisions, death penalty evaluations, domestic violence interventions, fitness for duty evaluations, and after a threat is made. The term dangerousness is not a psychiatric diagnosis; the concept of dangerousness is a legal judgment based on social policy. In other words, dangerousness is a broader concept than either violence or dangerous behavior; it indicates an individual's propensity to commit dangerous acts (Mulvey & Lidz, 1984).

Unfortunately, no psychological test or interview can predict future violence with high accuracy. Relatively infrequent events (e.g. homicide) are more difficult to predict than more common events (e.g. domestic violence) because they have a low base rate of occurrence. The accuracy of a clinician's assessment of future violence is related to many factors, including the circumstances of the evaluation and the length of time over which violence is predicted.

In a classic review of clinicians' accuracy at predicting violent behavior toward others, Monahan concluded in 1981 that psychiatrists and psychologists were accurate in no more than one out of three predictions of violent behavior among institutionalized patients followed over many years who had both committed violence in the past and who were diagnosed as mentally ill (Monahan & Steadman, 1994). However, more recent studies indicate that clinicians' accuracy in assessing future violence improves when the prediction is limited to briefer periods of time. For example, Lidz, Mulvey, and Gardner (1993), found that the accuracy of clinicians' predictions of violence by male patients (but not female patients) examined in an acute psychiatric emergency room significantly exceeded chance based on patient self-reports of violent incidents, corroborating information from someone who knew the patient well, and a review of official records.

When conducting a violence risk assessment, the clinician may find it helpful to divide the concept of dangerousness into five components. The first component is the magnitude of potential harm that is threatened. Behavior may involve physical harm to persons or property, as well as psychological harm to others. In addition to identifying the likely target of violence, the degree of anticipated harm should be understood. For example, threatening to shoot someone in the head foreshadows a much greater risk of serious harm than does threatening to kick someone in the leg.

The second component of dangerousness is the likelihood that a violent act will take place. Here it is important to clarify the seriousness of the person's intent to cause harm. A person's past history of acting on violent thoughts is the best predictor that violent intentions will be carried out. The third component is the imminence of the harm. For example, is the person threatening harm in the next ten hours or the next ten days? The fourth component examines the frequency of a behavior. Frequency is defined as the number of times a particular act has occurred over a specified period of time. The greater the frequency of an aggressive act, the higher the risk that the behavior will reoccur in the future. Situational factors constitute the fifth component of potential dangerousness. Situational factors that increase the risk of future violence include association with a criminally offending peer group, lack of financial resources and housing, easy access to weapons, and exposure to alcohol or illicit drugs.

RISK FACTORS ASSOCIATED WITH VIOLENCE

Demographic Factors and Violence Risk

The clinical assessment of dangerousness requires a review of several risk factors that have been associated with an increased likelihood of future violence (Humphreys, Johnstone, MacMillan & Taylor, 1992; Pearson, Wilmot & Padi, 1992; Swanson, Holzer, Ganju & Jono, 1990). For example, data from the Epidemiologic Catchment Area study showed violent behavior generally was associated with younger age groups. Swanson and colleagues found that the percentage of respondents reporting violent behavior in the past year was 7.34 percent among those between eighteen and twenty-nine years old, 3.59 percent among those between thirty and forty-four years old,

1.22 percent among those between forty-five and sixty-four years old, and less than 1 percent among those sixty-five years and older (Swanson et al., 1990).

Males perpetrate violent acts approximately ten times more often than females (Tardiff & Sweillam, 1980). In contrast, among people with mental disorders, men and women do not significantly differ in their base rates of violent behavior. In fact, rates are remarkably similar and in some cases slightly higher for women (Lidz et al., 1993; Newhill, Mulvey & Lidz, 1995).

The MacArthur Foundation's Violence Risk Assessment Study monitored male and female psychiatric inpatients (aged eighteen years to forty years) released from a psychiatric hospital with mental disorders for acts of violence toward others (MacArthur Foundation, 2001). During the one-year follow-up, men were "somewhat more likely" than women to be violent, but the difference was not large. Women were more likely than men were to target their aggression toward family members in the home environment. Violent acts by men were more likely to result in an arrest or the need for medical treatment (MacArthur Foundation, 2001). Research examining the relationship of gender and violence committed by psychiatric inpatients also concluded that both men and women have similar rates of aggression in this setting. In their study of 155 male and 67 female psychiatric inpatients, Krakowski and Czobor (2004) found that a similar percentage of women and men had an incident of physical assault in the hospital. However, women had a higher frequency of physical assaults during the first ten days of the study period, and men were more likely to perpetrate assaults that resulted in an injury.

The examiner should also consider the patient's economic status because violence is nearly three times as common among individuals in lower income brackets (Borum, Swartz & Swanson, 1996). However, one study (Silver, Mulvey & Monahan, 1999) reported that the actual socioeconomic status of individual patients was less predictive of violent behavior than was concentrated poverty in the neighborhood.

The risk of violence also increases for those with lower intelligence and mild mental retardation (Borum et al., 1996; Quinsey & Maquire, 1986). Hodgins (1992) reported that intellectually handicapped men were five times more likely to commit violent offenses, and intellectually handicapped women were twenty-five times more likely to commit violent offenses. In addition, persons with less education have also been shown to have a higher rate of violent acts (Borum et al., 1996; Link, Andrews & Cullen, 1992).

Evaluating Past Violence History

A past history of violence is the single best predictor of future violent behavior (Klassen & O'Connor, 1988). The MacArthur study found that all measures of prior violence—self-report, arrest records, and hospital records—

were strongly related to future violence (MacArthur Foundation, 2001). It is helpful to ask individuals about the most violent thing that they have ever done. Obtaining a detailed history of violence involves determining the type of violent behavior, why violence occurred, who was involved, the presence of intoxication, and the degree of injury.

Criminal and court records are particularly useful in evaluating the person's past history of violence and illegal behavior. For example, the age at first arrest for a serious offense is highly correlated with persistence of criminal offending (Borum et al., 1996). Each prior episode of violence increases the risk of a future violent act (Borum et al., 1996). Given four previous arrests, the probability of a fifth is 80 percent (Wolfgang, Thornberry & Figlio, 1987).

Additional sources of information relevant in assessing a person's potential for violence include a military and work history. For those individuals who have served in the military, the clinician should review any history of fights, absences without leave (AWOL), disciplinary measures (Article XV in the *Uniform Code of Military Justice*), as well as the type of discharge. An evaluation of the work history should review frequency of job changes and reasons for each termination. Frequent terminations increase the risk for violence. Persons who are laid off from work are six times more likely to be violent than are their employed peers (Catalano, Dooley, Novaco, Wilson & Hough, 1993).

A person who has used weapons against others in the past may pose a serious risk of future violence. The main difference between assault and homicide is the lethality of the weapon used. Loaded guns have the highest lethality of any weapon. An assault with a gun is five times more likely to result in a fatality than is an attack with a knife (Zimring, 1991). According to the Department of Justice, an estimated 40 percent of U.S. households contain a gun and 20 percent of all gun-owning households keep the gun loaded and unlocked (Cook & Ludwig, 1997). Subjects should be asked whether they own or have ever owned a weapon. The recent movement of a weapon, such as transferring a gun from a closet to a nightstand, is particularly ominous in a paranoid person. The greater the psychotic fear, the more likely the paranoid person is to kill someone he or she misperceives as a persecutor in misperceived self-defense.

Substance Use and Violence Risk

Drugs and alcohol are strongly associated with violent behavior (MacArthur Foundation, 2001; Pulay et al., 2008). Most people involved in violent crimes are under the influence of alcohol at the time of their aggression (Murdoch, Pihl & Ross, 1990). At least half of all violent events, including murders, were preceded by alcohol consumption by the perpetrator of the crime, the victim, or both (Roth, 1994). Stimulants, such as cocaine, crack, amphetamines, and phenylcyclidine (PCP), are of special concern. These drugs typically result in feelings of disinhibition, grandiosity, and paranoia. Among psychiatric patients, a coexisting diagnosis of substance abuse is strongly predictive of violence (MacArthur Foundation, 2001). In a study comparing discharged psychiatric patients to nonpatients in the community, substance abuse tripled the rate of violence in nonpatients and increased the rates of violence by discharged patients by up to five times (Steadman et al., 1998).

MENTAL DISORDERS AND VIOLENCE RISK

Studies examining whether individuals with mental illness are more violent than are the nonmentally ill have yielded mixed results (Steadman et al., 1998; Torrey, 1994). Reported prevalence rates of violence by mentally ill individuals have varied by the sample type studied and the time frame examined (Choe, Teplin & Abram, 2008). In a study of civilly committed psychiatric patients released into the community, most mentally ill individuals were not violent (Monahan, 1997). Although a weak relationship between mental illness and violence was noted, violent conduct was greater only during periods in which the person was experiencing acute psychiatric symptoms. Individuals with a diagnosis of schizophrenia had lower rates of violence compared to individuals with a diagnosis of depression or bipolar disorder. In addition, Monahan and colleagues noted that substance abuse was a much greater risk factor for violence than mental illness was (2001).

Psychosis and Violence Risk

Specific psychiatric symptoms and diagnoses should be carefully reviewed when conducting a violence risk assessment. The presence of psychosis is of particular concern when evaluating a person's risk of future violence. In paranoid psychotic patients, violence is often well-planned and in line with their false beliefs. The violence is usually directed at a specific person, who is perceived as a persecutor. Relatives or friends are often the targets of the paranoid individual. In addition, paranoid persons in the community are more likely to be dangerous because they have greater access to weapons (Krakowski, Volavka & Brizer, 1986).

Do specific delusions increase the risk that a person will behave violently? Research examining the contribution of delusions to violent behavior does not provide a clear answer to this question. Earlier studies suggested that persecutory delusions were associated with an increased risk of aggression (Wessely et al., 1993). Delusions noted to increase the risk of violence were those characterized by threat/control override symptoms. These delusions involve the following beliefs: that the mind is dominated by forces beyond the person's control; that thoughts are being put into the person's head; that people are wishing the person harm; and that the person is being followed (Link & Stueve, 1995). Similarly, Swanson, Borum, and Swartz, using data from the Epidemiologic Catchment Area surveys, found that people who reported threat/control override symptoms were about twice as likely to engage in assaultive behavior as those with other psychotic symptoms. (1996)

In contrast, results from the MacArthur Study of Mental Disorder and Violence (MacArthur Foundation, 2001; Monahan et al., 2001) showed that the presence of delusions did not predict higher rates of violence among recently discharged psychiatric patients. In particular, a relationship between the presence of threat/control override delusions and violent behavior was not found. In a study comparing male criminal offenders with schizophrenia found not guilty by reason of insanity to matched controls of nonoffending schizophrenics, Stompe, Ortwein-Swoboda, and Schande (2004) also found that threat/control override symptoms showed no significant association with the severity of violent behavior nor did the prevalence of threat/control override symptoms differ between the two groups. However, nondelusional suspiciousness, such as misperceiving others' behavior as indicating hostile intent, was associated with subsequent violence (Monahan et al., 2001).

The seemingly contradictory findings on the relationship of threat/control override delusions to violent behavior may be explained, in part, by gender. For example, in a reanalysis of the findings from the MacArthur Violence Risk Assessment study, researchers found men and women coped with threat delusions differently. In particular, men were significantly more likely to engage in violent behavior when experiencing threat delusions in contrast to women who were actually less likely to behave violently under the same circumstance (Teasdale, Silver & Monahan, 2006).

In addition to suspiciousness, the presence of other emotions associated with delusions and subsequent violence has been described. For example, when delusional beliefs make subjects unhappy, frightened, anxious, or angry, they are more likely to act aggressively (Appelbaum, Robbins & Roth, 1999). Finally, a propensity to act on delusions in general (not including violent actions) is significantly associated with a tendency to commit violent acts (Monahan et al., 2001). Therefore, the clinician should inquire not only about the relationship between prior acts of violence and delusions but also about any prior acts that resulted from delusional beliefs.

A careful inquiry about hallucinations is required to determine whether their presence increases the person's risk to commit a violent act. In general, the presence of hallucinations is not related to dangerous acts, but certain types of hallucinations may increase the risk of violence (Zisook, Byrd, Kuck & Jeste, 1995). Patients with schizophrenia are more likely to be violent if their hallucinations generate negative emotions (anger, anxiety, sadness) and if the patients have not developed successful strategies to cope with their voices (Cheung, Schweitzer, Crowley & Tuckwell, 1997).

In a review of seven controlled studies examining the relationship between command hallucinations and violence, no study demonstrated a positive relationship between command hallucinations and violence, and one found an inverse relationship (Rudnick, 1999). A positive relationship between violence in the presence of command hallucinations was found when the voice was familiar to the person and when the act commanded was less serious. In contrast, McNiel, Eisner and Binder (2000) reported that in a study of 103 civil psychiatric inpatients, 33 percent reported having had command hallucinations to harm others during the prior year and 22 percent of the patients reported that they complied with such commands. The authors concluded that patients in their study who experienced command hallucinations to harm others were more than twice as likely to be violent.

Junginger (1990) reported that command hallucinations were more likely to be followed in the presence of a delusion whose content was related to the hallucination. In the MacArthur Foundation's Violence Risk Assessment Study (MacArthur Foundation, 2001), there was no relationship between the presence of general hallucinations or nonviolent command hallucinations and violence. However, there was a relationship between command hallucinations to commit violence and actual violence (MacArthur Foundation, 2001; Monahan et al., 2001). In addition to evaluating positive symptoms of psychosis, clinicians should also assess their patients' insight into their illness and into the potential legal complications of their illness. Buckley and colleagues (2004) found that violent patients with schizophrenia had more prominent lack of insight regarding their illness and legal complications of their behavior when compared with a nonviolent comparison group. However, a subsequent research study of 209 schizophrenic patients followed for two years after hospital discharge found that aggressive behavior was more strongly associated with high scores for psychopathy traits and positive symptoms than with lack of insight (Lincoln & Hodgins, 2008).

Delusions and hallucinations are prominent symptoms of schizophrenia. Although most individuals with schizophrenia do not behave violently (Walsh, Buchanan & Fahy, 2002), there is emerging evidence that a diagnosis of schizophrenia is associated with an increase in criminal offending. In a retrospective review of 2861 Australian patients with schizophrenia followed over a twenty-five-year period, Wallace, Mullen, and Burgess (2004) found that patients with schizophrenia accumulated a greater total number of criminal convictions and were significantly more likely to have been convicted of a criminal offense (including violent offenses) relative to matched comparison subjects. These authors noted that the criminal behaviors committed by schizophrenic patients could not be entirely accounted for by comorbid substance use, active symptoms, or characteristics of systems of care (Wallace et al., 2004). In data from the Clinical Antipsychotic Trials of Intervention Effectiveness (CATIE) project, researchers clinically assessed and interviewed 1410 schizophrenia patients about violent behavior. The six-month prevalence of any violence was 19.1 percent with 3.6 percent of individuals reporting serious violence. Positive symptoms, including persecutory ideation, increased the risk of both minor and serious violence. In contrast, negative symptoms, such as social withdrawal, actually lowered the risk of serious violence (Swanson et al., 2006).

Mood Disorders and Violence Risk

Depression may result in violent behavior, particularly in depressed individuals who strike out against others in despair. After committing a violent act, the depressed person may attempt suicide. Depression is the most common diagnosis in murder-suicides (Marzuk, Tardiff & Hirsch, 1992), which is discussed in detail later.

Patients with mania show a high percentage of assaultive or threatening behavior, but serious violence itself is rare (Krakowski et al., 1986). Additionally, patients with mania show considerably less criminality of all kinds than do patients with schizophrenia. Patients with mania most commonly exhibit violent behavior when they are restrained or have limits set on their behavior (Tardiff & Sweillam, 1980). However, active manic symptoms appear to play a substantial role in criminal behavior. In a study of sixty-six inmates with bipolar disorder, 74 percent were manic and 59 percent were psychotic at the time of their arrest (Quanbeck et al., 2004).

Cognitive Impairment and Violence Risk

Brain injury or illness can also result in aggressive behavior. After a brain injury, formerly normal individuals may become verbally and physically aggressive (National Institutes of Health, 1998). Characteristic features of aggression resulting from a brain injury include reactive behavior triggered by trivial stimuli, lack of planning or reflection, nonpurposeful action with no clear aims or goals, explosive outbursts without a gradual build up, an episodic pattern with long periods of relative calm, and feelings of concern and remorse following an episode.

Personality Factors and Violence Risk

Violence is also associated with certain personality traits and disorders. Although borderline (Meloy, 1992; Tardiff & Sweillam, 1980) and sadistic (Meloy, 1992) personality disorders are associated with increased violence, the most common personality disorder associated with violence is antisocial personality disorder (APD) (MacArthur Foundation, 2001). The violence by those with APD is often motivated by revenge or occurs during a period of heavy drinking. Violence among these persons is frequently cold and calculated and lacks emotionality (Williamson, Hare & Wong, 1987). Low IQ and APD are a particularly ominous combination for increasing the risk of future violence (Heilbrun, 1990). It is important to assess for the presence of APDs in individuals with a major mental illness. When compared with schizophrenic patients without APD, offenders with both schizophrenia and APD are less likely to have violence that is prompted by psychotic symptoms. Their violence is more likely to be associated with alcohol use and an altercation with the victim prior to violence and be against a victim who is not a family member (Joyal, Putkonen, Paavola & Tiihonen, 2004).

Adults may have personality traits that increase their risk for violent behavior but may still not meet the criteria for a personality disorder. Personality traits associated with violence include impulsivity (Borum et al., 1996), low frustration tolerance, inability to tolerate criticism, repetitive antisocial behavior, reckless driving, a sense of entitlement, superficiality, and narcissism (Svindseth, Noettestad, Wallin, Roaldset & Dahl, 2008). The violence associated with these personality traits usually has a paroxysmal, episodic quality. When interviewed, these people often have poor insight into their behavior and frequently blame others for their difficulties (Reid & Balis, 1987).

In addition to *Diagnostic and Statistical Manual of Mental Disorders* (4th ed., text revision) (*DSM-IV-TR*) personality disorders or traits, the clinician should also be familiar with the psychological construct known as psychopathy. The term psychopath was described by Cleckley (1976) as an individual who is superficially charming, lacks empathy, lacks close relationships, is impulsive, and is concerned primarily with self-gratification. Hare and colleagues developed the Psychopathy Checklist-Revised (PCL-R) (Hare, 1991) as a validated measure of psychopathy in adults. The concept of psychopathy is important because the presence of psychopathy is a strong predictor of criminal behavior generally and violence among adults (Salekin, Rogers & Sewell, 1996). It is more predictive of violence than is a diagnosis of APD.

ASSESSING CURRENT DANGEROUSNESS

When conducting an assessment of current dangerousness, pay close attention to the individual's affect. Individuals who are angry and lack empathy for others are at increased risk for violent behavior (Menzies, Webster & Sepejak, 1985). In the MacArthur Study of Mental Disorder and Violence, subjects with high anger scores as measured by the Novaco Anger Scale were twice as likely to have engaged in violent behavior when compared with subjects with low anger scores (Monahan et al., 2001).

When evaluating a patient with persecutory delusions, the clinician should also inquire if the patient has employed "safety actions." Safety actions are specific behaviors (such as avoidance of a perceived persecutor or an escape from a fearful situation) that the individual has employed with the intention of minimizing a misperceived threat. In one study of 100 patients with current persecutory delusions, more than 95 percent reported using safety behaviors in the past month. In this study, individuals with a prior history of violence reported a greater current use of safety behaviors, and safety behaviors were significantly associated with acting on delusions (Freeman et al., 2007).

All threats should be taken seriously and details fully elucidated. Understanding how a violent act will be carried out and the expected consequences for the patient helps the clinician in assessing the degree of danger. In addition, fully considering the consequences of an act may help the patient elect an alternative coping strategy. For example, a patient may be focused on revenge against his wife because of her infidelity. When confronted with the likelihood of spending many years in prison, he may decide to divorce his wife instead. Additional information that should be elicited includes potential grudge lists, investigation of the subject's fantasies of violence (MacArthur Foundation, 2001), and a careful assessment of the future victim if one has been identified. Finally, the clinician should assess the suicide risk in any patient making a homicidal threat. Violent suicide attempts increase the likelihood of future violence toward others (Brizer, 1989; Convit, Jaeger, Lin, Meisner & Volavka, 1988). One study found that 91 percent of outpatients who had attempted homicide also had attempted suicide and that 86 percent of patients with homicidal ideation also reported suicidal ideation (Asnis, Kaplan, Hundorfean & Saeed, 1997).

When organizing strategies to decrease those risk factors that may contribute to future violence, clinicians should distinguish static from dynamic risk factors. By definition, static factors are not subject to change by intervention. Static factors include such items as demographic information and past history of violence. Dynamic factors are subject to change with intervention and include such factors as access to weapons, acute psychotic symptoms, active substance use, and a person's living setting. The clinician may find it helpful to organize a chart that outlines known risk factors, management and treatment strategies to address dynamic risk factors and the current status of each risk factor. This approach will assist in the development of a violence prevention plan that addresses the unique combination of risk factors for a particular patient.

EVALUATION OF SPECIAL POPULATIONS

Stalking

Approximately one in twelve women and one in forty-five men will be stalked at some point in their lifetime. Nearly 90 percent of stalkers are men, and most female and male victims know their stalker. Women are more likely than men (59% vs. 30%) to be stalked by an intimate partner. Although the average duration of stalking is 1.8 years, the duration increases to 2.2 years when the stalking relationship involves an intimate partner. More than 70 percent of current or former intimate partners verbally threaten their victim with violence. Eighty-one percent of women stalked by a current or prior partner are eventually physically assaulted; more than 30 percent will be sexually assaulted (Tjaden & Thoennes, 1998).

Stalking can occur in a variety of circumstances, including attempts to contact the victim directly or indirectly through the phone, mail, faxes, or personal notes left at a particular location. With the advent of electronic communication, stalkers may employ cyberspace technology and the Internet to maintain contact with their victim through emails. They may also gather information about the victim using common search engines (McGrath & Casey, 2002). Text messaging or short message service (SMS) via a mobile phone represents yet another developing method for the stalker to maintain communication with the victim without actual physical contact (Eytan & Borras, 2005).

All fifty states, the federal government, and the District of Columbia now classify stalking as a crime. Although precise statutory definitions vary, most stalking statutes incorporate the following elements:

- A course of conduct
- The conduct is directed at a specific person
- The conduct results in a reasonable person experiencing fear

The degree of danger posed by a stalker depends on a variety of factors. Intervention plans to curb or stop stalking behavior should be tailored to each specific case. General recommendations noted to reduce the impact of stalking include the following (Mullen, Pathe & Purcell, 2000):

- Communicating early and clearly that any contact and attention is unwanted
- Carefully protecting personal information, including limiting distribution of home address, telephone numbers, and cyberspace information
- Informing trusted others at home and work to prevent inadvertent disclosure of information and to protect their safety
- Contacting appropriate agencies such as police, victim support organizations, mental health clinics, and domestic and sexual violence programs when applicable
- Documenting and preserving all stalker contacts
- Recording all phone calls on an answering machine and keeping a separate private line for personal calls
- Obtaining self-defense training
- Avoiding all contact and confrontations

The decision to obtain a restraining order against the stalker is one that requires careful consideration and may be ineffective or actually inflammatory in certain situations. In particular, Orion (1997) emphasized that restraining orders are likely to be ineffective against exintimates, who are heavily invested in the relationship, and erotomanic or delusional stalkers, who view legal orders as not applicable to their situation. DeBecker (1997) notes that restraining orders are most likely to be effective in those situations that involve a casual acquaintance with limited emotional investment and no prior history of violence. If a decision is made to obtain a restraining order, the victim should be aware that stalkers are at higher risk to act violently immediately following the issuance of the order, so additional precautions should be taken. A protection order should be viewed as only one component of a comprehensive plan designed to minimize risk to the victim and may not be appropriate for every case.

Murder-Suicide

Murder-suicide occurs when an individual commits suicide after taking the life of another person. The National Violent Death Reporting System (NVDRS) defines a murder-suicide as including only those suicides that occur within a twenty-four-hour period after a murder (Bossarte, Simon & Barker, 2006), whereas other authors extend this period up to one week (Marzuk et al., 1992). Various labels have been used to describe the phenomenon of murderers who subsequently take their life and include homicide-suicide, dyadic death, doubly violent aggression, and despondent killers.

Because there is no national surveillance system for murder-suicide in the United States, the exact prevalence is difficult to determine. In most studies, murder-suicide rates have been reported to range from 0.2 to 0.3 per 100,000 persons (Coid, 1983; Marzuk et al., 1992; Milroy, 1995) although rates as high as 0.4 to 0.5 per 100,000 persons have also been noted (Hannah, Turf & Fierro, 1998; Hanzlick & Koponen, 1994).

Marzuk and associates (1992) proposed a murder-suicide typology based on the relationship between the perpetrator and the victim. The proposed categories of murder-suicide are (1) spousal/consortial, (2) familial, and (3) extrafamilial.

Spousal/Consortial Murder-Suicides

Numerous studies indicate that most murder-suicides involve male perpetrators who kill spouses or intimates (Aderibigbe, 1997; Felthous & Hempel, 1995; Malphurs & Cohen, 2002; Marzuk et al., 1992; Milroy, Dratsas & Ranson, 1997; Palermo et al., 1997). Nearly one third of men who kill their spouse or partner will commit suicide, a statistical phenomena not matched by females who kill intimate partners (Bossarte et al., 2006). Common psychiatric diagnoses in perpetrators of couple murder-suicides include depression (Rosenbaum, 1990) and alcohol intoxication or abuse (Comstock et al., 2005).

Marzuk, Tardiff, and Hirsch (1992) divide spousal/consortial murder-suicides into two subtypes: (1) *amorous-jealous* and (2) *declining health.* The amorous-jealous subtype is the most common, representing between 50 percent and 75 percent of all spousal/consortial murder-suicides. In the amorous-jealous subtype, the perpetrator is commonly a young man who kills his spouse or girlfriend with a firearm in a jealous rage during a period of actual or impending separation (Marzuk et al., 1992). More recent studies of homicide-suicide in older persons also note that interpersonal conflict remains a potential trigger for these deaths, particularly in an older man married to a younger woman (Cohen, Llorente, & Eisdorfer, 1998).

In the declining health subtype, the murderer is typically an older man (potentially in poor health) caring for his ailing wife. The perpetrator may believe his actions are altruistic and serve as a mercy homicide. Sometimes both parties view their deaths as a dual suicide pact, but usually the male is the decision maker.

Murder-Suicides of Family Members

Murder-suicides may involve a perpetrator who kills one or more family members other than a spouse or intimate partner. In an Australian study examining murder-suicides of children over a twenty-nine-year period, researchers found that when fathers killed their children, they were more likely to also kill their spouse in contrast to mothers who killed only their children. Furthermore, compared to men, women tended to use less violent methods to commit murder and suicide (Byard, Knight, James & Gilbert, 1999). Filicide is broadly defined as the murder of a child by a parent. Three types of filicide include (1) *neonaticide,* the murder of a child less than one day old; (2) *infancticide,* the murder of a child older than one day and less than one year old; (3) *pedicide-*murder of a child older than one year and less than age sixteen.

High rates of suicide following a filicide have been noted, with between 16 percent and 29 percent of mothers and 40 percent and 60 percent of fathers taking their life after murdering their child (Hatters Friedman, Hrouda, Holden, Noffsinger & Resnick, 2005; Marzuk et al., 1992; Rodenburg, 1971). In a study of thirty family filicide-suicide files, the most common motive involved an attempt by the perpetrator to relieve real or imagined suffering of the child, an action known as an altruistic filicide. Eighty percent of the parents in this study had evidence of a past or current psychiatric history, with nearly 60 percent suffering from depression, 27 percent with psychosis, and 20 percent experiencing delusional beliefs (Hatters-Friedman et al., 2005).

Familicide is defined as the murder of an entire family. These family annihilators are usually men suffering from depression, intoxication, or both (Dietz, 1986). Risk factors associated with family annihilation include ongoing marital conflict, anger over separation, illness in a child, and financial stress (Hatters-Friedman et al., 2005; Morton, Runyan, Moracco & Butts, 1998). In certain cases, the perpetrator believes that murdering the family members will alleviate future suffering and views his action as altruistic. Rare cases of depressed or psychotic adolescents have also been described in which children kill their entire family prior to taking their own life (Malmquist, 2006).

Because of the high rates of mental illness in parents who kill their children, evaluators should carefully consider the possibility that their depressed, suicidal, or psychotic patients who are parents may represent a potential risk of harm to their child. In addition to a standard suicide risk assessment, the clinician should explore areas that may assist in preventing a tragic death (Hatters-Friedman et al., 2005). Suggested questions include the following:

- What do you believe will happen to your child if you die or commit suicide?
- Do you have any fears or concerns that your child may be harmed by others?
- Do you have any worries regarding your child's health or unnecessary suffering?

• Are you having any thoughts about harming your child?
• Have you taken any steps to harm your child?
• If you have had thoughts of harming your child, what has kept you from doing so thus far?

Extrafamilial Murder-Suicides

Suicides following the murder of a nonfamily member or intimate partner are relatively rare. Murder-suicides outside the family have occurred in the workplace; schools; and public settings, such as malls or tourist locations. Such perpetrators have also been referred to as mass killers or rampage killers.

The perpetrator of a mass murder typically is a heavily armed male who randomly shoots individuals before turning the gun on himself. The murderer may initially target a person with whom he has a grudge and subsequently expand his rampage to random victims. Such perpetrators are likely to be depressed and may frequently suffer from obsessional traits with marked hypersensitivity and paranoia. Mullen (2004) found the following seven characteristics of perpetrators of autogenic massacres who survived despite their intent to commit suicide:

• male
• less than forty years of age
• social isolate without close relationships
• unemployed or minimally employed
• bullied or isolated as a child, or both
• fascinated with weapons
• collector of weapons

These murderers may provoke law enforcement personnel to kill them after their murders, a phenomena known as suicide by cop. One study of ninety-eight lone U.S. rampage killers found that those who were ultimately killed by police officers had the largest number of victims when compared with those who committed suicide or who were ultimately captured (Lester, Stack, Schmidtke, Schaller & Muller, 2005).

STRUCTURED RISK ASSESSMENTS OF VIOLENCE

Standardized risk assessment instruments for the prediction of violence are being used increasingly by clinicians in conjunction with their clinical violence risk assessments. The goals of these prediction schemes are to assist the clinician in gathering appropriate data and to anchor clinicians' assessments to established research. One of the most validated risk-assessment instruments is the PCL. The Hare PCL-R (Hare, 1991) is a clinical construct rating scale designed to measure psychopathic attributes in individuals. Individuals who score higher on this measurement of psychopathy have been shown to have higher rates of violent recidivism. The PCL-R uses a semi-structured interview, case-history information, and specific scoring criteria to rate each of twenty items on a three-point scale (0, 1, 2) according to the extent to which it applies to a given individual. Total scores (ranging from 0 to 40) reflect an estimate of the degree to which the individual matches the prototypical psychopath. In North America, the cutoff score for psychopathy is 30 or greater. A screening version of the PCL-R, known as the PCL-SV, has also been developed. The PCL-SV has been shown to have good predictive validity for institutional violence (Hill, Rogers & Bickford, 1996) and community violence (Monahan et al., 2001). Concerns about using the PCL-R as the sole assessment of dangerousness include its inability to capture protective, mediating, and moderating factors against future violent behavior (Rogers, 2000) and the potential to overpredict violent behavior (Freedman, 2001).

The Violence Risk Appraisal Guide (VRAG) is another actuarial risk assessment instrument that consists of twelve items, one of which is psychopathy as defined by the PCL-R. The VRAG instrument was derived from information about 618 patients at a maximum security hospital providing assessment and treatment services for persons received from the courts, correctional services, and other provincial psychiatric hospitals in Canada (Webster, Harris & Rice, 1994). A third risk assessment instrument is the HCR-20, which combines the assessment of historical risk factors and clinical judgment regarding risk management. The HCR-20 (Webster, Douglas, Eaves & Hart, 1997) is a broadband violence risk assessment instrument with twenty items divided into historical, clinical, and risk management items. One of the items is the presence or absence of psychopathy as determined by the PCL-R (Webster et al., 1997). An assessment tool commonly used in correctional settings is the Level of Service Inventory-Revised (LSI-R). The LSI-R is a combined risk and needs assessment tool developed in Canada whose measurements have been validated in North America. The LSI-R consists of fifty-four items and is composed of ten subscales. The LSI-R score indicates the likelihood of recidivism and suggests interventions based on the score (Andrews & Bonta, 1995).

A recent tool for the purpose of assessing the violence risk of individuals discharged from civil psychiatric facilities is known as the Iterative Classification Tree (ICT). This approach utilizes a sequence of questions related to risk factors for potential violence. Contingent on the answer to a question, one or another second question is posed, until the individual is classified into a category of high or low risk of future violence (Monahan et al., 2001). In a sample of 939 male and female civil psychiatric patients followed after hospital discharge, the ICT classified 72.6 percent of the sample as either low risk or high risk. This tool shows promise in the assessment of future violence for periods up to twenty weeks. However, the extent to which the accuracy of the ICT generalizes to other types of clinical settings such as from forensic hospitals is currently unknown.

Actuarial models have inherent limitations when used exclusively. Specific criticisms of actuarial instruments include the following: they provide only approximations of risk, their use is not generalizable beyond the studied populations on which they are based, they are rigid and lacking sensitivity to change and they fail to inform violence prevention and risk management (Douglas, Ogloff & Hart, 2003). Although actuarial models attempt to standardize the practice of dangerousness assessment, they are not designed to be the sole standard for violence assessment. Actuarial tools are useful in assisting clinicians in reaching reasonable conclusions based on research findings (Borum et al., 1996), but the evaluator must also consider the imminence and severity of violence that may not be reflected in an actuarial instrument alone (Glancy & Chaimowitz, 2005).

Mental health clinicians faced with large caseloads may not have sufficient time to complete the more time-consuming actuarial risk assessment instruments. To help address this concern, Wootton and associates (2008) followed 708 general psychiatric patients with a psychotic disorder for two years to determine if readily available clinical information was useful in predicting assaultive behavior. These researchers developed a simple screening tool based on age, sex, self-reported history of violence, and illicit drug use that had a level of predictive accuracy comparable to more detailed risk assessment tools.

DUTY TO POTENTIAL VICTIMS

The duty of clinicians to third parties (individuals with whom the clinician does not have a treating relationship) has expanded significantly during the last thirty years. In the United States, one person is not ordinarily responsible for the violence that a second person inflicts on a third, unless the first person had a special relationship with the second. The seminal U.S. case establishing that the outpatient-therapist relationship is such a "special" relationship is *Tarasoff v. Regents of the University of California* (1976).

In *Tarasoff* the court held that "When a therapist determines, or pursuant to the standards of his profession should determine that his patient presents a serious danger of violence to another, he incurs an obligation to use reasonable care to protect the intended victim against such danger. The discharge of this duty may require the therapist to take one or more of various steps. Thus, it may call for him to warn the intended victim, to notify police, or to take whatever steps are reasonably necessary under the circumstances."

Clinicians have various options in fulfilling their requirement to protect under the *Tarasoff* doctrine. When possible, the threat of violence should be handled as a treatment issue. In some cases, the patient can be involved in the notification of the victim. If necessary, the therapist may notify the intended victim and police against the patient's wishes. Another option is voluntary hospitalization of the patient. If the individual refuses and there is an imminent risk of harm, the clinician must consider involuntary commitment. If the patient does not meet involuntary commitment criteria, other "reasonable steps" that may be implemented include (1) increasing the frequency of outpatient appointments, (2) adjusting medications, (3) involving family or friends in an attempt to control the patient, and (4) removing weapons from the home (Tardiff, 1989).

CONCLUSION

The assessment of potential violence is an important area when evaluating psychiatric patients in both an outpatient and an inpatient setting. The clinician should be familiar with the relationship of various mental health symptoms to a patient's potential future aggression. Despite improvement in the field of risk assessment, the prediction of violence remains an inexact science. Predicting violence has been compared with forecasting the weather. Like a good weather forecaster, the clinician does not state with certainty that an event will occur. Instead, he or she estimates the likelihood that a future event will occur. Like weather forecasting, predictions of future violence will not always be correct. However, gathering a detailed past history and using appropriate risk assessment instruments help make the risk assessment as accurate as possible.

REFERENCES

Aderibigbe, Y.A. (1997). Violence in America: A survey of suicide linked to homicides. *Journal of Forensic Sciences, 42,* 662–665.

Andrews, D., and Bonta, J. (1995). *LSI-R: The Level of Service Inventory: Revised Users Manual.* Toronto: Multi-Health Systems.

Appelbaum, P.S., Robbins, P.C., and Roth, L.H. (1999). Dimensional approach to delusions: Comparison across types and diagnoses. *American Journal of Psychiatry, 156,* 1938–1943.

Asnis, G.M., Kaplan, M.L., Hundorfean, G., and Saeed, W. (1997). Violence and homicidal behaviors in psychiatric disorders. *Psychiatric Clinics of North America, 20*, 405–425.

Borum, R., Swartz, M., and Swanson, J. W. (1996). Assessing and managing violence risk in clinical practice. *Journal of Practical Psychiatry and Behavioral Health, 4*, 205–214.

Bossarte, R.M., Simon, T.R., and Barker, L. (2006). Characteristics of homicide followed by suicide incidents in multiple states, 2003-04. *Injury Prevention, 12 (Suppl 2)*, ii33–ii38.

Brizer, D.A. (1989). Introduction: overview of current approaches in the prediction of violence. In D.A. Brizer and M. Crowner (Eds.), *Current Approaches to the Prediction of Violence* (pp. 1–12). Washington, DC: American Psychiatric Press.

Buckley, P.F., Hrouda, D.R., Friedman, L., Noffsinger, S.G., Resnick, P.J., and Camlin-Shingler, K. (2004). Insight and its relationship to violent behavior in patients with schizophrenia. *American Journal of Psychiatry, 161*, 1712–1714.

Byard, R.W., Knight, D., James, R.A., and Gilbert, J. (1999). Murder-suicides involving children: A 29-year study. *American Journal of Forensic Medicine and Pathology, 20*, 323–327.

Tarasoff v. Regents of the University of California, 17 Cal 3d 425, 131 Cal Rptr 14, 551, Prd 334, 1976 C.F.R.

Catalano, R., Dooley, D., Novaco, R.W., Wilson, G., and Hough, R. (1993). Using ECA survey data to examine the effect of job layoffs on violent behavior. *Hospital and Community Psychiatry, 44*, 874–879.

Cheung, P., Schweitzer, I., Crowley, K., and Tuckwell, V. (1997). Violence in schizophrenia: Role of hallucinations and delusions. *Schizophrenia Research, 26*, 181–190.

Choe, J.Y., Teplin, L.A., and Abram, K.M. (2008). Perpetration of violence, violent victimization, and severe mental illness: balancing public health concerns. *Psychiatric Services, 59*, 153–164.

Cleckley, H.M. (1976). *The Mask of Sanity*. St. Louis, MO: Mosby.

Cohen, D., Llorente, M., and Eisdorfer, C. (1998). Homicide-suicide in older persons. *American Journal of Psychiatry, 155*, 390–396.

Coid, J. (1983). The epidemiology of abnormal homicide and murder followed by suicide. *Psychological Medicine, 13*, 855–860.

Comstock, R. D., Mallonee, S., Kruger, E., Rayno, K., Vance, A., and Jordan, F. (2005). Epidemiology of homicide-suicide events: Oklahoma, 1994-2001. *American Journal of Forensic Medicine and Pathology, 26*, 229–235.

Convit, A., Jaeger, J., Lin, S.P., Meisner, M., and Volavka, J. (1988). Predicting assaultiveness in psychiatric inpatients: A pilot study. *Hospital and Community Psychiatry, 39*, 429–434.

Cook, P.J., and Ludwig, J. (1997, May). Guns in America: National survey on private ownership and use of firearms [Online]. Retrieved March 18, 2008. Available: www.ncjrs.org/txtfiles/165476.txt.

deBecker, G. (1997). *The Gift of Fear: Survival Signals that Protect us from Violence*. London: Bloomsbury.

Dietz, P.E. (1986). Mass, serial and sensational homicides. *Bulletin of the New York Academy of Medicine, 62*, 477–491.

Douglas, K.S., Ogloff, J.R., and Hart, S.D. (2003). Evaluation of a model of violence risk assessment among forensic psychiatric patients. *Psychiatric Services, 54*, 1372–1379.

Eytan, A., and Borras, L. (2005). Stalking through SMS: A new tool for an old behavior? *Austra-lian and New Zealand Journal of Psychiatry, 39*, 204.

Felthous, A.R., and Hempel, A. (1995). Combined homicide-suicides: A review. *Journal of Foren-sic Sciences, 40*, 846–857.

Freedman, D. (2001). False prediction of future dangerousness: Error rates and psychopathy checklist–revised. *Journal of the American Academy of Psychiatry and Law, 29*, 89–95.

Freeman, D., Garety, P.A., Kuipers, E., Fowler, D., Bebbington, P.E., and Dunn, G. (2007). Acting on persecutory delusions: the importance of safety seeking. *Behavior Research and Therapy, 45,* 89–99.

Glancy, G.D., and Chaimowitz, G. (2005). The clinical use of risk assessment. *Canadian Journal of Psychiatry, 50,* 12–17.

Hannah, S.G., Turf, E.E., and Fierro, M.F. (1998). Murder-suicide in central Virginia: A descriptive epidemiologic study and empiric validation of the Hanzlick-Koponen typology. *Ameri-can Journal of Forensic Medicine and Pathology, 19,* 275–283.

Hanzlick, R., and Koponen, M. (1994). Murder-suicide in Fulton County, Georgia, 1988-1991. Comparison with a recent report and proposed typology. *American Journal of Forensic Medicine and Pathology, 15,* 168–173.

Hare, R. (1991). *The Hare Psychopathy Checklist-Revised.* Toronto: Multi-Health Systems.

Hatters Friedman, S., Hrouda, D.R., Holden, C.E., Noffsinger, S.G., and Resnick, P.J. (2005). Filicide-suicide: Common factors in parents who kill their children and themselves. *Journal of the American Academy of Psychiatry and Law, 33,* 496–504.

National Institutes of Health (1998). Rehabilitation of persons with traumatic brain injury [Online]. Retrieved March 18, 2008. Available: http://consensus.nih.gov/1998/1998 TraumaticBrainInjury109html.htm

Heilbrun, A.B., Jr. (1990). The measurement of criminal dangerousness as a personality construct: Further validation of a research index. *Journal of Personality Assessment, 54,* 141–148.

Hill, C.D., Rogers, R., and Bickford, M.E. (1996). Predicting aggressive and socially disruptive behavior in a maximum security forensic psychiatric hospital. *Journal of Forensic Sciences, 41,* 56–59.

Hodgins, S. (1992). Mental disorder, intellectual deficiency, and crime: Evidence from a birth cohort. *Archives of General Psychiatry, 49,* 476–483.

Humphreys, M.S., Johnstone, E.C., MacMillan, J.F., and Taylor, P.J. (1992). Dangerous behavior preceding first admissions for schizophrenia. *British Journal of Psychiatry, 161,* 501–505.

Joyal, C.C., Putkonen, A., Paavola, P., and Tiihonen, J. (2004). Characteristics and circumstances of homicidal acts committed by offenders with schizophrenia. *Psychological Medicine, 34,* 433–442.

Junginger, J. (1990). Predicting compliance with command hallucinations. *American Journal of Psychiatry, 147,* 245–247.

Klassen, D., and O'Connor, W.A. (1988). A prospective study of predictors of violence in adult male mental health admissions. *Law and Human Behavior, 12,* 143–158.

Krakowski, M., and Czobor, P. (2004). Gender differences in violent behaviors: Relationship to clinical symptoms and psychosocial factors. *American Journal of Psychiatry, 161,* 459–465.

Krakowski, M., Volavka, J., and Brizer, D. (1986). Psychopathology and violence: A review of literature. *Comprehensive Psychiatry, 27,* 131–148.

Lester, D., Stack, S., Schmidtke, A., Schaller, S., and Muller, I. (2005). Mass homicide and suicide deadliness and outcome. *Crisis, 26,* 184–187.

Lidz, C.W., Mulvey, E.P., and Gardner, W. (1993). The accuracy of predictions of violence to others. *Journal of the American Medical Association, 269,* 1007–1011.

Lincoln, T.M., and Hodgins, S. (2008). Is lack of insight associated with physically aggressive behavior among people with schizophrenia living in the community? *Journal of Nervous and Mental Disease, 196,* 62–66.

Link, B.G., Andrews, H., and Cullen, F. (1992). The violent and illegal behavior of mental patients reconsidered. *American Sociological Review, 57,* 275–292.

Link, B.G., and Stueve, A. (1995). Evidence bearing on mental illness as a possible cause of violent behavior. *Epidemiologic Reviews, 17,* 172–181.

MacArthur Foundation. (2001). The MacArthur Violence Risk Assessment Study Executive Summary [Online]. Retrieved March 18, 2008. Available: http://macarthur.virginia.edu/risk.html.

Malmquist, C.P. (2006). Combined murder-suicide. In R.I. Simon and R.E. Hales (Eds.), *Textbook of Suicide Assessment and Management* (pp. 495–509). Washington, DC: American Psychiatric Publishing, Inc.

Malphurs, J.E., and Cohen, D. (2002). A newspaper surveillance study of homicide-suicide in the United States. *American Journal of Forensic Medicine and Pathology, 23*, 142–148.

Marzuk, P.M., Tardiff, K., and Hirsch, C.S. (1992). The epidemiology of murder-suicide. *Journal of the American Medical Association, 267*, 3179–3183.

McGrath, M.G., and Casey, E. (2002). Forensic psychiatry and the internet: Practical perspectives on sexual predators and obsessional harassers in cyberspace. *Journal of American Academy of Psychiatry and Law, 30*, 81–94.

McNiel, D.E., Eisner, J.P., and Binder, R.L. (2000). The relationship between command hallucinations and violence. *Psychiatric Services, 51*, 1288–1292.

Meloy, J.R. (1992). *Violent Attachments.* Northvale, NJ: Jason Aronson Publishers, Inc.

Menzies, J.R., Webster, C.D., and Sepejak, D.S. (1985). The dimensions of dangerousness: Evaluating the accuracy of psychometric predictions of violence among forensic patients. *Law and Human Behavior, 9*, 49–70.

Milroy, C.M. (1995). The epidemiology of homicide-suicide (dyadic death). *Forensic Science International, 71*, 117–122.

Milroy, C.M., Dratsas, M., and Ranson, D.L. (1997). Homicide-suicide in Victoria, Australia. *American Journal of Forensic Medicine and Pathology, 18*, 369–373.

Monahan, J. (1997). Actuarial support for the clinical assessment of violence risk. *International Review of Psychiatry, 9*, 167–170.

Monahan, J., and Steadman, H.J. (1994). *Violence and Mental Disorder: Developments in Risk Assessment.* Chicago: University of Chicago Press.

Monahan, J., Steadman, H.J., Silver, E., Appelbaum, P.S., Clark-Robbins, P., Mulvey, E.P., et al. (2001). *Rethinking Risk Assessment: The MacArthur Study of Mental Disorder and Violence.* New York: Oxford University Press.

Morton, E., Runyan, C.W., Moracco, K.E., and Butts, J. (1998). Partner homicide-suicide involving female homicide victims: A population-based study in North Carolina, 1988-1992. *Violence and Victims, 13*, 91–106.

Mullen, P.E., Pathe, M., and Purcell, R. (2000). *Stalkers and Their Victims.* New York: Cambridge University Press.

Mulvey, E.P., and Lidz, C.W. (1984). Clinical considerations in the prediction of dangerousness in mental patients. *Clinical Psychology Review, 4*, 379–401.

Murdoch, D., Pihl, R.O., and Ross, D. (1990). Alcohol and crimes of violence: Present issues. *International Journal of Addiction, 25*, 1065–1081.

Newhill, C.E., Mulvey, E.P., and Lidz, C.W. (1995). Characteristics of violence in the community by female patients seen in a psychiatric emergency service. *Psychiatric Services, 46*, 785–789.

Orion, D. (1997). *I Know You Really Love Me: A Psychiatrist's Journal of Erotomania, Stalking, and Obesssive Love.* New York: Macmillan.

Palermo, G.B., Smith, M.B., Jenzten, J.M., Henry, T.E., Konicek, P.J., Peterson, G.F., et al. (1997). Murder-suicide of the jealous paranoia type: A multicenter statistical pilot study. *American Journal of Forensic Medicine and Pathology, 18*, 374–383.

Pearson, M.E., Wilmot, E., and Padi, M. (1992). A study of violent behavior among in-patients in a psychiatric hospital. *British Journal of Psychiatry, 149*, 232–235.

Pulay, A.J., Dawson, D.A., Hasin, D.S., Goldstein, R.B., Ruan, W.J., Pickering, R.P., et al. (2008). Violent behavior and DSM-IV psychiatric disorders: Results from the national epidemiologic survey on alcohol and related conditions. *Journal of Clinical Psychiatry, 69,* 12–22.

Quanbeck, C.D., Stone, D.C., Scott, C.L., McDermott, B.E., Altshuler, L.L., and Frye, M.A. (2004). Clinical and legal correlates of inmates with bipolar disorder at time of criminal arrest. *Journal of Clinical Psychiatry, 65,* 198–203.

Quinsey, V.L., and Maquire, A. (1986). Maximum security psychiatric patients: actuarial and clinical predictions of dangerousness. *Journal of Interpersonal Violence, 1,* 143–171.

Reid, W.H., and Balis, G.U. (1987). Evaluation of the violent patient. In R.E. Hales and A.J. Frances (Eds.), Psychiatric Update: American Psychiatry Annual Review (Vol. 6, pp. 491–509). Washington, DC: American Psychiatric Press.

Rodenburg, M. (1971). Child murder by depressed parents. *Canadian Psychiatric Association Journal, 16,* 41–48.

Rogers, R. (2000). The uncritical acceptance of risk assessment in forensic practice. *Law and Human Behavior, 24,* 595–605.

Rosenbaum, M. (1990). The role of depression in couples involved in murder-suicide and homicide. *American Journal of Psychiatry, 14,* 1036–1039.

Roth, J.A. (1994). Psychoactive substances and violence [Online]. Retrieved March 18, 2008. Available: http://www.ncjrs.gov/txtfiles/psycho.txt.

Rudnick, A. (1999). Relation between command hallucinations and dangerous behavior. *Journal of the American Academy of Psychiatry and Law, 27,* 253–257.

Salekin, R.T., Rogers, R., and Sewell, K.W. (1996). A review of meta-analysis of the Psychopathy Checklist and Psychopathy Checklist-Revised: Predictive validity of dangerousness. *Clinical Psychology: Science and Practice, 3,* 203–213.

Silver, E., Mulvey, E.P., and Monahan, J. (1999). Assessing violence risk among discharged psychiatric patients: toward an ecological approach. *Law and Human Behavior, 23,* 237–255.

Steadman, H.J., Mulvey, E.P., Monahan, J., Robbins, P.C., Appelbaum, P.S., Grisso, T., et al. (1998). Violence by people discharged from acute psychiatric inpatient facilities and by others in the same neighborhoods. *Archives of General Psychiatry, 55*(5), 393–401.

Stompe, T., Ortwein-Swoboda, G., and Schanda, H. (2004). Schizophrenia, delusional symptoms, and violence: the threat/control override concept reexamined. *Schizophrenia Bulletin, 30,* 31–44.

Svindseth, M.F., Noettestad, J.A., Wallin, J., Roaldset, J.O., and Dahl, A.A. (2008). Narcissism in patients admitted to psychiatric acute wards: Its relation to violence, suicidality and other psychopathology. *BMC Psychiatry, 8,* 13.

Swanson, J.W., Borum, R., and Swartz, M. (1996). Psychotic symptoms and disorders and risk of violent behavior in the community. *Criminal Behavior and Mental Health, 6,* 317–338.

Swanson, J.W., Holzer, C.E., 3rd, Ganju, V.K., and Jono, R.T. (1990). Violence and psychiatric disorder in the community: Evidence from the Epidemiologic Catchment Area surveys. *Hospital and Community Psychiatry, 41,* 761–770.

Swanson, J.W., Swartz, M.S., Van Dorn, R.A., Elbogen, E.B., Wagner, H.R., Rosenheck, R.A., et al. (2006). A national study of violent behavior in persons with schizophrenia. *Archives of General Psychiatry, 63,* 490–499.

Tardiff, K. (1989). *Assessment and Management of Violent Patients.* Washington, DC: American Psychiatric Press.

Tardiff, K., and Sweillam, A. (1980). Assault, suicide, and mental illness. Archives of *General Psychiatry, 37,* 164–169.

Teasdale, B., Silver, E., and Monahan, J. (2006). Gender, threat/control-override delusions and violence. *Law and Human Behavior, 30,* 649–658.

Tjaden, P., and Thoennes, N. (1998, April). *Stalking in America: Findings from the National Violence Against Women Survey.* Research in Brief. Washington, DC: U.S. Department of Justice.

Torrey, E.F. (1994). Violent behavior by individuals with serious mental illness. *Hospital and Community Psychiatry, 45,* 653–662.

Wallace, C., Mullen, P.E., and Burgess, P. (2004). Criminal offending in schizophrenia over a 25-year period marked by deinstitutionalization and increasing prevalence of comorbid substance use disorders. *American Journal of Psychiatry, 161,* 716–727.

Walsh, E., Buchanan, A., and Fahy, T. (2002). Violence and schizophrenia: Examining the evidence. *British Journal of Psychiatry, 180,* 490–495.

Webster, C.D., Douglas, K.S., Eaves, D., and Hart, S.D. (1997). *HCR-20: Assessing the Risk for Violence* (Version 2). Vancouver, BC: Mental Health, Law, and Policy Institute, Simon Fraser University.

Webster, C.D., Harris, G.T., and Rice, M.E. (1994). *The Violence Prediction Scheme: Assessing Dangerousness in High Risk Men.* Toronto: Centre of Criminology, University of Toronto.

Wessely, S., Buchanan, A., Reed, A., Cutting, J., Everitt, B., Garety, P., et al. (1993). Acting on delusions. I: Prevalence. *British Journal of Psychiatry, 163,* 69–76.

Williamson, S., Hare, R., and Wong, S. (1987). Violence: criminal psychopaths and their victims. *Canadian Journal of Behavioral Sciences, 19,* 454–462.

Wolfgang, M.E., Thornberry, T.P., and Figlio, R.M. (1987). *From Boy to Man, From Delinquency to Crime.* Chicago: University of Chicago Press.

Wootton, L., Buchanan, A., Leese, M., Tyrer, P., Burns, T., Creed, F., et al. (2008). Violence in psychosis: Estimating the predictive validity of readily accessible clinical information in a community sample. *Schizophrenia Research.*

Zimring, F. E. (1991). Firearms, violence, and public policy. *Scientific American, 265,* 48–54.

Zisook, S., Byrd, D., Kuck, J., and Jeste, D.V. (1995). Command hallucinations in outpatients with schizophrenia. *Journal of Clinical Psychiatry, 56,* 462–465.

Part B

DECEIT, MEMORY, AND CONFESSIONS

Chapter Five

THE DETECTION OF DECEIT

PÄR ANDERS GRANHAG AND LEIF A. STRÖMWALL

Deceit occurs in all walks of life and in many day-to-day situations it would make little sense to try to unmask the possible liar (e.g. is today's special really as fresh as the waitress claims?). However, in some situations, we may feel a need to carefully separate what is truthful from what is not (e.g. should I accept my partner's reason for coming home that late last night?). In this chapter, we will examine deception detection in legal contexts, with a particular focus on deceit in criminal investigations. It is a small task to recognize why deception is an important issue within legal settings: to correctly discriminate between truth and deceit will lead to much good (guilty suspects will be sentenced, and innocent suspects cleared of suspicion), whereas incorrect judgments may have very negative effects (guilty suspects can walk free, and innocent suspect may be convicted).

The topic of deception was studied already at the dawn of legal psychology. In 1908 Hugo Münsterberg published *On the Witness Stand*, in which he touches upon the issue of deception detection. The modern research on deception started at the end of the 1960s (Ekman & Friesen, 1969), and summing up forty years of research on deception, we face an impressive corpus of scientific papers (*see* Vrij, 2008, for an up-to-date overview). Because the field still expands quickly, it makes sense to take stock of the area.

Before we start the journey, it is good to agree on how to define deception. This is not an easy task, however. Deception has been studied within many different disciplines, such as linguistics, psychiatry, philosophy, and human communication, and scholars from these and other disciplines have suggested a number of different definitions (Granhag & Strömwall, 2004a). For the present context, however, we think it suffices to go with the definition offered by Vrij (2008): deception is "a successful or unsuccessful attempt, without

95

forewarning, to create in another a belief which the communicator considers to be untrue" (p. 15). Note that lying is an intentional act and that misremembering is not the same as lying.

The chapter is structured as follows. We start with a summary of the research conducted on objective nonverbal cues to deception; some underlying theoretical approaches are outlined; and the overall findings are reviewed together with some factors that moderate people's overt behavior. In the next section, we discuss research findings pertaining to subjective cues to deception (i.e. what people think characterizes deceptive behavior). We then summarize research on people's ability to detect deception, in terms of both overall findings and factors that are known to moderate a lie-catcher's performance. Next we review research on how to detect deception from verbal content, and we focus on two such methods: *Statement Validity Assessment* (SVA) and *Reality Monitoring* (RM). We then enter the much-debated issue of psychophysiological lie detection, and we describe and review research on the two most common forms of polygraph tests: the *Control Question Tests* (CQT) and the *Guilty Knowledge Test* (GKT). Next we briefly discuss some alternative methods for detecting deception: brain scanning, the *Scientific Content Analysis* (SCAN), and two forms of analysis of voice stress. We then introduce a new promising technique for detecting deception: the *Strategic Use of Evidence* (SUE) *technique*. The theoretical framework motivating the SUE technique is described, and we comment briefly on how psychological theory can be translated to interview tactics. We close the chapter by summarizing the most important findings.

OBJECTIVE NONVERBAL CUES TO DECEPTION

Theoretical Approaches

Trying to find a telltale sign of deceit (a "Pinocchio's nose") in human nonverbal behavior has been the subject of much research effort. Both in lay people's thinking and in, for example, police interrogation manuals there are numerous ideas about detecting deceit from cues such as eye contact or gestures (*see* Vrij, 2008). Included in the concept *nonverbal behavior* are body movements (e.g. gestures and leg movement), facial indicators (e.g. eye contact, smiling), and speech behaviors (sometimes called paraverbal behaviors; e.g. response latency and pitch of voice) (DePaulo et al., 2003; Sporer & Schwandt, 2006; Vrij, 2008).

There is not one solid theory to be used in order to predict how liars and truth-tellers differ with respect to their overt behavior (Granhag & Strömwall, 2004a). It is possible, however, to identify a number of different theoretical approaches, and five of these will be summarized here.

The Emotional Approach

This approach suggests that liars might be given away by their emotions (Ekman, 2001). Specifically, experiencing emotions when lying is predicted to have behavioral consequences. For example, fear of apprehension may cause liars to experience stress and arousal, the pitch of voice will rise, blushing and sweating will increase, and so on, whereas feelings of guilt and regret will cause gaze aversion.

The Attempted Control Approach

This approach suggests that liars are aware that internal processes (such as emotions) could result in cues to deception and that they therefore will try to minimize such cues (Vrij, 2008). However, controlling one's behavior may in itself result in cues to deception (DePaulo & Kirkendol, 1989). For example, trying to inhibit movements caused by nervousness may result in overcontrol, which in turn can lead to a rigid appearance.

The Content Complexity Approach

This approach was first outlined by Zuckerman, DePaulo, and Rosenthal (1981), and it departs from the hypothesis that lying is (sometimes) more cognitively demanding than telling the truth, and that engaging in cognitively complex tasks may result in behavioral cues. For example, it has been predicted that a cognitively demanding task will result in fewer body movements and long pauses within a statement as well as between the interviewer's question and the reply (Ekman & Friesen, 1972).

The New Cognitive Load Approach

This recent approach has been developed by Vrij and his colleagues (Vrij, Mann, Fisher & Leal, 2008), and draws to some extent on the attempted control approach and the content complexity approach (Vrij, 2008). However, the approach is original in its view of the cognitive load component. The core component is that lying is (sometimes) more difficult than telling the truth, and several reasons are put forward in order to support this claim (e.g. liars need to monitor both themselves and the people they are lying to, and they need to remind themselves to role-play). Interestingly, brain-scanning studies confirm this assumption by showing that lying (more than telling the truth) activates the higher brain center (Spence et al., 2006). The main prediction is that when lying results in heightened levels of cognitive load, signs of nervousness (e.g. blinking) will decrease.

The Self-Presentational Perspective

This approach is different because it emphasizes that liars and truth tellers have the same goal: to appear honest. Self-presentation is defined as regulating one's own behavior to create a particular impression (DePaulo, 1992). The major difference is that truth tellers have grounds for their claims and they stay within the boundaries of the truth. Hence, liars and truth tellers are predicted to differ cognitively and behaviorally. For example, due to the fact that liars are aware that their claims of honesty are illegitimate, it is predicted that they will embrace their statements to a lesser extent than truth tellers will, and, in turn, that this will lead to more negative feelings and make liars appear more tense (DePaulo et al., 2003).

Overall Findings

To find out about potential nonverbal correlates of deception, researchers instruct some people to lie or tell the truth, or both (the lies are most often "constructed" for the sake of the experiment), and videotape the truths and lies told in interviews or mock interrogations. If focus is on the speech-related variables, audiotapes are of course a sufficient source. Then these video-tapes are closely analyzed and the frequency or duration, or both, of a list of nonverbal behaviors are scored and then summarized for truths and lies separately. If statistical comparisons show significant differences, researchers conclude that there are systematic nonverbal signs of deceit and truthfulness. In this section, findings from several meta-analyses and research overviews are summarized (DePaulo et al., 2003; Vrij, 2008).

In general, nonverbal behaviors do not correlate strongly with either deception or truthfulness; very few reliable nonverbal cues to deception have been found. There is some evidence that liars tend to speak with a higher pitched voice, which might be the result of experienced arousal. However, differences in pitch between liars and truth tellers are usually small and detectable only with specialized equipment. Furthermore, sometimes liars' voices sound more tense than do truth tellers' voices, another result of arousal. Speech errors (for example, word and sentence repetition, sentence incompletions, slips of the tongue) occur more often during deception, and response latency is longer before giving deceptive answers. There is also some evidence for message duration being shorter for liars, who also tend to make fewer illustrators (hand and arm movements modifying what is said verbally). Moreover, compared with truth tellers, liars tend to sound vocally less expressive, more passive, and more uncertain. Liars also sound less involved and come across as being less cooperative, and tending to make more negative statements (DePaulo et al., 2003).

Perhaps the most remarkable outcome of the reviews is that several signs of nervousness, such as gaze aversion (eye contact) and fidgeting, are generally unrelated to deception. One reason why nervous behaviors do not seem to be systematically related to deception is that truth tellers could be nervous as well (DePaulo et al., 2003); a complementary reason is that liars work hard to suppress signs of nervousness.

Presented so far are results at the general level, across all available studies without taking into account presumably important differences in the experimental designs. There are however, a few moderating factors that have been studied often enough to allow for interesting reflections.

MODERATING FACTORS

Transgressions

A factor most relevant to the forensic context is the distinction between lies that were and were not about transgressions. Lies about transgressions are told to hide or deny acts, or both such as cheating, stealing, and committing other small and large crimes. Will differences between liars' and truthtellers' nonverbal behavior emerge when they have been interviewed about transgressions they have or have not committed? The results indicate that people lying about transgressions look more nervous than truthtellers do; they also blink more and have a faster speech rate. Additionally, they are more inhibited than truthtellers are in the sense that they move their feet and legs less often (DePaulo et al., 2003).

Motivation

In many experimental studies, the liars did not have any special motivation to tell a convincing lie and simply participated with no special rewards for succeeding or punishments for failing. It is of importance to separate those studies in which participants had some special motivation to do well from those in which they did not. The question, then, is: If people are motivated to get away with their lies, will there be fewer cues to deception because they are trying harder to tell a good lie, or will their lies become more obvious as the stakes are raised? Research shows that when participants had no special incentives there were no obvious nonverbal cues to deception, which, in turn, leads to the conclusion that when people do not have very much invested in their lies, others will have a very hard time detecting the deceit. However, when liars do worry about getting away with their lies, then several behaviors may betray them. It is only when participants are motivated to do well that they speak in a higher pitch when lying than when telling the truth. Although liars also seem more tense than truth tellers do regardless of level of motivation, the difference is pronounced for those who are highly motivated to get away with their lies. In the previous section, in which results were summarized over all studies, we found no differences in eye contact between liars and truthtellers. When participants are motivated to do well, however, then one stereotype about liars becomes a reality: They make less eye contact than truth tellers do. There is also some evidence that, under high motivational conditions, liars made fewer foot and leg movements than did truthtellers (DePaulo et al., 2003).

Preparation

Sometimes suspects know in advance that they are going to be interviewed, which gives them a chance to prepare their answers. Presumably, liars should manage to appear more like truthtellers when they can plan their answers in advance than when they cannot. The available research indicates that when liars have time to plan, they have shorter response latency than truthtellers do. When given no time to prepare, the opposite pattern is found. There is also some evidence that liars show shorter message duration than truthtellers do when they have time to prepare (Sporer & Schwandt, 2006).

Real-Life Cases

Although researchers have in some studies tried to raise the motivation of and stakes for lying by participants, the question still remains how the results from laboratory-based studies reflect what may happen in real-life high-stake situations such as police interviews. In a few studies, the behavior of real-life suspects, interviewed about serious crimes such as murder, rape and arson – for which suspects face long prison sentences if found guilty – has been examined. Results revealed that these suspects did not show the nervous behaviors typically believed to be associated with lying, such as gaze aversion and fidgeting. In fact, they exhibited an increase in pauses; a decrease in eye blinks; and (for male suspects) a decrease in finger, hand, and arm movements (Mann, Vrij & Bull, 2002; Vrij & Mann 2001).

In summary, the scientific research shows that under certain conditions there seem to be some – but very few – differences between truthtellers and liars in their nonverbal behavior. However, it is of great importance to realize that these differences, albeit significant in meta-analyses, are not large and the practical value may be quite low. None of the behaviors discussed here can be used as a fail-safe decision rule. The available research thus indicates that there are no nonverbal indicators of deception that always works – there is no "Pinocchio's nose."

SUBJECTIVE NONVERBAL CUES TO DECEPTION

This section deals with what people think is indicative of deception – the subjective cues to deception (sometimes referred to as belief about deception). Lots of research has been conducted on this issue, and the most straightforward approach is to simply ask participants to describe the cues they believe to occur more or less often when people are lying, compared with when people are telling the truth. These answers can be given on a series of rating scales as in most survey studies. Another method is to have people judging the veracity of stimuli material (most often videotaped interviews) and then writing down why they thought someone was lying or telling the truth. A third alternative is for the researcher to score the nonverbal behavior of the liars and truth tellers and to correlate these scores with the veracity judgments to see which cues to deception observers actually used (Anderson, DePaulo, Ansfield, Tickle, & Green, 1999; Vrij, 2008). Research has been carried out collecting the subjective cues to deception from both laypersons and practitioners within the legal arena.

Lay people

Research on subjective nonverbal indicators of deception has shown that people (community samples, college students) tend to associate lying with an increase in speech disturbances such as hesitations and speech errors, a slower speech rate, longer and more frequent pauses, more gaze aversion, and an increase in smiling and movements such as self-manipulations, gestures, hand and finger and leg and foot movements (Vrij, 2008). Generally, these subjective deception cues are indicators of nervousness. It seems as if people believe that a liar will feel nervous and act accordingly. In other words, because people tend to believe that liars are more nervous than truth tellers are, they infer deception from signs of nervousness. What emanates from the research on subjective cues to deception is a set of stereotypical beliefs (Vrij, 2008; Zuckerman, et al., 1981). The most commonly and strongly expressed cue to deception is the decrease in eye contact. This is the most favored subjective cue to deception on a worldwide scale, as shown in a large study collecting subjective deception cues from close to 5000 people in fifty-eight countries (Global Deception Research Team, 2006).

Practitioners

Certain groups of professionals are faced with deciding whether someone is lying or not on an everyday basis. It sounds plausible that this everyday experience, coupled with these practitioners' training and, probably, special interest in these issues, could affect their subjective cues to deception. A number of studies, mostly surveys, have examined this issue. The practitioners have been mostly police officers, but customs officers, prison guards, prosecutors, and judges, among others, have also been studied. These groups of professionals work in different countries: The United Kingdom (Akehurst, Köhnken, Vrij & Bull, 1996), Germany (Greuel, 1992), Sweden (Strömwall & Granhag, 2003), Spain (Masip & Garrido, 2001), The Netherlands (Vrij & Semin, 1996) and the United States (Kraut & Poe, 1980).

Although in some studies a few differences among the groups studied were found, it is fair to say that the practitioners have similar subjective cues to deception. They think that liars are more gaze aversive, fidget more, make more self-manipulations and body movements, and have less fluent speech compared with truthtellers. In the perhaps most valid study, in terms of human ecology, of police officers' beliefs, Mann, Vrij, and Bull (2004) showed fragments of real-life police interviews with suspects to British police officers. Most of the police officers claimed that searching for a decrease in eye contact is useful in detecting deception. Those police officers who were more correct used this cue to a lesser extent. The authors suggested that police officers rely upon cues that are general rather than idiosyncratic (Mann et al., 2004).

The practitioners, then, express the same subjective nonverbal cues to deception as laypersons do. In general, these beliefs are incorrect. Just like laypersons, the presumed experts consider nervous behaviors to indicate deception (Strömwall, Granhag & Hartwig, 2004). What indicator experts and laypeople alike rely on most is a decrease in eye contact when lying. It seems that participants in deception studies (both practitioners and lay persons), when stating their subjective cues to deception, visualizes a highly motivated liar. According to Anderson, and coworkers (1999), when people are asked to describe the cues they think are indicative of deceit, they do little more than recount the accepted cultural wisdom about such matters, also known as stereotypical beliefs.

Interestingly, one group of people has been shown to have different and more correct subjective cues to deception, namely criminals (Granhag, Andersson, Strömwall & Hartwig, 2004; Vrij & Semin, 1996). This "professional" group does, for example, not believe in decrease in eye contact as a reliable indicator of deception. Criminals' more calibrated beliefs have been explained by the fact that they live in more deceptive environments that provide them with clear, frequent, and (often) immediate feedback on the deception strategies that work and those that do not. That is, in contrast to many other groups, they learn the right lesson from their experience (Strömwall et al., 2004).

Lie-Catchers' Performance

Overall Findings

There are a few things to keep in mind when taking stock of results on lie-catchers' performance. First, one must make sure what the numbers presented actually refer to. In brief, one needs to separate (1) truth or lie discrimination (which refers to overall accuracy) from (2) deception detection accuracy (which refers to accuracy for detecting liars) and (3) truth detection accuracy (which refers to accuracy for detecting truthtellers). Obviously, truth or lie discrimination is the average of deception detection accuracy and truth detection accuracy. One should acknowledge, however, that a group of liecatchers can achieve high deception detection accuracy but poor truth detection accuracy (or vice versa). A second thing to consider is circumstances under which the liecatchers are tested (i.e. the ecological validity of the test).

To map people's ability to detect lies and truths has been the main research question for many deception scholars, and there is now a huge body of reports on this topic. A recent meta-analysis, based on more than 250 separate studies, showed an average truth or lie discrimination level of 54 percent (Bond & DePaulo, 2006). Interestingly, with very few exceptions, the accuracy levels fall between 45 percent and 60 percent. Considering that the level of chance is 50 percent, this is hardly an impressive performance. On the other hand, taking the scarcity and weakness of valid cues to deception into account, this result is not surprising.

This "a few percentages above chance level" result is an average over a variety of lie-catcher samples, sender samples, deception media, contexts, and so on. A closer look shows that there are a number of factors that moderate the lie-catchers' accuracy (Granhag & Strömwall, 2008b). In what follows we will discuss some of the moderators.

Moderating Factors

Preparation

Sometimes people have anticipated that they need to lie, and on other occasions, lies are told in response to an unanticipated need. This is an area worthy of much more work, but the available research suggests that liecatchers are better when judging unprepared than prepared messages and that prepared messages appear more truthful than do messages that are unprepared (Bond & DePaulo, 2006; Vrij, 2008).

Deception Medium

Lies and truths can be evaluated over different mediums, resulting in different accuracy rates for lies that have been seen, heard, or read. This line of research shows that lie or truth discrimination accuracy is lower if judgments are made with video only rather than with audiovisual or audio only media or written transcripts. It has also been found that messages are perceived as most truthful if judged from audiovisual or audio presentations, followed by written transcripts and video presentations (Bond & DePaulo, 2006). The medium may affect deception detection accuracy, lies being more evident when they can be heard. This is probably due to the stereotype of a liar (e.g. a person who is gaze aversive and fidgeting) being most strongly brought to mind by the video medium. Obviously, the stereotypical liar may very well be a nervous and uncomfortable truth teller.

Interaction

In some studies, the senders are alone and talk to a camera; in other studies, an experimenter asks a standardized list of questions. Sometimes, the interaction partner is attempting to judge the veracity (such as in a mock police interview); on other occasions, an observer may be making this judgment. The literature shows that interacting interviewers tend to assess the sender as truthful much more often than the passive observers do (Granhag & Strömwall, 2001). In a similar vein, passive live observers have been found to perceive both adult (Landström, Granhag & Hartwig, 2005) and child witnesses (Landström, Granhag & Hartwig, 2007) more positively compared to passive video observers. Furthermore, research suggests that observers are better than interaction partners are at discriminating lies from truths (Bond & DePaulo, 2006; Vrij, 2008). It seems as if people do not want to believe that someone just lied to them without their spotting it. Alternatively, the reluctance to assess interaction partners as liars could be the result of not wanting to insinuate that the partner is dishonest. In conclusion, research suggests that lies told in social interactions are better detected by observers than by interaction partners.

Baseline Familiarity

It makes sense to predict that a lie catcher should perform better if he or she has some familiarity with the sender. The rationale for this is that the more knowledge one has about the sender's (normal) behavior, the better the chance to detect deviations. In turn, this might lead to increased detection performance, but only if lying really causes deviations in behavior and if telling the truth does not. This line of research shows that baseline exposure does indeed improve lie or truth discrimination (Bond & DePaulo, 2006). However, one should be aware that senders who are familiar to the receiver are more likely to be judged as truthful. People seem to be unwilling to imply that someone familiar to them is lying.

Motivation

It has been argued that sender's motivation (to be assessed as honest) might influence their appearance and, in turn lie catchers' accuracy. Deception research has therefore investigated the effects of different levels of sender motivation. The so-called motivational impairment effect, states that the truths and lies of highly motivated senders will be more easily discriminated than those of unmotivated senders. Indeed, this hypothesis is supported by experimental studies (for more on this factor, *see* Vrij, 2008). However, it should be noted that this result is found for within-study comparisons and not for between-study comparisons. In brief, the reliable difference found is that motivated senders appear less truthful than those with little or no motivation to be assessed as honest. The combined evidence suggests that people who are very motivated to be assessed as honest seem to appear deceptive, whether or not they are lying (Bond & DePaulo, 2006).

Expertise

Those asked to assess veracity in deception experiments are usually college students with no special training or reason to succeed. Reasonably, people with more experience should be better at spotting lies, and researchers have therefore tested groups such as police officers, FBI agents, judges, psychiatrists, and customs officials. Vrij (2008) presents an overview of more than thirty published studies testing different groups of presumed deception-detection experts. The average accuracy rate over these groups was found to be 56 percent, which is in line with the performance of laypeople. However, it would probably be premature to conclude that, for example, police officers (the most commonly tested group) are poor at detecting deception. This note of caution is issued because the experimental setting used to test the presumed experts is not mirroring their real-life environment. This leads to our next section. (For a recent and interesting debate on lie-catching expertise, *see* Bond and Uysal (2007) and O'Sullivan (2007)).

A Critical Note

The paradigmatic task for presumed experts (or laypeople for that matter) who take part in studies on deception is to assess veracity on the basis of very short video clips in which an interviewer asks a few (or no) questions. The presumed experts under examination are without any form of background information and are not allowed to interact with the sender. Obviously, this is very far from the real-life settings in which these professionals have developed their (presumed) expertise. What deception research really shows is that presumed experts perform just above the level of chance when tested in a particular situation, characterized by low human ecological validity. It is true that sometimes professionals must assess veracity on the basis of a very brief interaction and without any form of background information (e.g. customs personnel in the field). Much more often, however, professional lie catchers will have information about the suspect at hand and opportunity to plan and conduct an actual interview with the suspect. As will be discussed later in this chapter, these circumstances might help the lie catcher to detect deception and truth, but only if using this background information in a strategic manner.

DETECTING DECEIT FROM VERBAL CONTENT

In a previous section, we have shown that there are not many reliable nonverbal indicators of deception, thereby making correct classifications of truths and lies on the basis of nonverbal behavior really difficult. This fact has led researchers as well as practitioners to turn to other deception-detection strategies. One such strategy is the analysis of the verbal content, that is, what people actually say and not how they say it. Discussed here will be two verbal assessment tools, SVA and RM.

Statement Validity Assessment

The presumably most popular, and definitely the most widely used, technique for assessing the veracity of verbal statements is SVA. The technique was developed in Germany to determine the credibility of children's testimonies concerning sexual offences. In such cases, it is usually difficult to determine the facts, as often there are no other witnesses or medical or physical evidence. Frequently, the alleged victim and the defendant give contradictory statements; as a result the perceived credibility of the defendant and alleged victim become important. To date, SVAs are accepted as evidence in criminal courts in several countries, such as Germany and The Netherlands (Vrij, 2008). However, the SVA does not stem from established scientific findings but rather from practice. According to the *Undeutsch hypothesis* (Steller, 1989), a child's statement that is derived from the memory of an actual experience will differ in content and quality from a statement based on invention or fantasy. Undeutsch, and later Steller and Köhnken, developed content criteria that are supposed to discriminate the different types of statements from each other (Steller & Köhnken, 1989).

A SVA consists of several stages (Vrij, 2008). First, the child (or the adult) is interviewed using a *semi-structured interview* in which the child provides his or her own account of the allegation. Of utmost importance is that the child tells the story without any influence or suggestions from the interviewer. These interviews are audiotaped and then transcribed. Second, a systematic assessment of the credibility of the written statement given during the interview is undertaken. This assessment, which is called criteria-based content analysis (CBCA), is based on the list of nineteen content criteria compiled and discussed by Steller and Köhnken (1989) (Table 5-1). The presence of CBCA criteria enhances the quality of the statement and strengthens the hypothesis that the account is based on an authentic personal experience. The CBCA, then, searches for the truth and not for signs of deceit. Third, alternative explanations for the CBCA outcomes are considered. For this purpose, a so-called validity checklist has been developed (Vrij, 2008). In the validity checklist, the SVA evaluator checks for example for inconsistencies with other evidence and statements and inappropriate use of language (i.e. more mature words used than one would expect from a child of a certain age).

Most research into the SVA has focused on the CBCA criteria. Do they actually differentiate truthful and deceptive accounts? Vrij (2005, 2008) has reviewed the available studies (more than fifty), conducted both in field settings and in the laboratory, and analyzed statements from both adults and children. On a general level, the Undeutsch hypothesis has found support; it has been found that the CBCA criteria do differentiate the truthful and the deceptive accounts because the criteria are more often found in truthful statements (Vrij, 2008). When examining the individual criteria, it is found that criteria 3 (quantity of details), 2 (unstructured production), 4 (contextual embeddings), and 6 (reproduction of conversation) are the ones receiving most support from research. At the level of total CBCA scores, and averaged over all available studies, just over 70 percent of all statements have been correctly classified, and lies and truths achieve similar accuracy rates (Vrij, 2008).

Table 5-1. CBCA Criteria (from Steller & Köhnken, 1989)

General characteristics
    1. Logical structure
    2. Unstructured production
    3. Quantity of details
Specific contents
    4. Contextual embedding
    5. Descriptions of interactions
    6. Reproduction of conversation
    7. Unexpected complications during the incident
Peculiarities of content
    8. Unusual details
    9. Superfluous details
    10. Accurately reported details misunderstood
    11. Related external associations
    12. Accounts of subjective mental states
    13. Attribution of perpetrator's mental state
Motivation-related contents
    14. Spontaneous corrections
    15. Admitting lack of memory
    16. Raising doubts about one's own testimony
    17. Self-deprecation
    18. Pardoning the perpetrator
Offence-specific elements
    19. Details characteristic of the offence

Reality Monitoring

Based on principles from well-established research findings on human memory, RM has been used as an alternative method to examine verbal differences between the truthful and deceptive. The fundamental idea is that memories of actually experienced events differ in quality from memories of imagined or fabricated events. Since memories of real experiences are obtained through perceptual processes, they are likely to contain certain types of information, such as *perceptual information* – details of smell, taste, and touch, and visual, and auditory details – and *contextual information* – spatial and temporal details. Accounts of imagined events are derived from an internal source and are therefore likely to contain *cognitive operations*, such as thoughts and reasoning ("I remember thinking to myself . . .") (e.g. Johnson & Raye, 1981, 1998). Reasonably, experienced events reflect truth telling (since a truthful witness has seen or heard something and tries to recapitulate the actual memory), whereas imagined events reflect deception (since a deceptive witness talks about something invented). Therefore, differences between truth tellers and liars could be expected regarding RM criteria (Sporer, 2004; Vrij, 2008).

Researchers have used somewhat different content criteria based on the RM way of thinking (Sporer, 2004). Table 5-2 contains the list of RM criteria most commonly applied in deception detection studies. The available research (which is not as comprehensive as the CBCA studies) has been reviewed by Masip, Sporer, Garrido, and Herrero (2004) and by Vrij (2008). At an individual criterion level, it is criteria 2 (*perceptual information*), 3 (*spatial information*) and 4 (*temporal information*) that best differentiate truthful and deceptive accounts. Unfortunately, the only lie criterion (*cognitive operations*) has not received much support. The overall result is that RM shows an accuracy rate of just below 70 percent correct classifications, with slightly better accuracy found for detecting truths than lies. These accuracy rates are comparable with the accuracy rates reported for CBCA evaluations.

Table 5-2. Reality Monitoring Criteria (from Sporer, 1997)

Truth criteria
 1. Clarity
 2. Perceptual information
 3. Spatial information
 4. Temporal information
 5. Affect
 6. Reconstructability of the story
 7. Realism
Lie criterion
 8. Cognitive operations

Note: Some researchers split criterion 2 into five separate criteria reflecting the five senses (Strömwall, Bengtsson, Leander & Granhag, 2004).

Verbal Content Analysis: Conclusions

The SVA and the RM techniques have certain similarities (e.g. they are both criteria-based tools that search for indicators of the truth) and certain differences (e.g. SVA stems from practice, RM from research). Both techniques require training before use and are therefore strictly speaking not comparable to the previously reviewed nonverbal method that usually involves untrained observers. One common problem for SVA and RM is standardization, both in definitions of the criteria (e.g. What is a cognitive operation?) and in the scoring and evaluation systems (e.g. What is scored as presence of a criteria? How many criteria need to be present for an evaluator to claim that a specific statement is truthful?). At this time, RM seems to be preferable, because RM analyses are much easier to conduct than are CBCA evaluations (Sporer, 1997) and work as well in terms of accuracy (Vrij, 2008).

Psychophysiological Lie Detection

So far we have discussed cues to deception in demeanor and in the verbal content of a statement. We will now shift focus to the psychophysiological aspects of deception and the polygraph as lie detector. The psychophysiological approach has a long history, and one of the first polygraphs to be used in forensic contexts was constructed in 1914 by William Marston in the United States. It measured the galvanic skin response, which, in turn, depends on sweating, for example from the palm. Marston's polygraph was used for interrogating suspected spies during the First World War (Teigen, 2006). The polygraph of today is more sophisticated, but the basic function is much the same (Grubin & Madsen, 2005). The modern polygraph measures different physiological systems, all governed by the autonomic nervous system: typically, galvanic skin response, cardiovascular activity (such as systolic and diastolic blood pressure), and breathing patterns.

The polygraph is used in a number of different contexts, such as in criminal investigations, as a condition for probation orders and as a release condition for convicted sexual offenders. Moreover, the polygraph is used in many parts of the world, such as the United States, Belgium, Israel, Japan, Korea, Thailand, and Turkey (Honts, 2004). It is important to distinguish between two main types of polygraph tests: the CQT (Honts, 2004) and the GKT (Lykken, 1959).

The Control Question Test (CQT)

The CQT, which is the most frequently used polygraph test when it comes to criminal investigations, starts with an introductory phase, after which the suspect is asked a number of questions belonging to one of three categories: (1) irrelevant questions ("Is soccer a sport?"), (2) relevant questions ("Did you stab Mr. Lee?"), or (3) control questions ("Before the age of twenty, did you ever steal something?"). The control questions concern transgressions in the past, designed to force the suspect to give a deceptive response. The core of CQT is to compare the responses registered when answering the control questions to the responses registered when answering the relevant questions (i.e. questions about the crime). The prediction is that guilty suspects will react more strongly to the relevant questions than to the control questions, whereas the opposite pattern is expected from innocent suspects (Fiedler, Schmid & Stahl, 2002).

There are a few overviews of CQT laboratory research, and these show an accuracy rate that ranges from 74 percent to 82 percent for classifying guilty suspects and an accuracy rate that ranges from 60 percent to 84 percent for classifying innocent suspects (Vrij, 2008). The different reviews published of

CQT field studies confirm this pattern by showing an accuracy rate that ranges from 83 percent and 89 percent for classifying guilty suspects, and an accuracy rate that ranges from 53 percent and 75 percent for classifying innocent suspects (Vrij, 2008). The main problem with field studies is, of course, to know whether the suspect is guilty or innocent (i.e. to establish ground truth). In sum, the evaluations show that the CQT has some discriminative value and that the technique is better at pinpointing liars than truth tellers. It should be noted, however, that CQT has been exposed to severe criticism (e.g. Ben-Shakhar & Furedy, 1990; Lykken, 1998), and particularly so with respect to the assumption that innocent suspects will give more aroused responses to control questions than to relevant questions. It simply may be incorrect to believe that an innocent suspect would react more strongly to a control question about a rather mild transgression in the past than to a relevant question about the crime for which he or she is being falsely accused.

The Guilty Knowledge Test

The GKT aims at detecting concealed knowledge by asking a number of questions, and for each question it presents a number of answer alternatives, one of which is correct (e.g. "Where was the body of Mr Lee found? Was it in the hall? In the kitchen? In the bedroom?" etc.). The assumption is that guilty suspects will try to conceal their knowledge and therefore experience more physiological arousal when the correct (vs. the incorrect) alternative is presented. Innocent suspects are, in contrast, expected to react similarly to all answer alternatives as they lack guilty knowledge (MacLaren, 2001).

The different overviews of GKT laboratory research show an accuracy rate that ranges from 76 percent to 88 percent for classifying guilty suspects, and an accuracy rate that ranges from 83 percent to 99 percent for classifying innocent suspects (Vrij, 2008). The published GKT field studies (which are very few) confirm this pattern by showing an accuracy rate that ranges from 42 percent to 76 percent for guilty suspects, and an accuracy rate that ranges from 94 percent to 98 percent for innocent suspects (Vrij, 2008). Taken together, research shows that the GKT has some discriminative value and that the technique is better at pinpointing truth tellers than liars. The GKT does not escape criticism; for example, the validity of the test depends very much on the fact that innocent suspects do not know the correct answer to the questions asked and the correct answer does not stand out in any way.

Countermeasures

If suspects are trained in countermeasures before being hooked up to a polygraph, this can pose a serious threat to the accuracy of the test (Honts,

Hodes & Raskin, 1985; Honts, Raskin & Kircher, 1994). Countermeasures can be of many different kinds, for example, physical (e.g. biting the tongue) or cognitive (e.g. counting backwards). For a detailed discussion on different forms of countermeasures, *see* Honts and Amato (2002).

ALTERNATIVE METHODS FOR DETECTING DECEIT

Brain Scanning

One of the more common methods for scanning the human brain is called functional magnetic resonance imaging (fMRI). During recent years, fMRI has been used for many purposes, and one is to study the brain activity taking place during deception. This line of research shows that there is an increased activity in the prefrontal cortex during deception (Spence et al., 2006). This has been interpreted as lying being more cognitively demanding than telling the truth. The studies on neural correlates of deception are intriguing, and the findings reported to date are rather promising. However, the view presented by the media is not always balanced, and it is important to acknowledge that the studies reported so far are very few. In addition, not only is the fMRI equipment extremely expensive, but it also requires that the target remain still and silent (and answer questions by pressing buttons). In brief, it is very hard to predict to what extent (if any) fMRI will be a useful tool for detecting deception in forensic contexts. On the other hand, it is safe to say that the technique already is very helpful in mapping the cognitive processes taking place during deception.

The Scientific Content Analysis

The underlying assumption of SCAN is that a statement based on memory of a personal experience differs in content from a statement based on fabrication (see the sections on CBCA and RM). The SCAN rests on an extensive list of criteria such as "change in language" and "denial of allegations" (Vrij, 2008). To date, there has been very little research on the diagnostic value of the SCAN, and the different criteria used are much less standardized compared with, for example, the CBCA. Vrij (2008) could only find three published studies on the SCAN, two field studies and one laboratory study. Critically, for both field studies the "ground truth" was unknown (Driscoll, 1994; Smith, 2001, both cited in Vrij, 2008), and the laboratory study showed that truthful and deceptive statements did not differ with regard to the criteria tested (Porter & Yuille, 1996). According to its advocates the technique is used worldwide, but one should be aware that there is not much scientific evidence supporting the SCAN.

Analysis of Voice Stress

Yet another suggested approach to deception detection is to analyze the voice as such. Broadly speaking, there are two such methods: voice stress analysis (VSA) and layered voice-stress analysis (LVA). Eriksson and Lacerda (2007) provide a summary of both these methods. The idea behind the VSA is to measure the activity in the muscles responsible for producing speech to infer the speaker's mental state. The key concept is so-called micro-tremors, which are described as weak involuntarily muscle activity, that can only be registered by fine electrodes. It is an easy task to show that tremors occur in large muscle groups, such as the biceps, but there is very little scientific evidence for the existence of tremors in the muscles producing speech (Shipp & Izdebski, 1981). If there is no tremor in the muscles producing speech, there is no tremor to measure in the voice. In addition, even if it was possible to find tremor in the voice, it would still remain to be decided to what extent (if any) such tremor is diagnostic for deception.

The second method, LVA, depends on the use of a computer program for analyzing errors occurring when a signal is digitized. It is argued that such errors can only be measured by sophisticated technology and that the LVA uses these errors to calculate a so-called truth value. However, such errors can be found for any type of sound, and by the LVA logic, a pair of roller-blades could be assessed as telling the truth and a distant bark as deceptive. In brief, there is no empirical research supporting the validity of the SVA or the LVA, and true experts in forensic phonetics do their best to debunk the nonsense (Eriksson & Lacerda, 2007).

Strategic Use of Evidence

As previously noted, research on deception has been heavily focused on the performance of lie catchers who, rather passively, watch short video clips of suspects. However, there is a new line of research that departs from the fact that there is often some potentially incriminating evidence against the suspect, for example, physical evidence or witness reports. The basic idea is that deception detection performance can be significantly improved if the investigator (1) is allowed to interrogate the suspect, (2) is given background information about the case and the suspect, and (3) knows how to strategically use this background information (Granhag & Strömwall, 2008b). The SUE technique provides basic principles on how to best use the available evidence to detect deception. In what follows we will describe some theoretical underpinnings of the SUE technique, provide empirical support for some core predictions, and offer a few words on how these predictions can be translated to interview tactics.

Theoretical Framework

The theoretical framework supporting the SUE technique rests on psychological notions from three domains: (1) the psychology of instrumental mind reading, (2) the psychology of self-regulation, and (3) the psychology of guilt and innocence (Granhag & Hartwig, 2008).

Instrumental Mind Reading

We perform acts of mind reading daily by using different methods to draw conclusions about other people's mental states. For the present context we are not concerned with attempts to read the actual content of a person's mind, which indeed is a very speculative form of mind reading. Instead, we are interested in instrumental mind reading, in which the goal is to make predictions about a person's future behavior. In a criminal investigation the interrogator should try to mind read the strategies and behavior of the suspect. This is, however, not an easy task. First of all, many interrogators are too occupied thinking about their own tactics and therefore neglect the suspect's strategies (Hartwig, Granhag & Vrij, 2005). In addition, biases such as false consensus, stereotyping, and the curse of knowledge might contribute to mind-reading failures (for a more detailed account of these problems, *see* Granhag & Hartwig, 2008b). However, basic psychological theory might help investigators to mind read their suspects.

The Psychology of Self-Regulation

The term self-regulation refers to the ways in which people try to control their behavior (Fiske & Taylor, 1991). It is well-known that self-regulatory strategies are evoked by threatening situations, and particularly when there is a lack of knowledge about the forthcoming event. Translated into an investigative context, it is reasonable to construe an upcoming interrogation as a threat for the suspect. Research on social cognition suggests that a suspect may use many forms of cognitive control, and it has been argued that one such form – decision control – is of particular relevance for an interrogative setting (Granhag & Hartwig, 2008a). Decision control refers to the control achieved when deciding how to engage in an upcoming aversive event.

At the most basic level both guilty and innocent suspects are assumed to view the upcoming interrogation as a threat, but there is an important difference in that guilty suspects will have exclusive knowledge about the crime, knowledge that innocent suspects lack. The threat for the guilty suspect is that the interrogator may come to know that the guilty suspect holds exclusive knowledge about the crime, whereas the threat for an innocent suspect is that the interrogator may not come to know that the innocent suspect does not hold exclusive knowledge about the crime. Hence, there is reason to believe that the use of the same self-regulatory strategy (decision control) will result in different outcomes depending on whether the suspect is guilty or innocent.

The Psychology of Guilt and Innocence

In short, guilty suspects need to decide what to admit, avoid and deny during the interrogation (e.g. a very basic counterinterrogation strategy is to admit what one believes the interrogator to already know). However, the more interesting part is to try to predict how the guilty suspect will handle the pieces of incriminating information that he is not certain the interrogator holds. Construing these as an aversive stimulus, the guilty suspect is left with two ways of acting: (1) to go for avoidance when asked to freely tell his story and (2) to go for denial in response to a direct question. Turning to innocent suspects, we have reason to believe that their decision control will be colored by basic psychological concepts such as the belief in a just world (i.e. one gets what one deserves; Lerner, 1980) and the illusion of transparency (i.e. the belief that one's inner feelings and states will manifest themselves on the outside; Savitsky & Gilovich, 2003).

Importantly, research on mock suspects' planning and strategies supports the previous reasoning. It has been found that a much higher proportion of guilty (vs. innocent) suspects (1) report having a strategy prepared before entering the interrogation room (Hartwig, Granhag & Strömwall, 2007); (2) avoid mentioning incriminating information during a free recall (Hartwig, Granhag, Strömwall & Vrij, 2005), and (3) deny holding incriminating information when asked specific questions addressing this particular information (e.g. Hartwig, Granhag, Strömwall & Kronkvist, 2006). The combined empirical evidence supports the assumptions that a suspect's strategy is a reflection of his mental state; and that a suspect's behavior is a reflection of his strategy.

FROM PSYCHOLOGICAL THEORY TO INTERVIEW TACTICS

In a still-ongoing research program we have outlined how these (and other) empirical findings can be used in order to formulate and implement the SUE technique for interrogating suspects (Granhag, Strömwall & Hartwig, 2007). The full SUE technique consists of a number of different components, and so far only some of these have been experimentally tested (e.g. withholding the evidence, asking for a free narrative, asking specific questions that concern – but do not reveal – the evidence). One of these tests was conducted at a police academy in Sweden, where a group of highly motivated police trainees received training in some core components of the SUE technique and an equally motivated group of trainees received no such training. The trained group received an overall accuracy rate of 85 percent, whereas the corresponding figure for the untrained group was 56 percent (Hartwig et al., 2006). A closer analysis showed that the trained interrogators – by interviewing in accordance with the SUE technique – managed to create and use a diagnostic cue to deception, namely statement evidence inconsistency.

Applications and Limitations

The application of the SUE technique is probably wide because the use of the technique only requires that the suspect is uncertain about what the interrogator knows (a situation very common in criminal investigations). The SUE technique is totally different from the confrontational techniques typically found in interrogation manuals (e.g. Inbau, Reid, Buckley & Jayne, 2001). However, the SUE technique stretches beyond pure and passive information gathering by drawing on the differences in information that innocent suspects volunteer and guilty suspects conceal and deny. It needs to be underscored that the SUE-technique is very much a project under progress. Future research will illuminate how the effectiveness of the technique is moderated by factors such as the order in which different pieces of evidence are disclosed and the different counterinterrogation methods used by (guilty) suspects.

CONCLUSION

We started out by briefly outlining five theoretical approaches to people's nonverbal behavior: the emotional approach, the attempted control approach, the content complexity approach, the new cognitive load approach, and the self-presentational perspective. It is very difficult to decide the exact amount of explanatory power that should be assigned to each approach (and we refrained from evaluating the approaches), but it is rather safe to say that no single approach can be used to predict liars' and truth tellers' nonverbal behavior over a variety of different situations and contexts. The overall finding from research on objective nonverbal cues is that there are few cues that correlate with deception, and those that do correlate (e.g. liars have a higher-pitched voice and use fewer illustrators) are only weakly related. In short, there is very meager scientific evidence backing up those criminal investigators (and other legal professionals) who feel smug about their ability to read a suspect's body language in order to detect deception. Furthermore, one needs to acknowledge that nonverbal behaviors might be differently correlated with truth status under certain conditions. For example, if the liar has had time to prepare the lie or not will show different correlations with some nonverbal behaviors. Research on subjective cues to deception show that it is common to believe that signs of nervousness are indicative of deception, this general misconception seems to hold for laypeople as well as professionals.

Considering that the nonverbal cues to deception are very few and weak – and that people seem to hold incorrect beliefs about these cues – it is of no surprise that people's ability to discriminate truth from lies is mediocre. A closer look reveals that there are some factors moderating lie-catcher's success; for example, lies that are prepared shown on video only (vs. in audio-visual or written format), and told by an unfamiliar person are more difficult to detect. We also concluded that presumed lie-catching experts do not perform better than laypersons, but we also acknowledged that these presumed experts have been tested in situations that are very different from their day-to-day work situations.

Considerable research effort has gone into finding correlates of truths and lies with the verbal content of a given statement. In this chapter, we reviewed two techniques, SVA and RM. Overall accuracy was around 70 percent if following either technique. Arguably, RM seems to be preferable over SVA, because RM analyses are easier to teach, learn, and conduct than are SVA evaluations, in addition to having a theory-based rationale.

We then turned to psychophysiological lie detection and described the CQT and the GKT. We summarized both laboratory and field research showing that the CQT seems to be better at catching liars than clearing innocent suspects, whereas the GKT seem to better at clearing innocent suspects than catching liars. Although we conclude that both tests seem to have some discriminative value, we also note that both tests have been severely criticized and that the polygraph as lie detector must be used with caution. We then discussed alternative methods for detecting deception and concluded that brain scanning (fMRI) is a somewhat promising method but that the wait is long before the method can be used in criminal investigations. With reference to research (or the lack thereof) we took a much more critical stand with respect to the other alternative methods: the SCAN, VSA, and LVA. Finally, we introduced the SUE technique, which is the result of a new line of research within deception detection. We outlined the theoretical basis for the SUE technique and provided evidence that the technique can help interviewers to discriminate between guilty and innocent suspects.

In conclusion, this chapter shows that detecting deceit in legal contexts is a difficult task and that legal professionals are well-advised to take a humble stand with respect to their own lie-catching ability. There is no single lie-detection technique that can be trusted to always generate the correct answer.

Different contexts demand different lie-detection methods, and none of the methods available are without problems. Nevertheless, it is possible to end on a positive note; professional lie catchers will, in the long run, make more correct judgments and reduce their number of mistakes if learning the lessons taught by science.

REFERENCES

Akehurst, L., Köhnken, G., Vrij, A., and Bull, R. (1996). Lay persons' and police officers' beliefs regarding deceptive behaviour. *Applied Cognitive Psychology, 10*, 461–471.

Anderson, D.E., DePaulo, B.M., Ansfield, M.E., Tickle, J.J., and Green, E. (1999). Beliefs about cues to deception: Mindless stereotypes or untapped wisdom? *Journal of Nonverbal Behavior, 23*, 67–89.

Ben-Shakhar, G., and Furedy, J.J. (1990). *Theories and Applications in the Detection of Deception: A Psychophysiological and International Perspective.* New York: Springer-Verlag.

Bond, C.F., Jr, and DePaulo, B.M. (2006). Accuracy of deception judgments. *Personality and Social Psychology Review, 10*, 214–234.

DePaulo, B.M. (1992). Nonverbal behavior and self-presentation. *Psychological Bulletin, 111*, 203–243.

DePaulo, B.M., and Kirkendol, S.E. (1989). The motivational impairment effect in the communication of deception. In J.C. Yuille (Ed.), *Credibility Assessment* (pp. 51–70). Dordrecht, The Netherlands: Kluwer.

DePaulo, B.M., Lindsay, J.J., Malone, B.E., Muhlenbruck, L., Charlton, K., and Cooper, H. (2003). Cues to deception. *Psychological Bulletin, 129*, 74–118.

Ekman, P. (2001). *Telling Lies: Clues to Deceit in the Marketplace, Politics and Marriage.* New York: Norton.

Ekman, P., and Friesen, W.V. (1969). Nonverbal leakage and clues to deception. *Psychiatry, 32*, 88–105.

Ekman P., and Friesen, W.V. (1972). Hand movements. *Journal of Communication, 22*, 353–374.

Eriksson, E., and Lacerda, F. (2007). Charlatanry in forensic speech science: A problem to be taken seriously. *The International Journal of Speech, Language and the Law, 14*, 169–193.

Fiedler, K., Schmid, J., and Stahl, T. (2002). What is the current truth about polygraph lie detection? *Basic and Applied Social Psychology, 24*, 313–324.

Fiske, S.T., and Taylor, E.T. (1991). *Social Cognition.* New York: McGraw-Hill.

Global Deception Research Team. (2006). A world of lies. *Journal of Cross-Cultural Psychology, 37*, 60–74.

Granhag, P.A., Andersson, L.O., Strömwall, L.A., and Hartwig, M. (2004). Imprisoned knowledge: Criminals' beliefs about deception. *Legal and Criminological Psychology, 9*, 103–119.

Granhag, P.A., and Hartwig, M. (2008). A new theoretical perspective on deception detection: On the psychology of instrumental mind-reading. *Psychology, Crime & Law.*

Granhag, P.A., and Strömwall, L.A. (2001). Deception detection based on repeated interrogations. *Legal and Criminological Psychology, 6*, 85–101.

Granhag, P.A., and Strömwall, L.A. (2004a). Deception detection in forensic contexts: Past and present. In P.A. Granhag and L.A. Strömwall (Eds.), *The Detection of Deception in Forensic Contexts* (pp. 3–12). Cambridge: Cambridge University Press.

Granhag, P.A., and Strömwall, L.A. (2004b). Deception detection in forensic contexts: Intersections and future challenges. In P.A. Granhag and L.A. Strömwall (Eds.), *The detection of deception in forensic contexts* (pp. 317–330). Cambridge: Cambridge University Press.

Granhag, P.A., and Strömwall, L.A. (2008a). Detection of deception in adults. In B. L. Cutler (Ed.), *Encyclopedia of Psychology and Law* (pp. 207–212). Thousand Oaks, CA: Sage Publication.

Granhag, P.A. and Strömwall, L.A. (2008b). Detection of deception: Use of evidence. In B.L. Cutler (Ed.). Encyclopedia of Psychology and Law (pp. 204-206). Thousand Oaks, CA: Sage Publication.

Granhag, P.A., Strömwall, L.A., and Hartwig, M. (2007). The SUE-technique: The way to interview to detect deception. *Forensic Update, 88*, 25–29.

Granhag, P.A., and Vrij, A. (2005). Deception detection. In N. Brewer and K.D. Williams (Eds.), Psychology and law. *An Empirical Perspective* (pp. 43–92). New York: The Guilford Press.

Greuel, L. (1992). Police officers' beliefs about cues associated with deception in rape cases. In F. Lösel, D. Bender, and T. Bliesener (Eds.), *Psychology and Law – International Perspectives* (pp. 234–239). Berlin: Walter de Gruyter.

Grubin, D., and Madsen, L. (2005). Lie detection and the polygraph: A historical review. *The Journal of Forensic Psychiatry and Psychology, 16*, 357–369.

Hartwig, M., Granhag, P.A., and Strömwall, L.A. (2007). Guilty and innocent suspects' strategies during police interrogations. *Psychology, Crime & Law, 13*, 213–227.

Hartwig, M. Granhag, P.A., Strömwall, L.A., and Kronkvist, O. (2006). Strategic use of evidence during police interviews: When training to detect deception works. *Law and Human Behavior, 30*, 603–619.

Hartwig, M., Granhag, P.A., Strömwall, L.A., and Vrij, A. (2005). Detecting deception via strategic disclosure of evidence. *Law and Human Behavior, 29*, 469–484.

Hartwig, M., Granhag, P.A., and Vrij, A. (2005). Police interrogation from a social psychology perspective. *Policing and Society, 15*, 401–421.

Honts, C.R. (2004). The psychophysiological detection of deception. In P.A. Granhag and L.A. Strömwall (Eds.), *The Detection of Deception in Forensic Contexts* (pp. 103–123). Cambridge: Cambridge University Press.

Honts, C.R., and Amato, S. (2002). Countermeasures. In M. Kleiner (Ed.), *Handbook of Polygraph Testing* (pp. 251–264). London: Academic.

Honts, C.R., Hodes, R.L., and Raskin, D.C. (1985). Effects of physical countermeasures on the physiological detection of deception. *Journal of Applied Psychology, 70*, 177–187.

Honts, C.R., Raskin, D.C., and Kircher, J.C. (1994). Mental and physical countermeasures reduce the accuracy of polygraph tests. *Journal of Applied Psychology, 79*, 252–259.

Inbau, F.E., Reid, J.E., Buckley, J.P., and Jayne, B.C. (2001). *Criminal Interrogation and Confessions.* Gaithersburg: Aspen Publishers.

Johnson, M. K., and Raye, C. L. (1981). Reality Monitoring. *Psychological Review, 88*, 67–85.

Johnson, M. K., and Raye, C. L. (1998). False memories and confabulation. *Trends in Cognitive Sciences, 2*, 137–145.

Kraut, R.E., and Poe, D. (1980). Behavioral roots of person perception: The deception judgements of customs inspectors and laymen. *Journal of Personality and Social Psychology, 39*, 784–798.

Landström, S., Granhag, P.A., and Hartwig, M. (2005). Witnesses appearing live vs. on video: How presentation format affect observers' perception, assessment and memory. *Applied Cognitive Psychology, 19*, 913–933.

Landström, S., Granhag, P.A., and Hartwig, M. (2007). Children appearing live vs. on video: Effects on adults' perception, assessment and memory. *Legal and Criminological Psychology, 12*, 333–347.

Lerner, M.J. (1980). *The Belief in a Just World.* New York: Plenum.

Lykken, D.T. (1959). The GSR in the detection of guilt. *Journal of Applied Psychology, 44*, 385–388.

Lykken, D.T. (1998). *A Tremor in the Blood: Uses and Abuses of the Lie Detector*. New York: Plenum Press.

MacLaren, V.V. (2001). A quantitative review of the guilty knowledge test. *Journal of Applied Psychology, 86*, 674–683.

Mann, S., Vrij, A., and Bull, R. (2002). Suspects, lies and videotape: An analysis of authentic high-stake liars. *Law and Human Behavior, 26*, 365–376.

Mann, S., Vrij, A., and Bull, R. (2004). Detecting true lies: Police officers' ability to detect deceit. *Journal of Applied Psychology, 89*, 137–149.

Masip, J., and Garrido, E. (2001, June). *Experienced and Novice Officers' Beliefs About Indicators of Deception*. Paper presented at the 11th European Conference of Psychology and Law, Lisbon, Portugal.

Masip, J., Sporer, S.L., Garrido, E., and Herrero, C. (2005). The detection of deception with the reality monitoring approach: A review of the empirical evidence. *Psychology, Crime & Law, 11*, 99–122.

Savitsky, K. and Gilovich, T. (2003). The illusion of transparency and the alleviation of speech anxiety. *Journal of Experimental Social Psychology, 39*, 618–625.

Spence, S.A., Hunter, M.D., Farrow, T.F.D., Green, R.D., Leung, D.H., Hughes, C.J., and Ganesan, V. (2006). A cognitive neurobiological account of deception: Evidence from functional neuroimaging. In S. Zeki and O. Goodenough (Eds), *Law and the Brain* (pp. 169–182). Oxford: Oxford University Press.

Sporer, S.L. (1997). The less travelled road to truth: Verbal cues in deception detection in accounts of fabricated and self-experienced events. *Applied Cognitive Psychology, 11*, 373–397.

Sporer, S.L. (2004). Reality monitoring and detection of deception. In P.A. Granhag & L.A. Strömwall (Eds.), *The Detection of Deception in Forensic Contexts* (pp. 64–102). Cambridge: Cambridge University Press.

Sporer, S.L., and Schwandt, B. (2006). Paraverbal indicators of deception: A meta-analytic synthesis. *Applied Cognitive Psychology, 20*, 421–446.

Steller, M., and Köhnken, G. (1989). Criteria-based content analysis. In D. C. Raskin (Ed.), *Psychological Methods in Criminal Investigation and Evidence* (pp. 217–245). New York, NJ: Springer-Verlag.

Strömwall, L.A., Bengtsson, L., Leander, L., and Granhag, P.A. (2004). Assessing children's statements: The impact of a repeated experience on CBCA and RM ratings. *Applied Cognitive Psychology, 18*, 653–668.

Strömwall, L.A., and Granhag, P.A. (2003). How to detect deception? Arresting the beliefs of police officers, prosecutors and judges. *Psychology, Crime, & Law, 9*, 19–36.

Strömwall, L.A., Granhag, P.A., and Hartwig, M. (2004). Practitioners' beliefs about deception. In P.A. Granhag & L.A. Strömwall (Eds.), *The Detection of Deception in Forensic Contexts* (pp. 229–250). Cambridge: Cambridge University Press.

Teigen, K.H. (2006). *En psykologihistoria* [A history of psychology]. Stockholm: Liber.

Vrij, A. (2005). Criteria-based content analysis: The first 37 studies. *Psychology, Public Policy and Law, 11*, 3–41.

Vrij, A. (2008). *Detecting Lies and Deceit: Pitfall and Opportunities* (2nd ed.). Chichester: John Wiley & Sons.

Vrij, A., and Mann, S. (2001). Telling and detecting lies in a high-stake situation: The case of a convicted murderer. *Applied Cognitive Psychology, 15*, 187–203.

Vrij, A., and Semin, G.R. (1996). Lie experts' beliefs about nonverbal indicators of deception. *Journal of Nonverbal Behavior, 20*, 65–80.

Zuckerman, M., DePaulo, B.M., and Rosenthal, R. (1981). Verbal and nonverbal communication of deception. In L. Berkowitz (Ed.) Advances in Experimental Social Psychology (Vol. 14, pp. 1–60). New York: Academic Press.

Chapter Six

EYEWITNESS MEMORY

Cara Laney and Elizabeth F. Loftus

Eyewitnesses play an important role in the legal system. They are the people, besides the necessarily biased perpetrators, who can claim that "I was there, and I saw what really happened." Because of this, they have substantial influence in investigations and trials that follow them. Unfortunately, eyewitnesses are far from perfect recorders of the events they witness. In particular, they make the same sorts of errors in perceiving and remembering that all humans do. The problem is that eyewitness errors, unlike other types of everyday human memory errors, can and do lead to the investigation, prosecution, and even conviction of innocent persons (*see* Scheck, Neufeld & Dwyer, 2003; Wells, Memon & Penrod, 2006).

In 1990, George Franklin was convicted of the murder of Susan Nason, a childhood friend of his daughter Eileen. The girl had been killed in 1969, and the only evidence against George was the eyewitness report of Eileen. The troubling aspect of this was that Eileen had reportedly repressed her memory of this event, only recovering her memory of witnessing the murder twenty years after the fact. This type of noncontinuous memory is suspicious because it could represent false memory. In this case, there was a pattern of errors and changes in her story that suggested that Eileen's memory of witnessing her father commit murder was probably false. Ultimately, George Franklin's conviction was overturned in 1995 (Loftus & Ketcham, 1996).

In 1989, Dwane Allen Dail was convicted of burglary and the rape of a twelve-year-old girl in North Carolina. The evidence against him was an identification made by the girl and the limited forensic analysis of a few hairs left at the scene of the crime. He was sentenced to two life terms plus fifteen years in prison. He served eighteen years of his sentence before a DNA test

– which had not been used as part of the original investigation – proved him innocent of the crimes (The Innocence Project, n.d.).

These two cases highlight some of the ways that eyewitness memory can go wrong. Eyewitnesses can incorrectly identify perpetrators. They can falsely remember not only the details of the events but also sometimes, the entirety of those events. A variety of additional errors are addressed later.

In this chapter we briefly discuss how human memory works. We then describe some of the most common and important memory errors, and the implications of these errors for the role of eyewitnesses. Eyewitness memory errors and their implications for jury decision-making and thus justice systems have been studied for more than thirty years, primarily by cognitive and social psychologists (e.g. Buckhout, 1977; Cutler, Penrod & Martens, 1987; Davis & Loftus, 2007; Loftus, 1975, 1979; Wells & Olson, 2003; Yuille & Cutshall, 1986). We discuss several key areas of this research, including the misinformation effect, false memories, and eyewitness identification errors. We also briefly touch on the smaller area of earwitness memory research.

REMEMBERING PEOPLE AND EVENTS

Human memory is amazing in that it enables us to retain and then recall information about events and people from moments, days, years, and decades ago. A tremendous amount of information is stored, and this storage, along with quick and precise access to it, is what allows us to function. Memory is not merely a storehouse of facts and events or a video recording of one's life experiences, however. Rather, it is a collection of several complex processes, that broadly include encoding, storage, and retrieval of information (Atkinson & Shiffrin, 1968).

The first step to memory encoding (that is, getting information into memory) is to pay attention (Schacter, 2001). Attention determines what information makes it from the wide, nonselective net of sensory memory into the smaller, more selective net of working memory. Sensory memory can hold a huge amount of information about the present state of one's world, but only for a fraction of a second at a time before being replaced by new information coming in from the senses. The information that is not attended to is immediately lost. The information that is attended to becomes part of working memory. Working memory is an active process rather than a storage facility, able to process about seven pieces of information at any one time (see Reisberg, 2001). Most of the information held in working memory does not make it into long-term memory. Instead, it is forgotten when it is no longer needed. Of course, a subset of the information from working memory does make it into long-term memory. Long-term memory is the largest storage facility for memories and is what most people think about when they refer to memory.

Memories can be formed through intentional learning or working specifically at remembering a particular bit of information (e.g. multiplication tables or important dates in world history), but they can also be formed through incidental learning, that is, with no specific intention to learn. Incidental learning can happen when one is repeatedly exposed to information, or when one interacts meaningfully with information (Reisberg, 2001). That is, people know their parents' names without ever having tried to memorize them and remember important people and events from their lives even if they happened only once. As a rule, deeper processing of information leads to more successful encoding, and better memory (Craik & Lockhart, 1972).

Once memories have been encoded, they are stored until they are needed. Memory storage does not work like library book storage or off-season clothing storage, however. That is, one cannot go back to the specific location (in the brain) where one left something (i.e. a memory) and pick it back up again. There are certain structures in the brain that are especially important for the encoding and storage of memory, in particular, the hippocampus and the amygdala (e.g. McGaugh et al., 1990; Scoville & Milner, 1957). Memories are not stored entirely within either of these bodies, however. Instead, memories are stored as patterns of activation in the brain (Rumelhart & McClelland, 1986).

The companion process to encoding is called retrieval, and it is through this process that information is brought back from long-term storage to be attended to and used. Just as information can be encoded in different ways, either intentionally or incidentally, it can be retrieved in different ways. Recall is the process of retrieval that occurs in response to an open question (e.g. "What happened after the robber said 'hands up?'") whereas recognition happens in response to closed questions, including multiple-choice questions (e.g. "Was the robber tall or short?" or "Is this man the robber?").

Retrieval cues are reminders that link us back to specific memories. These can come from the content of questions or from images, words, feelings, noises, or smells in the environment. One memory can also form a powerful retrieval cue for another memory. Some memories are easier to retrieve when one can match the circumstances in which the memory was encoded, a phenomenon termed state-dependent memory (Eich, 1980). This explains why going back to one's childhood hometown or school as an adult can bring up memories that one has not thought of for many years. Likewise, going back to the scene of the crime can allow witnesses to remember details that they had not recalled before (Swihart, Yuille & Porter, 1999).

Information can be lost (forgotten) at any stage of the encoding, storage, and retrieval process, and perhaps, contrary to intuition, this is a good thing.

As William James (1890) pointed out, "If we remembered everything, we should on most occasions be as ill off as if we remembered nothing" (p. 68). If the truth of this statement is not immediately apparent, consider for a moment what would happen if every memory of parking your car was as clear as every other memory of parking your car. That is to say, forgetting is as important a process as remembering.

As previously noted, lack of sufficient attention at encoding results in forgetting (consider how difficult it can be to find your keys or glasses if you did not pay sufficient attention when you set them down). Other memories are forgotten because they are not accessed sufficiently quickly or frequently after being put into long-term storage, a process called decay. Longer delays between an event and its recall, termed retention interval, make forgetting more likely (*see* Read and Connolly, 2007, for review). Finally, errors in recall and recognition are called retrieval failure. One important type of retrieval failure, termed interference, occurs when other, newer or older, memories preclude access to the desired memory.

MEMORY ERRORS IN EYEWITNESSES

As we have seen, human memory has an amazing ability to store and retrieve information. Human memory, including eyewitness memory, can also go very wrong. In this section, we describe some common and forensically relevant types of errors and the research that demonstrates them. Broadly, errors can occur during both the encoding and retrieval processes described before.

Eyewitness memory encoding often occurs at the complex (both physically and emotionally) scene of a crime. This scene complexity can lead to some types of information being insufficiently encoded. For example, some witnessed events happen very quickly, and leave very little time to properly encode people or actions. Other events go on for very long periods, leading to severe stress in witnesses, which makes full encoding of events difficult (see section on emotion and stress, later).

In addition, a wide range of features of events has been shown to affect eyewitnesses' initial encoding and later retrieval of those events. For example, the presence of a weapon or other surprising and meaningful objects at the scene of a crime can lead witnesses to focus on that object to such a degree that they fail to encode other aspects of the scene, including the face of the perpetrator (Loftus, Loftus & Messo, 1987; Steblay, 1992; *but see* Valentine, Pickering & Darling, 2003). Alcohol and drug use by witnesses can also dramatically affect their ability to encode and later recall details from events that they witness (Clifasefi, Takarangi & Bergman, 2006; Yuille & Tollestrup, 1990).

One particularly well-researched memory error is that caused by "misinformation" (*see* Davis & Loftus, 2007). In these studies, research subjects are asked to witness an event, typically a mock crime, usually presented via slides or video. They are then presented with incorrect information (termed misinformation) about this event, often in the form of misleading questions or erroneous information embedded in reports expressed by other witnesses. This misinformation often affects the subjects' memories for the original event, in what is termed the misinformation effect. That is, memory for the details of the event can be altered by misleading information that people are exposed to after the fact. Since memory is a process of reconstruction, the new, misleading information can be incorporated into subjects' memories for the prior event.

One important purpose of these studies is to show that the memories of eyewitnesses can be influenced by events that happen long after a crime takes place. When an eyewitness is interviewed by the police, and later by attorneys and even the media, his or her memory may incorporate information from leading questions and suggestions made by other individuals. This alteration of memory may occur without the knowledge of the eyewitness, such that he or she may swear to the truth of his or her memory on the witness stand and yet be inaccurate.

In an early study of the misinformation effect, Loftus and Palmer (1974) showed subjects a film depicting a car accident. Some subjects were asked how fast the two cars were going when they "smashed" into each other. Other subjects were asked how fast the cars were going when they "hit" each other. Control subjects were not asked about vehicle speed. Subjects queried about the cars smashing into each other reported higher rates of speed than those queried about the cars hitting each other. After a week's delay, all subjects were asked additional questions about the accident, including, critically, whether they had seen any broken glass. Those subjects who had been asked about the cars smashing into each other were more likely to remember seeing broken glass than were subjects asked about the cars hitting each other or the controls. These results demonstrate that even small changes in the wording of questions can affect memory – a serious worry considering how often real eyewitnesses are typically questioned about the events that they witnessed.

In a further demonstration of the power of even small amounts of misinformation, Loftus (1975) showed that replacing the word "a" in a question, as in "Did you see a broken headlight?" with the word "the" ("Did you see the broken headlight?") could make subjects far more likely to answer in the affirmative. Note that although these questions sound very similar, the second question is essentially informing the witness that there was a broken headlight and asking whether he or she managed to notice it. The first question does not carry any presumption about the existence of the headlight.

Loftus (1975) also got subjects to report seeing a barn in a scene that contained no such building by asking simple leading questions about a barn after subjects saw films containing the scene. Loftus, Miller, and Burns (1978) extended these findings by showing subjects a series of slides depicting a car moving down the street, then sitting at a yield sign (or, for other subjects, a stop sign), then hitting a pedestrian. Subjects were then asked a series of questions, including a critical question about an event that happened after the car stopped "at the stop sign" (or yield sign, depending on condition). After a short delay, the subjects were given a recognition test in which they were asked, in series, which of two slides had been part of the original set. One of these pairs was made up of the stop sign and yield sign slides. Again, subjects' memories were contaminated by the misinformation, with those subjects who were asked about the stop sign after seeing the yield sign picking the correct (yield sign) slide at significantly lower than chance levels.

Some authors have criticized studies of eyewitness memory that use staged slides or videos, advocating instead the use of real-life crime witnesses (Yuille & Cutshall, 1986). Yet, studies of witnesses who experience genuinely distressing events demonstrate that the witnesses' memories are likewise susceptible to errors (e.g. Morgan et al., 2007). In addition, the growing evidence provided by DNA exonerations shows that real crime witnesses make exactly the sorts of errors that are demonstrated in studies using mock witnesses (*see* Steblay & Loftus, in press).

In the last decade, eyewitness memory research has broadened significantly from its event plus leading question equals distortion roots, but some important themes have continued. The memory implications of the presence of cowitnesses to events have long been a fruitful area of research (e.g. Loftus, 1979; Loftus & Greene, 1980). Recent research in this area has demonstrated that real-life cowitnesses do discuss what they have witnessed (Paterson & Kemp, 2006) and reinforced the conclusion that discussions among cowitnesses can be detrimental to the truth by leading subjects to remember far more than they encoded to begin with (Gabbert, Memon & Allan 2003; Gabbert, Memon, Allan, & Wright, 2004; Hope, Ost, Gabbert, Healey & Lenton, 2008; Takarangi, Parker & Garry, 2006; Wright, Mathews & Skagerberg, 2005).

In one study (Gabbert et al., 2003), two sets of subjects watched two different versions of a short video, but were led to believe they were watching the same video. Both videos covered the same events, but those events were viewed from different angles (just as the real event might have been observed by witnesses with slightly different perspectives). After the videos, some subjects thought about the videos alone; others discussed them with "cowitnesses." Then all subjects completed an individual memory task. A majority

(71%) of the subjects who discussed their memories with cowitnesses incorporated elements of the discussion into their own memories, and 60 percent of relevant subjects reported the commission of a crime that they had not actually seen (because it had been visible only in the other version of the video).

One recent technique has been provided with particularly impressive demonstrations of cowitness effects. Called the "manipulation of overlapping rivalrous images by polarizing filters" (MORI) paradigm (Garry, French, Kinzett & Mori, in press), it allows for two research subjects to sit in front of a single screen to watch a video. The two subjects assume (quite reasonably) that they are seeing the same images, but because each subject is wearing a different type of polarized glasses, they are in fact watching different images (projected onto the same screen, much like for three-dimensional movies). Because the two subjects believe they have seen exactly the same event (just as in real-world eyewitnessing), they are particularly likely to allow their cowitness' memories of the video to affect their own.

In another variation on the misinformation paradigm, a recent series of studies has demonstrated just how influential postevent information may be in the real world (*see* Loftus & Castelle, 2000). In the first "crashing" memory study, Cronbag, Wagenaar, and van Koppen (1996) interviewed Dutch subjects about a horrible plane crash that had killed forty-three people and been major national news. One misleading question, "Did you see the television film of the moment the plane hit the apartment building?" led more than 60 percent of subjects to report that they had seen nonexistent television footage and answer additional questions about it. Other "crashing" memory studies have since been conducted, with subjects falsely remembering videos of other plane crashes, the car crash that killed Princess Diana, an assassination, and a sinking cruise ship (Granhag, Strömwall & Billings, 2002; Jelicic et al., 2006; Ost, Vrij, Costall & Bull, 2002; Smeets et al., 2006). These studies demonstrate that a single leading question can not only alter an existing memory, but also can create an entire secondary false memory. The subjects in the studies presumably heard news about the relevant major events, then imagined those events. With the addition of a suggestion that there had been a video, subjects came to believe that they saw the event in question happening, rather than merely imagined it. Having actually seen an event happen is subjectively (and legally) more meaningful than having merely imagined that event happening, and so subjects are likely giving their own memories for the details of the event far more credibility than they deserve.

FALSE MEMORIES FOR EVENTS

In what must be the most extreme sort of memory distortion, researchers have been able to implant wholly false memories into the minds of research subjects. The field of false-memory research evolved as an extension of the misinformation literature, largely in response to a rash of accusations and lawsuits in the late 1980s and early 1990s. These lawsuits were typically (though certainly not exclusively) brought by daughters accusing their fathers of horrible sexual abuse, spanning years, that the victims did not remember happening until they went into therapy in adulthood for problems such as depression and eating disorders. Their therapists then helped them to "recover" their memories of being brutalized as a path to curing their current ills (*see* Ofshe & Watters, 1994). More recently, many of the same techniques have been used to help adult Catholics to remember being abused by their priests in childhood. In both cases, severe criminal penalties have been levied and substantial awards have been made by juries, in the absence of forensic evidence corroborating the victims' statements.

These therapists (*see*, e.g. Claridge, 1992; Herman & Schatzow, 1987) started with the assertion, derived from the work of Freud, that when people experience repeated horrific events, they repress these experiences into the unconscious. Sometimes they even split their psyches into two separate parts, one that experiences the trauma and the other that continues to function normally with no awareness of the trauma. Decades later, when the person has adult skills and support structures that will allow the reintegration of these half-psyches (and this is necessary because the trauma has begun to leak out in some other way), therapists can help them to recover or reconstruct memories of the original trauma. When the memories are recovered, the person can finally "recover" from the abuse that has haunted his or her life, or at least that was the promise of this type of therapy.

This treatment typically involved a variety of techniques, including guided imagination, dream interpretation, repeated questioning, journaling, the use of family pictures to cue memories, and social pressure in the form of group therapy sessions. Some of the memories that were produced using these techniques were particularly bizarre (including satanic ritual abuse; Ofshe & Watters, 1994). Experimental psychologists have, since the mid-1990s, modeled these techniques in the laboratory and demonstrated that they can cause people to remember events that did not happen.

In an early study that implanted wholly false memories, Loftus and Pickrell (1995) used a repeated interview and journaling technique to get subjects to believe that as young children they had been lost in a shopping mall for an extended period of time and then rescued by an older adult. Subjects were presented with a summary of this (bogus) event, along with three other true events, and told that all four events had come from their parents or other relatives (authority figures who would have been in a position to know such things). Subjects were asked to write down what they remembered (if anything) about each of the four events. During two subsequent interviews, subjects were again asked to remember as many details as possible about each of the four events (including the critical shopping mall event, which relatives had specifically dismissed as false). Subjects remembered some 68 percent of the true memories learned about from their families, but six of the twenty-four subjects (25%) also remembered the critical *false* event. Some of these subjects went on to produce elaborate details of their (false) ordeal of being lost in the mall.

Subsequent studies replicated and extended these findings using similar methodologies. The false events produced in these studies ranged from being rescued by a lifeguard (Heaps & Nash, 1999) to spilling punch on the bride's parents at a family wedding (Hyman, Husband & Billings, 1995). Some authors have explicitly sought to produce false memories for traumatic events, such as being a victim of a vicious animal attack (e.g. Porter, Yuille & Lehman, 1999). In light of criticisms that these studies might be triggering genuine memories rather than actually producing false memories, some researchers have worked to give subjects false memories for highly implausible and even impossible events, such as witnessing demonic possession, or shaking hands with Bugs Bunny at Disneyland (e.g. Braun, Ellis & Loftus, 2002; Mazzoni & Memon, 2003; Wade, Garry, Read & Lindsay, 2002). Wade and Garry (2005) compiled data from ten peer-reviewed "lost in the mall" type studies and found a weighted mean of 37 percent of subjects reporting false memories.

The "lost in the mall" study and its descendents specifically emulated certain aspects of the therapeutic context, including repeated visits and proof of the existence of a childhood event originating with an authority figure (the parents in the studies, like the therapist in the real-life scenario). In point of fact, these techniques turn out to be particularly powerful types of suggestion, and their use has been disputed by some consumers of the research (e.g. Harvey, 1999; Ost, Foster, Costall & Bull, 2005). Specifically, some therapists have pointed out that they do not tell their clients that they have spoken with their parents and heard about specific instances of abuse from them. This is certainly true, but in addition to the similarities already mentioned between the two situations, other, very similar, suggestive techniques are used by therapists (Gore-Felton et al., 2000; Poole, Lindsay, Memon & Bull, 1995).

A number of these other therapy techniques have been specifically modeled in experimental studies that produced false memories. For example, therapists may instruct clients to imagine specific events happening to them as children, they may interpret clients' dreams, and they may even hypnotize clients. Garry, Manning, Loftus, and Sherman (1996) asked subjects to imagine four different events happening to them, and they subsequently became more confident that those events had indeed happened (*see also* Thomas & Loftus, 2002, for related data with documented original events). Mazzoni, Lombardo, Malvagia, and Loftus (1999) used a dream interpretation paradigm to convince subjects that they had been lost as young children. Scoboria, Mazzoni, Kirsch, and Milling (2002) used hypnosis and misleading questions to distort subjects' memories for a story. Both techniques produced memory errors, and their combination produced the most errors (*see also* Lynn, Lock, Myers & Payne, 1997; Mazzoni & Lynn, 2007). Group therapy techniques have been modeled in the cowitness studies described earlier.

Using family photographs as memory cues has been modeled in two ways. First, Wade and associates (2002) created pseudo-family photographs by combining true childhood photographs with a false hot air balloon setting. When these doctored photographs were shown to subjects along with some true photos, about half of subjects falsely remembered going on a hot air balloon ride. Lindsay, Hagen, Read, Wade, and Garry (2004) combined a false suggestion of childhood mayhem with an accurate age-appropriate class photograph to produce false memories in more than half of their subjects (*see* Strange, Gerrie & Garry, 2005, for additional false memory studies employing photographic evidence).

Recent research has shown that it is not necessary to go to such lengths to convince people that they experienced very specific events in the past. Recent studies have used a simple false feedback procedure to suggest to subjects that very specific events happened to them in their childhoods (Berkowitz, Laney, Morris, Garry & Loftus, in press; Bernstein, Laney, Morris & Loftus, 2005a, 2005b; Laney & Loftus, in press; Laney, Morris, Bernstein, Wakefield & Loftus, in press). In the false-feedback procedure, subjects are asked to fill out a set of questionnaires on a particular topic. They are then told (falsely) that their data will be entered into a special computer program that will provide specific feedback for them. After a delay, subjects are given their "feedback" (which is in fact not specific at all but is the false memory manipulation) and then asked to fill out more questionnaires. Subjects frequently become more confident that they have experienced a particular event that has been suggested by the false feedback. They may also produce very specific detailed memory descriptions that conform to the feedback suggestions.

This simple technique has been used to get subjects to believe that they had once become sick after eating a specific food, loved a specific food the first time they tried it, or had a specific interaction with a character at Disneyland (Berkowitz et al., in press; Bernstein et al., 2005a, 2005b; Laney et al., in press). Each of these false memories also had consequences for participants, such that they were more or less likely to eat the suggested food, or were not willing to pay as much for a Disney souvenir. The false feedback technique has also been used to plant in subjects' minds false memories for potentially traumatic childhood events, including witnessing a physically violent fight between their parents (Laney & Loftus, in press).

There is ample evidence that memory distortion and false memory production also happen outside the laboratory and the therapist's office (Sheen, Kemp & Rubin, 2001; Taylor, 1965). Even normal conversation can produce false memories. Research suggests that people make pragmatic inferences about the meaning of the words and phrases used by conversation partners (Brewer, 1977). Rather than remembering the specific words used by the speaker (and his or her specific intended meanings), people instead remember these inferences and their implications (e.g. Chan & McDermott, 2006).

EMOTION AND STRESS IN EYEWITNESSES

Emotion is another important factor in memory quality. The effects of emotion (which is here broadly defined to include arousal, stress, and even trauma) have been studied from a variety of perspectives. Various authors have demonstrated that emotional events are remembered better than are nonemotional (but otherwise equivalent) events (e.g. Cahill & McGaugh, 1995; Conway et al., 1994; Heuer & Reisberg, 1990; Laney, Campbell, Heuer & Reisberg, 2004; McNally, Clancy & Barrett, 2004; Reisberg, Heuer, McLean, & O'Shaughnessy, 1988). Other authors have argued that emotional content can be harmful to memory (e.g. Loftus & Burns, 1982; Morgan et al., 2004). Finally, a few authors have suggested that the relationships between emotion and memory are in fact much more complicated than these simple "better" or "worse" results imply and instead depend on factors like the type of emotion and type of to-be-remembered event (Burke, Heuer & Reisberg, 1992; Christianson & Loftus, 1990; Levine & Pizarro, 2004; Reisberg, 2006; Reisberg & Heuer, 2007).

The differing results are likely attributable to the researchers' different conceptualizations of emotion. Many studies conceptualize emotion along a single dimension ranging from neutral to arousing. For example, Heuer and Reisberg (1990) showed subjects a series of slides depicting a mother taking her son to visit his father at work. In the neutral version of the story, the father works as a garage mechanic, and he is shown fixing a car. In the arousing version of the story, the father works as a surgeon and a critical slide shows the severed and reattached legs of a child. Although the two sets of slides were matched as closely as possible, the arousing version was much better remembered than the neutral version was.

Other studies conceptualize emotion along a different dimension: stress. Studies of stress and emotion often come to very different conclusions than do studies of arousal and memory (*see* Reisberg & Heuer, 2007). Morgan and colleagues (2004) found that after food and sleep deprivation, soldiers who experienced forty minutes of extremely stressful interrogation were less able to identify their interrogators (who had been demanding direct eye contact) than other soldiers who experienced less stressful interrogation were (*see also* Lieberman et al., 2005; Southwick, Morgan, Nicolaou & Charney, 1997). That is, these highly stressed subjects had poor memories for the details of the interrogation that they had experienced. Deffenbacher, Bornstein, Penrod, and McGorty (2004) conducted a meta-analysis of studies of stress and memory and found that stress was a reliable impediment to accurate memory.

Even relatively mild acute stressors, like being asked to give a short speech, can have a negative effect on memory, as can drugs that work to mimic these stressors (Payne, Nadel, Britton & Jacobs, 2004). Reisberg and Heuer (2007) argue that this distinction between events that are arousing and those that are stressful is key. Essentially, arousing events seem to produce an orienting response that leads to more attention and better memory, whereas stressful events produce a defensive response that leads to diverted attention and worse memory. So stress is not merely a more severe form of arousal, and quantity of emotion does not by itself predict memory quality. Type of emotion (here, arousal versus stress) matters as well.

A few researchers have utilized more complex conceptualizations of emotion in their studies of memory (Laney et al., 2004; Levine & Bluck, 2004; Levine & Burgess, 1997). For example, Levine and Bluck (2004) borrowed from cognitive appraisal theories of emotion in their analysis of memory for the O. J. Simpson verdict. Cognitive appraisal theories propose specific functions for different specific emotions, and these functions have specific implications for memory. Levine and Bluck (2004) found that individuals who were happy about the verdict in the O. J. Simpson murder trial reported clearer memories for the verdict announcement and recalled more trial details but were less discriminating than were neutral and unhappy individuals in determining whether specific events had occurred. That is, happy individuals had clearer but not more accurate memories than unhappy individuals had.

Traumatic experiences fall at the extreme end of the emotional spectrum. The "traumatic memory argument" suggests that these memories will all be of poor quality. In particular, supporters of this argument claim that memories for trauma are fractured, not easily verbalized, and sometimes completely repressed (e.g. Herman, 1992; van der Kolk, 1997). Extensive research has demonstrated, however, that a competing theory, the "trauma superiority argument" is a much better fit to the data (Kihlstrom, 2006; McNally, 2003; Porter & Birt, 2001; Shobe & Kihlstrom, 1997). Indeed, most traumatic experiences are particularly difficult for people to forget and can even lead to intrusive memories of the event and flashbacks, as in posttraumatic stress disorder (PTSD) (McNally, 2003; McNally et al., 2004). Numerous studies have shown that people who experience trauma tend to have particularly vivid and complete memories of those events (e.g. Peace & Porter, 2004; Peterson & Whalen, 2001; Quas et al., 1999; Shobe & Kihlstrom, 1997; Wagenaar & Groeneweg, 1990). According to a study conducted by Alexander and associates (2005), victims of child sexual abuse who were particularly traumatized (as evidenced by greater PTSD symptomatology or their naming of their abuse as their most traumatic event) had better memory for the details of that abuse than did other victims who were less traumatized. This is not to say that traumatic memories are errorfree. Indeed, traumatic memories are susceptible to the same errors as other sorts of memories, and may be particularly fragile at the periphery (*see* McNally, 2003; Paz-Alonso & Goodman, 2008). These errors simply reinforce the notion that traumatic memories do not make up a special class of memory with separate rules (such as fragmentation or repression). Instead, they are an extreme form of normal autobiographical memory.

To summarize, the relationship between emotion and memory is complicated and depends on numerous contextual and extrasituational factors. It also depends on how "emotion" is defined. The important message, however, is that most kinds of emotion, and particularly trauma, lead to particularly good (though not flawless) memory for the emotional events themselves, rather than to repression of memory.

MISTAKEN INDENTIFICATION

At some point after witnessing a particular crime, an eyewitness is often called on to identify the perpetrator in a lineup. This may happen because the witness' description of the perpetrator has led to the identification of a suspect (*see* Meissner, Sporer & Schooler, 2007), because the witness has identified a suspect from a set of mugshots (Lindsay, Noswothy, Martin & Martynuck, 1994), or because the police have identified a particular suspect through forensic evidence or other means.

The research literature on eyewitness identifications is vast. Particular foci have been on two types of variables: those that are under the control of the justice system (called system variables) and those that cannot be controlled by the justice system (called estimator variables) (Wells & Olson, 2003).

Estimator variables include both the individual differences among witnesses and the characteristics of the witnessed event that make correct identification more or less likely. A variety of individual differences have been tested, including gender, race, age, and personality. Of these, just two have consistently shown differences in identification accuracy. With respect to age, young adults have proved to be less susceptible than children or the elderly are to making false identifications when the perpetrator is not in the lineup (Pozzulo & Lindsay, 1998). With respect to race, there is no overall advantage for one race over another, but almost forty years of research has demonstrated that individuals are more successful at identifying members of their own race than of other races (Malpass & Kravitz, 1969; Meissner & Brigham, 2001).

Research has also identified numerous aspects of the witnessed event that can affect identification accuracy. Some of these are aspects of the physical environment where the crime took place. Correct identifications are more likely when the witness has better opportunities, including sufficient time and attention, to see the perpetrator's face (e.g. Ellis, Davies, & Shepherd, 1977; Yarmey, 1986). Identifications are also better when the witness believes the crime to be more serious (Leippe, Wells & Ostrom, 1978).

Other factors have to do with the perpetrators themselves. Perpetrators are easier to identify if they are unusually attractive (or unattractive) or otherwise distinctive in appearance (Fleishman, Buckley, Klosinsky, Smith, & Tuck, 1976; Light, Kayra-Stuart & Hollander, 1979). Perpetrators (even distinctive-looking ones) become much more difficult to identify if they use even simple disguises (Cutler et al., 1987).

System variables are called this because the legal system has some power to change them for the better. System variables include the type of lineup used and the people involved in creating and administering it, the instructions given to witnesses, and the use of other evidence gathering procedures before and after lineups.

The first important consideration is what type of lineup should be used. In traditional, simultaneous lineups, several individuals or photographs are viewed at the same time, and the witness is asked whether the perpetrator is present in the group (Wogalter, Malpass & McQuiston, 2004). This lineup type, still commonly used in the United States and many other countries, has been criticized because it leads witnesses to make a relative judgment. That is, witnesses often decide which of the people present most closely matches their memory of the perpetrator, rather than deciding whether each individual is or is not the perpetrator (an absolute judgment). A newer type of lineup is now in use in some U.S. jurisdictions, exclusively in the United Kingdom, and elsewhere in the world. In the sequential lineup, the witness views only one individual or photograph at a time, and (with some local variation) must make a yes or no judgment about that person before the next person is viewed. This procedure is designed to eliminate the kind of relative judgments encouraged by simultaneous lineups (Lindsay, 1999). The superiority of the sequential procedure has been advocated in a survey of eyewitness testimony experts (Kassin, Tubb, Hosch & Memon, 2001) and supported by many studies, including one meta-analysis (Steblay, Dysart, Fulero & Lindsay, 2001; *but see* McQuiston-Surrett, Malpass & Tredoux, 2006).

How should the lineups be created, and who should administer them? A lineup or photospread is made up of one suspect and several foils, or known innocents. For it to be fair, the suspect should not stick out from the crowd (Brigham, Ready & Spier, 1990). Practically, this means that there should be enough foils in a lineup that the chance of an innocent suspect being selected is low and that the suspect is not distinctive looking within the group. Ideally, the foils should be chosen on the basis of the witness' description rather than on the looks of the suspect. If the foils are chosen to match the looks of the suspect, the suspect will always look more like himself or herself than like any of the foils. This makes the lineup inherently biased (Wells et al., 1998).

Sometimes witnesses are asked to identify the perpetrator from a book of mugshots before they see the lineup. Those witnesses who pick an innocent person from a book of mugshots are very likely to falsely identify the same person in a subsequent lineup (Brigham & Cairns, 1988; Dysart, Lindsay, Hammond & Dupuis, 2001). Thus one relatively minor error (thinking that a photograph in a book looks like the perpetrator) can lead quickly to a major error (falsely identifying an innocent suspect in a lineup) and a substantial risk of miscarriage of justice.

Another important consideration is who is present during the lineup administration. Just as double-blind drug studies (where neither the patient nor the person interacting with the patient knows whether the patient is receiving active drug or placebo) have been shown to be important in medical research, so double-blind lineup administration has been advocated in eyewitness research (Wells et al., 1998). Lineups are made double-blind simply by having them administered by someone who does not know who the suspect is. This is important because administrators who know who the suspect is may unknowingly send signals to the witness to suggest who the suspect is or may respond to correct identifications with approving feedback. This feedback has been shown not only to make witnesses unjustifiably confident of their identifications but also to make them more certain of their memories and overly optimistic about the circumstances in which they witnessed the crime (Wells & Bradfield, 1998; Wright & Skagerberg, 2007).

All of these different causes of eyewitness identification errors have significant consequences for innocent suspects. Of the more than 200 Americans who have so far been exonerated on the basis of postconviction DNA testing, eyewitness misidentification has been a factor in at least 75 percent (Garrett, 2008). That is, eyewitness misidentification has been a major cause of false convictions of innocent individuals.

EARWITNESSES

Some witnessed crimes take place in the dark, or while victims' or witnesses' eyes are covered or directed away from the events of the crime; other crimes, including some types of fraud, can actually take place on the phone. Some witnesses have impaired eyesight or less than optimal views of crime events for other reasons (perhaps because they are hiding from perpetrators or their view is obstructed). Beyond these relatively special cases, memory for conversations is relevant in a sizeable number of legal cases (Davis & Friedman, 2007). Because of these facts, witnesses' auditory memory for a crime can be just as important as their visual memory. Thus, there is a secondary area of study into the memories of earwitnesses, but this is a much smaller area of research than that of eyewitnesses.

One important problem for earwitnesses is that although familiar voices (one's spouse on the phone or a famous person on television) are generally quite easy to identify, unfamiliar voices are much more difficult (Yarmey, Yarmey, Yarmey & Parliament, 2001). What's more, unfamiliar voices are even harder to identify when they are whispered or muffled (Bull & Clifford, 1984), when they are speaking a foreign language (Philippon, Cherryman, Bull & Vrij, 2007), or when they change tone because of emotion (Saslove & Yarmey, 1980). All of these variations are relevant to crime scenes.

Researchers have compared voice identification accuracy with that of face identifications and found that subjects are worse at making identifications from auditory lineups than from visual lineups (McAllister, Dale & Keay, 1993). Subjects are also even more susceptible to misinformation in an earwitness paradigm than in an eyewitness one (McAllister, Bregman & Lipscomb, 1988). When witnesses have access to both facial and voice information, they seem to prefer to concentrate on faces rather than on voices. This (involuntary) preference leads to a face overshadowing effect, whereby voice identification suffers (Cook & Wilding, 1997, 2001). Despite this overall lack of reliability, research has shown that voice identifications have as much credibility with potential jurors as face identifications do (McAllister et al., 1993; Yarmey, 1995).

SUGGESTIONS FOR REFORM

What can be done to ameliorate the problems caused by faulty eyewitness memory? We have already hinted at several potential reforms. We address these more fully and present additional suggestions in this final section. In particular, we consider the variable nature of system variables and the usefulness of expert testimony about eyewitness memory.

Recall that system variables (as distinguished from estimator variables) are those factors over which the justice system has some control. The creation and administration of lineups were addressed in our earlier section on mistaken identifications. Other system variables include when and how witnesses are asked questions, the types of questions they are asked, and the other people and information to which witnesses are exposed. In order to fully preserve the quality of eyewitness memory (just as one would want to fully preserve the quality of physical evidence), all of these variables are important.

A variety of specific recommendations have been made by eyewitness researchers over the last several decades (e.g. Steblay & Loftus, in press; Technical Working Group for Eyewitness Accuracy, 1999; Wells et al., 1998). With respect to lineups, sequential lineups conducted in a double-blind fashion have been advocated over simultaneous and non-double-blind lineups for the reasons already discussed. Lineups should of course be nonbiased; that is, the perpetrator should not stand out in the lineup. It has also been suggested that witnesses should be warned that the perpetrator may not be present in the lineup, and thus an identification is not mandatory. Because eyewitness confidence, like eyewitness memory, is malleable, various authors have suggested that confidence should be measured immediately after witnesses make an identification and certainly before they receive any feedback about that identification (e.g. Wells et al., 1998; Wright & Skagerberg, 2007).

Other important recommendations have been made regarding contact with witnesses. The extensive research into the misinformation effect has led to recommendations that witnesses be questioned as quickly as possible after the crime, using questions that are open ended and unbiased (for details, *see* Fisher & Schreiber, 2007). Contact among co-witnesses should also be minimized, as should witnesses' contact with media reports of the events they witnessed (Davis & Loftus, 2007; Gabbert et al., 2003).

Because of the demonstrated problems with eyewitness memory, many scientists have argued that jurors would benefit if they were given scientific information about the factors that affect eyewitness accuracy. Research has shown that many would-be jurors (and some judges) sometimes have beliefs that are not supported by science or are even contradicted by the scientific findings (Benton, Ross, Bradshaw Thomas, & Bradshaw, 2006; Wise & Safer,

2004). As such, expert testimony designed to assist juries with assessing the reliability of eyewitness testimony has long been advocated and provided (Leippe, 1995; Loftus & Ketcham, 1991; Steblay & Loftus, in press). Unfortunately, because the admissibility of this testimony is at the discretion of individual judges (in the United States, at least), it is often disallowed on the grounds that the research findings offer no more than common sense, that the expert testimony is prejudicial rather than probative, or that the testimony may usurp the jury's role (Wells et al., 2006). On the other hand, some criminal convictions have been overturned when expert psychological testimony has been excluded. Further exploration into the usefulness of expert testimony, or other means of educating jurors about eyewitness science, might assist in a goal that we all should seek, namely fewer convictions of the innocent and more convictions of the truly guilty.

In summary, more than three decades of research into eyewitness memory has demonstrated that eyewitnesses tend to err in predictable ways. This research has led to a variety of specific recommendations for investigative and courtroom practice. Unfortunately, this advice has not been uniformly adopted, and so eyewitnesses (and earwitnesses) tend to exert more power in the legal system than their accuracy justifies.

REFERENCES

Alexander, K.W., Quas, J.A., Goodman, G.S., Ghetti, S., Edelstein, R.S., Redlich, A.D., et al. (2005). Traumatic impact predicts long-term memory for documented child sexual abuse. *Psychological Science, 16,* 33–40.

Atkinson, R.C., and Shiffrin, R.M. (1968). Human memory: A proposed system and its control processes. In K.W.S. Spence and J.T. Spence (Eds.), *The Psychology of Learning and Motivation* (pp. 89–105). New York: Academic Press.

Benton, T.R., Ross, D.F., Bradshaw, E., Thomas, W.N., and Bradshaw, G.S. (2006). Eyewitness memory is still not common sense: Comparing jurors, judges and law enforcement to eyewitness experts. *Applied Cognitive Psychology, 20,* 115–129.

Berkowitz, S.R., Laney, C., Morris, E.K., Garry, M., and Loftus, E.F. (in press). Pluto behaving badly: False beliefs and their consequences. *American Journal of Psychology.*

Bernstein, D.M., Laney, C., Morris, E.K., and Loftus, E.F. (2005a). False beliefs about fattening foods can have healthy consequences. *Proceedings of the National Academy of Sciences, 102,* 13724–13731.

Bernstein, D.M., Laney, C., Morris, E.K., and Loftus, E.F. (2005b). False memories about food can lead to food avoidance. *Social Cognition, 23,* 11–34.

Braun, K.A., Ellis, R., and Loftus, E.F. (2002). Make my memory: How advertising can change our memories of the past. *Psychology & Marketing, 19,* 1–23.

Brewer, W.F. (1977). Memory of the pragmatic implications of sentences. *Memory and Cognition, 5,* 673–678.

Brigham, J.C., and Cairns, D.L. (1988). The effect of mugshot inspections on eyewitness identification accuracy. *Journal of Applied Social Psychology, 18,* 1394–1410.

Brigham, J.C., Ready, D.J., and Spier, S.A. (1990). Standards for evaluating the fairness of photographic lineups. *Basic and applied social psychology, 11*, 149–163.

Buckhout, R. (1974). Eyewitness testimony. *Scientific American, 231*, 23–31.

Bull, R., and Clifford, B.R. (1984). Earwitness voice recognition accuracy. In G.L. Wells and E.F. Loftus (Eds.), *Eyewitness Testimony, Psychological Perspectives* (pp. 92-–123). Cambridge: Cambridge University Press.

Burke, A., Heuer, F., and Reisberg, D. (1992). Remembering emotional events. *Memory and Cognition, 20*, 277–290.

Cahill, L. and McGaugh, J.L. (1995). A novel demonstration of enhanced memory associated with emotional arousal. *Consciousness and Cognition, 4*, 410–421.

Chan, J.C.K. and McDermott, K.B. (2006). Remembering pragmatic inferences. *Applied Cognitive Psychology, 20*, 633–639.

Christianson, S.-Å. and Loftus, E.F. (1990). Some characteristics of people's traumatic memories. *Bulletin of the Psychonomic Society, 28*, 195–198.

Claridge, K.E. (1992). Reconstructing memories of abuse: A theory-based approach. *Psychotherapy: Theory, Research, Practice, Training, 29*, 243–252.

Clifasefi, S.L., Takarangi, M.K., and Bergman, J.S. (2006). Blind drunk: The effects of alcohol on inattentional blindness. *Applied Cognitive Psychology, 20*, 697–704.

Conway, M.A., Anderson, S., Larsen, S., Donnelly, C., McDaniel, M., McClelland, A. G.R., et al. (1994). The formation of flashbulb memories. *Memory and Cognition, 22*, 326–343.

Cook, S., and Wilding, J. (1997). Earwitness testimony 2: Voice, faces, and context. *Applied Cog-nitive Psychology, 11*, 527–541.

Cook, S., and Wilding, J. (2000). Earwitness testimony: Effects of exposure and attention on the face overshadowing effect. *British Journal of Psychology, 92*, 617–629.

Craik, F.I.M., and Lockhart, R.S. (1972). Levels of processing: A framework for memory research. *Journal of Verbal Learning and Verbal Behavior, 11*, 671–684.

Cronbag, H.F.M., Wagenaar, W.A., and van Koppen, P.J. (1996). Crashing memories and the problem of "source monitoring." *Applied Cognitive Psychology, 10*, 95–104.

Cutler, B.L., Penrod, S.D., and Martens, T.K. (1987). The reliability of eyewitness identification: The role of system and estimator variables. *Law and Human Behavior, 11*, 233–258.

Davis, D., and Loftus, E.F. (2007) Internal and external sources of misinformation in adult witness memory. In M.P. Toglia, J.D. Read, D.F. Ross and R.C.L. Lindsay (Eds), *The Handbook of Eyewitness Psychology: Vol. II: Memory for Events* (pp. 195–237). Mahwah, NJ: Erlbaum.

Davis, D., and Friedman, R.D. (2007). Memory for conversation: The orphan child of witness memory researchers. In M.P. Toglia, J.D. Read, D.F. Ross, R.C.L. Lindsay (Eds.), *The Handbook of Eyewitness Psychology: Vol.e 1: Memory for Events* (pp. 3–52). London: Lawrence Erlbaum.

Deffenbacher, K.A., Bornstein, B.H., Penrod, S.D., and McGorty, E.K. (2004). A meta-analytic review of the effects of high stress on eyewitness memory. *Law and Human Behavior, 28*, 687–706.

Dysart, J.E., Lindsay, R.C.L., Hammond, R., and Dupuis, P. (2001). Mug shot exposure prior to lineup identification: Interference, transference, and commitment effects, *Journal of Applied Psychology, 86*, 1280–1284.

Eich, J.E. (1980). The cue-dependent nature of state dependent retrieval. *Memory & Cognition, 8*, 157–173.

Ellis, H.D., Davies, G.M., and Shepherd, J.W. (1977). Experimental studies of face identification. *Journal of Criminal Defense, 3*, 219–234.

Fisher, R.P., and Schreiber, N. (2007). Interview protocols for improving eyewitness memory. In M.P. Toglia, J.D. Read, D.F. Ross, and R.C.L. Lindsay (Eds) *The Handbook of Eyewitness Psychology: Vol. II: Memory for Events* (pp. 53–80). Mahwah, NJ: Erlbaum.

Fleishman, J.J., Buckley, M.L., Klosinsky, M.J., Smith, N., and Tuck, B. (1976). Judged attractiveness in recognition of women's faces. *Perceptual & Motor Skills, 43*, 709–710.

Gabbert, F., Memon, A., and Allan, K. (2003). Memory conformity: Can eyewitnesses influence each other's memories for an event? *Applied Cognitive Psychology, 17*, 533–543.

Gabbert, F., Memon, A., Allan, K., and Wright, D.B. (2004). Say it to my face: Examining the effects of socially encountered misinformation. *Legal and Criminological Psychology, 9*, 215–227.

Garrett, B.L. (2008, January). Judging innocence. *Columbia Law Review, 108.*

Garry, M., French, L., Kinzett, T., and Mori, K. (in press). Eyewitness memory following discussions: Using the MORI technique with a Western sample. *Applied Cognitive Psychology.*

Garry, M., Manning, C.G., Loftus, E.F., and Sherman, S.J. (1996). Imagination inflation: Imagining a childhood event inflates confidence that it occurred. *Psychonomic Bulletin and Review, 3*, 208–214.

Gore-Felton, C., Koopman, C., Thoresen, C., Arnow, B., Bridges, E., and Spiegel, D. (2000). Psychologists' beliefs and clinical characteristics: Judging the veracity of childhood sexual abuse memories. *Professional Psychology: Research and Practice, 31*, 372–377.

Granhag, P.A., Strömwall, L.A., and Billings, J.F. (2002, September). *"I'll Never Forget the Sinking Ferry": How Social Influence Makes False Memories Surface.* Paper presented at the 12th European Conference on Psychology and Law, Leuven, Belgium.

Harvey, M.R. (1999). Memory research and clinical practice: A critique of three paradigms and a framework for psychotherapy with trauma survivors. In L.M. Williams and V.L. Banyard (Eds.), *Trauma and Memory.* (pp. 19–29). Thousand Oaks, CA: Sage.

Heaps, C., and Nash, M. (1999). Individual differences in imagination inflation. *Psychonomic Bulletin and Review, 6*, 313–138.

Herman, J.L. (1992). *Trauma and Recovery.* New York: Basic.

Herman, J.L. and Schatzow, E. (1987). Recovery and verification of memories of childhood sexual trauma. *Psychoanalytic Psychology, 4*, 1–14.

Heuer, F. and Reisberg, D. (1990). Vivid memories of emotional events: The accuracy of remembered minutiae. *Memory and Cognition, 18*, 496–506.

Hope, L., Ost, J., Gabbert, F., Healey, S., and Lenton, E. (2008). "With a little help from my friends . . .": The role of co-witness relationshiop in susceptibility to misinformation. *Acta Psychologica, 12*, 76–484.

Hyman, I.E., Jr., Husband, T.H., and Billings, F.J. (1995). False memories of childhood experiences. *Applied Cognitive Psychology, 9*, 181–197.

Innocence Project, The. (n.d.). *Know the Cases* [Online]. Retrieved March 29, 2008. Available: http://www.innocenceproject.org/know/Browse-Profiles.php

James, W. (1890). *The Principles of Psychology* (Vol. 1). New York: Holt.

Jelicic, M., Smeets, T., Peters, M.J.V., Candel, I., Horselenberg, R., and Merckelbach, H. (2006). Assassination of a controversial politician: Remembering details from another nonexistent film. *Applied Cognitive Psychology, 20*, 591–596.

Kassin, S.M., Tubb, V.A., Hosch, H.M., and Memon, A. (2001). On the "general acceptance" of eyewitness testimony research. *American Psychologist, 56*, 405–416.

Kihlstrom, J.F. (2006). Trauma and memory revisited. In B. Uttl, N. Ohta, and A.L. Siegenthaler (Eds.) *Memory and Emotion: Interdisciplinary Perspectives* (pp. 259–291). Malden, MA: Blackwell.

Laney, C., Campbell, H.V., Heuer, F., and Reisberg, D. (2004). Memory for thematically arousing events. *Memory and Cognition, 32*, 1149–1159.

Laney, C., and Loftus, E.F. (in press). Emotional content of true and false memories. *Memory.*

Laney, C., Morris, E.K., Bernstein, D.M., Wakefield, B.M., and Loftus, E.F. (in press). Asparagus, a love story: Healthier eating could be just a false belief away. *Experimental Psychology.*

Leippe, M.R. (1995). The case for expert testimony about eyewitness memory. *Psychology, Public Policy, and Law, 1,* 909–959.

Leippe, M.R., Wells, G.L., and Ostrom, T.M. (1978). Crime seriousness as a determinant of accuracy in eyewitness identification. *Journal of Applied Psychology, 63,* 345–351.

Levine, L.J., and Bluck, S. (2004). Painting with broad strokes: Happiness and the malleability of event memory. *Cognition and Emotion, 8,* 559–574.

Levine, L.J., and Burgess, S.L. (1997). Beyond general arousal: Effects of specific emotions on memory. *Social Cogntion, 15,* 157–181.

Levine, L.J., and Pizarro, D.A. (2004). Emotion and memory research: A grumpy overview. *Social Cognition, 22,* 530–554.

Lieberman, H.R., Bathalon, G.P., Falco, C.M., Kramer, F.M., Morgan, C.A., III, and Niro, P. (2005). Severe decrements in cognition function and mood induced by sleep loss, head, dehydration, and undernutrition during simulated combat. *Biological Psychiatry, 57,* 422–429.

Light, L.L., Kayra-Stuart, F., and Hollander, S. (1979). Recognition memory for typical and unusual faces. *Journal of Experimental Psychology: Human Learning and Memory, 5,* 212–228.

Lindsay, D.S., Hagen, L., Read, J.D., Wade, K.A., and Garry, M. (2004). True photographs and false memories. *Psychological Science, 15,* 149–154.

Lindsay, R.C.L. (1999). Applying applied research: Selling the sequential line-up. *Applied Cognitive Psychology, 13,* 219–225.

Lindsay, R.C.L., Nosworthy, G.J., Martin, R.R., and Martynuck, C. (1994). Finding suspects in mugshots. *Journal of Applied Psychology, 79,* 121–130.

Loftus, E.F. (1975). Leading questions and the eyewitness report. *Cognitive Psychology, 7,* 560–574.

Loftus, E.F. (1979). *Eyewitness Testimony.* Cambridge, MA: Harvard University Press.

Loftus, E.F., and Burns, T.E. (1982). Mental shock can produce retrograde amnesia. *Memory and Cognition, 10,* 318–323.

Loftus, E.F., and Castelle, G. (2000). Crashing memories in legal cases. In P.J. VanKoppen and N.H.M. Roos (Eds.), *Rationality, Information and Progress in Law and Psychology* (pp. 115–127). Maastricht: Maastricht University Press.

Loftus, E.F., and Greene, E. (1980). Warning: Even memory for faces can be contagious. *Law and Human Behavior, 4,* 323–334.

Loftus, E.F., and Ketcham, K. (1991). *Witness for the Defense: The Accused, the Eyewitness, and the Expert Who Puts Memory on Trial.* New York: St. Martin's Press.

Loftus, E.F., and Ketcham, K. (1996). *The Myth of Repressed Memory: False Memories and Allegations of Sexual Abuse.* New York: St. Martin's Griffin.

Loftus, E.F., Loftus, G.R., and Messo, J. (1987). Some facts about "weapon focus." *Law and Human Behavior, 11,* 55–62.

Loftus, E.F., Miller, D. G., and Burns, H.J. (1978). Semantic integration of verbal information into a visual memory. *Journal of Experimental Psychology: Human Learning & Memory, 4,* 19–31.

Loftus, E.F. and Palmer, J.C. (1974). Reconstruction of automobile destruction. *Journal of Verbal Learning and Verbal Behavior, 13,* 585–589.

Loftus, E.F. and Pickrell, J.E. (1995). The formation of false memories. *Psychiatric Annals, 25,* 720–725.

Lynn, S.J., Lock, T.G., Myers, B., and Payne, D. (1997). Recalling the recallable: Should hypnosis be used to recover memories in psychotherapy? *Current Directions in Psychological Science, 6,* 79–83.

Malpass, R.S., and Kravitz, J. (1969). Recognition for faces of own and other race. *Journal of Personality and Social Psychology, 13,* 330–334.

Mazzoni, G.A.L., Lombardo, P., Malvagia, S., and Loftus, E.F. (1999). Dream interpretation and false beliefs. *Professional Psychology: Research & Practice, 30*, 45–50.

Mazzoni, G.A.K., and Lynn, S.J. (2007). Using hypnosis in eyewitness memory: Past and current issues. In M.P. Toglia, J.D. Read, D.F. Ross, and R.C.L. Lindsay (Eds.), *The Handbook of Eyewitness Psychology: Vol. 1: Memory for Events* (pp. 321–338). London: Lawrence Erlbaum.

Mazzoni, G.A.L., and Memon, A. (2003). Imagination can create false autobiographical memories. *Psychological Science, 14*, 186–188.

McAllister, H.A., Bregman, N.J., and Lipscomb, T.J. (1988). Speed estimates by eyewitnesses and earwitnesses: How vulnerable to postevent information? *Journal of General Psychology, 115*, 25–35.

McAllister, H.A., Dale. R.H.I., and Keay, Cynthia E. (1993). Effects of lineup modality on witness credibility. *Journal of Social Psychology, 133*, 365–376.

McGaugh, J.L., Introini-Collison, I.B., Nagahara, A.H., Cahill, L., Brioni, J.D., and Castellano, C. (1990). Involvement of the amygdaloid complex in neuormodulatroy influences on memory storarage. *Neuroscience & Biobehavioral Reviews, 14*, 425–431.

McNally, R.J. (2003). *Remembering Trauma*. Cambridge, MA: University of Harvard Press.

McNally, R.J., Clancy, S.A., and Barrett. (2004). Forgetting trauma? In D. Reisberg and P. Hertell (Eds.), *Memory and Emotion* (pp. 129–154). New York: Oxford University Press.

McQuiston-Surrett, D., Malpass, R.S., and Tredoux, C.G. (2006). Sequential vs. simultaneous lineups: A review of methods, data, and theory. *Psychology, Public Policy, and Law, 12*, 137–169.

Meissner and Brigham (2001). Thirty years of investigating the own-race bias in memory for faces: A meta-analytic review. *Psychology, Public Policy, and Law, 7*, 3–35.

Meissner, C.A., Sporer, S.L., and Schooler, J.W. (2007). Person descriptions as eyewitness evidence. In M.P. Toglia, J.D. Read, D.F. Ross, and R.C.L. Lindsay (Eds.) *The Handbook of Eyewitness Psychology: Vol. II: Memory for People* (pp. 3–34). London: Lawrence Erlbaum.

Morgan, C.A., Hazlett, G., Baranoski, M., Doran, A., Southwich, S., and Loftus, E.F. (2007). Accuracy of eyewitnesses identification is significantly associated with performance on a standarized test of face recognition. *International Journal of Law and Psychiatry, 30*, 213–223.

Morgan, C.A., Hazlett, G., Doran, A., Garrett, S., Hoyt, G., Thomas, P., et al. (2004). Accuracy of eyewitness memory for persons encountered during exposure to highly intense stress. *International Journal of Law and Psychiatry, 27*, 265–279.

Ofshe, R., and Watters, E. (1994). *Making Monsters: False Memories, Psychotherapy, and Sexual Hysteria*. Berkeley: University of California Press.

Ost, J., Foster, S., Costall, A., and Bull, R. (2005). False reports of childhood events in appropriate interviews. *Memory, 13*, 700–710.

Ost, J., Vrij, A., Costall, A., and Bull, R. (2002). Crashing memories and reality monitoring: Distinguishing between perceptions, imaginations and "false memories." *Applied Cognitive Psychology, 16*, 125–134.

Paterson, H.M., and Kemp, R.I. (2006). Co-witnesses talk: A survey of eyewitness discussion. *Psychology, Crime & Law, 12*, 181–191.

Payne, J.D., Nadel, L., Britton, W.B., and Jacobs, W.J. (2004). The biopsychology of trauma and memory. In *Memory and Emotion. Series in Affective Science* (pp. 76–128). New York: Oxford University Press.

Paz-Alonso, P.M., and Goodman, G.S. (2008). Trauma and memory: Effects of post-event misinformation, retrieval order, and retention interval. *Memory, 16*, 58–75.

Peace, K.A. and Porter, S. (2004). A longitudinal investigation of the reliability of memory for trauma and other emotional experiences. *Applied Cognitive Psychology, 18*, 1143–1159.

Peterson, C., and Whalen, N. (2001). Five years later: Children's memory for medical emergencies. *Applied Cognitive Psychology, 15,* S7–S24.

Philippon, A.C., Cherryman, J., Bull, R., and Vrij, A. (2007). Earwitness identification performance: The effect of language, target, deliberate strategies and indirect measures. *Applied Cognitive Psychology, 21,* 539–550.

Poole, D.A., Lindsay, D.S., Memon, A., and Bull, R. (1995). Psychotherapy and the recovery of memories of childhood sexual abuse: U.S. and British practitioners' beliefs, practices, and experiences. *Journal of Consulting and Clinical Psychology, 6,* 426–437.

Porter, S., Yuille, J.C., and Lehman, D. R. (1999). The nature of real, implanted, and fabricated memories for emotional childhood events: Implications for the recovered memory debate. *Law and Human Behavior, 23,* 517–537.

Pozzulo, J.D., and Lindsay, R.C.L. (1998). Identification accuracy of children versus adults: A meta-analysis. *Law and Human Behavior, 22,* 549–570.

Quas, J.A., Goodman, G.S., Bidrose, S., Pipe, M.-E., Craw, S., and Ablin, D.S. (1999). Emotion and memory: Children's long-term remembering, forgetting, and suggestibility. *Journal of Experimental Child Psychology, 72,* 235–270.

Read, J.D., and Connolly, D.A. (2007). The effects of delay on long-term memory for witnessed events. In M.P. Toglia, J.D. Read, D.F. Ross, and R.C.L. Lindsay (Eds.), *The Handbook of Eyewitness Psychology; Vol. 1: Memory for Events* (pp. 117–156). London: Lawrence Erlbaum.

Reisberg, D. (2001). *Cognition: Exploring the Science of the Mind* (2nd ed.). New York: W. W. Norton.

Reisberg, D. (2006). Memory for emotional episodes: The strengths and limits of arousal-based accounts. In B. Uttl, N. Ohta, and A.L. Siegenthaler (Eds.), *Memory and Emotion: Interdisciplinary Perspectives* (pp. 15–36). Malden, MA: Blackwell.

Reisberg, D., and Heuer, F. (2007). The influence of emotion on memory in forensic settings. In M.P. Toglia, J.D. Read, D.F. Ross, and R.C.L. Lindsay (Eds.), *The Handbook of Eyewitness Psychology: Vol. 1: Memory for Events* (pp. 81–116). London: Lawrence Erlbaum.

Reisberg, D., Heuer, F., McLean, J., and O'Shaughnessy, M. (1988). The quantity, not the quality, of affect predicts memory vividness. *Bulletin of the Psychonomic Society, 26,* 100–103.

Rumelhart, D.E., and McClelland, J.L. (Eds.), (1986). *Parallel Distributed Processing, Vol 1.* Cambridge, MA: MIT Press.

Saslove, H., and Yarmey, A.D. (1980). Long-term auditory memory: Speaker identification. *Journal of Applied Psychology, 65,* 111–116.

Schacter, D.L. (2001). *The Seven Sins of memory: How the Mind Forgets and Remembers.* New York: Houghon Mifflin.

Scheck, B., Neufeld, P., and Dwyer, J. (2003). *Actual Innocence: When Justice Goes Wrong and How to Make it Right.* New York: New American Library.

Scoboria, A., Mazzoni, G.A.L., Kirsch, I., and Milling, L.S. (2002). Immediate and persisting effects of misleading questions and hypnosis on memory reports. *Journal of Experimental Psychology: Applied, 8,* 26–32.

Scoville, W.B., and Milner, B. (1957). Loss of recent memory after bilateral hippocampal lesions. *Journal of Neurology, Neurosurgery & Psychiatry, 20,* 11–21.

Sheen, M., Kemp, S., and Rubin, D. (2001). Twins dispute memory ownership: A new false memory phenomenon. *Memory and Cognition, 29,* 779–788.

Shobe, K.K., & Kihlstrom, J.F. (1997). Is traumatic memory special? *Current Directions in Psychological Science, 6,* 70–74.

Smeets, T., Jelicic, M., Peters, M.J.V., Candel, I., Horselenberg, R., and Merckelbach, H. (2006). "Of course I remember seeing that film:" How ambiguous questions generate crashing memories. *Applied Cognitive Psychology, 20,* 779–789.

Southwick, S.M., Morgan, C.A., Nicolaou, A.L., and Charney, D.S. (1997). Consistency of memory for combat-related traumatic events in veterans of Operation Desert Storm. *American Journal of Psychiatry, 154,* 173–177.

Steblay, N.M. (1992). A meta-analytic review of the weapon focus effect. *Law and Human Behavior, 16,* 413–424.

Steblay, N.M., Dysart, J., Fulero, S., and Lindsay, R.C.L. (2001). Eyewitness accuracy rates in sequential and simultaneous lineup presentations: A meta-analytic comparison. *Law and Human Behavior, 25,* 459–473.

Steblay, N.M., and Loftus, E.F. (in press). Eyewitness memory and the legal system. In E. Shafir (Ed.), *The Behavioural Foundations of Policy.* Princeton, NJ: Princeton University Press.

Strange, D., Gerrie, M. P., and Garry, M. (2005). A few seemingly harmless routes to a false memory. *Cognitive Processing, 6,* 237–242.

Swihart, G., Yuille, J., and Porter, S. (1999). The role of state-dependent memory in "red-outs." *International Journal of Law and Psychiatry, 22,* 199–212.

Takarangi, M.K.T., Parker, S., and Garry, M. (2006). Modernizing the misinformation effect: The development of a new stimulus set. *Applied Cognitive Psychology, 20,* 583–590.

Taylor, F.K. (1965). Cryptomnesia and plagiarism. *British Journal of Psychiatry, 4,* 1111–1118.

Technical Working Group for Eyewitness Accuracy (1999). *Eyewitness Evidence: A Guide for Law Enforcement.* Research Report. Washington, DC: U.S. Department of Justice; *A Trainer's Manual for Law Enforcement,* published 2003.

Thomas, A.K. and Loftus, E.F. (2002). Creating bizarre false memories through imagination. *Memory and Cognition, 30,* 423–431.

Valentine, T., Pickering, A., and Darling, S. (2003). Characteristics of eyewitness identification that predict the outcome of real lineups. *Applied Cognitive Psychology, 17,* 969–993.

van der Kolk, B.A. (1997). The psychobiology of posttraumatic stress disorder. *Journal of Clinical Psychiatry, 58,* 16–24.

Wade, K.A., and Garry, M. (2005). Strategies for verifying false autobiographical memories. *American Journal of Psychology, 118,* 587–602.

Wade, K.A., Garry, M., Read, J.D., and Lindsay, S.A. (2002). A picture is worth a thousand lies. *Psychonomic Bulletin and Review, 9,* 597–603.

Wagenaar, E., and Groeneweg, J. (1990). The memory of concentration camp survivors. *Applied Cognitive Psychology, 4,* 77–87.

Wells, G.L., and Bradfield, A.L. (1998). "Good, you identified the suspect": Feedback to eyewitnesses distorts their reports of the witnessing experience. *Journal of Applied Psychology, 83,* 360–376.

Wells, G.L., Memon, A., and Penrod, S.D. (2006). Eyewitness evidence: Improving its probative value. *Psychological Science in the Public Interest, 7,* 45–75.

Wells, G.L., and Olson, E. (2003). Eyewitness testimony. *Annual Review of Psychology, 54,* 277–295.

Wells, G.L., Small, M., Penrod, S., Malpass, R.S., Fulero, S.M., and Brimacombe, C.A.E. (1998). Eyewitness identification procedures: Recommendations for lineups and photospreads. *Law and Human Behavior, 22,* 603–647.

Wise, R.A., and Safer, M.A. (2004). What US judges know and believe about eyewitness testimony. *Applied Cognitive Psychology, 18,* 427–443.

Wright, D.B., Mathews, S.A., and Skagerberg, E.M. (2005). Social recognition memory: The effect of other people's responses for previously seen and unseen items. *Journal of Experimental Psychology: Applied, 11,* 200–209.

Wright, D.B., and Skagerberg, E.M. (2007). Postidentification feedback affects real eyewitnesses. *Psychological Science, 18,* 172–178.

Wogalter, M.S., Malpass, R.S., and McQuiston, D.E. (2004). A national survey of U.S. police on preparation and conduct of identification lineups. *Psychology, Crime & Law, 10*, 69–82.

Yarmey, A.D. (1986). Verbal, visual, and voice identification of a rape suspect under different levels of illumination. *Journal of Applied Psychology, 71*, 363–370.

Yarmey, A.D. (1995). Earwitness speaker identification. *Psychology, Public Policy, and Law, 1*, 792–816.

Yarmey, A.D., Yarmey, A.L., Yarmey, A.J., and Parliament, L. (2001). Common sense beliefs and the identification of familiar voices. *Applied Cognitive Psychology, 15*, 283–300.

Yuille, J.C., and Cutshall, J. L. (1986). A case study of eyewitness memory of a crime. *Journal of Applied Psychology, 71*, 291–301.

Yuille, J.C., and Tollestrup, P.A. (1990). Some effects of alcohol on eyewitness memory. *Journal of Applied Psychology, 75*, 268–273.

Chapter Seven

COGNITIVE INTERVIEWING

CORAL J DANDO AND REBECCA MILNE

The cognitive interview (CI) is a multidisciplinary forensic interview technique concerned exclusively with the retrieval of information from memory. It is one of the most-researched and widely acknowledged interview procedures for enhancing eyewitness memorial performance and has been described as "one of the most exciting developments in psychology in the last ten years" (Memon, 2000, p. 343). Indeed, the CI has been fundamental in shaping the prevailing approach to investigative interviewing in the United Kingdom,[1] as well as many other countries (e.g. Australia, United Statesa, and Canada). This chapter will commence by outlining the importance of witness information to the investigation of crime, followed by a brief introduction to some of the problems associated with police interviews prior to the formation of the CI. The CI procedure will then be described and the development process will be outlined, including a review of the relevant theory and empirical research. Finally, research pertaining to police officers' application of the procedure will be introduced.

WITNESS INFORMATION

During a criminal investigation police officers strive to answer two primary questions, namely what has occurred and who is responsible (Milne & Bull, 2006). When attempting to answer these questions and in order to bring the perpetrators of crime to justice, police officers require information. One of the primary sources of such information are witnesses and victims (the

---

1. For ease of reading United Kingdom has been used throughout this chapter. However, it should be noted that we are primarily referring to England, Wales, and Northern Ireland.

term "witness" will hereafter be used to describe both an onlooker and a victim of crime). Indeed, it is well-accepted that witnesses are a "central and important" feature of any criminal investigation (Sanders, 1986). Not only do they generally provide the central leads within an enquiry (Berresheim & Weber, 2003; Kebbell & Milne, 1998), but they also provide information that directs the entire investigatory process from the very outset (Milne & Bull, 2001; Milne & Shaw, 1999). For example, in the initial stages, witnesses report what has occurred and frequently provide a description of the perpetrator. Further, they often signal additional lines of enquiry and even indicate other potential sources of information. As the investigatory process progresses, witnesses can be asked to identify perpetrators, objects, or places, and in the final stages of bringing an offender to justice, witness evidence is central to most court cases (Kebbell & Milne, 1998; Zander & Henderson, 1993). Moreover, in an adversarial system, as governs the criminal justice system in England and Wales (and many other English-speaking countries), it is not unusual for the prosecution to view witness testimony as more important to their case than an offender's confession (Wolchover & Heaton-Armstrong, 1996). Certainly, when presented at a court of law, witness testimony is extremely powerful; research indicates that jurors rely heavily on witness accounts of what they have experienced (e.g. Cutler, Penrod & Dexter, 1990). Not surprisingly, witness testimony has also been found to increase the likelihood that a perpetrator will be not only apprehended but also prosecuted (Lieppe, 1980; Visher, 1987).

In light of the significance of witness information to the process of criminal justice, from the very beginning of an investigation through to any subsequent court case, it is clear that incomplete and inaccurate witness information can result in serious negative outcomes (Savage & Milne, 2006). Therefore, obtaining as full and as accurate an account as possible of what a witness has experienced is of paramount importance.

Police Interviewing

It is police officers who are generally tasked with gathering witness information and this is usually done by way of an interview. An interview (a conversation with a purpose) can be conducted over a wide gamut of situations ranging from an initial brief conversational exchange at the scene of a crime to a more formal in-depth interview conducted at a police station, a witness's home or workplace. An interview is, therefore, a fundamental information-gathering opportunity (ACPO, 2001; Milne & Bull, 2006) and a frequent "bread and butter" daily activity for all police officers from the very beginning of their police careers.

Interviewing is acknowledged as a complex skill. It is a process of conversational exchange (Shepherd, 1991) in which both the witness and the interviewing officer play an integral role. During an interview, witnesses are asked to work hard in terms of searching their memory and explaining, in detail, what they can remember about a previously experienced event, and it is the interviewer's task to help each witness to give the fullest and most accurate account of his or her experience. Remembering a crime event, such as a robbery or an assault, is essentially a constructive process, and there exists a large body of research that indicates that the manner in which a witness' memory of a to be remembered (TBR) event is accessed and constructed can be a significant determinant, not only of the amount of information he or she recalls but also of the accuracy of that information. It is very important that any information recalled is, in fact, correct. For example, the types of questions asked, the manner in which they are asked, and the structure of the retrieval process (in this case the interview) have all been found to have an impact on witness memorial performance in terms of both quantity (amount) and quality (accuracy) (e.g. *see* Loftus, 1975, 1979; Milne & Bull, 2001; Tulving, 1991).

Unfortunately, however, prior to the early 1990s, police officers throughout the world typically received a very limited amount of witness interview training (*see* Milne & Bull, 2001). For example, Sanders (1986) found that only 2 percent of his sample of U.S. police officers had undergone any witness interview training. George (1991) surveyed several U.K. police forces and found that some provided no witness interview training at all and others provided just one day. Furthermore, when training was provided it tended to be highly programmatic, focusing purely on the "mechanics" of the interview process: the who, what, where, when, why, and how. In essence, police officers were being trained as report takers rather than as information gatherers. Where no formal training was provided, officers simply learned on the job by observing their peers who, themselves, had generally undergone little or no training and who, although experienced, were not necessarily competent. Unfortunately, reflecting this lack of training, witness interviews were generally found to be poorly conducted. They tended to be interviewer-driven statement-taking exercises during which interviewer-interviewee communication was often found to be ineffective. Moreover, it was clear that witness memorial performance was frequently compromised by officers employing interview techniques that actually impeded, rather than assisted, the memory process (e.g. Fisher, Geiselman & Raymond, 1987; George, 1991; McLean, 1995). Thus, there was a clear need for a witness interview method to be developed.

THE COGNITIVE INTERVIEW

In the early 1980s, in response to many requests by American police investigators and other legal professionals for a method of improving witness memory, American psychologists Ron Fisher and Ed Geiselman developed the CI procedure. Devised as a practical forensic tool, the CI was designed for use with any cooperative interviewee (witnesses, victims, and suspects) and was concerned exclusively with the retrieval of information from memory, specifically with how the retrieval (remembering) process might be optimized during an interview situation. Initially presented in 1984, the procedure evolved over several ensuing years with further refinements and enhancements being reported in a series of subsequent papers. This development process is well-documented and falls into two fairly distinct phases, with the initial procedure being referred to as the original CI and the second as the enhanced CI (ECI).

The Original Cognitive Interview

The original CI (Geiselman et al., 1984) comprised four retrieval components, namely (1) mental reinstatement of context (MRC), (2) report everything, (3) recall in a variety of temporal orders (CTO), and (4) change perspective (CP) techniques. Each of these components, generally referred to as the "cognitive" components, will now be described, as will their theoretical underpinnings and the empirical research available at the time, that evidenced their suitability for inclusion in the original CI.

The MRC technique is one of the principle components of the original CI. When applying this technique the interviewer encourages the witness to mentally reinstate both the psychological and the physical environments that existed at the time of the TBR event in order that they might act as retrieval cues (triggers) for that event. The procedure comprises a series of "mini" instructions whereby the interviewer encourages the interviewee to recreate the context of the TBR event one step at a time. In between each of the mini instructions, the interviewer pauses for several seconds to allow the witness sufficient time to reinstate the context as instructed. For example:

> I would like to try and help you to remember as much as you can. As I talk to you I want you to think about each of the things I say, as I say them. Closing your eyes or staring or looking at a blank wall may help you. To begin I would like you to try to think back to the day the event happened. Think about that day . . . what had you been doing . . . what was the weather like. . . . Think about the place that the event happened . . . try and get a picture of it in your mind. Think about the layout of the place . . . think of all the objects that were there . . . think about the colors. Think about the smells. How did you feel at the time? Now think about the event and the people involved . . . focus on what happened . . . when you are ready I would like

you to tell me everything that you can remember, in your own time and at your own pace.

This component emanates from the encoding specificity principle (Tulving & Thomson, 1973), which provides a theoretical framework for understanding the power of contextual information and how it can affect (trigger) memory. It has been suggested that just because something cannot be remembered, it does not necessarily follow that it has been lost completely. The memory in question may simply be inaccessible (still present in memory but not able to be accessed or found; Tulving & Pearlstone, 1968). This was illustrated in a series of word association experiments in the 1970s (Thomson & Tulving, 1970; Tulving & Thomson, 1973). The results indicated that memory could indeed be improved when information present at the time of learning (encoding) was presented again at the time of remembering (retrieval). Presenting such material had apparently facilitated conscious remembering of aspects of the original event that were not remembered in the absence of that material (in the case of this research, words). However, it is not always possible or advisable for a witness to return to the scene of a crime (this may prove too traumatic, which can interfere with recall, and the crime scene may have altered). Further, context may not always be external (physical). A witness's subjective state (mood and feelings) can also be an important aspect of the encoding environment (Schacter, 1996). Thus, the MRC instruction attempts to facilitate maximum recall by helping the witness to mentally reinstate the contextual information (both physical and mental) that was present at the time of encoding.

The report everything component instructs witnesses to not edit any details about the TBR event, even those details they believe to be insignificant or irrelevant. For example:

> Some people hold back information because they are not quite sure that it is important, or you may think that I already know this information. Please do not leave anything out. I am interested in absolutely everything that you remember, anything that pops into your head. Even partial memories and things you think may not be important. Please tell, just tell me it all.

Memory for an event is believed to be stored as a series of coded representations (Bower, 1967) whereby what is stored in memory is not an exact replica of the TBR event itself but a multiplicity of interconnected codes that preserve the experience. Hence, there are likely to be several means of retrieving or cueing witness memory of the TBR event (Melton & Martin, 1972). Furthermore, interviewees often feel ill at ease or apprehensive in a formal interview setting. They may be of the opinion that the police are already knowledgeable about the event and are only likely to be interested in "important" and fully remembered information. Consequently, information is often held back. In light of this, the report everything instruction aims to lower a witness's subjective criteria for reporting information, the hope being that even partial or apparently insignificant features of an event may trigger previously inaccessible memory codes. The report everything instruction is also viewed as a useful method for increasing the overall amount of information collected from all witnesses to a particular event, and lots of small, apparently insignificant pieces of information collected from several witness accounts can be of investigative value when pieced together.

The multicomponent view of a memory trace suggests that there are several ways of accessing memory codes. Thus, the CTO component was included as an additional method of accessing memory codes that may have been previously irretrievable. The CTO technique is also based on the theoretical assumption that the retrieval of information from memory can be influenced by prior knowledge and the application of schemas and scripts (Schank & Abelson, 1977). It is suggested that predictive schemas act as organizing structures for knowledge and that script-based understanding fills in aspects of an event according to previous experiences. New information is, therefore, understood in terms of old information. Hence, script guided retrieval can result in limited retrieval due to the filtering of recalled information that does not fit the script or erroneous filling of gaps when recall is poor or scant. Encouraging an interviewee to recall the TBR event from the end, or even the middle, is therefore aimed at limiting script-consistent recall by interfering with forward-only recall. For example:

> It is natural to go through the incident in your own order. However, I would like to try something which sometimes helps people to remember more. What I would like you to do is to tell me what happened backwards. I know it sounds hard but I am going to help you. To start, what is the very last thing that you remember happening . . . what happened before that . . . what happened just before that (this prompt can be repeated, if necessary, until the interviewee reaches the beginning of the TBR event).

Research had indicated that a backward search through autobiographical memory was more effective than either a forward or a random search because it led to less recall failure (Whitten & Leonard, 1981). Other researchers have also reported that a reverse-order recall elicited more details of a TBR event (especially actions) when compared with a forward-order recall (Geiselman, Fisher, MacKinnon & Holland, 1986; Geiselman & Callot, 1990).

The CP component of the CI aims to access memory codes that may have been irretrievable using the three previous techniques (Bower, 1967). The CP technique encourages witnesses to recall the TBR event from a variety of personal perspectives. For example witnesses are instructed as follows:

Try to recall the incident from the perspective of another person involved in the incident. Think about where he or she was and isolate everything that you can remember about them, as if they are in a spotlight. Describe what he or she would have seen.

It was research by Anderson and Pichert (1978) that prompted the inclusion of this technique. Participants were asked to read a narrative passage from the perspective of either a burglar or a house purchaser, after which they were instructed to write down everything they could remember about the story. After a distracter task, participants were then instructed to recall the story a second time from a different perspective (those who had initially read the passage from a burglar's perspective then changed to a home buyer's perspective and vice versa). It was found that when participants had changed perspective, additional information important to their new perspective was recalled. This could not be explained in terms of the encoding process (the process of perceiving and transforming experienced events into memory codes) because the perspective shift had occurred after the passage had been read and initially recalled. It appears that participants had selectively attended to, and subsequently remembered, elements of the story that were significant according to the perspective in operation at the time. However, more information must have been encoded than was initially recalled because participants were able to recall more information after a shift of personal perspective.

Empirical Evaluation of the Original Cognitive Interview

Between 1984 and 1987 Geiselman and colleagues conducted several empirical research studies designed to investigate the efficacy of the original CI. In the initial evaluation (Geiselman et al., 1984), mock witnesses viewed a short (non-violent) staged event and forty-eight hours later were asked to write down everything they could remember in a booklet. Participants in the CI condition were provided with instructions for each of the four cognitive retrieval components on a large board, whereas those in the control condition received no instructions. Analysis of participants' recall performance revealed that those in the CI condition recalled significantly more correct items of information than did those in the control, with no concomitant increase in the amount of incorrect recall.

This initial evaluation indicated that the original CI had promise as a procedure for enhancing the quantity of correct recall without compromising the quality (the amount of correct recall as a percentage of total recall) of that information. However, questionnaires had been used in this initial evaluation, so there had been no interviewer-interviewee interaction, as is the case when witnesses are interviewed in real life. Furthermore, student participants had administered the procedure themselves, and, therefore, it was not known whether they had utilized each of the individual components. Finally, there had been no comparison with any other interview methods.

Geiselman, Fisher, Mackinnon, and Holland (1985), therefore, completed a follow-up study comparing the effectiveness of the original CI with two other interview methods, namely a standard police interview (SI) and a hypnosis interview (HI). Participants initially viewed a violent crime film (used to train Los Angeles Police Department [LAPD] police officers). Forty-eight hours later they were interviewed, face-to-face, by law enforcement officers recruited from agencies in the United States (CIA, police, private detectives, and polygraph specialists) using either a CI, SI, or HI. SI interviewers used their normal everyday interview procedure. The HI interviewers followed the guidelines, in operation at the time, for conducting hypnosis interviews. The CI interviewers described the four CI components to each interviewee prior to the interview. These were then listed and placed in full view of the interviewee during the entire interview. The results of this study closely replicated those previously obtained (Geiselman et al., 1984). Both the CI and the HI conditions elicited an average of approximately 30 percent more correct information compared with the SI condition with no concomitant increase in the number of errors. However, the CI was viewed as the preferable technique because it was free from the legal concerns surrounding the use of forensic hypnosis (at that time in the United States) and, furthermore, the CI took less time to learn. These results not only provided further support for the superiority of the CI procedure *per se* but also gave some indication as to its efficacy in more ecologically valid conditions.

In light of the fact that the previous research had been conducted with a student population, which is not representative of the general population, Geiselman, Fisher, MacKinnon, and Holland (1986) then conducted a third study in an attempt to increase the human ecological validity of the CI technique, to further examine its efficacy, and to extend its generalizability. Adults between the ages of twenty and fifty-two years from the general population viewed one of the violent training films used in the previous study and were interviewed forty-eight hours later using either a SI or a CI interview procedure. Interviews were conducted by nine serving police officers who had been trained to use the CI. Again, it was found that the memorial performance of those interviewed using the CI was superior (for the amount of correct information recalled) to those in the SI condition by an average of more than 17 percent. Further, there were no effects of age, annual income, or ethnic group on the results of the adult participants.

The combined results of these initial three studies strongly supported the CI superiority effect for enhancing both the quality and quantity of eyewitness recall. However, there were some elements of the CI procedure that were also similar to forensic hypnosis (e.g. instructions to mentally reinstate the context, and forensic hypnosis had been found to not only increase the amount of inaccurate recall but also to negatively affect witnesses' responses to misleading questions (Sanders & Simmons, 1983; Sheenhan, Grigg & McCann, 1984). Hence, a fourth study was conducted (Geiselman, Fisher, Cohen, Holland & Surtes, 1986) to investigate eyewitness responses to leading and misleading questions during a CI. Both of these types of questions suggest the answer; for example, "he had black hair didn't he?" However, the former leads the interviewee to the correct response, whereas the latter leads the interviewee to an incorrect response. Employing similar methodology to that of the previously reported research (Geiselman et al., 1984), the CI was compared with a SI. Results revealed that the CI did not enhance the negative effect of either type of question but instead decreased the effect of both leading and misleading question types on incorrect responding.

In sum, the results of the aforementioned studies combined to offer strong empirical support for the superiority of the CI procedure compared with a SI and forensic hypnosis. The CI procedure had significantly increased correct eyewitness recall without a concomitant increase in the amount of erroneous information recalled. Further, this effect held (1) in controlled laboratory settings; (2) using students, law enforcement agency workers, and police officers as interviewers; and (3) when interviewing student and nonstudent interviewees. In addition, the CI also appeared to reduce the effects of both leading and misleading questions on recall. However, although this original CI procedure comprised a set of memory enhancing components to be given at the start of the interview, there was very little guidance concerning the method of presentation, the structure of the interview, the sequencing of questions, or interviewer behavior. Moreover, because the procedure had been devised as a practical forensic tool, it was necessary that future research should make the transition from the laboratory to more applied settings.

The Enhanced Cognitive Interview

As indicated earlier, field research investigating the techniques employed by police officers when interviewing real witnesses (Fisher et al., 1987) had revealed some idiosyncratic shortcomings. Almost without exception the interviews lacked a uniform structure. Officers used questioning techniques that resulted in brief witness responses either confirming or contradicting the officers' intuition. Of particular note were three interviewer behaviors, common to all the interviews, which had the potential to seriously hinder witness recall. First, every officer asked the witness to describe in a narrative fashion what he or she had experienced but were then constantly interrupted throughout that initial account. Second, all of the interviews were constructed using a series of direct short-answer questions that requested specific information. Finally, interviewers displayed a general lack of communication skills, for example using inappropriate language, judgmental comments, nonneutral wording of questioning, and negative phrasing. Similar findings were also found in the United Kingdom (George, 1991; McLean, 1995).

In light of these findings it became clear that the efficacy of the memory enhancing cognitive components, as previously described, was likely to be compromised due to an apparent lack of social and communication skills. Accordingly, Fisher, Geiselman, Raymond, Jurkevich, and Warhaftig (1987) made a set of recommendations that they believed would significantly enhance officers' interview technique in general. The resultant ECI procedure retains the original four cognitive components (mental reinstatement of context, report everything, recall in a variety of temporal orders, and change perspective) and adds a conversational element to the interview process. In addition, Fisher, Geiselman, Raymond, and colleagues (1987) recommend that the interview itself should be conducted in an appropriate environment as people have limited mental resources with which to process information (Baddeley, 1986), thus, disruptions and distractions should be minimized to ensure maximum concentration and attention during retrieval (Johnston, Greenberg, & Fisher, 1970). Having listened to an interviewee's initial recall of an event, it was further suggested that the interviewer should only then ask questions in a manner relevant to the mental representation that a particular interviewee has of the event in question.

Because previously introduced memory of an event is not the literal input stimulus but rather is thought to be a series of coded representations (Bower, 1967), each witness's stored mental representation is likely to be unique. Thus, it follows that interviewers should tailor their questioning accordingly. A rigid sequencing of requests for information imposes a "police report" style of organization on the retrieval process that may limit witness recall. To that end, *witness-compatible questioning* dictates that the interviewer should actively listen to each interviewee's account of what he or she has experienced and ask questions in the same order as the interviewee initially recounted the event. Guided imagery is also recommended as a method of inducing recall by helping the interviewee to recall specific details of an event. Guided imagery differs from MRC in that it helps an interviewee to imagine in his or her mind's eye highly detailed minute parts of the event as opposed to the more global approach of MRC. For example, a witness may be asked by the interviewer to generate in his or her mind a detailed image of the perpetrator and then to develop or sharpen that image so that it is as detailed as possible. Having been allowed as much time as necessary to develop that image (at least several seconds), the witness will then be asked to probe the image by concentrating on each specific part (e.g. the head, hair, face, eyes, etc.).

However, this is an interviewer-led technique. Recently it has been suggested that a more molecular approach should be adopted whereby the interviewee is allowed to dictate what he or she imagined rather than be guided by the interviewer (for more on molecular context, *see* Bekerian & Conway, 1988).

In an attempt to improve the social and communication aspects of the witness interview process it was also recommended that extra time be taken to establish rapport with the interviewee, so reducing his or her anxiety about the interview process. This should be done by commencing the interview with innocuous and easily answered questions. In addition, officers should tailor their language appropriately by avoiding (1) judgmental and personal comments, (2) rememorized patterns of language, and (3) jargon. Instead, simple straightforward language should be employed, thus addressing interviewer behaviors and procedures thought to negatively affect the overall success of the interview process. Several straightforward interviewer behaviors were included that aimed to encourage focused retrieval. First, the interviewer should explain or convey to the interviewee that it is his or her effort that will affect the outcome of the interview and that ultimately the success of the interview will depend on the interviewee's mental effort. This is done by encouraging the interviewee to both concentrate and actively participate. For example, the interviewer should both allow and encourage the interviewee to do most of the talking by the use of open-ended questions whenever possible and by the strategic use of pauses. Open-ended questions are particularly beneficial for information-gathering purposes because they elicit some of the most accurate information (e.g. Dent, 1991; Poole & Lamb, 1998) and invite longer and more detailed responses.

Indeed, open-ended questions (e.g. tell me everything about the robbery) are associated with longer response latencies (longer time spent thinking before answering) compared with specific closed questions (e.g. those that tend to start with what, where, when, etc.). This suggests that, when asked an open question, interviewees may well be conducting a more detailed and thorough memory search. Pauses and periods of silence used in conjunction with open-ended questions also provide an interviewee with an opportunity to continue developing his or her answer. Conversely, specific closed questions should be used sparingly because these generally invite limited narrowly defined responses that only concern the specific request (Bull, 1992). Further, the interviewer should never interrupt the interviewee but instead wait until he or she has finished and only then ask questions because interruptions disrupt concentration and distract the interviewee from his or her memory search. Finally at the end of the interview, the interviewee's account of what he or she has experienced should be reviewed by the interviewer, thus, providing an opportunity for the interviewee to add or change any details and for the interviewer to check the accuracy of his or her notes (*see* Fisher & Geiselman, 1992, for an in-depth description of the ECI).

It can be seen that the ECI concentrates on three core perspectives, namely the representation of knowledge, the memory retrieval process, and communication skills. One important further refinement of the interview procedure was the recommendation that it should follow a sequence of stages, the expectation being that each stage would contribute both individually and incrementally to the overall efficacy of the enhanced procedure.

Empirical Evaluation of the Enhanced Cognitive Interview

The first empirical investigation of the efficacy of the ECI (Fisher, Geiselman, Raymond et al., 1987) compared the original CI to the ECI. Undergraduates were interviewed two days after having viewed one of the LAPD training films (as used in Geiselman et al., 1985) employing either the original CI or ECI. The original CI comprised the four memory retrieval components that were described to the participant at the beginning of the interview in the following order (1) mental reinstatement of context, (2) report everything, (3) change temporal order, and (4) change perspective. The ECI, in addition to the four original components, included witness compatible questioning and focused retrieval. Further, the components were to be used in the following sequence. First, the interviewer should invite an initial free recall account using an open-ended question or invitation, during which the interviewer should not interrupt the witness. After this initial recall account the interviewer should return to specific episodes within the initial account to probe specific details with open and specific closed questions, and finally, the interviewer should end the interview by summarizing what the interviewee said. Results revealed that the ECI elicited 45 percent more correct items of information compared with the original CI with no differences between the two conditions in the amount of erroneous recall. Because the original CI had previously been found to be approximately 30 percent more effective than a SI (Geiselman et al., 1985) it was thus concluded that the ECI produced 75 percent more correct recall compared with a SI.

Having demonstrated the effectiveness of the ECI in the laboratory, Fisher, Geiselman, and Amador (1989) then tested the procedure in the field. American police detectives tape-recorded several interviews with real-life crime victims or witnesses using SI procedure. The detectives were then assigned to one of two interview conditions, namely untrained or ECI. Those in the latter condition underwent ECI training, whereas the untrained group served as a control comparison. After training, detectives from each group tape-recorded several more interviews with a number of witnesses. Analysis of the resultant interviews revealed that the ECI-trained detectives elicited, on average, 47 percent more information after training compared to before training.

As was the case with the previous laboratory-based studies, it was not only the amount of information recalled that was important but also the accuracy of that information. Data from laboratory studies had revealed no significant differences in accuracy rates between the original CI and a SI (Geiselman et al., 1985, 1986). However, field studies with real witnesses and victims did not allow such a measure because what exactly had occurred was not known. Therefore, accuracy could only be estimated by comparing witness reports with other sources of information such as other witness and victim reports, confessions, and CCTV footage. Overall 94 percent of information was corroborated, but more importantly corroboration rates were similar for the pretrained and posttrained interviews (93 percent cf. 94.5 percent) indicating that, as in the laboratory, the increase in information elicited by the ECI was not accompanied by a concomitant increase in the amount of erroneous recall.

In addition to the aforementioned research, which had all been conducted in the United States by the same group of researchers, numerous independent research studies have been carried out in both the laboratory and the field (e.g. Ascherman, Mantweill & Köhnken, 1991; Clifford & George, 1996; Köhnken, Thurer & Zoberbier, 1994), the most recent of which (Stein & Memon, 2006) investigated the efficacy of the procedure in a developing country. Stein and Memon report that, compared to a "Brazilian" SI, the CI procedure again elicited significantly more correct recall with no concomitant increase in erroneous recall or drop in accuracy rate.

Thus, from an applied perspective, there is a significant body of research to support the superiority of both the original and the ECI procedure over a SI procedure (as previously described). However, the type of control/comparison interview used in CI research can vary according to the researcher's perspective. Generally, the "applied" research approach has been one of comparing the ECI with the method being employed by police interviewers at the time (as was the case in the aforementioned empirical research conducted during the development process). From this perspective, it is argued that it is only necessary for the ECI to outperform the SI. However, from a theoretical perspective, it is suggested that, because SI have been found to be less than adequate, it may be that the ECI superiority effect is simply as a result of its comparison to such poorly conducted standard interviews (Köhnken et al., 1994). Therefore, a more theoretical approach tends to be that of employing a structured interview as the control. This is a variant of the ECI procedure which is of comparable quality (matched for recall attempts, structure, question types, and communication, etc.), but minus the "cognitive" mnemonic components. Employing this more theoretical approach, research conducted in Germany (Köhnken et al., 1994; Mantwell, Köhnken & Aschermann, 1995) and the United Kingdom (Memon, Wark, Bull & Köhnken, 1997) has found similar results in terms of enhancing correct recall without a concomitant increase in errors. Although some studies have reported a slight increase in the amount of incorrect information recalled using the ECI, nevertheless, the overall accuracy rates (proportion of correct details relative to the total amount of details reported) have been found to be almost identical. Therefore, irrespective of the control interview, research has consistently found that the CI/ECI enhances the quantity of information recalled by witnesses without jeopardizing its quality.

These positive effects have also been found in several countries: the United Kingdom (e.g. Clifford & Gwyer, 1999), United States (e.g. Brock, Fisher & Cutler, 1999), Canada (e.g. Turtle, Lawrence & Leslie, 1994), Germany (e.g. Köhnken et al., 1994), and Spain (e.g. Campos & Alonso-Quecuty, 1999). Moreover, the CI/ECI has also been found to be effective across various populations (e.g. children: Akehurst, Milne & Köhnken, 2003; Holliday, 2003; children with mild learning difficulties: Robinson & McGuire, 2006; and the elderly: Wright & Holliday, 2007). For a meta-analysis, see Köhnken, Milne, Memon, and Bull (1999).

THE COGNITIVE INTERVIEW AS A PRACTICAL FORENSIC TOOL

There appears to be little doubt that the CI is an effective witness interview procedure. Furthermore, research has indicated that the procedure is well-received by those tasked with applying it (Kebbell & Milne, 1998), and, as far as the authors are aware, the use of the CI procedure has not been viewed as contentious in a court of law. Moreover, in the United Kingdom, the CI underpins the current investigative interview model and is taught to all police recruits and expert interviewers alike (*see* Griffiths & Milne, 2005 for an introduction to the tiered approach to interview training in the United Kingdom). Likewise many officers in the United States, Canada, and Australia are taught the procedure. However, despite all of this and the fact that it was designed as a practical tool, in terms of its forensic application, there is much to suggest that the CI is not regularly or fully applied.

For example, in the United Kingdom experienced police investigators (with more than ten years experience) have consistently reported that they apply some of the individual CI components they are taught far more frequently (e.g. uninterrupted free recall, establish rapport, and report everything) than they do others (e.g. CP and MRC) and that often they do not apply the CI procedure at all (e.g. Kebbell, Milne & Wagstaff, 1999;

Longford, 1996; Wright & Holliday, 2005). More recently, the authors of this chapter (Dando, Wilcock & Milne, 2008) surveyed a large sample of the least-experienced police investigators (less than two years police service), and they too found that this group of officers reported applying some of the CI components far more frequently (e.g. establish rapport, uninterrupted free recall account, explain, and report everything) than they did others (e.g. MRC, witness compatible questioning, and never guess). Moreover, not one officer reported applying the CI procedure in its entirety, despite it being the only witness interview procedure they are currently taught.

Field research investigating officers' application of the CI procedure is sparse. However, what is available appears to support the aforementioned research pertaining to officers' perceptions of their witness interview behavior. Two field studies carried out in the early 1990s (Clifford & George, 1996; George, 1991) found that none of the officers applied the CI procedure as a whole. More recently, a national evaluation of investigative interviewing in England and Wales, conducted by the second author of this chapter (Clarke & Milne, 2001), reviewed 75 "real life" witness interviews. There was no evidence at all that the CI procedure was used in 83 percent of these witness interviews. Similarly, research conducted in Canada, the United States, and Australia (e.g. Wright & Alison, 2004) suggests that a similar situation may also exist in these countries. Thus, the question arises as to why such a widely researched and generally accepted method of enhancing witness recall appears to be so infrequently applied by those whose core function is to investigate crime and to, thus, interview witnesses. It is to this question that the concluding part of this chapter now turns.

Further consideration of the aforementioned empirical research, conducted during the development process, does reveal some important contraindicators that may go some way to addressing this question. Undoubtedly, there is much agreement that the CI in its current (enhanced) form is a superior interview procedure, in terms of witness memorial performance outcomes compared with a SI. However, leaving this fact aside, it does take longer to conduct, and it is well-documented that police officers experience considerable time constraints while on duty. Equally, it is acknowledged, that the CI makes extensive cognitive demands on the interviewer (e.g. Fisher et al., 1987). For example, there are increased demands on working memory, whereby the interviewer has to store questions until an appropriate time so as not to interrupt the witness while listening attentively in order to understand each witness's organization of knowledge. Further, any pre-established sequencing of questions has to be abandoned; thus, the interviewer is required to display considerable flexibility. In addition, the CI is viewed by some police interviewers as a time-consuming and bulky procedure that is not always appropriate, especially for less-serious crime.

Equally, the type of training provided may also account, albeit in part, for the apparently patchy application of the CI. For example, in the United Kingdom, police officers are initially taught the CI during a one-week interview training course. This course combines the teaching of both suspect and witness interview techniques. Thus, the average amount of time spent teaching officers to apply the CI is just two days. It may be that this is not long enough. Certainly, recent research has indicated that officers believe the training to be insufficient to equip them with the skills necessary to confidently apply the procedure (Dando et al., 2008). This was borne out by the findings of research, conducted with novice police officers immediately post training (Dando, Wilcock & Milne, in press), which found that no officer applied or attempted to apply the procedure in its entirety. That said, many of the individual components were applied or attempted, indicating that officers had acquired some CI interview skills. Indeed, research has long indicated that CI training should be separate from suspect interview training, rather than combined (e.g. Clifford & George, 1996), because this has been found to be more effective in terms of officers' application of the procedure post training.

In sum it appears that there are many factors associated with the practical application of the CI procedure that seem to constrain its forensic application. Furthermore, these factors are both complex and interlinked. This is both unfortunate and of concern. It is of concern because, if incorrectly applied, the CI has the potential to hinder and even interfere with witness memorial performance; something the CI was designed to counter. It is unfortunate, because a great deal of time and money has been invested by the relevant government departments (i.e. Home Office) in the United Kingdom and many other countries since the early 1990s to ensure that the shortcomings associated with witness interviewing, as introduced earlier in this chapter, are addressed.

On a positive note, witness interviewing in the United Kingdom has, undoubtedly, improved since the implementation of the investigative interview model in the early 1990s. However, it is accepted that there is still room for improvement. Witness interviews have recently been highlighted as possible information leakage points along the investigative trail (ACPO, 2004), and it may be that simply ensuring that officers correctly and fully apply the CI procedure may go some way to reducing this information leakage.

In response to the findings of the aforementioned national evaluation of investigative interviewing in the United Kingdom (Clarke & Milne, 2001) and the resultant recommendations made by the second author of this chapter, ACPO is currently introducing a tiered approach to CI training (for more on tiers *see* Griffiths & Milne, 2005; Milne & Bull, in press). The CI procedure is now being taught to police officers using a building block approach within a tiered interview training framework ranging from Tier 1 to Tier 5. All police officers in England and Wales now commence their police career as a Tier 1 CI interviewer. They are taught a basic CI procedure that is commensurate not only with their limited experience and training but also with the types of witness interviews they conduct (i.e. with the witnesses of less serious crime). Should their duties and interviewing competency warrant it, officers are then able to undertake further training and can progress through the tiers, ultimately becoming a Tier 5 interview advisor (Tier 5 interviewers being the most trained and most skilled interview strategists).

There is also a considerable amount of research, currently being conducted, surrounding various modifications of the CI and its constituent components. This research is attempting to address some of the problems formerly introduced (particularly the cognitive demands the process makes of the interviewer) while retaining its superiority. For example, both of the authors of this chapter are involved in investigating how the CI might be adapted to form a short CI/frontline CI specifically for some of the least-experienced and least-trained police officers (who conduct a vast amount of witness interviews, often on a daily basis) and for situations in which police officers are under severe time constraints (e.g. Dando, Wilcock & Milne 2007; Dando, Wilcock, Milne, & Henry, 2007). Equally, much research is also being conducted concerning the suitability of the CI for use by the Criminal Law Solicitor's Association (Davis, 1997) and the U.K. National Health Service and as a method of enhancing group decision making in business (Fisher & Castano, 2007).

CONCLUSION

This chapter commenced by outlining the importance of the witness interview situation in terms of its being the primary method used by police officers to collect witness information. The cognitive interview has been described, as has the relevant theory and research pertaining to the development process. Having been adopted for use by many police forces across the world the CI represents, arguably, the most successful example of the marrying of psychological theory and research to the practical world. This is especially the case in the United Kingdom, where it underpins the current witness interview model and is taught to all police officers. Certainly, there are some problems associated with its forensic application, and these problems have been introduced and briefly discussed. That said, progress continues to be made concerning how best to ensure that the CI procedure is as user friendly as possible for all police investigators, irrespective of experience or the interview situation. However, these problems should not detract the reader from the fact that, to date, the CI is one of the most influential methods for improving witness memorial performance.

REFERENCES

ACPO. (2001). *Investigative Interviewing Strategy.* Wybosten: National Centre for Policing Excellence.

ACPO. (2004). *Management of Volume Crime.* Bramshill: National Centre for Policing Excellence.

Akehurst, L., Milne, R., and Köhnken, G. (2003). The effects of children's age and delay on recall in a cognitive and structured interview. *Psychology, Crime, & Law, 9,* 97–107.

Anderson, R.C., and Pichert, J.W. (1978). Recall of previously unrecallable information following a shift of perspective. *Journal of Learning and Verbal Behavior, 17,* 1–12.

Ascherman, E., Mantwell, M., and Köhnken, G. (1991). An independent replication of the effectiveness of the cognitive interview. *Applied Cognitive Psychology, 5,* 489–495.

Baddeley, A. (1986). *Working Memory.* New York: Oxford University Press.

Bekerian, D.A., and Conway, M.A. (1988). Everyday contexts. In G.M. Davies, and D.M. Thompson (Eds.), *Memory in Context: Context in Memory.* Chichester: John Wiley & Son.

Berresheim, A., and Weber, A. (2003). Structured witness interviewing and its effectiveness. *Kriminalistik, 57,* 757–771.

Bower, G. (1967). A multicomponent theory of a memory trace. *Psychology of Learning and Motivation, 1,* 230–325.

Brock, P., Fisher, R.P., and Cutler, B.L. (1999). Examining the cognitive interview in a double-test paradigm. *Psychology, Crime, & Law, 5,* 29–45.

Bull, R. (1992). Obtaining information expertly. *Expert Evidence, 1,* 5–12.

Campos, L., and Alonso-Quecuty, M. (1999). The cognitive interview: Much more than simply "try again." *Psychology, Crime, & Law, 5,* 47–60.

Clarke, C., and Milne, R. (2001). *National evaluation of the PEACE investigative interviewing course.* London: Home Office.

Clifford, B.R., and George, R. (1996). A field evaluation of training in three methods of witness or victim investigative interviewing. *Psychology, Crime, & Law, 2,* 231–248.

Clifford, B.R., and Gwyer, P. (1999). The effects of the cognitive interview and other methods of context reinstatement on identification. *Psychology, Crime, & Law, 5,* 61–80.

Cutler, B.L., Penrod, S.D., and Dexter, H.R. (1990). Juror sensitivity to eyewitness identification evidence, *Law and Human Behavior, 14,* 185–191.

Dando, C.J., Wilcock, R., and Milne, R. (2007). *The Cognitive Interview: The Efficacy of a Modified Mental Reinstatement of Context Procedure for Frontline Police Investigators.* Manuscript under revision.

Dando, C.J., Wilcock, R., and Milne, R. (2008). The cognitive interview: Inexperienced police officers' perceptions of their witness interviewing behavior. *Legal and Criminological Psychology, 13,* 59–70.

Dando, C.J., Wilcock, R., and Milne, R. (in press). The cognitive interview: Novice police officers' witness/victim interviewing practices. *Psychology, Crime, & Law.*

Dando, C.J., Wilcock, R., Milne, R., and Henry, L. (2007). *An adapted Cognitive Interview Procedure for Frontline Police Investigators.* Manuscript under revision.

Dent, H.R. (1991). Experimental studies of interviewing child witnesses. In D. John (Ed.), *The Suggestibility of Children's Recollections.* Washington: American Psychological Society.

Fisher, R., and Castano, P. (2007). *Cognitive Interviewing to Enhance Recall of Group Decision-Making.* Paper presented at the Society for Applied Research in Memory and Cognition (SARMAC) VII conference, July 25–29, 2007, at Bates College, Lewiston, Maine.

Fisher, R., and Geiselman, R. (1992). *Memory-Enhancing Techniques for Investigative Interviewing: The Cognitive Interview.* Springfield, IL: Charles C. Thomas.

Fisher, R.P., Geiselman, R.E., and Amador, M. (1989). Field test of the cognitive interview: Enhancing recollection of actual victims and witnesses of crime. *Journal of Applied Psychology, 74,* 722–727.

Fisher, R.P., Geiselman, RE., and Raymond, D.S. (1987). Critical analysis of police interviewing techniques. *Journal of Police Science and Administration, 15,* 177–185.

Fisher, R.P., Geiselman, R.E., Raymond, D.S., Jurkevich, L., and Warhaftig, M.L. (1987). Enhancing enhanced eyewitness memory: Refining the cognitive interview. *Journal of Police Science and Administration, 15,* 291–297.

Geiselman, R.E., and Callot, R. (1990). Reverse versus forward order recall of script based texts. *Applied Cognitive Psychology, 4,* 141–144.

Geiselman, R.E., Fisher, R.P., Cohen, G., Holland, H., and Surtes, L. (1986). Eyewitness responses to leading and misleading questions under the cognitive interview. *Journal of Police Science and Administration, 14,* 31–39.

Geiselman, R.E., Fisher, R.P., Firstenberg, I., Hutton, L., Sullivan, S.J., Avetissian, I.V., and Prosk, A.L. (1984). Enhancement of eyewitness memory: An empirical evaluation of the cognitive interview. *Journal of Police and Science Administration, 12,* 74–80.

Geiselman, R.E., Fisher, R.P., MacKinnon, DP., and Holland, H. L. (1985). Eyewitness memory enhancement in the police interview: Cognitive retrieval mnemonics versus hypnosis. *Journal of Applied Psychology, 70,* 401–412.

Geiselman, R.E., Fisher, R.P., Mackinnon, D.P., and Holland, H.L. (1986). Enhancement of eyewitness memory with the cognitive interview. *American Journal of Psychology, 99,* 354–401.

George, R. (1991). *A Field Evaluation of the Cognitive Interview.* Unpublished masters thesis, Polytechnic of East London, London, U.K.

Griffiths, A., and Milne, R. (2005). Will it all end in tiers? Police interviews with suspects in Britain. In T. Williamson (Ed.), *Investigative Interviewing. Rights, Research, Regulation.* Devon: Willan Publishing.

Holliday, R.E. (2003). Reducing misinformation effects in children with cognitive interviews: Dissociating recollection and familiarity. *Memory, 74,* 728–751

Johnston, W.A., Greenberg, S.N., and Fisher, R.P. (1970). Divided attention: A vehicle for monitoring memory processes. *Journal of Experimental Psychology, 83,* 164–171.

Kebbell, M., and Milne, R. (1998). Police officers' perceptions of eyewitness factors in forensic investigations. *Journal of Social Psychology, 138,* 323–330.

Kebbell, M., Milne, R., and Wagstaff, G. (1999). The cognitive interview: A survey of its forensic effectiveness. *Psychology, Crime, & Law, 5,* 101–115.

Köhnken, G., Milne, R., Memon, A., and Bull, R. (1999). The cognitive interview: A meta-analysis. *Psychology, Crime, & Law, 5,* 3–27.

Köhnken, G., Thurer, C., and Zoberbier, D. (1994). The cognitive interview: Are the investigators' memories enhanced too? *Applied Cognitive Psychology, 8,* 13–24.

Leippe, M.R. (1980). Effects of integrative and memorial processes on the correspondence of eyewitness accuracy and confidence. *Law and Human Behavior, 4,* 261–74.

Loftus, E.F. (1975). Leading questions and eyewitness reports. *Cognitive Psychology, 7,* 560–572.

Loftus, E.F. (1979). *Eyewitness Testimony.* Cambridge: Harvard University Press.

Longford, G.P. (1996). *The Use of the Cognitive Interview by Police Officers Trained on the National Investigative Interviewing Course.* Unpublished master's thesis, Institute of Police and Crimino-logical Studies, University of Portsmouth, Portsmouth, U.K.

McLean, M. (1995). Quality investigation? Police interviewing of witnesses. *Medicine, Science, and Law, 35,* 116–122.

Melton, A.W., and Martin, E. (1972). *Coding Processes in Human Memory.* Washington, DC: Winston.

Memon, A. (2000). Interviewing witnesses: The cognitive interview. In A. Memon & R. Bull (Eds.), *The Handbook of the Psychology of Interviewing.* Chichester: Wiley.

Memon, A., Wark, L., Bull, R., and Köhnken, G. (1997). Isolating the effects of the cognitive interview techniques. *British Journal of Psychology, 88,* 179–197.

Milne, R., and Bull, R. (2001). Investigative Interviewing: Psychology and Practice. Chichester: John Wiley & Son.

Milne, R., and Bull, R. (2006). Interviewing victims of crime, including children and people with intellectual disabilities. In M.R. Kebbell and G. Davies (Eds.), *Practical Psychology for Forensic Investigations and Prosecutions.* Chichester: Wiley.

Milne, R., and Bull, R. (in press). Investigative Interviewing: Psychology and Practice (2nd Ed.). Chichester: John Wiley & Son.

Milne, R., and Shaw, G. (1999). Obtaining witness statements: Best practice and proposals for innovation. *Medicine, Science, and the Law, 39,* 127–138.

Poole, D. A., and Lamb, M.E. (1998). Children as witnesses: The tragedy and the dilemma. In D.A. Poole and M.E. Lamb (Eds.), *Investigative Interviews with Children: A Guide for Helping Professionals.* Washington: American Psychological Association.

Robinson, J., and McGuire, J. (2006). Suggestibility and children with mild learning disabilities: The use of the cognitive interview. *Psychology, Crime & Law, 12,* 537–556.

Sanders, G.S. (1986). *The Usefulness of Eyewitness Research from the Perspective of Police Investigators.* Unpublished manuscript, State University of New York at Albany.

Sanders, G.S., and Simmons, W.L. (1983). Use of hypnosis to enhance eyewitness accuracy: Does it work? *Journal of Applied Psychology, 68,* 70–77.

Savage, S., and Milne, R. (2006). Miscarriages of justice – the role of the investigative process. In T. Newburn, T. Williamson, and A.Wright (Eds.), *Handbook of Criminal Investigation.* Cullompton: Willan.

Schacter, D.L. (1996). *Searching for Memory: The Brain, the Mind and the Past.* New York: Basic Books.

Schank, R.C., and Abelson, R.P. (1977). *Scripts, Plans, Goals, and Understanding: An Enquiry into Human Knowledge Structures.* Hillsdale: Erlbaum.

Sheenhan, P.W., Grigg, L., and McCann, T. (1984). Memory distortion following exposure to false information in hypnosis. *Journal of Abnormal Psychology, 93,* 259–265.

Shepherd, E. (1991). Ethical interviewing. *Policing, 7,* 42–60.

Stein, L.M. and Memon, A. (2006). Testing the efficacy of the cognitive interview in a developing country. *Applied Cognitive Psychology, 20,* 597–605.

Thomson, D.M., and Tulving, E. (1970). Associative encoding and retrieval: Weak and strong cues. *Journal of Experimental Psychology, 86,* 255–262.

Tulving, E. (1991). Concepts of human memory. In L.R. Squire, N.M. Weinberger, G. Lynch, and J.L. McGaugh (Eds.), *Memory: Organization and Locus of Change,* New York: Oxford University Press.

Tulving, E., and Pearlstone, Z. (1968). Availability versus accessibility of information in memory for words. *Journal of Verbal Learning and Verbal Behavior, 5,* 381–391.

Tulving, E., and Thomson, D.M. (1973). Encoding specificity and retrieval processes in episodic memory. *Psychological Review, 80,* 352–373.

Turtle, J., Lawrence, C., and Leslie, V. (1994). *Exercising Cognitive Interview Skills with Police: A Research/Training Success Story.* Paper presented at the APLS Mid-Year Conference, Santa Fe.

Visher, C.A. (1987). Incapacitation and crime control: Does a "Lock em up" strategy reduce crime? *Justice Quarterly 4*, 513–543.

Whitten, W.B., and Leonard, J.M. (1981). Directed search through autobiographical memory. *Memory and Cognition, 9*, 556–579.

Wolchover, D., and Heaton-Armstrong, A. (1996). *Confession Evidence.* London: Street and Maxwell.

Wright, A.M., and Alison, L. (2004). Questioning sequences in Canadian police interviews: Constructing and confirming the course of events. *Psychology, Crime, & Law, 10*, 137–154.

Wright, A.M., and Holliday, R.E. (2005) Police officers' perceptions of older eyewitnesses. *Legal and Criminological Psychology, 10*, 211–223.

Wright, A.M., and Holliday, R.E. (2007) Enhancing the recall of young, young-old, and old-old adults with cognitive interviews. *Applied Cognitive Psychology, 21*, 19–43.

Zander, M., and Henderson, P. (1993). Crown court study. Royal Commission on Criminal Justice. *Research Study, 19.* London: HMSO.

Chapter Eight

FORENSIC HYPNOSIS

John W. Thompson, Jr., and Alan W. Newman

Throughout history, criminal cases have been solved using a plethora of methods, including the collection of forensic evidence, confessions, capture, and eyewitness accounts. When hard evidence is not available, other more novel techniques may be sought. Hypnosis has been used for many years to attempt to enhance witness and victim memories and assist in solving crimes (Reiser, 1980). This chapter will discuss the evolution of hypnosis as a technique to obtain legal information or to enhance memory. The school of thought that led to the rise in hypnosis in the 1960s and 1970s in the United States will also be discussed. Finally, the chapter will discuss why the abuse of hypnosis in the United States' legal system has led to strict guidelines regarding its limited use in criminal cases. Lack of compliance with these guidelines may lead to Daubert-type challenges of experts in court (Moenssens, Starrs, Henderson & Inbau, 1995).

HYPNOSIS OVERVIEW

Hypnosis can be defined as that state or condition in which an individual is able to respond to appropriate suggestions by experiencing alterations of perception, memory, or mood (Orne & Dinges, 1993). Hypnosis has been used as a method of treating a variety of psychiatric conditions since the early 1800s and was pivotal in the early work of many noted psychiatrists (Wong, 1993). The role that suggestion plays in the hypnotic phenomenon was studied by Hippolyte Bernheim, who used hypnosis with many of his patients as a means of suggesting that pathological symptoms would cease to be problems (Bernheim, 1973). Bernheim's observations differed from those

169

of Jean Charcot, who viewed the ability to be hypnotized as evidence of neuropathology in patients with hysteria (Bernheim, 1973). Sigmund Freud and Josef Breuer utilized hypnosis not as a method of suggesting that symptoms resolve but as a way of accessing traumatic early life events that they perceived to be at the root of the patient's problems (Bernheim, 1973; Wong, 1993). Although Freud abandoned the use of hypnosis by 1896 for other methods, hypnosis was instrumental in shaping his beliefs that hysterical phenomena were due to trauma, thinking that eventually led to his views on repression. Hypnosis has since been applied to the treatment of numerous psychiatric problems and has been recognized as a therapeutic modality by the American Medical Association since 1958 (American Medical Association, 1986).

USES OF HYPNOSIS IN FORENSIC INVESTIGATIONS

The free recall of memories may be hampered by the stress or anxiety associated with being a witness of a crime. An eyewitness of a murder may feel extremely anxious when reporting the details of a crime. An assault victim may also be unable to provide important details that would lead to the solution of a crime secondary to feelings of panic or posttraumatic stress. Memory problems may also affect those accused of a crime, who may have difficulty remembering details that could exonerate them or provide mitigating factors helpful in their defense (Orne, 1979). Police have long been thwarted by faulty leads by poor witnesses, and the absence of reliable witnesses has led to many unsolved cases. This problem, which Hibbard calls the nemesis of the law enforcement officer, creates a demand for better ways of improving eyewitness recall (Hibbard & Worring, 1980). Hypnosis was one method to address this problem that gained increased popularity in the 1960s and 1970s.

Despite claims that hypnosis is effective in improving memory, the exact mechanism of how this actually occurs is unclear. Although some think that hypnosis simply relaxes a witness in order to enhance his or her ability to report events, others view that hypnosis somehow allows for the recovery of memories that have been repressed by trauma (Loftus & Loftus, 1980; Monaghan, 1980; Reiser, 1980).

There are three common uses of hypnosis in a criminal investigation. One use of hypnosis is to enhance the memory of an accused defendant in a criminal case about events surrounding the crime. Although hypnosis may be used by the defense team to generate evidence to help exculpate their client, it could also be used by the police or prosecutors to generate evidence that would lead to a conviction. Second, hypnosis could also be used with eyewitnesses to allow them to provide details concerning the behavior or physical appearance of a perpetrator. This might be done in anticipation of viewing a police lineup or in assisting a police sketch artist. A third use of hypnosis would be to assist in the generation of leads for forensic investigators.

In the third example just mentioned, physical evidence independent from the information recalled under hypnosis can be obtained and evaluated on its own merit, whereas the information generated by hypnosis in the first two cases replaces the evidence. If hypnosis is not a valid method of obtaining consistent and accurate memories, the usefulness of eyewitness information generated by hypnosis is highly suspect. The fact that individual cases have been solved by the discovery of investigatory leads associated with the use of hypnosis does not necessarily mean that hypnosis is a valid and consistent method of obtaining evidence.[1]

Advocates of Hypnosis in Criminal Investigations

Several guidebooks have been written with the goal of providing detailed instruction and theory to police investigators for their use of hypnosis as an aid to criminal investigations (Gerber & Schroeder, 1972; Hibbard & Worring, 1980; Monaghan, 1980). Many of these guidebooks were written by police investigators and hypnotists who based their views on experiences accumulated in investigations over many years (Hibbard & Warring, 1880; Reiser, 1980). These police-oriented writers cite numerous examples of the usefulness of hypnosis as a tool for investigation. Hibbard cited studies from the Los Angeles Police Department and the New York Police Department from the late 1970s, suggesting that hypnosis provided valuable new information more than 65 percent of the time (Hibbard & Warring, 1880). The rapid dissemination of hypnosis in police investigations in the 1960s led to widespread use in many courts of law, with many convictions resulting from eyewitness memory recovered with hypnosis (Loftus, 1979).

A consistent theme found throughout these guides is the view that all memories are stored intact in the brain but are frequently inaccessible due to repression. Hypnosis is offered as a way to lift the repression in order to access these memories. Martin Reiser (1980), Director of Behavioral Sciences Services for the Los Angeles Police Department, illustrates this view in the *Handbook of Investigative Hypnosis*:

> The subconscious mind is alert and on duty 24 hours a day, seven days a week; it never sleeps. . . . Cheek's work in recovering memories around the birth experience suggests that both pre and perinatal experiences are recorded reflexively by the active subconscious of the baby. (Reiser, 1980, p. 11)

---

1. For example, psychics have been used by police to solve crimes. Although some crimes have reportedly been solved after the use of psychics, there has been no demonstrated scientific evidence that psychic powers should be constituted as evidence (Randi, 1996).

Reiser considers the cause of poor memory in eyewitnesses to be due to repression and dissociation which functions to ward off emotionally disturbing memories (Reiser, 1980) Monaghan also shows belief in the view that memory is recorded intact:

> Theoretically, human memory is perfect. The infallibility of memory is demonstrated over and over by facts revealed through hypnotic age regression. . . . Amnesias represent a separation between conscious and unconscious, and a failure in communications between the two. (Monaghan, 1980, p. 52)

Furthermore, Hibbard and Worring state:

> most authorities on hypnosis and researchers of human behavior believe that everything a human being takes in through the five senses is permanently recorded in the brain . . . [and] these experts also agree, however, that this stored information can largely and accurately be retrieved through hypnosis. (Hibbard & Worring, 1980)

The reported causal link between repression and amnesia in crime eyewitnesses is a consistent theme in these manuals (Bragin, 1981; Hibbard & Worring, 1980; O'Hara & O'Hara, 1994). Some of these views are consistent with contemporaneous psychoanalytic literature on repression. Infantile amnesia, as described in the American Psychoanalytic Association's *Psychoanalytic Terms and Concepts* (Moore & Fine, 1990), represents the ego's defensive effort to deal with early life events and reactions that would otherwise be traumatic. Through the process of repression, events, ideas, and affects involved in such experiences become unconscious (Moore & Fine, 1990). Rather than the lack of memory of childhood events being due to an immature nervous system or ordinary forgetting, the American Psychoanalytic Association says:

> Though it is often thought of as normal forgetting attributable to the immaturity of the child's mind, infantile amnesia represents the ego's defensive effort to deal with early-life events and reactions that would otherwise be traumatic. (Moore & Fine, 1990, p. 13)

The psychoanalytic literature also supports the view that memories of traumas sustained during adulthood can also be lost due to the effect of repression. According to Wolberg:

> . . . even in adulthood, intensely traumatic experiences may shock the organism into a revival of the mechanism of repression. This move is motivated by a need to ward off a threat to the self. There are no better examples of this than those seen in the neuroses of war in which traumatic incidents may be blotted from the mind. (Wolberg, 1988, p. 739)

Hypnosis is listed as one of several methods that can be used to recover such memories (Wolberg, 1975, 1988).

There are some important differences between the psychoanalytic literature reviewed and the claims made in the works by and for police investigators. Although the police guides are very definitive in their views on repression and the use of hypnosis to lift it (Monaghan, 1980), Wolberg notes that:

> It is essential not to take memories and experiences recounted in the trance at face value. The productions elaborated by a person during hypnosis generally are a fusion of real experiences and fantasies, (Wolberg, 1975, p. 247).

This blend of fact and fantasy may not be as much a concern in a therapeutic context, where "we are more concerned with a patient's ideas about his past rather than what actually happened in the past" but could pose dangers when used to uncover the truth, as would be desired in a forensic setting (Wolberg, 1988). Despite these differences, the reviewed works for police investigators clearly intend to frame their works in the context of psychoanalytic theory.

In addition to citing psychoanalytic theories of repression, many advocates of the view that all memories are stored permanently in the brain cite the works of neurosurgeon Wilder Penfield (Hibbard & Worring, 1980; Loftus & Loftus, 1980). Penfield was a neurosurgeon who specialized in removing damaged areas in the brains of epileptic patients. During stimulation of brain areas with an electrode, Penfield observed that certain types of stimulation caused patients to hear voices and song, and even to experience the sensation of reexperiencing a past event (Loftus & Loftus, 1980). Penfield described the process as follows:

> When, by chance, the neurosurgeon's electrode activates past experience, that experience unfolds progressively, moment by moment. This is a little like the performance of a wire recorder or a strip of cinematographic film on which are registered all those things of which the individual was once aware, the things he selected for his attention in that interval of time. Absent from it are the sensations he ignored, the talk he did not heed. (Penfield & Roberts, 1959, p. 53)

Penfield believed that every detail in awareness left a permanent mark on the brain, and his work was widely cited in psychology textbooks and the media, leading to what has been called the videorecorder model of memory (Loftus & Loftus, 1980).

Survey research by Elizabeth Loftus in the late 1970s gives evidence of the widespread acceptance of the videorecorder model view of memory during that time (Loftus & Loftus, 1980). This survey showed that 69 percent of nonpsychologists believed that everything learned is stored in the mind and potentially accessible by hypnosis while 23 percent supported the view that some memories may be permanently lost from memory and not recoverable by special techniques. Interestingly, 84 percent of psychologists who were given the same survey believed that all information is stored in long-term memory. Loftus noted that many of the psychologists surveyed told her that their views on memory were shaped by knowledge of Penfield's work, as well as their views on memory recovered by analysis, hypnosis, and other therapeutic techniques (Loftus & Loftus, 1980).

Methods Used by Police Investigators

Two predominant techniques are described in the police literature to help obtain memories: the age-regression technique and hypermnesia by direct suggestion technique (Orne, 1979). Orne describes age-regression as the most common technique used in hypnosis. Using this method, the hypnotist induces hypnosis and suggests that the subject will return to an earlier age. Monaghan demonstrates this technique as follows:

> The next time I speak to you, you will be at a very happy time and place, and you will be four-years-old. You are going back to a time and place when you were four-years-old. You will be able to tell me everything that you see and hear, without interfering in any way with your recall or your relaxation. (Monaghan, 1980, p. 51)

In the case of age-regression for crime witnesses, the regression goes back to the time that the crime occurred.

One technique used as an adjunct during age-regression is the television technique. Reiser describes this technique in the following way:

> While the subject views the crime event on the imaginary television screen during the TV technique, the hypnoinvestigator, as desired, can suggest that the film will go into slow motion, stop completely or reverse. The subject can also be told that when the camera zooms in on the suspect's face, the frame will freeze and although there was originally only a short time to look at the suspect, there will now be all the time in the world to look at the close-up on TV and to describe every feature very vividly, and accurately. (Reiser, 1980, p. 117)

This technique, acording to Reiser, is particularly useful in obtaining details from street signs, license plates, and other factual information.

In addition to age-regression, another technique involves hypermnesia (enhanced memory) by direct suggestions. With this technique, the hypnotist gives the subject a direct suggestion to do something to enhance the memory. A frequent suggestion given to the subject is that he or she will remember what was discussed during hypnosis upon awakening (Orne, 1979; Tayloe, 1995). This particular suggestion is quite relevant. If details can only be recalled while the subject is under hypnosis and forgotten when awake, the ability of the subject to testify on the memory is limited.

Although Hibbard provides warnings to police investigators about possible pitfalls in administering hypnosis in an investigatory setting, few of the guides for police investigators list potential hazards, despite a growing body of evidence of problems that can arise when recovering memories with hypnosis (Hibbard & Worring, 1980).

HYPNOTIC MEMORY THEORY

Constructive Model of Memory

As discussed earlier, advocates for forensic hypnosis utilize two major techniques: age-regression and direct suggestion. The age-regression technique, particularly when used with the imagery of watching a TV and being able to go into slow motion, stop completely, or reverse, strongly suggests the idea that memory is indeed like a videorecorder (Reiser, 1980). Orne and others have directly challenged this model of memory (Orne, 1979).

In reference to age-regression, Orne notes that the appearance of regression does not guarantee that actual regression is occurring. One study done by Orne and colleagues involved the regression of a group to elementary school age. Orne noted that when the information obtained by the regressions was checked with verifiable data, some interesting findings were noticed:

> The subjects would describe their classmates so vividly and with such conviction that we were surprised indeed to find, when we went to the trouble of checking the actual school records, that some of these individuals had not been members of the subject's class; nor was the factual recall better than that of unhypnotized controls. (Orne, 1979, p. 317)

Orne warns that questioning about specific details (such as when subjects are told to freeze on an image as if they are watching a TV) puts pressure on the subject to provide information for which few, if any, actual memories are available. This situation may jog the subject's memory and produce some increased recall, but it will also cause him or her to fill in details that are plausible but consist of memories or fantasies from other times (Orne, 1979). This can be likened to confabulation in the alcoholic patient with short-term memory loss. Laurence reports that if an individual is asked to zoom in on an image that, in the original experience, the retina could not resolve, there is no other source but fantasy for enhanced detail (Laurence & Perry, 1983). This task requires the subject to see something beyond his or her capacity and is a powerful and indirect suggestion to hallucinate.

Fantasy may not be the only source of recovered detail. Orne warns that when the subject is given guided instructions during this kind of questioning, such a procedure maximizes the potential input of the hypnotist about what is wanted, making it even more likely that the subject's memories will more closely resemble the hypnotist's prior conceptions than would ordinarily be the case (Orne, 1979). Although acknowledging the success of using this technique to recall license plate numbers, Orne notes that many license plate numbers recalled under hypnosis have led to cars that could not have been involved in the alleged crime.

The Videotape Model of Memory Refuted

In addition to providing evidence supporting a constructive view of memory, memory researchers have challenged some of the conclusions derived by supporters of the videotape model of memory. As discussed before, the primary evidence supporting the videotape model includes the psychoanalytic theory of repression, case studies of memory recovered by therapeutic techniques (like hypnosis and analysis), spontaneous recovery of memories, and the experiments of Wilder Penfield (Penfield & Roberts, 1959).

Despite the vividness of memories recovered via analysis, hypnosis, or spontaneous recall, it does not necessarily follow that memories retrieved by these methods provide evidence of the permanent storage of memory. A question rarely asked by the proponents of the videotape model is "Did the event in the memory actually occur?" In the absence of independent corroboration of the memories reported, a report of a memory does not provide proof that the memory is an accurate depiction of truth, or that it even occurred (Loftus, 1993). Therefore, even when independent corroboration is available, that does not prove that what is described by the patient is an actual memory. Additionally, even if it can be shown that a specific recovered memory is accurate, it does not prove that: (1) every memory from birth to death is recorded in the brain and (2) these memories can accurately be recovered by psychiatric techniques.

The view that memories from birth are stored in the brain and are recoverable is mentioned in many texts written for police investigators and has been advocated by some recovered memory therapists (*Frontline*, 1995; Monaghan, 1980; Reiser, 1980). For example, a *Frontline* documentary demonstrated scenes from actual age-regression sessions, where one client was regressed all the way to a previous life, and another client was regressed to a preimplantation embryo, where she allegedly was temporarily stuck in the fallopian tube, causing her future psychiatric problems (*Frontline*, 1995). From a scientific perspective, the view that one could have memories from a stage in development during which there is no nervous system appears untenable, and the concept of past lives is simply untestable by scientific methods. This exposes a major problem with some of the thinking of exact-copy memory advocates: If one assumes that the memories recovered from past lives or prenatal development are invalid, how can we rely on the validity of memories obtained when the same age-regression techniques are used for other purposes, such as recovering memories in crime witnesses?

Another problem with the videorecorder view of memory is its reliance on untestable psychoanalytic concepts. Many proponents of the videorecorder model note that their views are supported by the theory of repression. Consistency with the theory of repression, however, hardly proves the claims of the videorecorder model unless there is better evidence that repression itself is a valid concept. One criticism of the scientific status of repression is that:

> . . . despite some incredibly innovative attempts, the psychoanalytic defense mechanism of repression has never been clearly proven in the laboratory. In addition, there are those who believe that it cannot be. Most psychoanalytic notions are generally unfalsifiable. That is, no scientific evidence can clearly refute or prove the existence of repression. Given the definition of repression as forgetting without conscious knowledge that the material is forgotten, laboratory proof of the phenomenon is likely impossible. It is also difficult to imagine an experiment that could provide conclusive proof of repression. (Earleywine & Gann, 1995, p. 1101)

Although the psychoanalytic theory is accepted in many clinical settings, numerous problems occur when attempting to find scientific evidence to support these concepts.

Unlike the reliance on unverifiable case studies and theories of repression, Penfield's experiments on electrically stimulated brains appeared to some to provide strong evidence for the permanent storage of memories. Loftus' review of his data, however, challenges this conclusion (Loftus & Loftus, 1980). She notes that no attempts were made by Penfield to corroborate any of the memories with verifiable events, and only 3 percent of his patients who underwent electrical stimulation experienced phenomena more complex than hearing music or voices or seeing a familiar face or object. Loftus and others conclude that the experiences are more consistent with reconstructed experiences, such as dreams (Loftus & Loftus, 1980).

It is important to remember that Penfield's studies were on patients with tumors and epilepsy, especially since the phenomena that Penfield described sound suspiciously similar to the hallucinations experienced by many patients with partial complex seizures. According to neurologist David Kaufman:

> tumors, strokes, and other structural lesions can produce partial elementary, frontal lobe, or complex seizures with visual symptoms. These hallucinations are seen in both eyes and can even appear in an hemianopic area. They range from simple geometric forms in partial simple seizures to detailed visions accompanied by sounds, thoughts, emotions, and characteristically, impairment of consciousness in partial complex seizures. (Kaufman, 1995)

The view that Penfield might be inducing hallucinatory phenomena is not entertained in his works or by advocates of his theories. The evidence that Penfield's work demonstrates the permanent storage of memories in the brain remains unpersuasive.

CRITICISM AND CONCERNS ABOUT FORENSIC HYPNOSIS

Despite the widespread use of hypnosis to solve crimes and prosecute cases in the 1970s, concerns about the problems of using hypnosis for finding the truth are hardly new. The ability of hypnosis to suggest false memories was recognized by Bernheim in the ninteenth century; he referred to the phenomenon as a retroactive hallucination (Bernheim, 1973).

Wong (1993) notes that Freud utilized hypnosis in his early practice but abandoned it as a temporary fix that frequently encouraged acting out to please the hypnotist. Controlled experiments as early as 1932 demonstrated that hypnotized subjects had an increase in the number of memories reported, both accurate and confabulated, than did nonhypnotized subjects (Orne, 1979).

In part due to concerns generated by the increased use of hypnosis in forensic settings in the 1960s, there was a marked increase in the amount of scrutiny given the claims promoted by advocates of hypnosis for memory enhancement. During the 1970s, a considerable body of research was performed that provided evidence that the effect of hypnosis on memory is substantially different from what was previously thought (Loftus & Loftus, 1980; Orne, 1979; Putnam, 1979).

The view of memory postulated by many police investigators, advocates of the concept of repression, and others has been given a variety of names, including the videotape model, the exact copy theory, or the implicit theory of memory (Loftus & Loftus, 1980; Putnam, 1979). This view suggests not only that all information is stored permanently in the brain but also that subsequent information coexists with but does not alter the original memories.

In contrast to the videorecorder model of memory, some memory researchers have postulated that, rather than working like a videorecorder, memories are stored in a manner that allows them to be reconstructed at a later time (Putnam, 1979). This model, which implies that memories can be altered by a variety of factors subsequent to the original memory, is supported by a considerable body of research.

Several concerns can be raised about the use of suggestions by the hypnotist. The most obvious is that being told to provide details when none are present may lead to confabulation by the subject (Orne, 1979). Furthermore, the amount of knowledge the hypnotist has about the case can affect the subject in a variety of ways. Putnam's studies on subjects who were hypnotized after viewing an accident involving a car and a bicycle showed that although there was no difference between hypnotized and nonhypnotized subjects in answering objective, nonleading questions, hypnotized subjects were significantly more likely to make errors when given leading questions (Putnam, 1979). Loftus reports many studies showing how the wording of questions, even in nonhypnotized subjects, makes a large difference in what kind of answer is obtained from the subject (Loftus, 1979).

The risk of leading questions is particularly high when the hypnotist is the investigator and is aware of the details of an alleged case (*New Jersey v. Hurd,* 1980). In some documented cases, the hypnotist suggested distinguishing features of the prime suspect or asked if specific suspects were present (Kirkwood, 1968; Loftus, 1979; *New Jersey v. Hurd,* 1980).

The hypnotist may use suggestions to accomplish other goals. For example, one hypnotist recommends suggesting that the subject will confess if he is guilty (Bragin, 1981). While acknowledging that most courts do not admit confessions made during hypnosis, Bragin sees no problem with a confession that occurs once the hypnotic session has ended (Bragin, 1981). He recommends a posthypnotic suggestion that intimates that bad feelings will result if the subject keeps the crime to himself, and good feelings will result if the subject "lets it out" (i.e. confesses). Bragin does not discuss the effect such a suggestion would have on the defendant's Fifth Amendment rights or the danger such a suggestion could play on an innocent defendant, particularly if administered by a police hypnotist who might have preconceived views about the subject's guilt.

Other research on hypnosis exposes its potential dangers when used in an investigative setting. Orne summarizes these dangers as follows:

> Hypnosis has no utility to assure the truthfulness of statements since, particularly in a forensic context, subjects may simulate hypnosis and are able to willfully lie even in deep hypnosis; most troublesome, actual memories cannot be distinguished from confabulations either by the subject or by the hypnotist without full and independent corroboration. (Orne, 1979, p. 311)

Orne further adds that:

> . . . hypnosis may readily cause the subject to confabulate the person who is suspected into his hypnotically enhanced memories. These pseudomemories, originally developed in hypnosis, may come to be accepted by the subject as his actual recall of the original events; they are then remembered with great subjective certainty and reported with conviction. Such circumstances can create convincing, apparently objective eyewitnesses rather than facilitating actual recall. (Orne, 1979, p. 311)

This belief in the certainty of pseudomemories was reinforced by the research findings of Laurence, who implanted false memories of having been awakened by loud noises in thirteen of twenty-seven highly hypnotizable subjects (Laurence & Perry, 1983). Six of these thirteen subjects were absolutely certain that the suggested event occurred. This phenomenon, warned psychiatrist David Spiegel, could lead to the creation of the "honest liar," a witness who asserts pseudomemories as truth in the courtroom (Orne, Dinges & Orne, 1990).

Given the previous arguments, it can be demonstrated that hypnosis, although testable, is not a reliable and valid method of obtaining information from witnesses or refreshing witness testimony.

REBUTTALS TO RESEARCH FINDINGS ON HYPNOSIS

After the increase in scientific evidence challenging the validity of hypnotically recovered memories and the subsequent investigative guidelines and court changes that followed, some proponents of forensic hypnosis offered rebuttals. These rebuttals typically followed two patterns: (1) criticism of the generalization of laboratory experiments to actual patients and (2) a reliance on case studies demonstrating the usefulness of forensic hypnosis in solving cases.

Criticism of Research Findings

Butler and Spiegel (1997) list several criticisms that can be applied to most of the research studies on hypnosis and memory. For example, (1) laboratory events used in memory research tend to be artificial (slides, movies, staged events) and might not affect the subjects the same way that a real event would. (2) Laboratory events are intrinsically nontraumatic. Traumatic events may affect memory differently than nontraumatic events do. (3) Laboratory studies of memory tend to test memory hours to days after the initial stimulus, not years as frequently occurs in many real-life cases. (4) Many of the laboratory studies, especially those using college students as subjects, rely on a young and well-educated population that may not directly generalize to the population at-large (Butler & Spiegel, 1997).

Hibbard acknowledges Loftus' findings concerning evidence that leading or suggestive questions decrease the accuracy of memory and convince a witness of the truthfulness of his or her memories, but he makes the interesting comment that by "regressing the witnesses or victim to the crime event he neutralizes, bypasses, or obviates any memory alteration or contamination subsequent to the event" (Hibbard & Worring, 1980). His view provides a good illustration of the belief that memories are laid down chronologically like recordings on a videotape, where even if contamination occurs in the future, age-regression can simply "rewind the tape" to a point in time before the contamination occurred. This view, unsupported by any cited evidence, assumes that age-regression produces unaltered, uncontaminated memories and does not consider the possibility that it is precisely during the age-regression that memory can be altered by suggestion (Putnam, 1979).

Case Studies Promoting the Usefulness of Forensic Hypnosis

Even when advocates for the liberal use of forensic hypnosis concede some of the findings discovered in a research setting, they frequently argue that evidence from case studies provides proof of the concept of repression and demonstrates the usefulness of forensic hypnosis. Tayloe (1995), a psychiatrist who practices forensic hypnosis for the courts, provides evidence of this thinking. Tayloe notes that with forensic hypnosis the critical question is whether or not the concept of repressed memories is valid, and if the memories are valid, can they be accurately recalled through hypnosis. His "proof" is found in the statement: "That psychologically traumatic events can be repressed from conscious recall is incontrovertible. The weight of case histories describing verifiable repression is too heavy to support any other conclusions" (Tayloe, 1995, p. 26). Unfortunately, one case he cites is the George Franklin murder trial, a case that readily lends itself to a conclusion opposite to that of Tayloe's.[2] Tayloe also provided an example of a man he hypnotized who had no memory of shooting himself and killing his wife. During the hypnotic session, Tayloe told the subject (Mr. Bains), "You will be able to remember any of this story that is helpful to you, but will be unable to remember anything that is not helpful or would be harmful to you" (Tayloe, 1995, p. 28).

Although this did not resolve the subject's amnesia, Tayloe later "successfully" age-regressed the subject with hypnosis, and he then testified that the death of the wife was an accidental shooting. Tayloe concluded that since some of the details of the subject's recovered memories were consistent with physical evidence at the scene, the case provided evidence of the validity of hypnotically recovered memories.

Unfortunately, Dr. Tayloe did not consider another possibility: The fact that the subject reported details consistent with the physical evidence at the scene may have been because he never forgot them; in other words, his amnesia may have simply been malingering. The memory "recovered" by hypnosis just happened to be one that helped exculpate the defendant of a first-degree murder charge. Rather than questioning whether malingering was the cause of the alleged memory loss, Tayloe believed that the amnesia was genuine because "in this case, the setting lends credence to the creation of amnesia as a defense mechanism against severe emotional trauma. Mrs.

---

2. George Franklin was convicted of murder in 1990 solely on the basis of testimony by his daughter Eileen, who alleged her memories of seeing the crime were repressed for more than twenty years (Loftus, 1993). The jury was impressed by the detailed nature of Eileen's memory, but the case was overturned on appeal on the grounds that the trial judge refused to admit evidence that the verifiable details Eileen provided were in fact available in newspaper accounts of the crime (*Skeptic*, 1996). Eileen, who underwent hypnosis to recover memories, also "remembered" other crimes allegedly committed by her father, for which he was ultimately cleared.

Bain's death was an accident without premeditation or financial gain" (Tayloe, 1995). This explanation, however, is directly contradicted by Tayloe's own report that immediately before the killing Mr. Bains, who had suspected his wife of being unfaithful, had just seen his wife in her car with a male friend.

Mutter (1990) also challenges the results of memory research by citing cases in which hypnosis was perceived to be useful in investigations. Like Tayloe, Mutter's case examples ignore the possibility of malingering or other explanations.[3] The role of the expert is particularly relevant in this context. If one can lie under hypnosis, the defendant can not only feign amnesia for certain details but also recover an exculpatory explanation that might not be believed if offered by the defendant but will be believed if pronounced as accurate by a forensic expert.

Some problems with relying on case studies are that (1) it is difficult to generalize from individual instances, (2) cases are rarely validated with physical evidence supporting the claims made by the subject, and (3) cases involving memories are not controlled; therefore, it is not possible to know if the subject would have recalled the repressed memory with a different technique or spontaneously. It is impossible to know the qualitative differences between memories recalled by hypnosis and memories recalled by other techniques because each patient has different life experiences, and once memories are recovered by one method, it is impossible to take the patient back in time to his or her previous amnestic state and compare the different methods for accuracy.

GUIDELINES AND WARNINGS ON THE USE OF FORENSIC HYPNOSIS

As a consequence of concerns about the dangers associated with the liberal use of hypnosis in legal settings, several official statements were issued. The Federal Bureau of Investigation (FBI) revised its 1968 guidelines on hypnosis in 1979, requiring authorization to use hypnosis in FBI cases and mandating that certain safeguards be in place, including the recording of hypnotic sessions (Ault, 1979). The International Society of Hypnosis and the Society for Clinical and Experimental Hypnosis issued identical statements

---

3. The *a priori* belief in the validity of repression is a common theme in rebuttals to the research findings. Watkins (1989) demonstrates this faith in the validity of repression, saying "the forensic examiner, unlike a researcher, must often lift a psychogenic amnesia for a traumatic event before hypermnesia takes place." Although critical of laboratory methods examining memory, Watkins makes no attempt to examine evidence supporting the concept of "psychogenic amnesia" or "repression."

acknowledging alarm at the increase in the use of hypnosis by laypeople, particularly police officers using hypnosis as a part of a police investigation (International Society of Hypnosis, 1979). These resolutions acknowledged the dangers of accepting statements made under hypnosis at face value and warned of the effect that police biases can have on the memories of hypnotized subjects.

Orne formulated his own guidelines, which had a profound influence on the courts and contributed to the recommendations ultimately promulgated by the American Medical Association's Council of Scientific Affairs (American Medical Association, 1986; *New Jersey v. Hurd,* 1980; Orne, 1979). These guidelines are summarized as follows:

1. Hypnosis should be carried out by a psychiatrist or psychologist with special training in its use. He should not be informed about the facts of the case verbally; rather, he should receive a written memorandum outlining whatever facts he is to know, carefully avoiding any other communication which might affect this opinion.

2. All contact of the psychiatrist or psychologist with the individual to be hypnotized should be videotaped from the moment they meet until the entire interaction is completed. The casual comments that are passed before or after hypnosis are every bit as important to get on tape as the hypnotic session itself. . . . Prior to the induction of hypnosis, a brief evaluation of the patient should be carried out and the psychiatrist or psychologist should then elicit a detailed description of the facts as the witness or victim remembers them. . . . Only after this has been completed should the hypnotic session be initiated. The psychiatrist or psychologist should strive to avoid adding any new elements to the witness's description of his experience, including those that he had discussed in his wake state, lest he inadvertently alter the nature of the witness's memories.

3. No one other than the psychiatrist or psychologist and the individual to be hypnotized should be present in the room before and during the hypnotic session. . . .

4. Because the interactions that have preceded the hypnotic session may well have a profound effect on the sessions themselves, tape recordings of prior interrogations are important to document that a witness has not been implicitly or explicitly cued pertaining to certain information which might then be reported for apparently the first time by the witness during hypnosis. (pp. 335–336)

Although Orne (1997) proposed these guidelines to provide minimal safeguards for the admission of hypnotic testimony in the courts, he eventually concluded that hypnotically refreshed testimony is unreliable and advocated its use only when a defendant's constitutional rights were in jeopardy (Orne et al., 1990; Udolf, 1990).

IS HYPNOSIS A SCIENTIFIC METHOD THAT CAN BE USED IN THE COURTS IN LIGHT OF *DAUBERT*?

The controversy over the scientific status of hypnosis provides an illustration of the conflict that can occur when well-established beliefs of clinicians and investigators are challenged by experimental research. The conflicting views on the nature of hypnosis are explained by John Watkins as a conflict between credulous believers who "feel that skeptics are rigid and naive concerning the complexities of human behavior" and skeptics who hold that "believers are soft and easily persuaded by small, uncontrolled samples" (Watkins, 1989). Furthermore, he adds that whereas skeptics tend to be researchers in academia, the believers tend to be clinicians who "wouldn't be good therapists (if) they didn't believe in the phenomena which they evoke and use."

Although both could be characterized as credulous believers, clinicians have different motivations than investigators have. The clinician is interested in relieving the pain and suffering of a patient; the investigator's goal is to obtain the truth. In that sense, the research on hypnosis popularized in the 1970s and 1980s was not intended to challenge the clinical utility of hypnosis as a means to resolve psychiatric problems. Rather, the research was clearly intended to question the underlying beliefs associated with hypnosis, in other words, the presumption that memories obtained by hypnosis are true.

Unfortunately, it is not clear that this work has had a substantial impact on the practices of those who train police investigators. Despite the previous twenty years of research, the 1994 edition of Fundamentals of Criminal Investigation by O'Hara makes an even more dramatic claim of the recording powers of the mind than that of older police guidebooks, saying that:

> . . . at the subconscious level, the mind continuously records images even while the subject is sleeping, intoxicated, or his mind is otherwise inattentive. The subconscious serves as a storehouse of sensory impressions that, when accessed, will supply the hidden details of a crime. (O'Hara & O'Hara, 1994, p. 120)

Nevertheless, even if some police investigators have not followed the scientific debate, there is little question that the controversy over the scientific status of hypnosis has resulted in changes in the way hypnosis is treated by the courts (Orne et al., 1990). Testimony obtained as a result of hypnosis is considered inadmissible in almost all cases, due not only to the unreliability of such information but also to the risk that such testimony poses on a defendant's constitutional rights (Newman & Thompson, 1999).

CONCLUSION

Investigatory forensic hypnosis is based on a well-intentioned but scientifically untenable position, that is, that detailed memories could be accurately retrieved and utilized in criminal investigations. Courts have recognized the inherent risk that hypnotically elicited memories, although anecdotally helpful in some cases, could pose to the rights of a defendant in a criminal case.

Forensic hypnosis was based on untested theories of repression and misdirected conclusions drawn from the pioneering neurosurgical work of Penfield. The work of Orne, Loftus, and other researchers has identified the pitfalls associated with relying on hypnotically retrieved memories, influencing many courts to follow suit in denying the admissibility of such hypnotically derived memories.

An unfortunate irony of the scientific debate over the validity of hypnotically refreshed memories is that the scientific and judicial discrediting of refreshed memories in a criminal setting actually preceded the more recent and well-publicized abuse of patients by therapists utilizing "recovered memory therapy." These cases have involved the retrieval of memories of alleged sexual abuse and, in more dramatic cases, "memories" of ritual satanic cult abuse (Nathan & Snedeker, 1995). Advocates for the use of hypnosis in criminal cases have also tended to support the theory of repression in child abuse cases. The quest by many zealous therapists to uncover "repressed memories" of childhood sexual abuse through the use of memory recovery techniques has led to a spate of lawsuits detailing the invalidity of these abuse claims. Had the therapists involved been better informed by the discussion involving the use of forensic hypnosis, many potentially abusive treatments and related legal actions may well have been avoided.

A recent and perhaps more interesting debate is whether or not the use of forensic hypnosis in the courts could lead to an expert being excluded for failure to meet the Daubert standard of admissibility (*Daubert v. Merrell Dow Pharmaceuticals*, 1993). Although the Daubert case was originally a civil case, it places the trial judge as the ultimate gatekeeper of the admissibility of expert testimony. According to *Daubert*, the expert testimony proffered must be based on a reliable body of scientific knowledge. This reliability standard must be grounded in scientific methods and meet professional standards of reliability, validity, and acceptability within the field. Since *Daubert* applies to scientific experts and the methods they employ, the challenge could be introduced when an expert uses hypnosis in the course of his or her evaluation of the defendant in a criminal case. Although the use of hypnosis for these purposes may be testable, it is not a reliable and valid means of enhancing memory of victim and witness testimony, as demonstrated by the lack of consistent scientific evidence in its favor.

By the time that the *Daubert* decision was made in 1993, forensic hypnosis as a mechanism to recover memory was already in decline due to the influence of earlier court decisions. Whereas the 1980 decision *New Jersey v. Hurd* (1980) imposed limitations on the admissibility of hypnotically refreshed testimony, other cases such as the 1982 California case *People v. Shirley,* rendered the use of hypnotically refreshed memory inadmissible in most cases (Newman & Thompson, 1999). Although the U.S. Supreme Court acknowledged that a defendant could not be barred from testifying on his or her own behalf, despite having been previously hypnotized, the impact of the Hurd and Shirley cases significantly decreased the likelihood that a prosecution would benefit from the utilization of hypnotically refreshed memory (Newman & Thompson, 1999; Udolf, 1980). The trend of general inadmissibility of most hypnotically refreshed testimony has become the norm in most jurisdictions (Webert, 2003), and New Jersey itself shifted away from the procedural guidelines established in *New Jersey v. Hurd* toward a more restrictive standard of general inadmissibility in the 2006 case of *New Jersey v. Moore* (2006).

In states that use a Frye general acceptance test, there continue to be decisions that restrict the admissibility of forensic hypnosis. In the 2004 Illinois Supreme Court Case *People v. Sutton,* a critical potential eyewitness of a murder who had post injury amnesia underwent hypnosis and subsequently testified against the defendant, who was convicted of the murder. In this case, the trial court allowed the refreshed testimony to be admitted and excluded the testimony of a defense expert about the unreliability of hypnotically enhanced memories. The Court, utilizing the Frye-like admissibility standard in Illinois, as well as a previous ruling excluding the use of hypnosis by nondefendants, vacated the murder conviction (*People v. Sutton,* 2004). A 2004 Texas Appellate Court case *Texas v. Medrano* (2004) affirmed the decision of a trial court to exclude the hypnotically refreshed testimony of the single eyewitness in a capital murder case.

One case in which the *Daubert* standards were clearly applied to the issue of forensically refreshed testimony was the 1995 case of *Borawick v. Shay* (1995), decided by the U.S. Court of Appeals for the Second Circuit. In the lower court case, Joan Borawick filed a civil action against her aunt and uncle, alleging that they had sexually abused her as a child, the memories of which were elicited by way of hypnosis. The trial court, a U.S. District Court in Connecticut, heard the case and ruled in favor of the defendant's motion to exclude the hypnotically refreshed memories of the plaintiff. Shortly after this, *Daubert* was decided, and the plaintiff Borawick moved that the judge reconsider the earlier exclusion on the grounds that the use of hypnosis and the subsequent recollections satisfied the requirements of the *Daubert* decision. The trial court held to their earlier ruling excluding the use of hypnosis, and the District Court refused to have an evidentiary hearing and subsequently granted a summary judgment in favor of the accused defendants.

In the appeal to the Second Circuit Court of Appeals, the Court reviewed the admissibility of post hypnotic testimony, as well as whether the *Daubert* rules applied. The Court noted that this was distinct from cases such as *State v. Hurd* in that rather than addressing the use of hypnosis as an investigative tool to assist with recollection of a known specific event, it related to the recollection of memories of childhood sexual abuse purportedly recalled later by way of therapeutically applied hypnosis. The Court supported the findings of the lower court, noting that even if the lower court had had a more thorough evidentiary hearing before issuing its summary judgment, the final decision to exclude the admissibility was valid based on a number of factors, including the lack of formal training by the hypnotist, the lack of a permanent record of the sessions, the lack of credibility of the plaintiff Borawick, as well as the general problems with hypnotically refreshed memories raised in other legal cases. However, the Court ruled that *Daubert* did not apply in this case, because the question at hand was not the admissibility of either scientific data or an expert's opinion, but rather whether the plaintiff Borawick herself was a competent witness. Because she was a layperson, they concluded that *Daubert* was inapplicable, but added that "even if Daubert were of direct application, noting in Daubert is inconsistent with our outlined approach" (*Borawick v. Shay*, 1995).

Despite the ruling in the *Borawick* case that *Daubert* only applies to the testimony of experts rather than to the testimony of laypersons, other commentators have concluded that the tradition of *per se* inadmissibility of hypnotically refreshed recollections may eventually be challenged by the framework of *Daubert* in jurisdictions that utilize the *Daubert* standard (Martin, 2003; Webert, 2003). Martin further recommends that any attorney who is in a *Daubert* jurisdiction be prepared to support any testimony involving hypnosis utilizing the framework established by the *Daubert* case (Martin, 2003).

In the authors' opinion, even if the *Daubert* standards allow for a broader consideration of the potential admissibility of testimony related to hypnotically refreshed memories, nothing in the fifteen years since the *Daubert* case has significantly challenged the science that demonstrates the risks associated with the use of hypnosis as a tool to refresh memories in an accurate manner. For this reason, in our opinion the use of hypnosis in any circumstance has the potential to lead to false information that could result in false convictions and false exculpations and as such should be excluded.

ACKNOWLEDGMENT

Dr. Newman and I would like to express our sincere gratitude and appreciation to Gina Manguno-Mire, Ph.D., for her significant contributions to the information contained in this chapter. Dr. Mire spent countless hours conducting a review of the pertinent literature and making key revisions to the content contained in the chapter. In addition, her work editing and organizing the material was significant. We are extremely grateful to Dr. Mire for her attention to detail and her effort in editing the chapter for both content and style. Her assistance on the writing and submission of the project was an invaluable asset.

REFERENCES

American Medical Association Council, on Scientific Affairs (1986). Scientific status of refreshing recollection by the use of hypnosis. *The International Journal of Clinical and Experimental Hypnosis 34*, 1–12.

Ault, R.L. (1979). FBI guidelines for use of hypnosis. *The International Journal of Clinical and Experimental Hypnosis, 27*, 449–51.

Bernheim, H. (1973). *Hypnosis & suggestion in psychotherapy.* Northvale, NJ: Jason Aronson Inc.

Borawick v. Shay, 68 F. 3d U.S. 597 (1995).

Bragin, R. (1981). Hypnosis in the criminal justice system. In J.J. Grau (Ed.), *Criminal and Civil Investigation Handbook.* (pp. 135-145) New York: McGraw-Hill.

Butler, L.D., and Spiegel, D. (1997). *Trauma and Memory.* In D. Spiegel (Ed.), *Repressed Memories.* Washington, DC: American Psychiatric Press, Inc.

Daubert v. Merrell Dow Pharmaceuticals, Inc., 509 U.S. 579 (1993).

Earleywine, M., and Gann, M. (1995). *Challenging Recovered Memories in the Courtroom, In J. Ziskin (Ed.) Coping with Psychiatric and Psychological Testimony.* Los Angeles: Law and Psychology Press.

Frontline (1995). Divided Memories, Part 1: The Hunt for Memory [transcript]. Boston: Corporation for Public Broadcasting.

Gerber, S.R., and Schroeder, O. (1972). *Criminal Investigation and Interrogation.* Cincinnati: W. H. Anderson.

Hibbard, W.S., and Worring, R.W. (1980). *Forensic Hypnosis: The Practical Application of Hypnosis in Criminal Investigations.* Springfield, IL: Charles C Thomas.

International Society of Hypnosis (1979) August Resolution Adopted August. *The International Journal of Clinical and Experimental Hypnosis, 27*, 453.

Kaufman, D. (2001). *Clinical Neurology for Psychiatrists* (5th Ed.). Philadelphia: W.B. Saunders Company.

Kirkwood, J. (1968). *American Grotesque: An Account of the Clay Shaw-Jim Garrison Affair in the City of New Orleans.* New York: Simon and Schuster.

Laurence, J.R., and Perry, C. (1983). Hypnotically created memory among highly hypnotizable subjects. *Science 222*, 523–524.

Loftus, E.F. (1979). *Eyewitness Testimony.* Cambridge, MA: Harvard University Press.

Loftus, E.F. (1993). The reality of repressed memories. *American Psychologist, 48*, 518–37.

Loftus, E.F., and Loftus, G.R. (1980). On the permanence of stored information in the human brain. *American Psychologist, 35*, 409–420.

Martin, E. (2003). A Daubert test of hypnotically refreshed testimony in the criminal courts. *Texas Wesleyan Law Review, 9,* 151–179.

Moenssens, A.A., Starrs, J.E., Henderson, C.E., and Inbau, F.E. (1995). *Scientific Evidence in Civil and Criminal Cases* (4th Ed) Westbury, NY: The Foundation Press, Inc.

Monaghan, F.J. (1980). *Hypnosis in Criminal Investigation.* Dubuque: Kendall/Hunt.

Moore, B.E., and Fine, B.D. (1990). *Psychoanalytic Terms and Concepts.* New Haven: Yale University Press.

Mutter, C.B. (1990). Hypnosis with defendants: Does it really work? *American Journal of Clinical Hypnosis, 32,* 257–262.

Nathan, D., and Snedeker, M. (1995). Satan's Silence. New York: Basic Books.

Newman, A.W,. and Thompson, J.W., Jr. (1999). Constitutional rights and hypnotically elicited testimony. *Journal of the American Academy of Psychiatry and the Law, 27,* 149–154.

New Jersey v. Hurd, 173 N.J. Super. 333, 414 A.2d 291 (1980).

New Jersey v. Moore, 188 N.J. 182 (2006)

O'Hara, C.E., and O'Hara, G. (1994). *Fundamentals of Criminal Investigation.* Springfield, IL: Charles C Thomas.

Orne, M.T. (1979). The use and misuse of hypnosis in court. *International Journal of Clinical and Experimental Hypnosis, 27,* 311–341.

Orne, M.T., and Dinges, D.F. (1993). Hypnosis. In H.I. Kaplan and B.J. Sadock (Eds.), *Comprehensive Textbook of Psychiatry* (5th ed.). (pp. 1501-1516) Baltimore: Williams & Wilkins.

Orne, M.T., Dinges, D.F., and Orne, E.C. (1990). *Rock v. Arkansas:* Hypnosis, the defendant's privilege. *The International Journal of Clinical and Experimental Hypnosis, 38,* 250–265.

Penfield, W., and Roberts, L. (1959). Speech and Brain-Mechanisms. Princeton: Princeton University Press.

People v. Shirley, 31 Cal. 3d. 18 (1982)

People v. Sutton, 349 IL. App. 3d608, 622, 812 N.E.2d 543 (2004).

Putnam, W.H. (1979). Hypnosis and distortions in eyewitness memory. *The International Journal of Clinical and Experimental Hypnosis, 27,* 437–448.

Randi, J. (1996). "Twas Brillig." Skeptic, 4: 10–1.

Reiser, M. (1980). *Handbook of Investigative Hypnosis.* Los Angeles: LEHI.

Tayloe, D.R. (1995). The validity of repressed memories and the accuracy of their recall through hypnosis: A case study from the courtroom. *American Journal of Clinical Hypnosis, 37,* 25–31.

Texas v. Medrano, 127 S.W.3d 781, 785 (Tex. Crim. App. 2004).

Udolf, R. (1990). *Rock v. Arkansas:* A critique. *The International Journal of Clinical and Experimental Hypnosis, 38,* 239–249.

Watkins, J.G. (1989). Hypnotic hypermnesia and forensic hypnosis: A cross-examination. American Journal of Clinical Hypnosis, 32, 71-83.

Webert, D. (2003). Are the courts in a trance? Approaches to the admissibility of hypnotically enhanced witness testimony in light of empirical evidence. *American Criminal Law Review, 40,* 1301–1327.

Wolberg, L.R. (1975). *The Psychosocial Therapies, in Treatment* (2nd ed.). New York: Basic Books, Inc.

Wolberg, L.R. (1988). *The Technique of Psychotherapy* (4th ed.). New York: Harcourt Brace Jovanovich.

Wong, N. (1993). Classical psychoanalysis. In H.I. Kaplan, & B.J. Sadock (Eds.), *Comprehensive Textbook of Psychiatry,* (5th ed.). (pp. 356-402) Baltimore: Williams & Wilkins.

Chapter Nine

FALSE CONFESSIONS

CHRISTIAN A. MEISSNER, ALLYSON J. HORGAN,
AND JUSTIN S. ALBRECHTSEN

Jeff Deskovic was sixteen years of age when he falsely confessed to the rape and murder of a fifteen-year-old classmate. He confessed to this crime after an intense interrogation that was conducted by multiple police investigators and lasted more than six hours. Police first suspected Deskovic because he was late to school the day after the girl had disappeared and because he appeared overly emotional and distraught when asked about her death. During his interrogation, investigators lied to Deskovic, accused him of failing a series of polygraph examinations, stated that they were convinced of his guilt, and offered him rationalizations for his apparent violent behavior. The pressures of the interrogation finally led Deskovic to confess to the brutal murder as he sobbed inconsolably and lay in the fetal position underneath a table.

Investigation into the murder and rape of Deskovic's classmate revealed semen on the body that was later tested against his DNA sample. Deskovic was informed by investigators that if his DNA failed to match that of the specimen collected, he would be released. Unfortunately, Deskovic underestimated the power that his confession would have. Although the DNA evidence excluded him as the donor of the semen, Deskovic was prosecuted for murder and rape based on the statement he had provided to investigators. A jury convicted Deskovic, and he spent more than fifteen years in prison until he was finally exonerated in 2006 through the use of more sophisticated DNA technology. The actual perpetrator of the crime, Steven Cunningham, was later identified through a DNA database.

FREQUENCY OF FALSE CONFESSIONS

Similar examples of false confessions leading to wrongful conviction can be found in the United States, Canada, Great Britain, Australia, and elsewhere around the world. In the United States, organizations such as the Innocence Project (*see* www.innocenceproject.org) have worked to identify instances of wrongful conviction and to delineate the causes. To date, more than 215 wrongful convictions have been discovered, and nearly 25 percent of these cases have included false confession evidence. Other studies of wrongful conviction have produced similar estimates (Bedau & Radelet, 1987; Scheck, Neufeld & Dwyer, 2000), and it appears that juveniles may be particularly vulnerable to the power of the interrogation room. In a study of 328 wrongful convictions in the United States, Gross, Jacoby, Matheson, Montgomery, and Patil (2005) found that 44 percent of juveniles provided a false confession when compared with only 13 percent of adults in the sample. Among the youngest, those twelve to fifteen years of age, the incidence of false confession rose to 75 percent.

There has been a notable surge in the frequency of false confessions discussed in the media, but the actual rate of false confessions in practice is difficult to determine (cf. Leo & Ofshe, 1998). In a recent review of the literature, Gudjonnson (in press) examined the frequency of false confessions reported by individuals who had been interrogated in actual cases. Prisoners reported false confession rates between 12 and 24 percent, whereas community samples reported incidence rates between 1 and 14 percent. Viljoen, Klaver, and Roesch (2005) found that 6 percent of juvenile defendants reported having provided a false confession, while studies conducted by Redlich and colleagues (Redlich, 2007) found that 22 percent of defendants with serious mental illness reported having provided a false confession. Finally, a survey of police investigators in the United States who regularly conduct interrogations estimated that 5 percent of "innocent" suspects provide a false confession (Kassin et al., 2007). Although it may be difficult to estimate the precise incidence rate of providing a false confession, these studies make clear that the phenomenon occurs and is regularly reported by suspects and police investigators alike.

In an archival study, Drizin and Leo (2004) located and analyzed 125 cases of "proven" false confessions in the United States that occurred between 1971 and 2002. More than 90 percent of these cases involved charges of murder or rape. One third of the cases examined by Drizin and Leo concerned juvenile offenders (under the age of seventeen), 10 percent of the sample was considered "mentally ill," and 22 percent of the sample had been diagnosed as "mentally retarded". Nevertheless, most of the cases investigated by the authors involved adults of normal mental health and mental capacity. Owing to the power of confession evidence, Drizin and Leo found that 81 percent of defendants were convicted at trial based on a false confession. An additional 11 percent chose to plead "guilty" prior to trial in order to avoid the possibility of receiving the death penalty. Following conviction, 80 percent of these innocent defendants were sentenced to more than ten years in prison and 61 percent spent more than five years incarcerated prior to exoneration.

Taken together, these data demonstrate that the false confession phenomenon occurs in our criminal justice system to a significant degree and that it is associated with severe consequences for the innocent suspect. Several decades of research have now examined false confessions both from the field and, more recently, within the laboratory (*see* Gudjonsson, 2003; Kassin & Gudjonsson, 2005; Lassiter & Meissner, in press). This chapter will review our current knowledge of the false confession phenomenon, including the typology of false confessions most frequently observed, the situational and psychological factors that lead to the phenomenon, and recent attempts at reducing the likelihood of false confessions in practice. The chapter will conclude with empirically-based recommendations for best practice in the interrogation room.

TYPOLOGY OF FALSE CONFESSIONS

Analysis of the variety of false confessions observed in the real world led Kassin and Wrightsman (1985) to delineate three types of false confessions: voluntary, coerced-compliant, and coerced-internalized. First, a *voluntary false confession* is one in which a person falsely confesses to a crime absent any pressure or coercion from police investigators. Gudjonsson (2003) discusses a number of reasons why someone might provide a voluntary false confession, including the desire to protect someone else, a desire for notoriety or attention, or an inability to distinguish reality from fantasy. Research indicates that the desire to protect someone else is likely to be the most common motivation behind a voluntary false confession (cf. Sigurdsson & Gudjonsson, 1996). A recent example of a voluntary false confession was that of John Mark Karr, who confessed to the murder of JonBenet Ramsey in 2006. Karr had become obsessed with the Ramsey murder and ultimately made statements implicating his involvement in her death. Ultimately, DNA evidence from the Ramsey murder failed to match Karr's samples and testimony from relatives was provided to conclude that he was elsewhere when the incident occurred.

Coerced-compliant false confessions occur when a person falsely confesses to a crime for some immediate gain and in spite of the conscious knowledge that he or she is actually innocent of the crime. Individuals may falsely confess to escape the pressure of the interrogation or because they believe (or have been led to believe) that they will be allowed to go home, to sleep or eat, to call their family or that doing so will alleviate them of the charges against them. In general, suspects come to believe that the short-term consequences of confessing (e.g. ending the interrogation) will outweigh the long-term consequences of confessing. Most false confessions observed to date likely fall into this category. For example, many are familiar with the "Central Park jogger case" in which five teenage boys (aged fourteen to sixteen) confessed to attacking a twenty-eight-year-old woman in New York City. The interrogation of these boys lasted between fourteen and thirty hours, and the suspects would subsequently claim that they had provided the investigators what they wanted to hear and that they were led to believe that they would be sent home thereafter. Subsequent investigation led to identification of the true perpetrator, Matias Reyes. DNA testing exonerated the five boys and led to Reyes' conviction.

The final type identified by Kassin and Wrightsman (1985) is referred to as a *coerced-internalized false confession.* This occurs when a person falsely confesses to a crime and truly begins to believe that he or she is responsible for the criminal act. Researchers have suggested that internalized false confessions result from interrogation tactics that manipulate or distort the memories of individuals, causing them to develop false memories of their involvement in the crime (Bem, 1966; Henkel & Coffman, 2004). For example, suspects may be asked to imagine, visualize, or speculate how the crime might have occurred. They may be provided with details of the crime by the investigator, who encourages them to continue constructing a version of the crime. If the suspects fail to remember the event, they may be offered reasons to distrust their memories, including the notion of a blackout or repression of the event or the potential effects of drug or alcohol inducement on memory (cf. Gudjonsson, 2003). Along these lines, Kassin (1997) suggested that two factors may be common to all coerced-internalized false confession cases. First, the suspect's memory must be vulnerable in some way, such as by the use of certain substances, being fatigued during the interrogation, or as a result of a particular vulnerability (such as being young in age, of low intelligence, or highly suggestible). Second, the suspect must be confronted with false evidence of his or her guilt by the investigator; for example, individuals might be told that they failed a polygraph exam or that their DNA was found at the scene of the crime. Kassin (1997) has argued that the presence of these two factors will likely cause the suspect to question their memory and thereby open the door for suggestive interview tactics to have their influence (*see* Henkel & Coffman, 2004).

Although relatively uncommon, numerous case examples of coerced-internalized false confessions are available. The most well-known case is likely that of Paul Ingram (*see* Wright, 1993a, 1993b). Ingram was a deputy sheriff who was accused of the satanic ritual abuse of his two daughters. Although Ingram initially denied the charges, he would eventually confess and provide memories of the abuse over the course of five months as he was repeatedly interrogated, hypnotized to facilitate his memory, and encouraged to recall the abuse by his church pastor (Olio & Cornell, 1998). Following this internalization of the crime, Ingram pleaded guilty to the charges against him, although he would later recant his confession and seek to withdraw his plea. His request was denied, and he was sentenced to twenty years of imprisonment. Evidence was amassed to suggest that the abuse never occurred and that Ingram had falsely confessed to the crime. He was released from prison in 2003, although he has not been exonerated of the charges.

MODERN POLICE INTERROGATION TACTICS

To better understand the psychological and situational factors that lead to false confessions, one must first appreciate the psychological pressures and tactics placed upon any suspect that enters the interrogation room. A variety of interrogation approaches and manuals have been advocated to law enforcement over the past few decades, and it is beyond the scope of this chapter to review each separately. Nevertheless, these techniques can generally be described as involving two distinct phases. First, a preinterrogation interview is conducted in which investigators will probe for signs of deceit on the part of the suspect and assess his or her culpability. Once an investigator is convinced of the likely guilt of the suspect, the interrogation phase of the interview begins. Interrogation manuals, such as that of Inbau, Reid, Buckley, and Jayne (2001) in the United States, suggest three general tactics be employed during an interrogation: (1) *custody and isolation*, (2) *confrontation and maximization*, and (3) *minimization*.

The manuals suggest that, upon initiating an interrogation, investigators induce a period of isolation in which the suspect is detained in a small room and left to experience the anxiety, insecurity, and uncertainty associated with police interrogation. They should be separated from family, friends, and other support mechanisms and thereby be made to feel alone and uneasy about their situation. The ultimate goal of the interrogation is to encourage suspects to rely on the interrogator and to believe that going along with his or her suggestions (in this case, providing a confession) is in their best interest.

In the second phase of an interrogation, the investigator generally confronts the suspects with a firm belief in their culpability for the crime and attempts to maximize their perception of the evidence against them and the consequences associated with the act. For example, investigators may lie to a suspect regarding the extent to which evidence supporting their guilt exists (e.g. "We have a witness who has identified you." "The fingerprints left at the scene match those you provided us. How could this be?"). Investigators may also exaggerate the consequences associated with the crime and will attempt to prevent the suspect from denying his or her involvement. This approach is often thought of as the "bad cop" routine, and, of course, this is followed up with the "good cop" perspective.

In the third phase of an interrogation, a now sympathetic investigator will attempt to gain the suspect's trust, offer the suspect face-saving excuses or justifications for the crime, and imply that a confession might bring about more lenient consequences. Often referred to as theme development or minimization, the objective is to provide suspects with a way out of the interrogation room that minimizes both their perception of culpability and their beliefs regarding the consequences associated with confession. For example, an interrogator might say: "I know you are a good person, and this was simply an accident. Accidents happen, and the courts don't treat accidents the same as they would an intentional act of violence."

It is important to note that modern interrogations rarely involve physical abuse or threats on the part of the interrogator; rather, the interrogator attempts to psychologically manipulate the suspect's perception of the situation. Given the "soft" nature of these psychological techniques, many interrogation manuals, such as the Reid technique (Inbau et al., 2001), argue that these methods will not induce an innocent person to confess. This statement is often the result of a belief that these methods will not be applied against an innocent person, assuming that a preinterrogation assessment of the suspect's guilt (or likely deception) will exclude the innocent from the subsequent interrogation phase. Unfortunately, scientific evaluation of this interrogation process, from deception detection to psychological manipulation, suggests that these techniques place innocent suspects at risk.

THREE FACTORS THAT LEAD TO A FALSE CONFESSION

Social science researchers have begun to systematically examine the false confession phenomenon over the past several decades both from the field and within the laboratory (for reviews, *see* Gudjonsson, 2003; Kassin, 1997, 2005; Kassin & Gudjonsson, 2005; Redlich & Meissner, in press). Researchers have employed two broad methods to study interrogations and confessions, namely field research and laboratory research. Field research (e.g. observational studies of actual police interrogations or archival reviews of wrongful convictions) carries the distinct advantage of high external validity and generalizability. For example, in a seminal study of U.S. police interrogations, Leo (1996) observed more than 300 live and videotaped interviews in an effort to systematically document the techniques employed by investigators. Similar field studies have also been conducted in Great Britain (Baldwin, 1993; Irving; 1980; Irving & McKenzie, 1989; Moston, Stephenson & Williamson, 1992; Softley, 1980). Archival studies, such as those conducted by Drizin and Leo (2004) and Leo and Ofshe (1998), have similarly provided insights regarding the factors associated with false confessors in real cases, although they do not provide a comparable sample of true confessors from which to distinguish these effects.

Although field studies have certainly increased our understanding of police interrogations, like most field research methodologies, these approaches suffer from issues of internal validity in that they lack the experimental controls necessary to eliminate all confounds that might enable researchers to draw causal conclusions regarding the factors responsible for the false confession phenomenon. Because of the limitations of field research methods, a number of researchers have begun to employ experimental laboratory research methods (*see* Meissner, Russano & Narchet, in press). For example, researchers have investigated the ability of lay individuals and police investigators to distinguish truths from lies in the context of forensic interviews (for a review, *see* Bond & DePaulo, 2006; Vrij, 2008), the influence of preinterrogative beliefs of guilt on suspect interviews and perceptions of those interviews (*see* Meissner & Kassin, 2004) and the effects of certain interrogation techniques on the likelihood of true versus false confessions (Kassin & Keichel, 1996; Russano, Meissner, Narchet & Kassin, 2005). Although limited by issues of external validity, laboratory research benefits from a high degree of experimental control and internal validity that allows researchers to explore cause and effect relationships. To understand the process of interrogation and the psychology of false confessions, researchers have relied on both of these approaches in attempting to build a bridge from the laboratory to the field and ultimately to improving practice in the interrogation room.

Taken together, the overwhelming data from these studies suggest that three primary factors appear to be associated with the elicitation of false confessions. First, investigators attempting to detect deception on the part of the suspect appear to demonstrate a bias toward perceiving guilt, and research suggests that this *investigative bias* may lead to a pressure-filled, guilt-presumptive interrogation that places innocent suspects at risk. Second, both field and laboratory studies have demonstrated the use of *psychologically manipulative interrogation techniques* both increases the likelihood of false confession and reduces the overall diagnostic value of interrogative information. Third, certain characteristics or *psychological vulnerabilities* have been shown to make some suspects more susceptible to providing a false confession. In the following sections we briefly review the research supporting each of these factors.

Investigative Biases

The reader will recall that the first phase of any suspect interview frequently involves a preinterrogation interview in which investigators will attempt to detect deception on the part of the suspect. In a recent study by Kassin and colleagues (2007), police investigators reported that, on average, they were 77 percent accurate in distinguishing truth versus deception in a forensic interview. This degree of confidence in their ability to detect deception is not uncommon; in fact, Reid and associates claim to be able to train investigators to distinguish truth and deception at an 85 percent level of accuracy (http://www.reid.com).

Unfortunately, research shows that neither lay individuals nor law enforcement officials are particularly adept at detecting deception, even those who have been trained. For example, Bond and DePaulo (2006) conducted a meta-analysis of more than 200 studies in the deception detection literature and found that individuals correctly distinguish truths and lies with 54% accuracy. Furthermore, the analysis of expert (e.g. law enforcement) vs. naïve (e.g. student participants) found no significant differences in deception performance; in fact, the pattern of means suggested that naïve participants performed somewhat better than the experts.

Meissner and Kassin (2002) further examined the effects of experience and training on deception detection capabilities. When participants were asked to assess the veracity of statements (denials of involvement in a criminal act) that were provided in the context of a pseudoforensic interview, they found that investigators and trained participants, relative to naïve controls, exhibited a proclivity to judge targets as deceptive rather than as truthful. Although neither experience (as an investigator) nor training improved participants' ability to correctly distinguish between true and false statements, both experience and training did correlate with a deception response bias, a finding that the authors referred to as "investigative bias."

In a follow-up study, Kassin, Meissner, and Norwick (2005) tested a common collateral assumption about the ability to detect truth and deception in an interrogation setting, namely the commonly expressed belief by police investigators that "I'd know a false confession if I saw one." The authors compared the performance of police investigators and laypersons who attempted to distinguish between true and false confessions provided by actual prison inmates in a state correctional facility. Overall, the investigator bias effect was replicated such that police were predisposed to believe both the true and the false confessions. That is, the response bias did not lead police to see deception *per se*, but to infer *guilt,* an inference that rested upon a tendency to believe false confessions. Once again, this investigative bias to perceive guilt was enhanced among those with extensive law enforcement experience and those who had received training in interviewing and interrogation.

The remaining question regards the extent to which such an investigative bias might influence the conduct of an interrogation. Could a bias toward perceiving guilt in a preinterrogation interview lead an investigator to conduct a more aggressive, pressure-filled interrogation? Kassin, Goldstein, and Savitsky (2003) investigated whether a presumption of guilt might influence the conduct of student interrogators, the behavior of their suspects, and ultimately the judgments made by neutral observers. Participant suspects were asked to complete a mock crime or to complete a related, but innocent, act. These suspects were then subsequently interviewed by other subjects playing the role of investigators, who were led to believe that the suspect was either guilty or innocent of the crime. Kassin and colleagues (2003) found that investigators who were led to expect guilt rather than innocence asked more guilt-presumptive questions, employed more interrogation techniques, exerted more pressure on the suspects to confess, and were more likely to believe that the suspect was guilty. Furthermore, this investigative bias toward perceiving guilt caused the innocent suspects to act more defensively and to be perceived as more guilty by third-party observers.

In a recent study conducted by Narchet, Meissner, and Russano (2008), the impact of investigative bias was further examined for its influence on the elicitation of true versus false confessions. Using a "cheating paradigm" developed by Russano and colleagues (2005), the authors led student interrogators to believe that participants were either guilty or innocent of sharing information on a problem-solving task with another participant (who was a confederate to the study). The student interrogators had been trained in fifteen different interrogation techniques (including aspects of maximization and minimization), and the authors examined the influence of the preinterrogative information on the conduct of the interrogations, the perceptions of the participant suspects, and the resulting true versus false confession. Narchet and colleagues (2008) found that an investigative bias towards perceiving guilt led investigators to conduct longer interrogations involving a greater number of pressure-filled tactics. Innocent suspects perceived greater pressure to confess resulting from this manipulation and were more likely to falsely confess as a result. Finally, investigators' initial belief in guilt ultimately led them to perceive that these false confessions were more likely attributable to guilty suspects.

Together, this line of research suggests that investigative biases toward perceiving guilt are prevalent among investigators, particularly those with greater experience and training in deception detection approaches. Given that most interrogation manuals encourage a finding of deception or guilt prior to initiating an interrogation, these studies further suggest that a presumption of guilt sets in motion a process in which investigators conduct longer, more pressure-filled and guilt presumptive interrogations that can lead to the elicitation of a false confession when lodged against an innocent suspect. In the next section, we turn our attention to the specific interrogation tactics that are brought about by this process.

Psychologically-Coercive Interrogation Tactics

Interrogation of a suspect is one of the most difficult tasks in a police investigation, and throughout history investigators have resorted to a wide variety of techniques intended to break down a suspect's resistance and yield a confession. Interrogation techniques have evolved from overtly coercive, third degree tactics (e.g. beatings, sleep deprivation; *see* Leo, 2004) to modern-day practices that involve more subtle, yet effective, psychologically based techniques (White, 2003). These modern interrogation practices, described before, are believed to be effective in eliciting true confessions, but could they also be responsible for the false confessions observed in recent cases of wrongful conviction?

Both field and laboratory research has led to the conclusion that common police interrogation tactics, such as minimization and maximization, increase the likelihood of false confession when applied against innocent suspects. For example, research by Kassin and Keichel (1996) found that the presentation of false evidence, a classic maximization technique, increased the likelihood of false confession. A study by Russano and colleagues (2005) observed that minimization tactics, in which a sympathetic interrogator provides a face-saving excuse and implies leniency to a suspect, increased false confession rates. Combining these techniques, Klaver, Rose, and Lee (2003) and Narchet and colleagues (2008) found that the use of both minimization and maximization techniques increased the likelihood of false confession. Both observational studies (e.g. Leo, 1996) and case-based examples (e.g. Leo & Ofshe, 1998; Ofshe & Leo, 1997) confirm both the use and the risks associated with such techniques for the innocent suspect.

In its landmark decision of *Miranda v. Arizona* (1966), the U.S. Supreme Court explicitly acknowledged that "The atmosphere and environment of incommunicado interrogation as it exists today is inherently intimidating and works to undermine the privilege against self-incrimination" (p. 384). It is clear that the context in which the interrogation takes place is believed to play a large role in the success of obtaining a confession, but could this also work against the innocent suspect? Research has suggested that several situational factors inherent to the interrogation may be associated with false confessions (*see* Kassin & Gudjonnson, 2005). For example, interrogators are trained to remove suspects from their familiar surroundings and to question them in a sparsely furnished, dimly lit interrogation room. This process of isolation increases anxiety and insecurity on the part of the suspect (Zimbardo, 1967), and studies suggest that a preexisting state of stress can increase the likelihood of an innocent suspects providing a false confession (Forrest, Wadkins & Miller, 2002). In addition, false confessions have been found to be associated with lengthy interrogations. For example, Drizin and Leo (2004) found that among their 125 cases of proven false confession, 34 percent lasted between six and twelve hours, and 39 percent lasted between twelve and twenty-four hours, with an average interrogation length of approximately sixteen hours. Such lengthy interrogations are likely to involve deprivations of food or sleep, and research suggests that interrogative suggestibility significantly increases when individuals are deprived of sleep (*see* Blagrove, 1996).

The psychological processes initiated by an interrogation have been variously described and evaluated (Gudjonsson, 2003; Hilgendorf & Irving, 1981; Ofshe & Leo, 1997), with a general consensus that the pressures of the interrogation room led to a seemingly rational decision for the innocent suspect. In particular, suspects appear to undergo a natural decision-making process when evaluating the alternatives presented to them in the context of an interrogation. As so eloquently described by Ofshe and Leo (1997):

> Psychological interrogation is effective at eliciting confessions because of a fundamental fact of human decision-making—people make optimizing choices given the alternatives they consider. Psychologically-based interrogation works effectively by controlling the alternatives a person considers and by influencing how those alternatives are understood. The techniques interrogators use have been selected to limit a person's attention to certain issues, to manipulate his perceptions of his present situation and to bias his evaluation of the choices before him. The techniques used to accomplish these manipulations are so effective that if misused they can result in decisions to confess from the guilty and innocent alike. Police elicit the decision to confess from the guilty by leading them to believe that the evidence against them is overwhelming, that their fate is certain (whether or not they confess), and that there are advantages that follow if they confess. Investigators elicit the decision to confess from the innocent in one of two ways: either by leading them to believe that their situation, though unjust, is hopeless and will only be improved by confessing; or by persuading them that they probably committed a crime about which they have no memory and that confessing is the proper and optimal course of action. (pp. 985-986)

In summary, research examining the use of psychologically based interrogation methods has confirmed that these methods, although powerfully effective in eliciting confessions from guilty individuals, also place the innocent suspect at risk. In particular, the context of an interrogation works to increase the anxiety experienced by the innocent suspect, while the interrogative methods alter the suspect's perception of reality. Together, these factors ultimately produce a "rational decision" that providing a false confession is the only manner in which to alleviate the pressures of the interrogation room.

Psychological Vulnerabilities of the Suspect

Finally, research has suggested that some individuals may be more vulnerable than others are in the interrogation room, and particularly with regard to providing a false confession. Specifically, there appear to be certain characteristics that render an individual more susceptible to interrogation, including the age, mental capacity, suggestibility, and physical or psychological state of the suspect at the time of the interrogation. First, a number of field studies (e.g. Baldwin & McConville, 1980; Leiken, 1970; Phillips & Brown, 1998; Softley, 1980; for a review, *see* Drizin & Colgan, 2004) and several empirical studies (Billings et al., 2007; Redlich & Goodman, 2003; *see* Redlich, Silverman, Chen & Steiner, 2004) have demonstrated that younger suspects, and in particular children, are more likely to falsely incriminate themselves or confess, or both, during an interrogation than are older persons or adults. Indeed, 32 percent of the false confessions discussed by Drizin and Leo (2004) involved juveniles under the age of eighteen.

Second, studies have suggested that police routinely interrogate persons of low intelligence or IQ (*see* Gudjonsson, 1993) and that such individuals may be more suggestible and less able to cope with the pressures of the interrogation room (Gudjonsson, 1990, 2003). For example, Drizin and Leo (2004) found that 19 percent of their sample of false confessors could be classified as "mentally retarded." It appears that both decision-making abilities and heightened suggestibility in this population may result in the increased risk of falsely confessing.

Third, interrogative suggestibility (or the unique characteristic of a given individual to demonstrate increased suggestibility in a forensic interview setting) has been associated with false confessions (Gudjonsson, 2003; Gudjonsson & Clark, 1986). The Gudjonsson Suggestibility Scale (GSS) (Gudjonsson, 1984) has been developed and utilized to assess suggestibility in a number of studies, with suggestibility often being associated with poor memory, low self-esteem, high levels of anxiety, and a greater likelihood of confession (*see* Gudjonsson, 1991, 2003). Compliance (or the degree to which a given individual may yield to social requests), as measured by the Gudjonsson Compliance Scale (GCS) (Gudjonsson, 1989, 1991), has also been shown to be associated with a greater likelihood of confession.

Finally, the psychological state (e.g. due to drug use or mental illness) of a suspect at the time of interrogation may also be linked to the likelihood of false confession (Pearse, Gudjonsson, Clare & Rutter, 1998; Redlich, 2004). For example, studies have indicated that suspects undergoing alcohol withdrawal at the time of interrogation are more likely to provide a false confession (Gudjonsson et al., 2004). Furthermore, individuals suffering from mental illness, including depression and anxiety disorders, may be increasingly susceptible to interrogative pressures (*see* Gudjonsson, 2003). For example, 10 percent of the Drizin and Leo (2004) sample of false confessors were described as "mentally ill."

In summary, it is important to consider the variety of unique characteristics that may cause a particular suspect to be vulnerable to the power of the interrogation room. While some of these factors may be readily apparent to the investigator (e.g., the age of the suspect), others may be more difficult to discern (e.g., the degree of interrogative suggestibility, or the presence of mental illness). Nevertheless, the investigator must be ever mindful of the individual and his/her susceptibility to the power of the interrogation room.

A NEW MODEL OF INTERROGATION

Identifying interrogation strategies that minimize the likelihood of obtaining false confessions without compromising the ability of interrogators to elicit true confessions is a challenge faced by law enforcement and researchers alike. In assessing what progress law enforcement has made in this area, it may be informative to examine the interrogation practices of Great Britain. Although interviewing practices in the United States and Great Britain were on par with one another through the 1980s, these two countries now differ greatly in their approaches (Bull & Milne, 2004).

In Great Britain, public response to recurrent miscarriages of justice involving proven false confessions became a catalyst for change (*see* Gudjonsson, 2003). In 1981, the Royal Commission on Criminal Procedure (RCCP) was established to assess pretrial criminal procedures and to generate suggestions for reform in England and Wales. To achieve its goal the RCCP commissioned several researchers to carry out programs of research exploring events in the interrogation room (Gudjonsson, 2003). After concluding that the police frequently relied on interrogation techniques that were both physically and psychologically manipulative (which resemble methods currently employed in the United States) and that the police had no existing protocol or training on interrogations (Irving, 1980; Irving & Hilgendorf, 1980), the Police and Criminal Evidence (PACE) Act of 1984 was created. The primary goal of the PACE Act was to reduce the use of psychologically manipulative tactics and to require that all interrogations be audiorecorded (Bull & Milne, 2004). The move to PACE appears to have been successful.

A post-PACE study conducted by Irving and McKenzie (1989) found that the use of psychologically manipulative tactics had significantly declined and, more importantly, that the frequency of confessions did not decrease.

In 1993, the Royal Commission on Criminal Justice further reformed British interrogation methods by proposing the PEACE model. Each letter of the acronym PEACE represents a phase of interrogation that investigators should adhere to. In the "preparation and planning" phase, interrogators focus on organizing evidence and constructing a plan for the interview. During the "engage and explain" phase, the goal is to build rapport and to make the suspect aware of the purpose of the interview. The third phase, "account," is the core of the interview. Contrary to the United States style of interrogation, these interrogations maintain the goal of fact finding rather than obtaining a confession, and investigators are not permitted to deceive suspects. After initiating the interview, suspects are encouraged to provide a complete account of their involvement or relation to the crime, and they are encouraged to speak freely; close-ended questions are kept to a minimum (Bull & Milne, 2004; Mortimer & Shepherd, 1999). Once the suspect has completed his or her narrative, the investigator provides the opportunity to correct any discrepancies (the "closure" phase). Finally, the investigator compares the suspect's statements to evidence, tries to clear up any inconsistencies, and draws conclusions based on evidence and facts that have been gathered during the "evaluate" phase.

Thus far, evaluations of PEACE have been limited to observational research like that of Clarke and Milne (2001). They observed that the PEACE model appeared to succeed in yielding confession evidence in real cases, but officers seemed to forget their training rather quickly and that only 10 percent of the cases they reviewed were likely in violation of the PACE Act. Clarke and Milne concluded that when compared with pre-PEACE interviews, the post-PEACE interviews were more ethical and preferable overall. Once again, despite moving to a noncoercive approach, investigators using PEACE are able to secure confessions. Police in New Zealand have now also adopted the PEACE protocol after the successes of Great Britain (New Zealand Herald, 2006).

RECOMMENDATIONS FOR BEST PRACTICE

This chapter has attempted to review current research on the false confessions phenomenon in an attempt to delineate factors that likely increase the risks to innocent suspects. Although empirical research on interrogations and confessions continues to evolve, we believe that several best practice recommendations can be offered to police investigators.

Transparency of the Interrogation Process

First and foremost, the interrogation should be made "transparent" through the use of videotaping. Law enforcement personnel often fear that the videotaping of an interrogation will to some degree limit their discretion or effectively reduce the likelihood of achieving a confession from the suspect. In fact, research has demonstrated that the recording of interrogations does not significantly lower the frequency of confessions produced (Geller, 1992; Grant, 1987; Willis, Macleod & Naish, 1988), and investigators have found that videotaping can enhance the perceived strength and voluntary nature of the evidence while protecting the investigator against unfounded allegations of wrongdoing (Sullivan, in press). In a recent survey of U.S. law enforcement, 81 percent of investigators advocated the recordings of custodial interrogations (Kassin et al., 2007). Those seeking to institute such a policy should consider two key issues. First, recording should include all interactions between a suspect and an investigator. Second, the angle of recording should adhere to recommendations based on research by Lassiter and colleagues (*see* Lassiter & Geers, 2004).

Be Wary of Suspect Vulnerabilities

Investigators should evaluate suspects for characteristics that are likely to place them at risk in the interrogation room. As discussed earlier, the age, mental ability, and psychological state of the suspects are important factors to consider prior to initiating any interrogative scenario. Juveniles, and especially young children, should be interviewed in the presence of counsel or parental supervision. Individuals of questionable mental status should be evaluated prior to interrogation. The interview of suspects under the influence of alcohol or drugs or those undergoing withdrawal symptoms should be withheld until treatment has been provided and a state of normal cognitive functioning has returned.

Assess the Reliability of the Confession Statement

Leo and Ofshe (1998) have recommended that investigators evaluate the suspect's postadmission narrative to determine the extent to which the details provided in the statement are consistent with known facts in the case. Given that the goal of an interrogation is to yield evidence of the crime directly from the suspect, it is important that investigators (1) withhold details of the case from the media or third parties that might otherwise contaminate a suspect's knowledge of case-related information and (2) not provide a suspect with details of the case during the course of an interrogation (including evidentiary materials, crime scene photographs, or visits to the crime scene) such that a true assessment of the suspect's knowledge might be gleaned from the confession statement. In addition, investigators should assess whether any novel evidence was obtained during the course of the interrogation that might independently corroborate the confession statement.

CONCLUSION

False confessions occur in our criminal justice system with some regularity and are responsible for the wrongful conviction of innocent individuals around the world. This phenomenon is a troublesome reality, but researchers have begun to delineate factors that may be responsible for its occurrence, including the role of investigative biases stemming from preinterrogation interviews, the psychological pressures placed on an innocent suspect using modern-day interrogation methods, and the individual characteristics that make certain suspects more vulnerable to the power of the interrogation room. Given the maturity of our scientific understanding, we are also now in a position to recommend certain best practice approaches that will assist investigators in achieving true confessions while protecting the innocent. We believe that further research into alternative methods of interrogation that might yield more diagnostic confession evidence (i.e. a greater likelihood of true vs. false confessions) is warranted, particularly with regard to the non-coercive approaches advocated in Great Britain. Ultimately, it will be important for researchers and practitioners to work together on this critical issue.

REFERENCES

Baldwin, J. (1993). Police interviewing techniques: Establishing truth or proof? *The British Journal of Criminology, 33*, 325–352.

Bedau, H.A., and Radelet, M.L. (1987). Miscarriages of justice in potentially capital cases. *Stanford Law Review, 40*, 21–179.

Bem, D.J. (1966). Inducing belief in false confessions. *Journal of Personality & Social Psychology, 3*, 707–710.

Billings, F.J., Taylor, T., Burns, J., Corety, D.L., Garven, S., and Wood, J.M. (2007). Can reinforcement induce children to falsely incriminate themselves? *Law & Human Behavior, 31*, 125–139.

Blagrove, M. (1996). Effects of length of sleep deprivation on interrogative suggestibility. *Journal of Experimental Psychology, 2*, 48–59.

Bond, C.F., Jr., and DePaulo, B.M. (2006). Accuracy of deception judgments. *Personality & Social Psychology Review, 10*, 214–234.

Bull, R., and Milne, R. (2004). Attempts to improve the police interviewing of suspects. In G. D. Lassiter (Ed.), *Interrogations, Confessions, and Entrapment* (pp. 182–196). New York: Kluwer Academic Publishers.

Clarke, C., and Milne, R. (2001). *National Evaluation of the PEACE Investigative Interviewing Course.* Police Research Award Scheme. London: Home Office.

Drizin, S.A., and Colgan, B.A. (2004). Tales from the juvenile confession front: A guide to how standard police interrogation tactics can produce coerced and false confessions from juvenile suspects. In G.D. Lassiter (Ed.), *Interrogations, Confessions, and Entrapment* (pp. 127–162). New York: Kluwer Press.

Drizin, S.A., and Leo, R.A. (2004). The problem of false confessions in the post-DNA world. *North Carolina Law Review, 82,* 891–1007.

Forrest, K.D., Wadkins, T.A., and Miller, R.L. (2002). The role of pre-existing stress on false confessions: An empirical study. *Journal of Credibility Assessment & Witness Psychology, 3,* 23–45.

Forrest, K.D., Wadkins, T.A., and Larson, B.A. (2006). Suspect personality, police interrogations, and false confessions: Maybe it is not just the situation. *Personality & Individual Differences, 40,* 621–628.

Geller, W.A. (1992). *Police Videotaping of Suspect Interrogations and Confessions.* Wilmette, IL: Police Executive Forum.

Grant, A. (1987). Videotaping police questioning: a Canadian experiment. *Criminal Law Review,* 375–383.

Gross, S.R., Jacoby, K., Matheson, D.J., Montgomery, N., and Patil, S. (2005). Exonerations in the United States, 1989 through 2003. *Journal of Criminal Law & Criminology, 95.*

Gudjonsson, G.H. (1984). A new scale of interrogative suggestibility. *Personality & Individual Differences, 5,* 303–314.

Gudjonsson, G.H. (1989). Compliance in an interrogative situation. *Personality & Individual Differences, 10,* 535–540.

Gudjonsson, G.H. (1990). One hundred alleged false confession cases: Some normative data. *Journal of Clinical Psychology, 29,* 249–250.

Gudjonsson, G.H. (1993). Confession evidence, psychological vulnerability and expert testimony. *Journal of Community & Applied Social Psychology, 3,* 117–129.

Gudjonsson, G.H. (2003). *The Psychology of Interrogations and Confessions: A Handbook.* West Sussex, England: John Wiley & Sons, Ltd.

Gudjonsson, G.H. (in press). The psychology of false confessions: A review of the current evidence. In G.D. Lassiter and C. Meissner's (Eds.), *Interrogations and Confessions: Research, Practice, and Policy.* Washington, DC: American Psychiatric Association.

Gudjonsson, G.H., and Clark, N.K. (1986). Suggestibility in police interrogation: A social psychological model. *Social Behaviour, 1,* 83–104.

Gudjonsson, G.H., Hannesdottir, K., Agustsson, T., Sigurdsson, J.F., Gudmundsdottir, A., Pordarttir, P., Tyrfingsson, P., and Petursson, H. (2004). Personality predictors of the failure of alcoholics to come for follow-up assessment. *Personality & Individual Differences, 37,* 805–813.

Henkel, L.A., and Coffman, K.J. (2004). Memory distortion in coerced false confessions: A source monitoring framework analysis. *Applied Cognitive Psychology, 18,* 567–588

Hilgendorf, E.L., and Irving, B. (1981). A decision-making model of confessions. In M.A. Lloyd-Bostock (Ed.), *Psychology in Legal Contexts: Applications and Limitations.* London: MacMillan, 67–84.

Inbau, F.E., Reid, J.E., Buckley, J.P., and Jayne, B.C. (2001). *Criminal Interrogation and Confessions* (4th ed.). Gaithersberg, MD: Aspen.

Innocence Project, The. (2007). Causes and remedies. Retrieved November 9, 2007. Available: http://www.innocenceproject.org/causes/index.php

Irving, B. (1980). *Police Interrogation: A Case Study of Current Practice* (Royal Commission on Criminal Procedure Research Study No. 2). London: Her Majesty's Stationery Office.

Irving, B., and Hilgendorf, L. (1980). *Police Interrogation. A Case Study of Current Practice*. Research Studies No. 2. London: Her Majesty's Stationery Office.

Irving, B., and McKenzie, I.K. (1989). *Police Interrogation: The Effects of the Police and Criminal Evidence Act*. London: Police Foundation of Great Britain.

Kassin, S.M. (1997). The psychology of confession evidence. *American Psychologist, 52*, 221–233.

Kassin, S.M. (2005). On the psychology of confessions: Does innocence put innocents at risk? *American Psychologist, 60*, 215–228.

Kassin, S.M., Goldstein, C.J., and Savitsky, K. (2003). Behavioral confirmation in the interrogation room: On the dangers of presuming guilt. *Law & Human Behavior, 27*, 187–203.

Kassin, S.M., and Gudjonsson, G.H. (2005). The psychology of confessions: A review of the literature and issues. *Psychological Science in the Public Interest, 5*, 33-67.

Kassin, S.M., and Kiechel, K.L. (1996). The social psychology of false confessions: Compliance, internalization, and confabulation. *Psychological Science, 7*, 125–128.

Kassin, S.M., Leo, R. A., Meissner, C.A., Richman, K.D., Colwell, L.H., Leach, A-M., and LaFon, D. (2007). Police interviewing and interrogation: A self-report survey of police practices and beliefs. *Law & Human Behavior*.

Kassin, S.M., Meissner, C.A., and Norwick, R.J. (2005). "I'd know a false confession if I saw one": A comparative study of college students and police investigators. *Law & Human Behavior, 29*, 211–228.

Kassin, S.M., and Wrightsman, L.S. (1985). Confession evidence. In S.M. Kassin and L.S. Wrightsman (Eds), *The Psychology of Evidence and Trial Procedures* (pp. 67–94). London: Sage.

Klaver, J., Rose, V.G., and Lee, Z. (2003, July). *Effect of Different Interrogation Techniques and the Role of Plausibility in a False Confession Paradigm*. Paper presented at the 2003 International Psychology & Law Conference, Edinburgh, Scotland.

Lassiter, G.D., and Geers, A.L. (2004). Evaluation of confession evidence: Effects of presentation format. In G.D. Lassiter (Ed.), *Interrogations, Confessions, and Entrapment* (pp. 197–214). New York: Kluwer Press.

Lassiter, G. D., and Meissner, C. A. (in press). *Interrogations and Confessions: Research, Practice, and Policy*. Washington, DC: American Psychological Association.

Leiken, L.S. (1970). Police interrogation in Colorado: the implementation of Miranda. *Denver Law Journal, 47*, 1–53

Leo, R.A. (1996). Inside the interrogation room. *The Journal of Criminal Law & Criminology, 86*, 266–303.

Leo, R.A. (2004). The third degree and the origins of psychological interrogation in the United States. In D. Lassiter (Ed.), *Interrogations, Confessions, and Entrapment*. Kluwer Academic / Plenum Press.

Leo, R.A., and Ofshe, R. (1998). The consequences of false confessions: Deprivations of liberty and miscarriages of justice in the age of psychological interrogation. *Journal of Criminal Law & Criminology, 88*, 429–496.

Meissner, C.A., and Kassin, S.M. (2002)."He's guilty!": Investigator bias in judgments of truth and deception. *Law & Human Behavior, 26*, 469–480.

Meissner, C.A., and Kassin, S.M. (2004). "You're guilty, so just confess!" Cognitive and behavioral confirmation biases in the interrogation room. In D. Lassiter (Ed.), *Interrogations, Confessions, and Entrapment*. Kluwer Academic / Plenum Press.

Meissner, C.A., Russano, M.B., and Narchet, F.M. (in press). The importance of laboratory science for understanding the psychological processes underlying interrogations and confessions. In G. D. Lassiter & C. Meissner (Eds.), *Interrogations and Confessions: Research, Practice, and Policy*. Washington, DC: American Psychiatric Association.

Miranda v. Arizona, 384 U. S. 436 (1966).

Mortimer, A., and Shepherd, E. (1999). Frames of mind: Schemata guiding cognition and conduct in the interviewing of suspected offenders. In A. Memon and R. Bull (Eds.), *Handbook of the Psychology of Interviewing* (pp. 293–315). Chichester, England: Wiley.

Moston, S., Stephenson, G.M., and Williamson, T.M. (1992). The incidence, antecedents and consequences of the use of the right to silence during police questioning. *Criminal Behavior & Mental Health, 3,* 30–47.

Narchet, F.M., Meissner, C.A., and Russano, M.B. (2008). *Modeling the Effects of Investigator Bias on the Elicitation of True and False Confessions.* Manuscript under review.

Ofshe, R., and Leo, R.A. (1997). The decision to confess falsely: Rational choice and irrational action. *Denver University Law Review, 74,* 979–1122.

Olio, K.A., and Cornell, W.F. (1998). The facade of scientific documentation: A case study of Richard Ofshe's analysis of the Paul Ingram case. Psychology, *Public Policy, & Law, 4,* 1182–1197.

Pearse, J., Gudjonsson, G.H., Clare, I.C.H., and Rutter, S. (1998). Police interviewing and psychological vulnerabilities: Predicting the likelihood of a confession. *Journal of Community & Applied Social Psychology, 8,* 1–21.

Phillips, C., and Brown, D. (1998). *Entry Into the Criminal Justice System: A Survey of Police Arrests and Their Outcomes.* London: Home Office.

Redlich, A.D., and Appelbaum, P.S. (2004). Mental illness, police interrogations, and the potential for false confession. *Psychiatric Services, 55,* 19–21.

Redlich, A.D., and Goodman, G.S. (2003). Taking responsibility for an act not committed: The influence of age and suggestibility. *Law & Human Behavior, 27,* 141–156.

Redlich, A. D., and Meissner, C.A. (in press). Techniques and controversies in the interrogation of suspects: The artful practice versus the scientific study. To appear in J. Skeem et al. (Eds.), *Psychological Science in the Courtroom: Controversies and Consensus.* Guilford Press.

Redlich, A.D., Silverman, M., Chen, J., and Steiner, H. (2004). The police interrogation of children and adolescents. In G.D. Lassiter (Ed.), *Interrogations, Confessions, and Entrapment* (pp. 107–125). New York: Kluwer Press.

Russano, M.B., Meissner, C.M., Narchet, F.M., and Kassin, S.K. (2005). Investigating true and false confessions within a novel experimental paradigm. *Psychological Science, 16,* 481–486.

Scheck, B., Neufeld, P., and Dwyer, J. (2000). *Actual Innocence.* Garden City, NY: Doubleday.

Sigurdsson, J.F., and Gudjonsson, G.H. (1996). Psychological characteristics of "false confessors": A study among Icelandic prison inmates and juvenile offenders. *Personality & Individual Differences, 20,* 321–329.

Softley, P. (1980). *Police Interrogation: An Observational Study in Four Police Stations.* London, England: Her Majesty's Stationery Office.

Sullivan, T.P. (in press). The wisdom of custodial recording. In G.D. Lassiter, and C. Meissner (Eds.), *Interrogations and Confessions: Research, Practice, and Policy.* Washington, DC: American Psychiatric Association.

Viljoen, J.L., Klaver, J., and Roesch, R. (2005). Legal decisions of preadolescent and adolescent defendants: Predictors of confessions, pleas, communication with attorneys, and appeals. *Law & Human Behavior, 29,* 253–277.

Vrij, A. (2008). *Detecting Lies and Deceit: Pitfalls and Opportunities.* West Sussex, England: John Wiley & Sons Ltd.

White, W. (2003). *Miranda's Waning Protections: Police Interrogation Practices After Dickerson.* Ann Arbor, MI: University of Michigan Press.

Willis, C.F., Macleod, J., and Naish, P. (1988). *The Tape Recording of Police Interviews with Suspects: A Second Interim Report.* Home Office Research Study No. 97. London: Her Majesty's Stationery Office.

Wright, L. (1993a). Remembering Satan, Part I. *The New Yorker, 69*, 60–81.
Wright, L. (1993b). Remembering Satan, Part II. *The New Yorker, 69*, 54–76.
Zimbardo, P.G. (1967). The psychology of police confessions. *Psychology Today, 1*, 17–20, 25–27.

Part C

INVESTIGATING OR RESPONDING TO CRIME

Chapter Ten

CRIMINAL PROFILING

RICHARD N. KOCSIS

Criminal profiling can be understood as a psychological technique where-by behaviors evident in a crime or series of related crimes are evaluated typically for the purpose of inferring attributes about probable offenders (Kocsis, 2006). A few examples of such attributes can include, but are not limited to, the age of the offenders, their gender, level of education, and general appearance; and even aspects of their personality (Rossi, 1982; Vorpagel, 1982). The amalgamation of these characteristics is, in colloquial parlance, referred to as a *criminal profile,* and individuals who compile them are often referred to as *profilers* (Douglas, Burgess, Burgess & Ressler, 2006; Jeffers, 1992; Campbell & DeNevi, 2004). This conversion of a specific task into a vocation is something of a peculiarity given that a universally accepted standard denoting who may engage in constructing a criminal profile does not currently exist (Bekerian & Jackson, 1997; Bumgarner, 2007; Kocsis & Palermo, 2007).

To fully understand what criminal profiling is also requires some explanation of what it is not, given the existence of a number of other similarly entitled techniques. One example is DNA profiling, which entails the analysis of organic matter typically found at a crime scene to establish whether the genetic code corresponds with that of a person or persons of interest in relation to that crime (Lazer, 2004). Another example is that of racial profiling (also know as actuarial profiling) (Harcourt, 2007) which, as a technique, predominantly involves the conglomeration of demographic characteristics believed to be commonly shared by individuals who engage in a particular form of crime to potentially identify similar future offenders. An illustration of such profiling involves the identification of supposedly typical character-

213

istics of individuals engaged in smuggling narcotics through airports that customs officers may proactively use as a guide to select and search travelers. In contrast, criminal profiling is reactive via the examination of behaviors exhibited at crime scenes. Additionally, the attributes predicted for an offender in a criminal profile are determined by the interpretation of the exhibited behaviors in the particular crime under examination. Consequently, the content of criminal profiles can be quite varied, whereas the attributes contained in racial profiles are reflective of a fixed set of aggregated demographics.

Criminal profiling has also developed a number of semantic variations in nomenclature, including offender profiling, psychological profiling, and criminal personality profiling to name only a few. The precise basis of such variations in terminology is unclear, but their use predominantly appears related to the linguistic preferences of differing regions of the world. Thus, offender profiling appears to be commonly used in the United Kingdom and Europe (e.g. Boon, 1995; Canter, 1989; Jackson & Bekerian, 1997) whereas criminal profiling seems more common in North America (Hicks & Sale, 2006; Holmes & Holmes, 2002). For convenience, however, the technique will continue to be referred to herein as criminal profiling or simply profiling.

The basic purpose of criminal profiling is to act as a tool that may assist with lines of inquiry in a criminal investigation (Douglas & Burgess, 1986; Douglas, Ressler, Burgess & Hartman, 1986; Holmes & Holmes, 2002). A number of differing avenues exist whereby this objective may be achieved. Possibly the most common method is for a profile to serve as a tool for prioritizing the investigation of known suspects. Thus, suspects who possess characteristics matching those of a profile are prioritized for greater scrutiny by investigators in comparison to suspects who do not match the profile (Douglas & Burgess, 1986). In this context it should be noted that the use of criminal profiles are only recommended as a method by which investigative resources, in terms of which leads to pursue first, can be ordered. The degree of congruence that a suspect may have with the predicted attributes of a criminal profile is not advocated as a means by which suspects are eliminated from an investigation (Douglas et al., 1986).

The context in terms of what types of crime criminal profiling may be applied to is something of a contested issue. Traditionally, criminal profiling has been recommended as most beneficial to the investigation of intractable crimes (Douglas & Oleshaker, 1995; Fisher, 1993; Ressler & Shachtman, 1992), which are suggestive of some form of psychopathology or aberrant psychological drive(s), or both, within the offender(s) (Geberth, 1983; Holmes & Holmes, 2002; Rossi, 1982; Vorpagel, 1982). This is not to suggest that profiling is not potentially applicable to more conventional forms of crime. However, it is in the context of intractable, aberrant, violent crimes where profiling is seen as being of optimal benefit in practical (i.e. operational) terms (Nowikowski, 1995). Whereas some scholars appear to endorse this perspective (e.g. Campbell & DeNevi, 2004; Hickey, 2001; Holmes & Holmes, 2002; Kocsis, 2006) others seem to view profiling as broader in application and extending potentially to a wider variety of offences beyond intractable violent crimes (e.g. Alison, 2005; Canter, 2004).

Perhaps one of the greatest myths surrounding criminal profiling is the belief that it is a recent innovation. In contrast to popular media depictions, the concept of criminal profiling – that is, examining behavioral patterns evident in a crime to glean some impression of the probable offender – has been in use for well over a century. Beyond analogies between criminal profiling and Sir Arthur Conan Doyle's consummate fictional detective Sherlock Holmes (Doyle, 1891), examples of profiling can be found throughout history dating back as far as 1888 and the investigation of the Whitechappel murderer, also known as Jack the Ripper (Whittington-Egan, 1975). Other instances in which criminal profiling has been used (typically via the consultation of a mental health professional) appear throughout history and involve some of the world's most infamous cases. A few such examples include the kidnapping of Charles Lindbergh, Jr., in the 1920s (Shoenfeld, 1936), the evaluation of Adolf Hitler by the U.S.. Office of Strategic Services (Langer, 1972), the Mad Bomber of New York, and the Boston Strangler in the 1950s and 1960s (Brussel, 1968; Frank, 1966). Although research and development into dedicated methods for criminal profiling have certainly flourished over approximately the past three decades (Dowden, Bennell & Bloomfield, 2007), the historical realities indicate that the fundamental concept of profiling, that is, evaluating crime behaviors to infer attributes about the probable offender, is in fact very old.

APPROACHES TO CRIMINAL PROFILING

Criminal profiling has evolved over time, and as a consequence what can be described as differing schools of thought or approaches to the task of constructing a criminal profile have also developed (Kocsis, 2007a). In this context, the practice of criminal profiling can be viewed as somewhat analogous to the field of personality theory. In attempting to understand human behavior there is common agreement among scholars in the fundamental construct of the mind (Gregory, 2004). However, although there is a general consensus in this basic construct, various rivaling theoretical perspectives (e.g. psychodynamic, cognitive behaviorism, gestalt) exist that endeavor to explain the operation of the mind (Monte, 1995). Within the topic of criminal profiling there is, akin to the field of personality theory, general agreement with the fundamental notion of evaluating crime behaviors to gain some insight into the probable perpetrator. Also akin to the field of personality theory are differing views concerning the best methods and principles to employ when profiling crimes (Palermo & Kocsis, 2005). Consequently, to explain the process of profiling requires a brief overview of these differing approaches as well as some examination of the clinically oriented origins of criminal profiling and the discrete topic of geographic profiling. It must be noted, however, that the parameters of this chapter do not allow for any comprehensive coverage of the underlying principles inherent to each of the approaches. As a consequence, the following material is primarily focused on highlighting some of the key themes and features that typically characterize each approach.

Diagnostic Evaluations: Clinical Perspectives on Profiling Crimes

As previously indicated, the historical origins of criminal profiling largely emanate from the endeavors of various mental health professionals who have been consulted on an intermittent basis to render an evaluation of a crime that may be of some assistance to police investigators. This circumstance in which the task of profiling has occurred has been referred to as diagnostic evaluations (DE) (Wilson, Lincoln & Kocsis, 1997). It needs to be clarified that DE are largely an artifact of the practical application of psychiatry/psychology rather than being a coherent research based approach to profiling *per se*. The term DE is best viewed as a descriptor for the aforementioned circumstance in which a criminal profile is sought from a mental health professional. Consequently, the theoretical basis for DE is the common method by which profiles are constructed. That is, with DE mental health professionals draw on their disciplinary knowledge, typically from psychiatry or psychology, to profile the crime. Thus, a profile is produced via an attempt to relate or diagnose possible psychopathologies indicative of the behaviors evident in a crime and from this to extrapolate some understanding of the probable offender (e.g. Badcock, 1997; Britton, 1997; Boon, 1997; Girod, 2004: Kent, 1999; Palermo, 2004; Proulx, Beauregard, Cusson & Nicole, 2007; Revitch & Schlesinger, 1989). It is from this diagnostic-like process of assessing possible psychopathology that the term diagnostic evaluation was derived (Palermo & Kocsis, 2005).

The legacy and importance of DE should not be underestimated because a number of significant dimensions to the contemporary practice of criminal profiling originate from DE. Foremost among them is that all approaches to profiling share a fundamental disciplinary grounding in psychology/psychiatry in attempting to understand human behaviors, motivations, and psychopathological factors that may explain exhibited patterns of behavior. Additionally, DE remain one of the most readily accessible means by which a criminal profile may be obtained. That is, investigators to this day may simply elect to consult mental health professionals regarding a particular crime to ascertain whether they can offer some useful insight into the crime and its perpetrator(s) (Wilson et al., 1997). Indeed, what have been hailed as some of the most remarkably perspicuous criminal profiles have originated from individuals who could arguably be viewed as proponents of the diagnostic evaluation approach (Palermo & Kocsis, 2005).

Criminal Investigative Analysis

What arguably constitutes the first systematic research-based approach to criminal profiling is the collective work of personnel affiliated with the Behavioral Sciences Unit (BSU) of the Federal Bureau of Investigation's (FBI) training academy (Ressler, Douglas, Groth & Burgess, 1980; van Zandt, 1994). The BSU approach to criminal profiling has been termed criminal investigative analysis (CIA) (Douglas & Oleshaker, 1995; Hazelwood, Ressler, Depue & Douglas, 1995). In response to a perceived prevalence of aberrant violent crime and a desire to assist in the investigation of such crimes agents attached to the BSU began a research program in the late 1970s to study the behavioral patterns manifest in these offences (Ressler, Burgess & Douglas, 1988). The ultimate purpose of this research was to garner a better understanding of the *modus operandi* and psychological mechanisms driving the perpetrator of these crimes. Integral to these research endeavors, however, was an operational agenda for law enforcement to identify features specifically focused on the needs of investigative personnel (Ressler & Shachtman, 1992). Previous research in the area was viewed as predominantly clinical in perspective and thus oriented toward topics that were not considered particularly relevant to the objectives of investigators (e.g. rehabilitation) and thus superfluous in attempting to apprehend the perpetrators of such offences (Ressler, 1985).

The method for constructing a criminal profile using the CIA method is somewhat akin to DE in that it involves a process that can be regarded as similar to the formulation of clinical judgment by a mental health practitioner (Dietz, 1985; Douglas et al., 1986). What differentiates CIA, however, is that instead of drawing upon diagnostic criteria for mental disorders, it draws on its own body of research concerning crime patterns, related offender characteristics, motivations, and avenues for the investigation of offences (e.g. Douglas et al., 2006). The modes of crime that have been studied by the BSU are quite diverse but have predominantly focused on crimes of interpersonal violence, such as sexual assault (Hazelwood, 1995; Hazelwood & Burgess,

1987), arson (Icove & Estepp, 1987), and homicide (Ressler et al., 1988).

Possibly the most renowned piece of research developed in the CIA sphere is the *organized/disorganized* offender typology that was originally derived from the study of sexual murderers and their crime scenes (Ressler, Burgess, Douglas, Hartman & D'Agostino, 1986). The premise underpinning this dichotomy is that crime scenes are distinguishable and thus interpretable by their degree of behavioral sophistication. Thus, an organized crime scene is indicative of a high degree of behavioral sophistication on the part of the offender, such as planning and precautionary measures undertaken in respect of the offense. A constellation of distinguishable offender characteristics has been identified as being commonly associated with these organized crime scene behaviors. A few examples of such offender characteristics include a higher standard of education, having a skilled job, and possessing a vehicle. In contrast to the patterns indicative of the organized category are the features of the *disorganized* category. Thus, a disorganized crime scene is characterized by behaviors that are viewed as being indicative of a low or minimal degree of behavioral sophistication on the part of the offender(s). In this respect, disorganized crimes are described as featuring comparative disarray and are viewed as being perpetrated in a spontaneous/opportunistic manner suggestive of no real planning. Akin to the organized category, a constellation of commonly occurring characteristics inherent to offenders who perpetrate crimes in a disorganized fashion have also been identified. Some of these attributes typically include a low standard of education, limited or no employment, and being slovenly in appearance (Ressler et al., 1988).

The construction of a criminal profile via the CIA approach involves an assessment of the behaviors exhibited in the crime as compared with the organized/disorganized dichotomy. Thus, some interpretation is made as to whether the exhibited behaviors correspond with the behavioral attributes of either the organized or disorganized category. Once such a determination is made the process of predicting offender characteristics is determined from the corresponding offender characteristics previously developed as indicative of either an organized or disorganized offender (Ressler et al., 1986).

Investigative Psychology

Another research-based approach to profiling is that known as investigative psychology (IP), which appears to advocate the creation of a disciplinary specialization focused on psychological principles specifically applicable to the investigation of crime (Canter, 1995, 2000). In this context what may traditionally be viewed as criminal profiling constitutes only one of a range of topics encapsulated by IP. Justification for developing the nomenclature IP is debatable, given the prior existence of other analogous specializations. That is, a number of disciplinary fields already exist, such as forensic, police, and criminal psychology, which arguably already embody the topics that appear to form the basis of IP (Arrigo & Shipley, 2005; Aumiller et al., 2008; Bull et al., 2007; Raskin, 1989).

Regardless, a coherent body of empirical research has developed in IP whereby crime behaviors have been studied for the purpose of gaining some understanding about the attributes of a probable offender that may be used in an investigative capacity. One of the characteristic features of IP research is that it advocates the analysis of crime behaviors independent of the inference of motivations attached to those behaviors. The inference of motivations with behaviors is argued as being a methodological limitation to previous research in the area (Canter & Heritage, 1989). Another common feature of IP research is the use of ideographic methods of analysis and the use of quite specialized statistics such as multidimensional scaling (MDS) (Coxon, 1982).

Figure 10-1

SSA Diagram of Homicide Crime Scene Behaviors with Offense Patterns Identified

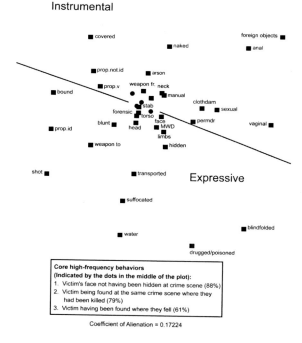

From Salfati, G.C. (2000). The nature of expressive and instrumentality in homicide. *Homicide Studies*, Vol. 4(3), pp. 265-293 (figure 1). © Sage Publications, Inc. Reprinted with permission of Sage Publications, Inc.

The findings of IP studies often focus on the identification of discernible themes that characterize particular behavioral styles exhibited in various forms of crime. As a simple example, an analysis of exhibited behaviors in domestic homicides may reveal cogent patterns indicative of either an instrumental or expressive purpose in the typically enacted behaviors of these crimes (Salfati, 2000, *see* Figure 10-1). From the identification of these patterns general theorems can then be advanced that characterize and explain the criminal behavior observed. The development of these theorems can in turn inform any predictions concerning the probable offender of similar future crimes. Akin to other approaches to criminal profiling IP's research efforts have examined a range of crime modalities including arson (e.g. Canter & Fritzon, 1998), serial murder (e.g. Godwin, 2000), and sexual assault (e.g. Canter & Heritage, 1989).

Crime Action Profiling

Possibly the most recent research-based approach to criminal profiling is that of crime action profiling (CAP). In many respects, CAP is a hybrid of its predecessors and thus, akin to CIA, endeavors to focus on issues more pertinent to the operational goals of investigators. Additionally, CAP makes use of similar methods of statistical analysis (i.e. MDS) akin to IP and the initial premise of analyzing crime behaviors independent of inferring motives in an offender.

Where CAP markedly differs from other approaches, however, is in the development of models in which crime behaviors are correlated with various offender characteristics and thus operate as mechanisms by which the perpetrators of future crimes may be profiled. The use of CAP models is conceptually similar to the process of reading time from a nondigital wristwatch. The models feature diagrams displaying various crime behaviors as denoted by a range of icons. The crime behaviors exhibited in the offence under consideration are then examined for their correspondence with those in the relevant CAP model. Thereafter, various arrows that have been superimposed onto a CAP model serve as guides, dependent upon their proximity to the identified behaviors in the model to attributes about the offender that may be predicted. Thus, through a somewhat mechanized process comparisons can be drawn with displayed behaviors in a crime, and from the interpretation of the CAP model, predictions can be made about various attributes that may be related to the probable offender. One component of a CAP model is displayed in Figure 10-2.

As a final point, the CAP approach adopts a refined perspective in the application of profiling to crimes of an aberrant violent nature. In this respect only three CAP models have thus far been developed: one that is designed for the profiling of sexual murders, another focused upon the profiling of serial rape offences, and a third for the profiling of serial arson offenses. This is not to suggest that the concepts inherent to CAP may not be adaptable to more conventional modes of crime but rather that the key focus is on aberrant crimes, which profiling is arguably better suited to in terms of assisting criminal investigators beyond standard investigative procedures. The various principles and procedures inherent to the CAP approach to profiling crimes are best summarized in Kocsis (2006).

Figure 10-2
VICTIM CHARACTERISTICS CLUSTER VECTORS FITTED TO THE TWO DIMENSIONAL HOMICIDE SCENE BEHAVIOR MDS COORDINATES

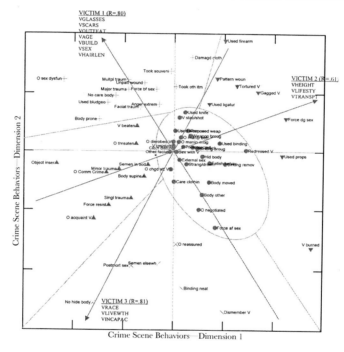

Source: Kocsis, R. N., Cooksey, R. W., & Irwin, H. J. (2002). Psychological profiling of sexual murders: An empirical model. *International Journal of Offender Therapy and Comparative Criminology.* 46(3), 532-553. (Fig. 3). Sage Publications, Inc. Reprinted with permission of Sage Publications, Inc.

Geographic Profiling

Although not a comprehensive approach to the profiling of crimes, geographic profiling is a discrete topic within the field that is focused on the geographic relevance of offense locations. The geographic examination of crime is not a recent concept to the discipline of criminology (e.g. Brantingham & Brantingham, 1981; Rengert & Wasilchick, 1985; Reppetto, 1974). Similarly, the examination of offense localities to garner some insight about a perpetrator is not a recent innovation (Kind, 1987). However, with the surge of interest in the development of criminal profiling, as well as computerized mapping programs known as Geographic Information Systems (GIS), a reinvigoration of interest in the topic has developed under the conceptual label of *geographic profiling* (Palermo & Kocsis, 2005). The objective of geographic profiling is the analysis of related crime locations for the purpose of identifying a specific region that may possess some relationship or nexus with the perpetrator(s) of the offenses (Rossmo, 1997). The nature of the nexus between the identified geographic region and the offender can manifest itself in a host of differing circumstances, including the general location of the offender's residence, workplace, or even the residence of a significant other party (e.g. parents, girlfriend). The application of this information to assist in an investigation is not unlike how other information in criminal profiles is used. As a hypothetical example, a geographic profile may identify a region of approximately two square miles containing three distinct suburbs. Investigators can then use this information as a means by which suspects may be prioritized for further investigation. That is, suspects who hold some connection with the identified region, such as their home being situated within any one of the three identified suburbs, can be prioritized for further inquiry over other suspects who do not possess such a nexus with the identified region.

Analogous to the general area of criminal profiling there are a number of rivaling approaches (e.g. Canter, 2004b; Levine, 2000; Rossmo, 2000; Young, 2003) with respect to the calculations and measurements employed in developing geographic profiles, each of which possesses its own rivaling merits and limitations (Stangeland, 2005; van der Kemp & van Koppen, 2007). In spite of their differences, however, there are some fundamental commonalties among the approaches. At a basic level, all approaches involve the plotting of known offense locations on some form of map. Similarly, all approaches operate on the premise that offense locations possess some form of causality with the offender, who is typically not itinerant and thus enjoys some stability in his or her own lifestyle, location, and movement patterns. From these core principles, differing methods have been developed for how offense locations are mapped and used as points of measurement from which the prediction area indicative of a geographic profile is then developed.

The differences among these theorems for geographic profiling appear to stem, to some extent, from the disciplinary origins of the differing proponents as well as their reliance on geographic information systems for undertaking certain computations. Thus, the work by Rossmo (2000) predominantly derives from disciplinary principles indicative of geography, whereas the work of Canter (2004b) is more sourced in the disciplinary specialization referred to as *environmental psychology* (Lundrigan & Canter, 2001). The methods advocated by Rossmo (2000) initially emphasized the use of GIS and thus a semiautomated approach for developing geographic profiles; an example of which is displayed in Figure 10-3. In contrast, Canter's work (2004b) originally used traditional mapping techniques; however, in subsequent years, this has developed to include GIS programs for generating geographic profiles.

Figure 10-3
GEOGRAPHIC PROFILE PREDICTION AREA
DEPICTED WITH PROBABILITIES VALUE

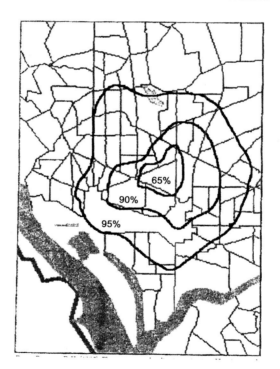

From: Rossmo, D.K. (1995). Place, space and police investigation: Hunting serial violent criminals. In: J.E. Eck and D.A. Weisburd (Eds.), *Crime and Place: Crime Prevention Studies*, Vol. 4, pp. 217-235. Monsey, NYL Criminal Justice Press Reproduced with permission of Criminal Justice Press.

THE VALIDITY AND UTILITY OF CRIMINAL PROFILING

Given the renown criminal profiling enjoys in popular media portrayals (Boon, 1995; Herndon, 2007) and true crime literature (Britton, 1997, Canter, 1994; Douglas & Oleshaker, 1995; Hazelwood & Michaud, 1999; McCrary & Ramsland, 2003; Ressler & Shachtman, 1992; Vorpagel & Harrington, 1998), it is difficult to reconcile the paucity of scientifically grounded evidence supporting the technique. This is not to assert that research into the development of criminal profiling has progressed independently of considerations concerning the fundamental validity of the technique. However, only in approximately the past two decades have some concerted attempts been made to test the accuracy (*vis-à-vis* validity) of profiles via scientifically controlled experiments.

What is arguably the largest available source of evidence relied upon in support of the merits of criminal profiling are anecdotal accounts (such as those contained in true crime literature) in which profiling is used and almost invariably judged to be useful and therefore accurate. Unfortunately, such accounts of profiling successes appear to have given rise to a phenomenon whereby the perceived benefits derived from the use of criminal profiles and thereby their continued use have come to be interpreted as a proxy indicator of their accuracy (Poythress, Otto, Darkas & Starr, 1993). This circumstance has been referred to as the *operational utilitarian argument* (Kocsis, 2006). The development of this argument is ironically simply a manifestation of the old saying "the proof is in the pudding." Simply put, if criminal profiles were not deemed accurate and beneficial to police investigators, law enforcement would not continue to use them. Because police investigators continue to request profiles, this circumstance is cited as an indicator that profiles must therefore be accurate (Jeffers, 1992; Poythress et al., 1993).

Although the logic of the operational utilitarian argument is intuitively appealing, its rationale relies on the assumption that perceptions concerning profiles are, in fact, reliable. Unfortunately, a number of recent studies have suggested otherwise and have revealed some troubling aspects regarding the perceived merits of criminal profiles. Firstly, a study by Alison, Smith, and Morgan (2003) demonstrated the ambiguity of information contained in profiles. In this particular study participants were asked to gauge the relative merits of two profiles, one of which was genuine; the other was deliberately contrived to be similar but inaccurate. Alarmingly, in examining the two profiles, participants judged both to be equally meritorious, indicating that even an incorrect profile could be perceived to possess some merit. Possibly the most confronting research to challenge the operational utilitarian argument however arose from a series of studies that examined the relationship between the belief (i.e. confidence) individuals possess, or were induced to possess in criminal profiling, and their evaluations concerning the merit (i.e. accuracy) of a profile (Kocsis, 2006). These studies found an incremental relationship between belief in profiling and the perceived merits of a criminal profile. Thus, the more an individual believed in the value of criminal profiling, the more meritorious a criminal profile was perceived to be.

These studies provide some troubling evidence that collectively serve to suggest that the perceptions of criminal profiles (such as those from anecdotal accounts) should not be relied on as a measure of their merit.

Quasi-Experimental Studies on Profiler Accuracy

At a cursory level, empirically testing the accuracy of criminal profiles would seem to be a relatively straightforward task of comparing the predictions contained in a criminal profile with the characteristics of the apprehended offender. Unfortunately, developing a suitably robust research methodology wherein such measurements can be objectively undertaken is surprisingly problematic. The difficulties are based partly on the diversity of the information potentially to be found in criminal profiles and partly on the circumstances (i.e. different modes and complexity of differing crimes) under which a criminal profile is sought. As a consequence, it is questionable how methodologically robust and representative any study may be that endeavors to combine and then measure data imbued with such potential vagaries.

A small number of quasi-experiments have been conducted that simulate the profiling of a crime and thus endeavor to impartially test the abilities of profilers, *vis-à'-vis* the accuracy of the profiles constructed by them. Accordingly, through this experimental procedure, many of the aforementioned methodological problems surrounding the evaluation of profiles are minimized or avoided as participants profile the same crime within roughly the same parameters. The first example of such an experiment occurred as a subcomponent of a study by Pinizzotto and Finkel (1990). This experiment compared groups of various skill-based participants, including police detectives, psychologists, students, and trained profilers, on a simulated profiling task of a rape and a murder. Case files for a murder and a rape offence were presented to these participants who were then asked to predict (i.e. profile) the characteristics of the probable offender for each of the crimes via a multiple-choice questionnaire that itemized and thus quantified possible responses (i.e. predicted characteristics). Both the rape and the murder cases had been solved, with the respective offender convicted. The identity of the offenders in terms of the correct responses to the multiple-choice questionnaires presented to the participants were known; consequently, the responses (i.e. the profiled characteristics of the offenders) could be objectively scored for accuracy.

The findings of Pinizzotto and Finkel's (1990) study were somewhat mixed with the trained profilers surpassing the other groups in accurately predicting (i.e. profiling) the characteristics of the offender in the rape case but not in the murder case. Subsequent to their study, another series of studies adopting a similar experimental design further tested the capabilities of profilers via a simulated profiling exercise requiring the prediction of an offender's characteristics via a multiple-choice questionnaire that could be objectively scored (Kocsis, 2006). The overall findings of this research provide some tentative support for the capabilities of profilers to accurately predict the characteristics of the unknown offender at a generally superior standard to that of the compared groups (Kocsis, 2007b).

The studies by Pinizzotto and Finkel (1990) and Kocsis (2007b) represent promising beginnings in empirically testing the accuracy (i.e. validity) of profiling. Although their findings are encouraging, they must nonetheless be interpreted conservatively because further replication and exploration of their findings will be needed in the future (e.g. Gogan, 2007; Hodges & Jacquin, 2008). In this context, the research thus far should be viewed as merely a tentative start in lending support to the potential of criminal profiling. Unfortunately, however, these modest findings appear to have been long surpassed by the apparent reputation and claims of accuracy that profiling already seems to enjoy (Herndon, 2007).

The Utility of Criminal Profiles

In the wake of the paucity of scientific evidence attesting to the validity of criminal profiles, one issue that occasionally seems to be overlooked is the utility of profiling in assisting with the resolution of crime (Oleson, 1996). Assuming that a criminal profile can, hypothetically, accurately predict various attributes about an offender does not necessarily imply that the knowledge of these attributes will tangibly assist in the investigation and apprehension of the offender and thus effect some meaningful reduction in crime (Farrington, 2007). Ironically, the evidence considering the utility of criminal profiling is, arguably, equally as scant as that examining the accuracy of profiles. A large part of this problem is that identifying and thus quantifying utility is a conceptually difficult task in terms of ascertaining precisely how a profile may have been of some material assistance (Kocsis & Palermo, 2007). Although anecdotal examples are readily available where profiles have been used during the course of an investigation and, in retrospect, the predictions of these profiles are viewed as corresponding with the apprehended offender, how exactly these profiles assisted in apprehending the offender is not always clear (Kocsis, 2007; Pinizzotto, 1984). This has led some in the field of profiling to comment that to the best of their knowledge a profile has yet to be directly instrumental in solving a crime (Ressler & Shachtman, 1992).

Nonetheless, an interesting source of information concerning the utility of profiles can be found in the various surveys that have sought to gauge the satisfaction police personnel have derived from the use of criminal profiles during the course of an investigation (e.g. Copson, 1995; Jackson, van Koppen & Herbrink, 1993; Pinizzotto, 1984; Trager & Brewster, 2001). It is important to note, however, that these studies do not measure utility *per se* but rather the surveyed usefulness of a profile by police personnel who have used them. The common theme to emerge from these studies is that police personnel generally consider criminal profiles beneficial and of some assistance, but ironically, indications of precisely how the profiles were of assistance is less clear.

PROFILERS AS EXPERT WITNESSES

Although the use of profiling in criminal investigations is well chronicled (e.g. Britton, 1997; Canter, 1994; Douglas & Oleshaker, 1995; Hazelwood & Michaud, 2001; Ressler & Shachtman, 1992), there have been some comparatively recent attempts to admit into evidence the testimony of profilers in evaluating criminal behaviors. The general view from legal scholars on this issue appears to be one of trepidation (Meyer, 2007; Ormerod, 1999; Risinger & Loop, 2002), which is evidently shared by members of the judiciary around the world when considering the admissibility of such evidence. Judicial comment for example, from the United Kingdom on profiling has opined: "psychological [i.e. criminal] profiling as an aid to police investigations is one thing, but its use as a means of proof in court is another" (*R. v. Guilfoyle*, 2001, p. 68). Similar reservations concerning profiling and in particular some of its proponents were expressed in Australia where it was observed that:

> . . . courts must exercise constant vigilance to ensure that they are not unwittingly misled. Amongst the many factors which may lead an expert witness into error is a malady which, if encountered in a new car salesperson, might be described as gross product enthusiasm. Some witnesses seem to become so fervid about the potential of their chosen discipline that they lose sight of its limitations and are borne by their enthusiasm into making claims that could not be supported by more sober and objective assessment. (*R. v. Hillier*, 2003, p. 10)

Within the United States, efforts to have the testimony of profilers admitted into evidence has experienced a somewhat checkered reception because testimony has either been excluded from the outset or initially admitted and then subsequently disallowed upon appeal (*Commonwealth of Pennsylvania v. DiStefano*, 1999; *State v. Fortin*, 1999; 2004). The present chapter does not allow for a detailed exposition of the legal reasoning underpinning this circumstance. Suffice it to say, without delving too deeply into legal doctrine such as general acceptance (*Frye v. United States*, 1923) or other criteria in the form of the *Federal Rules of Evidence* (2004), the admission of criminal profiling within the United States and abroad appears to be hampered by its inherently probabilistic (i.e. speculative) nature. Within most western common law legal systems there is an imperative to assess whether the *probative* value of any posited evidence will outweigh any *prejudicial* impact of that testimony (Davis & Follette, 2002; Kirkpatrick, 1998). Simply put, western common law legal systems chiefly function on the basis of the assessment of directly pertinent factual information evident in the specific case before the court. The obstacle confronting criminal profiling and the testimony that profilers may offer is that they cannot, for example, sufficiently attest to the fact that their predictions relate to the particular person charged and tried for a crime. The testimony derived from profiling can only attest that the characteristics of the probable offender match, or do not match, those of the accused. They cannot however, unequivocally claim that due to any correspondence, or lack thereof, the accused is likely guilty or innocent. For this reason the evidence of profilers has in the main thus far been excluded and described as "evidence intended to address guilt by likening a defendant to a profile or stereotype of those likely to commit the crime in question" and as a consequence "has great potential for introducing bias and error" (Davis & Follette, 2002, p. 152).

Perhaps in response to the apparent aversion of courts to admitting profiling testimony, ways of introducing similar alternative testimony has increasingly been explored. These alternative avenues appear to involve testimony that seeks to avoid making inferences about the probable offender but nonetheless provides some form of analysis of the behaviors evident in the specific crime(s). Interestingly, this approach appears to have enjoyed, thus far, some limited success in Canadian jurisdictions in terms of the admission of such testimony (e.g. *R. v. Ranger*, 2003; *R. v. Clark*, 2004). However, these alternatives have not gone unnoticed and have also attracted criticism as merely being "a different suit on the same animal" and as "a distinction without a difference" (Grezlak, 1999, p. 2). As a consequence, further examination and testing of the legal merits of this type of testimony in future legal proceedings will invariably occur.

CONCLUSION

The technique of criminal profiling is indicative of a long-held fascination the human race has had with attempting to understand criminal behaviors and the perpetrators of crime. Although fictional analogies describing profiling can be found in classical literature, historical examples involving the use of some external expert, typically a mental health professional, to examine crimes for the purpose of offering investigators some insight into the probable offender date back to the previous century.

In recent decades, there has been a significant increase in interest in the development of criminal profiling techniques. This heightened interest has, analogous to the field of personality theory, spawned a number of rivaling schools of thought concerning how the prediction (i.e. profiling) of offender characteristics from exhibited crime behaviors may be undertaken. At this time there does not appear to be any clear indication of the best way to profile crimes because each approach possesses its own inherent strengths and weaknesses. What is increasingly apparent from research into the topic of profiling however are the difficulties in assessing the fundamental merits of profiling in terms of its validity and utility. Although some tentative empirical research has emerged to support the capabilities of profilers, these modicums of evidence seem to be eclipsed by the favorable reputation the technique appears to enjoy universally.

In the wake of this apparent popularity it is perhaps unsurprising that in recent years an increasing number of attempts to admit, in some capacity, profiles into evidence for legal proceedings have occurred. In the judicial arena at least, however, the scientific merits of criminal profiling appear to have come under far more critical scrutiny than ever before and in this context has generally been considered unsuitable as a reliable form of evidence in the context of criminal proceedings.

REFERENCES

Alison, L. (2005). From trait-based profiling to psychological contributions to apprehension methods. In L. Alison, (Ed.), *The Forensic Psychologists Casebook: Psychological Profiling and Criminal Investigation* (pp. 3–22), Devon: Willan Publishing.

Alison, L., Smith, M., and Morgan, K. (2003). Interpreting the accuracy of offender profiles. *Psychology, Crime and Law, 9*, 185–95.

Arrigo, B.A., and Shipley, S.L. (2005). *Introduction to Forensic Psychology* (2nd ed). NY: Elsevier Academic Press.

Aumiller, G.S., Corey, D., Brewster, J., Allen, S., Gupton, H., Cuttler, M., and Honig, A. (2008). Defining the field of police psychology: Core domain & proficiencies. *Journal of Police and Criminal Psychology, 22*, 65–76.

Badcock, R. (1997). Developmental and clinical issues in relation to offending in the individual. In J.L. Jackson and D.A. Belcerian (Eds.), *Offender Profiling: Theory, Research and Practice.* (pp. 9-42). New York: John Wiley & Sons.

Bekerian, D.A., and Jackson, J.L. (1997). Critical issues in offender profiling. In J.L. Jackson, and D.A. Bekerian, (Eds.), *Offender Profiling: Theory, Research and Practice.* (pp. 209–220). New York: John Wiley & Sons.

Boon, J.C.W. (1995). Offender profiling: Distinguishing the media prurience from the real-life science. *Inter Alia, 1*, 31–35.

Boon, J.C.W. (1997). The contribution of personality theories to psychological profiling. In J.L. Jackson, and D.A. Bekerian, (Eds.) *Offender Profiling: Theory, Research and Practice.* (pp. 43–60). New York: John Wiley & Sons.

Britton, P. (1997). *The Jigsaw Man.* London: Bantam Press.

Brantingham, P.L., and Brantingham, P.J. (1981). *Environmental Criminology.* Beverly Hills, CA: Sage.

Brussel, J. (1968). *Casebook of a Criminal Psychiatrist.* NY: Howard Geis.

Bull, R., Cookie, C., Hatcher. R., Woodhams, J., Bilby, C., and Grant, T. (2007). *Criminal Psychology: A Beginner's Guide.* London: Oneworld Publications

Bumgarner, J. (2007). Criminal profiling and public policy. In Kocsis, R.N. (Ed.), *Criminal Profiling: International Theory, Research and Practice.* (pp.273-288). Tottowa, NJ: Humana Press.

Campbell, J.H., and DeNevi, D. (2004). *Profilers: Leading Investigators Take You Inside the Criminal.* NY: Prometheus Books.

Canter, D., and Heritage, R. (1989). A multivariate model of sexual offence behavior: Developments in "offender profiling" – I. *Journal of Forensic Psychiatry, 1,* 185–212.

Canter, D., and Fritzon, K. (1998). Differentiating arsonists: A model of firesetting actions and characteristics. *Legal and Criminological Psychology, 3,* 73–96.

Canter, D. (1989). Offender profiles. *The Psychologist, 2,* 12–16.

Canter, D. (1994). Criminal shadows. London: Harper Collins.

Canter, D. (1995). Psychology of offender profiling. In R. Bull and D. Carson (Eds.). *Handbook of Psychology in Legal Contexts.* (pp. 343–355). Chichester, UK: John Wiley & Sons.

Canter, D. (2000). Offender profiling and criminal differentiation. *Legal and Criminological Psychology, 5,* 23–46.

Canter, D. (2004a). Offender profiling and investigative psychology. *Journal of Investigative Psychology and Offender Profiling, 1,* 1–15.

Canter, D. (2004b). *Mapping Murder.* London: Harper Collins.

Commonwealth of Pennsylvania v. DiStefano. [1999]. No. 96-CR-737

Copson, G. (1995). *Coals to Newcastle? Part 1: A study of offender profiling (paper 7).* London, Police Research Group Special Interest Series, Home Office.

Coxon, A.P.M. (1982). *The User's Guide to Multidimensional Scaling.* London: Heinman Educational Books.

Davis, D., and Follette, W.C. (2002). Rethinking the probative value of evidence: Base rates, intuitive profiling, and the "*post-diction*" of behavior. *Law and Human Behavior, 26,* 133–158.

Dietz, P.E. (1985). Sex offender profiling by the FBI: A preliminary conceptual model. In M.H. Ben-Aron, S.J. Hucher, and C.D. Webster (Eds.), *Clinical Criminology* (pp. 207–219). Toronto: M & M Graphics.

Douglas, J.E., and Burgess, A.W. (1986). Criminal profiling: A viable investigative tool against violent crime. *FBI Law Enforcement Bulletin, 55,* 9–13.

Douglas, J.E., Burgess, A.W., Burgess, A.G., and Ressler, R.K. (Ed.)(2006). *Crime Classification manual* (2nd Ed.). San Francisco: Joseey-Bass.

Douglas, J.E., and Oleshaker, M. (1995). *Mindhunter.* New York: Scribner.

Douglas, J.E., Ressler, R.K., Burgess, A.W., and Hartman, C.R. (1986). Criminal profiles from crime scene analysis. *Behavioral Sciences and the Law, 4,* 401–421.

Dowden, C., Bennell, C., and Bloomfield, S. (2007). Advances in offender profiling: A systematic review of the profiling literature published over the past three decades. *Journal of Police and Criminal Psychology, 22,* 44–56.

Doyle, A.C. (1891). *The Original Illustrated Sherlock Holmes.* Secaucus, NJ: Castle.

Farrington, D. P. (2007). Book review. *International Journal of Offender Therapy and Comparative Criminology, 4,* 486–487.

Federal Rules of Evidence. (2004). Washington, DC: U.S. Government Printing Office.

Fisher, A.J. (1993). *Techniques of Crime Scene Investigation* (5th Ed.). NY: Elsevier.

Frank, G. (1966). *The Boston Strangler.* NY: New American Library.

Frye v. United States, 54 App. D.C. 46, 293F. 103 (1923).

Geberth, V.J. (1983). *Practical Homicide Investigation: Tactics, Procedures and Forensic Techniques.* Boca Raton, FL: CRC Press.

Girod, R. (2004). *Profiling the Criminal Mind: Behavioral Science and Criminal Investigative Analysis.* NY: iUniverse Inc.

Gogan, D. (2007). Investigative experience and profile accuracy: A replication study. In Kocsis, R.N. (Ed.), *Criminal profiling: International theory, practice and research.* (pp. 383–392), Tottowa, NJ: Humana Press.

Gregory, R.L. (Ed.) (2004). *The Oxford Companion to the Mind.* New York: Oxford University Press.

Grezlak, H. (1999, April 12). Profiling testimony inadmissible in murder trial: Too speculative, prejudicial judge says. *Pennsylvania Law Weekly,* 1–2.

Harcourt, B. (2007). *Against Prediction: Profiling, Policing and Punishing in an Actuarial Age.* Chicago: The University of Chicago Press.

Hazelwood, R.R. (1995). Analyzing the rape and profiling the offender. In R.R. Hazelwood and A.W. Burgess (Eds.), *Practical Aspects of Rape Investigation: A Multidisciplinary Approach.* (2nd ed.)(pp. 115-126). Boca Raton, FL: CRC Press.

Hazelwood, R.R., and Burgess, A.W. (1987). An introduction to the serial rapist research by the FBI. *FBI Law Enforcement Bulletin, 56,* 16–24.

Hazelwood, R., and Michaud, S.G. (2001). *Dark Dreams.* New York: St. Martins Press.

Hazelwood, R.R., Ressler, R.K., Depue, R.L., and Douglas, J.C. (1995). Criminal investigative analysis: An overview. In R.R. Hazelwood, and A.W. Burgess, (Eds.), *Practical Aspects of Rape Investigation: A Multidisciplinary Approach.* (2nd ed.). (pp. 115–126). Boca Raton, FL: CRC Press.

Herndon, J.S. (2007). The image of profiling: Media treatment and general impressions. In R.N. Kocsis (Ed.), *Criminal Profiling: International Theory, Practice and Research* (pp. 290–303), Tottowa, NJ: Humana Press.

Hickey, E. (2001). *Serial Murderers and Their Victims* (3rd ed.). Belmont, CA: Wadsworth.

Hicks, S.J., and Sale, B.D. (2006). *Criminal Profiling: Developing an Effective Science and Practice.* Washington: APA.

Hodges, E. P., and Jacquin, K.M. (2008). Psychological skills and criminal profile accuracy. In Kocsis, R.N. (Ed.), *Serial Murder and the Psychology of Violent Crimes.* (pp. 259–276), Tottowa, NJ: Humana Press.

Holmes, R.M., and Holmes, S.T. (2002). *Profiling Violent Crimes: An Investigative Tool* (3rd ed.). Thousand Oaks, CA: Sage.

Icove, D.J., and Estepp, M.H. (1987). Motive-based offender profiles of arson and fire-related crimes. *FBI Law Enforcement Bulletin, 56,* 17–23.

Jackson, J.L., and Bekerian, D.A. (1997). *Offender Profiling: Theory, Research and Practice.* New York: John Wiley & Sons.

Jackson, J.L., van Koppen, P.J., and Herbrink C.M. (1993). *Does the Service Meet the Needs? An Evaluation of Consumer Satisfaction with the Specific Profile Analysis and Investigative Advice as Offered by the Scientific Research Advisory Unit of the National Criminal Intelligence Division (CRI).* The Netherlands: NISCALE Report NSCR 93-05.

Jeffers, H.P. (1992). *Profiles in Evil.* London: Warner Brothers.

Kent, J. (1999, September 12). *Monsters in the making. The Sunday Mail Sunday Magazine,* 4–5.

Kind, S.S. (1987). Navigational ideas and the Yorkshire Ripper investigation. *Journal of Navigation, 40,* 385–393.

Kirkpatrick, L.C. (1998). Profile and syndrome evidence: Its use and admissibility in criminal prosecutions. *Security Journal, 11,* 255–257.

Kocsis, R.N. (2006). *Criminal Profiling: Principles and Practice.* Tottowa, NJ: Humana Press.

Kocsis, R.N. (2007a). Schools of thought related to criminal profiling. In R.N. Kocsis, (Ed.), *Criminal Profiling: International Theory, Practice and Research.* (pp. 393–404), Tottowa, NJ: Humana Press.

Kocsis, R.N. (2007b). Skills and accuracy to criminal profiling. In R.N. Kocsis, (Ed.), *Criminal Profiling: International Theory, Practice and Research.* (pp. 335–358), Tottowa, NJ: Humana Press.

Kocsis, R.N., and Palermo, G.B. (2007). Contemporary problems with criminal profiling. In R.N. Kocsis, (Ed.), *Criminal Profiling: International Theory, Practice and Research* (pp. 335–358) Tottowa, NJ: Humana Press.

Langer, W. (1972). *The Mind of Adolf Hitler.* New York: New American Library.

Lazer, D. (Ed.) (2004). *DNA and the Criminal Justice System: The Technology of Justice.* Boston: MIT Press.

Levine, N. (2000). *Crimestat: A Spatial Statistics Program for the Analysis of Crime Incident Locations* (Version 1.1). Washington, DC: National Institute of Justice.

Lundrigan, S., and Canter, D. (2001). A multivariate analysis of serial murderers' disposal site location choice. *Journal of Environmental Psychology, 21,* 423–432.

McCrary, G.O., and Ramsland, K. (2003). *The Unknown Darkness: Profiling the Predators Among Us.* New York: Harper Collins.

Meyer, C.B. (2007). Criminal profiling as expert evidence. In R.N. Kocsis, (Ed.), *Criminal Profiling: International Theory, Research and Practice* (pp. 207–248) Tottowa, NJ: Humana Press.

Monte, C. (1995). *Beneath the Mask: An Introduction to Personality* (5th ed.). New York: Harcourt Brace.

Nowikowski, F. (1995). Psychological offender profiling: An overview. *The Criminologist, 19,* 255–273.

Oleson, J.C. (1996). Psychological profiling: Does it actually work? *Forensic Update, 46,* 11–14.

Ormerod, D. (1999). Criminal profiling: Trial by judge and jury, not criminal psychologist. In D.V. Canter and L.J. Alison (Eds.), *Profiling in Policy and Practice* (pp. 207–261). Aldershot: Ashgate.

Palermo, G.B. (2004). *The Faces of Violence* (2nd ed). Springfield, IL: Charles C Thomas.

Palermo, G.B., and Kocsis, R.N. (2005). *Offender Profiling: An Introduction to the Sociopsychological Analysis of Violent Crime.* Springfield, IL: Charles C Thomas.

Pinizzotto, A.J. (1984). Forensic psychology: Criminal personality profiling. *Journal of Police Science and Administration, 12,* 32–40.

Pinizzotto, A.J., and Finkel, N.J. (1990). Criminal personality profiling: An outcome process study. *Law and Human Behavior, 14,* 215–233.

Poythress, N., Otto, R.K., Darkes, J., and Starr, L. (1993). APA's expert panel into the Congressional review of the USS Iowa incident. *American Psychologist, 48,* 8–15.

Proulx, J., Beauregard, E., Cusson, M., and Nicole, A. (Ed.) (2007). *Sexual Murderers: A Comparative Analysis and New Perspectives.* New York: Wiley.

Raskin, D.C. (Ed.) (1989). *Psychological Methods in Criminal Investigation and Evidence.* New York: Springer-Verlag.

Rengert, G.F., and Wasilchick, J. (1985). *Suburban Burglary.* Springfield, IL: Charles C Thomas.

Reppetto, T.A. (1974). *Residential Crime.* Cambridge, MA: Ballinger.

Ressler, R.K. (1985). Violent crimes. *FBI Law Enforcement Bulletin. 54,* 1–31.

Ressler, R.K., Burgess, A. and Douglas, J.E. (1988). *Sexual Homicide: Patterns and Motives.* NY: Lexington Books.

Ressler, R.K., Burgess, A.W., Douglas, J.E., Hartman, C.R., and D'Agostino, R.B. (1986). Sexual killers and their victims: Identifying patterns through crime scene analysis. *Journal of Interpersonal Violence, 1,* 288–308.

Ressler, R.K., Douglas, J.K., Groth, N., and Burgess, A.W. (1980). Offender profiles: A multi-disciplinary approach. *FBI Law Enforcement Bulletin, 49,* 16–20.

Ressler, R.K., and Shachtman, T. (1992). *Whoever Fights Monsters.* London: Simon & Schuster.

Revitch, E., and Schlesinger, L. B. (1989). *Sex Murder and Sex Aggression: Phenomenology, Psychopathology, Psychodynamics and Prognosis.* Springfield, IL: Charles C Thomas.

Risinger, D.M., and Loop, J.L. (2002). Three card monte, monty hall, modus operandi and "offender profiling": Some lessons of modern cognitive science for the law of evidence. *Cardoza Law Review, 24,* 193–285.

R. v. Clark [2004]. 182 CCC (3d) 1 (Canada)

R. v. Guilfoyle [2001]. 2 Cr. App. Rep. 57. (United Kingdom)

R. v. Hillier [2003]. ACTSC 50, 25 June 2003 (Australia)

R. v. Ranger [2003]. 178 CCC (3d) 375 (Canada)

Rossi, D. (1982). Crime scene behavioral analysis: Another tool for the law enforcement investigator. *Police Chief, 18,* 152–155.

Rossmo, K. (1997). Geographic profiling. In Jackson, J.L., and Bekerian, D.A. (Eds.), *Offender Profiling: Theory, Research and Practice.* (pp. 159–176). NY: John Wiley & Sons.

Rossmo, K. (2000). *Geographic Profiling.* Boca Raton: FL: CRC Press.

Salfati, C.G. (2000). The nature of expressiveness and instrumentality in homicide. *Homicide Studies, 4,* 265–293.

Shoenfeld, D. (1936). *The Crime and the Criminal: A Psychiatric Study of the Lindbergh Case.* New York: Convici-Friede.

Stangeland, P. (2005). Catching a serial rapist: Hits and misses in criminal profiling. *Police Practice and Research, 6,* 453–469.

State v. Fortin. 162 NJ 517, 745 A.2d 509 (2000).

State v. Fortin. 178 NJ 540; 843 A.2d 974 (2004).

Trager, J., and Brewster, J. (2001). The effectiveness of psychological profiles. *Journal of Police and Criminal Psychology, 16,* 20–28.

van der Kemp, J.J., and van Koppen, P.J. (2007). Fine-tuning geographical profiling. In R.N. Kocsis, (Ed.), *Criminal Profiling: International Theory, Practice and Research.* (pp. 347–364), Tottowa, NJ: Humana Press.

van Zandt, C.R. (1994). The real silence of the lambs: The National Center for the Analysis of Violent Crime (NCAVC). *Police Chief, 61,* 45–46.

Vorpagel, R.E. (1982). Painting psychological profiles: Charlatanism, coincidence, charisma or new science? *Police Chief, 3,* 156–159.

Vorpagel, R.E., and Harrington, J. (1998). *Profiles in Murder.* New York: Plenum.

Whittington-Egan, R. (1975). *A Casebook on Jack the Ripper.* London: Wiley.

Wilson, P.R., Lincoln, R., and Kocsis, R.N. (1997). Validity, utility and ethics of profiling for serial violent and sexual offenders. *Psychiatry, Psychology and Law, 4,* 1–12.

Young, G. (2003, August). *Mapping Mayhem: The Geography of Crime.* Computeredge.

Chapter Eleven

PSYCHOLOGICAL AUTOPSY

RICHARD N. KOCSIS

Explaining the concept of psychological autopsy is not as easy as one might expect. This difficulty appears to arise from the varying connotations the term seems to imply. In one context, such as those in a coroner's investigation, psychological autopsy is commonly recognized as a mechanism for assessing the likely circumstances that led to an individual's death. In another context, psychological autopsy is recognized as a research paradigm by which patterns in the perpetration of suicide may be studied (Sanborn & Sanborn, 1976).[1]

Another factor clouding the clear understanding of the technique is the variation in terminology used to refer to it, such as *psychiatric autopsy, equivocal death analysis* or *reconstructive psychological evaluations*. The nuances that are argued to justify these differences in terminology are debatable. For example, Bendheim (1979) suggests that a psychiatric autopsy is different from a psychological autopsy because it is inclusive of a psychiatric evaluation including consideration of the deceased's genetic history, environmental background, personal experiences, and history as determined by numerous sources. Similarly, equivocal death analysis is suggested to be distinguished by its examination of physical evidence and behaviors (Hazelwood, Dietz & Burgess, 1982). However, Litman (1989) challenges the distinctions between psychiatric and psychological autopsies as being little more than semantic in nature. Similarly, the suggested differentiation of equivocal death analysis appears derivative of the psychological autopsy concept and thus a similarly questionable distinction (Ebert, 1987; Jacobs & Klein, 1993; Poythress, Otto,

---

1. There is also a third suggested use of the psychological autopsy as a quality assurance mechanism when assessing the suitability of treatment programs subsequent to a patient committing suicide. Although an interesting application, this role appears to have achieved limited coverage in the published literature (e.g. Neil, Benesohn, Farber & Resnick, 1974.)

Darkes & Starr, 1993; Review of Navy Investigation of the USS Iowa Explosion, 1989; Shneidman, 1969, 1994). Perhaps the most strident criticism of such postulated distinctions comes from Ogloff and Otto (1993) who contend that differences between *psychiatric* and *psychological* autopsy appear to be based more on guild interests than on substantive differences in the processes and objectives of the undertaken technique.

Setting aside these arguments, for conceptual ease, the technique in the context of this chapter will simply be referred to as psychological autopsy and within an operational application be conceived as:

> a postmortem, postdictive psychological investigative procedure by which a person's circumstances and psychological state of mind at the time leading up to his/her death are reconstructed, in order to help determine the manner of death. (Aumiller et al., 2008, p. 74)

In light of such definitions, it is perhaps not surprising that psychological autopsy has been likened to the reconstruction a historian or biographer undertakes when offering some narrative of the probable thoughts and emotions of a historical figure (Canter, 2005; Shaffer, Perlin, Schmidt & Himmelfarb, 1972). Similarly, psychological autopsy is not unlike in conception a form of indirect personality assessment (Meloy, 2004). In this respect, although the operational application of psychological autopsy originally emerged from coroner's investigations it also appears to have developed broader application as a general means to evaluate a deceased person's state of mind (e.g. Ebert, 1987). As an apparent consequence of this broader conception, psychological autopsy has been used in a diverse range of circumstances. Some examples include aircraft crash investigations, evaluation of staff behavior before death, homicide investigations, the mental status of geriatric patients, and the consideration of persons of political importance (e.g. Jones, 1977; Yanowitch, Mohler & Nichols, 1972; Neill et al., 1979; Bendheim, 1979; Selkin & Loya, 1979).

THE PSYCHOLOGICAL AUTOPSY PROCESS

Despite the renown and use psychological autopsy seems to enjoy (Jacobs & Klein, 1993), it is surprising that it does not appear, at present, to feature uniformly recognized procedures in terms of precisely how the technique is to be undertaken. The term psychological autopsy describes as much a goal of inquiry as it does a tangible process (Ogloff & Otto, 1993). This is not to imply that the overall process of undertaking a psychological autopsy does not involve any coherent structure, but rather that, the process of a psychological autopsy in collating and then evaluating information about a deceased person appears to be somewhat varied. A number of procedural models for undertaking a psychological autopsy have been proposed over the years, however (e.g. Shneidman, 1969; Snider, Hane & Berman, 2006). One of the most thorough expositions for conducting a psychological autopsy is that proposed by Ebert (1987), and this appears in the Appendix to this chapter.

Irrespective of the particular procedural model adopted, there appear to be a number of underlying generic commonalties that can be discerned from the various advocated procedures in undertaking a psychological autopsy. First and foremost, the technique involves the collection of information about the deceased person from a wide variety of sources. It is in the range of sources and the extent of information examined that a substantial degree of variation occurs. Some common sources of information may include interviews with the parents of the deceased; the spouse or partner of the deceased; or work colleagues, friends, or the treating physician of the deceased, or a combination of these. In addition to interviews, psychological autopsies may also draw upon a wide range of archival sources of data about the deceased, including, but not limited to, medical, school, police, and military records.

From the collation of information from these differing sources, various preliminary attributes concerning the deceased are identified. Thus, the second general phase of a psychological autopsy typically involves the evaluation of a number of common factors. A few examples include the general mental status and psychological history of the deceased, any antecedent events or possible stress factors in the life of the deceased, and possible motives as to why the deceased may have committed suicide (Ebert, 1987; Jacobs & Klein, 1993). With the initial determination of these issues about the deceased considered, the third and typically final phase of a psychological autopsy largely appears to be guided by the actual purpose for undertaking the technique. As will be discussed shortly, one well-known use of psychological autopsy is in assisting a coroner to classify an individual's death in equivocal (uncertain) circumstances. In this context, the issues under examination largely center around the likely intention of the deceased to actively and consciously bring about his or her own demise. The precise procedural parameters concerning how such determinations are ultimately made vary and are again influenced by the particular circumstances of each matter under consideration in combination with the clinical judgment of the individual(s) undertaking the psychological autopsy.

Finally, the procedure concerning how the evaluations inherent to a psychological autopsy are ultimately arrived at is also somewhat variable. Some authors appear to advocate that the process be undertaken by a single individual (Jacobs & Klein-Benheim, 1995; Schlesinger, 2006); others suggest a collaborative approach whereby colleagues may review each other's conclusion, thus offering a final determination arrived at through a process of consensus in opinion (Litman, Curphey, Shneidman, Farberow & Tabachnick, 1963). A good collection of sample psychological autopsies that serve to illustrate the technique in an operational context of coroners' investigations can be found in Shneidman and Faberow (1976).

Psychological Autopsy in an Operational Context

The coining of the term psychological autopsy is generally credited to Litman and colleagues (1963) and their endeavors to assist the L.A. County Coroner's Office in the examination of persons found dead in equivocal circumstances (Shneidman, 1981). One of the key tasks of coroners is to render some determination as to the mode of death of a deceased person. This determination within the United States generally follows a system of categorizing the circumstance of a death as being attributable to either natural causes, homicide, accidental death, suicide, or a circumstance that cannot be established (Shneidman, 1981). However, significant difficulties arise in performing this task reliably when circumstances surrounding an individual's death are ambiguous, or what is more technically referred to as equivocal in nature. Indeed, Litman and coworkers (1963, p. 102) describe such cases as being where "suicide is a possibility but in which there could be more than one interpretation and therefore, the decision is uncertain and doubtful."

The hazards with incorrectly classifying an individual's circumstance of death are well-recognized. These problems appear to begin when the boundaries of medical science (e.g. pathology, toxicology) are reached and thereafter assessment of the psychological factors inherent to the circumstances surrounding the death require consideration. For example, both Curphey (1968) and Shneidman (1981) warn of the particular difficulties in classifying circumstances of death related to the ingestion of tranquilizers or barbiturates, or both. A toxicology examination can, for example, ascertain that the mode of death was due to a lethal overdose of a particular drug that induced respiratory failure, but the toxicology examination cannot necessarily establish whether the deceased knowingly consumed the particular amount of drug to deliberately induce their death. Compounding these problems are potential misperceptions that can innocently arise among the coroner's staff. For example, Jobes, Berman, and Josselson (1986) found a bias in coroners who unjustifiably classify certain circumstances of death as suicide, such as those in which individuals were playing Russian Roulette or were simply identified as suffering from psychosis.

In light of these problems with the classification of death, particularly in equivocal circumstances, one of the earliest operational applications of psychological autopsy was realized. As noted by Litman (1984), the pivotal issue in the evaluation of an equivocal death, and whether the circumstances are suggestive of suicide as opposed to some other cause, largely centers around the probable intention of the deceased. Thus, pivotal to the psychological autopsy in this context is considering whether the deceased appreciated and was knowingly cognizant of his or her self-destructive behavior. Evaluation of this element of intention, however, is neither a simplistic categorical issue nor as easy or straightforward as one might expect. Specifically, careful consideration needs to be given to the extent to which a deceased may have intended his or her own death. In adjudicating on these concepts, Shneidman (1981) indicates that an intentional death is one in which "the deceased plays a direct conscious role in effecting their own demise." Unfortunately, complicating the assessment of intention are situations in which the deceased may exhibit what Shneidman (1981) refers to as some "sub-intentional" or unconscious role in effecting their own death.

An illustration of the complexity associated with these issues can be seen in the hypothetical scenario proposed by Litman (1984) wherein an individual places a gun to their head and then shoots themself. An autopsy of the deceased would likely determine that the cause of death was a gunshot wound to the head. The exhibited behaviors of this circumstance would also normally suggest that the intention of the deceased was to commit suicide. Similarly, it can be seen that voluntarily placing a loaded gun to one's head is a harmful act to an individual's own welfare. However, mitigating these factors may be evidence that the individual actually intended to live even though engaging in such action. For example, the deceased may not have believed that the gun was actually loaded. Alternatively, the deceased may have been engaging in a party trick, pretending to play Russian Roulette believing that when the trigger was pulled the revolver (i.e. the gun) would rotate onto an empty chamber and not the one that actually contained the bullet. If such issues were established, then the death would in fact be more suggestive of an accident than a suicide.

One key avenue by which the intent of the deceased may be ascertained comes from an analysis of behavioral features inherent in his or her life that may be suggestive of suicidal intent. A variety of studies have found various commonly recurring premonitory and prodromol indicators within individuals who commit suicide (e.g. Faberow, 1968; Farberow & Shneidman, 1961; Jacobs & Klein, 1993; Roy, 1981). In this context, the evaluative process inherent to psychological autopsy in the operational context to assist a coroner's investigation appears to be oriented toward determining the congruence, or otherwise, with identifiable risk factors associated with the perpetration of suicide. Generally, the greater prevalence of known suicide risk factors concerning the deceased, the more suggestive of possible suicide it may be. Conversely, the fewer or absence of such risk factors is less suggestive of an intention to commit suicide, and thus the individual's death may be attributable to another reason such as an accident.

Psychological Autopsy as a Research Mechanism

As previously indicated, psychological autopsy also enjoys an alternate role as a mechanism for the study of etiologic patterns inherent in the perpetration of suicide. This role of psychological autopsy as a research tool is in no way trivial and in some respects the volume of scholarly literature concerning psychological autopsy in this capacity rivals that of the technique used in an operational context. Interestingly, although the legacy of the operational use of psychological autopsy dates back to the work of Litman and associates (1963), indications of the research application of the technique in the study of self-destructive behavior generally are suggested to date as far back as the 1920s (Isometsa, 2001).

Suicide is an issue of concern for the medical, and mental health professions and for the general community alike. Despite the significance of this phenomenon, the precise reasons as to why individuals continue to commit suicide remain elusive (Jacobs & Klein-Benhelm, 1995). This circumstance is not altogether unsurprising, however, because research into the underlying drives associated with suicide is difficult as potentially the most valuable source of data (i.e. the deceased person) cannot be interviewed. When there is such an impasse, the psychological autopsy is the method by which various antecedents to the commission of suicide can be studied. Thus the aforementioned methodological impasse can, to some extent, be overcome (Cavanagh, Carson, Sharpe & Lawrie, 2003).

Isometsa (2001) has classified the research into suicide using psychological autopsy as falling into one of two broadly conceived generations. The first generation is generally characterized by studies that provide qualitatively rich descriptions of self-destructive behavior patterns but that are also, unfortunately, often imbued with various methodological limitations. The second generation of studies, however, is characterized by a higher use of case-control methodological designs or use of standardized interviewing procedures, or both. Although a marked improvement, this second generation of research is not without its limitations. Further complicating the suicide research that employs the psychological autopsy method are some generic problems with respect to the conceptual parameters of how variables (i.e. certain behaviors etc) are uniformly measured. For example, the communication of an individual's intent to commit suicide represents a commonly agreed indicator of suicidal intent. Rudestam (1971) examined the communication of suicidal intent and found that 62 percent of persons who committed suicide communicated their intent. Unfortunately, the problem that arises from such research is the potential discordance among differing studies as to what is commonly considered or measured as communication of the individual's intent to commit suicide (Isometsa, 2001).

Notwithstanding these issues, psychological autopsy as a research tool has contributed to the study and identification of some common precursors in the perpetration of suicide. As previously indicated, these precursors and common variables can be beneficial in anticipating and deciphering circumstances of suicide (Shneidman, 1981). In one of the most thorough reviews of research utilizing psychological autopsy and encompassing a sample pool of 154 papers, Cavanagh and associates (2003) concluded that the strongest variable associated with the perpetration of suicide was the presence of mental disorder (*see also* Hawton et al., 1998). The predominant pathology is the presence of depression (Appleby, Cooper, Amos & Faragher, 1999; Aranto, Demeter, Rihmer & Somogyi, 1988; Beskow, 1979; Cheng, 1995; Foster, Gillespie and McClelland, 1997; Lesage et al., 1994; Shaffer, et al., 1996). Other common disorders associated with the perpetration of suicide include alcoholism and schizophrenia (Hawton et al., 1998). Furthermore, a high comorbidity of such disorders have also been clearly observed across the research findings (Conwell et al., 1996; Foster et al., 1997; Henriksson et al., 1993; Isometsa, 2001).

In addition to recurring psychopathologies, psychological autopsy research has also revealed a number of demographic patterns. Thus, successful perpetrators of suicide, in comparison with failed attempts, are twice as likely to be male than female (Clark & Horton-Deutsch, 1992). Furthermore, simply being male, having a history of past suicide attempts, having a nonsupportive partner and a variety of psychosocial factors (Gould, Fisher, Parides, Flory & Shaffer, 1996) have all been found to be highly significant indicia for an increased likelihood of suicide in adult life. Finally, sickness or poor health have also been found to be notable risk factors for suicide among the elderly (Carney, Rich, Beerke & Fowler, 1994; Henriksson et al., 1995).

CAUTIONS AND CONCERNS SURROUNDING PSYCHOLOGICAL AUTOPSY

Although the reputation and use of psychological autopsy has steadily grown, this progress has not gone without reservations being expressed by some commentators (e.g. Canter, 2005; Ogloff & Otto, 1993). The foremost concern is possibly its fundamental validity, particularly in the context of its operational application in the assessment of equivocal deaths. Indeed, well over three decades ago Shaffer and colleagues (1972, p. 309) poignantly noted that in psychological autopsy there is:

. . . the need to explain phenomenon on a plausible, causal, usually psychodynamic basis. Unfortunately, the plausibility of any such explanation is no guarantee of its validity.

In this context, psychological autopsy is somewhat analogous to hypothesis testing wherein plausible explanations are generated to explain observed phenomena. However, simply because an espoused hypothesis is intuitively appealing does not necessarily imply that it is valid. Some support for this proposition emerges from the work of Canter (2005), who challenges some of the long-held prodromal cues regarded as indicative of the perpetration of suicide and relied upon when undertaking psychological autopsy of equivocal deaths. The various concerns surrounding psychological autopsy can be broadly summarized into two categories. First, there are concerns of a methodological nature principally relating to the procedures and how psychological autopsies are undertaken. Second, there are concerns of a conceptual nature relating to the validity and essential accuracy of the evaluations derived through the adoption of psychological autopsy techniques. Both of these categories will be discussed in turn.

Methodological Concerns

Possibly the most examined methodological concern relating to psychological autopsies in the published literature relates to the reliability and interpretation of the collated information (Barraclough, Bunch, Nelson & Sainsbury, 1974; Fisher & Shaffer, 1984). There are numerous facets to this seemingly single issue. First is the reliability of information garnered from informants in a state of bereavement, such as parents mourning the death of a child. Such information must be considered with caution. That is, to what extent may the perceptions of the deceased be biased, influenced, or distorted due to this emotional state? Unfortunately, Barraclough and colleagues (1974) clearly forewarn of two distinct possibilities that may be encountered with informants in this circumstance, or more specifically the information such parties may provide. First, informants may exaggerate the presence of any symptomology or even mental disorder due to the suicide. Alternatively, informants may glorify the deceased and thus minimize or deny the presence of any irregularity or disorder.

Moving beyond possible perceptual distortions due to bereavement, another concern is that informants may provide unreliable information due to simple ignorance or some ulterior motive. Thus, informants may be genuinely ignorant and thus simply unaware of certain factors that may be present within the deceased (Hawton et al., 1998). One hypothetical example is parents who may be unaware of their child's history of recreational drug use. Unfortunately, a more contrived alternative is that informants may have some vested interest in deliberately distorting, manipulating, or withholding information (Selkin & Loya, 1979). The predominant motive for informants to deliberately distort information emerges when there is a vested interest concerning the payment of a life insurance policy (Selkin, 1994). Many life insurance policies do not pay claims in the circumstance of intentional acts of death such as suicide. This circumstance therefore generates an incentive for some informants to distort information in an effort to ensure that the demise of the deceased is determined to be something other than suicide.

In addition to the previously mentioned issues there are also procedural concerns surrounding the reliability of gathered information. Despite the history of psychological autopsy, the published literature is surprisingly bereft of indications concerning what time delays may have on an informant's recollection and therefore at what time juncture they should be interviewed. Similarly, guidelines as to the optimal method for the collection of information and what weightings, if any, different sources of information should be given is also absent from the literature. As a simple illustration of this issue, in the circumstance of trying to establish the presence of various symptomologies in a deceased prior to their death, whose perception is more reliable – that of the deceased's parents, the spouse or partner of the deceased, or a close friend?

Finally, one surprising source of concern involving psychological autopsy does not relate to informants *per se* but rather to the individual(s) undertaking the psychological autopsy. Issues of concern in this circumstance relate to disciplinary perspectives of those undertaking the psychological autopsy and any emotional empathy that may develop toward grieving relatives of a deceased. For example, Gavin and Rogers (2006) argue that there is an emphasis in psychological autopsies to focus on links between mental illness and suicide that potentially limit the conceptual scope of the evaluation in not giving adequate consideration to the deceased's social environment, which may also account for his or her death. Alternatively, Litman and associates (1963) have observed the emotional rapport investigators often develop with members of a victim's family and how sympathy can readily arise and then innocently interfere with judgments concerning the deceased. Similarly, Selkin and Loya (1979) have stressed the need for impartiality and a nonpartisan role by those conducting a psychological autopsy. Perhaps one of the most ardent comments on this point comes from Shneidman (1994, p. 76) who opines that psychological autopsy cannot be properly undertaken by "a detective, a prosecutor, or a 'hired gun' psychologist (or psychiatrist)."

Solutions

In light of these concerns a number of countermeasures have been suggested over the years in an attempt to minimize or nullify these problems. For instance, to address the issue of empathy among investigators, Litman and coworkers (1963) have suggested a review process whereby determinations are checked by colleagues who have had minimal or no personal contact with informants. Similarly, to counter some of the potential distortions arising from informants, both Dregne (1982) and Hawton and colleagues (1998) have emphasized the need for interviewing multiple informants. Additionally, cross-referencing gathered information with official records whenever possible is also strongly advocated to ensure consistency and thus improve the reliability of gathered information. Other nominated measures include the use of standardized (i.e. structured) protocols for interviewing and data collection (e.g. Blau & Alberts, 2004; Rudestam, 1979; Werlang & Botega, 2003) as well as the use of psychometric instruments. For example, Shaffer and colleagues (1972) have suggested the use of the Katz Adjustment Scales (KAS)-R forms in which relatives can complete the instrument and, via the scales of the KAS, provide information about a deceased's personality attributes in a more quantifiable and replicable manner.

Finally, some research endeavors have also been undertaken to address some of the procedural concerns. A study by Brent, Pepper, Kolko, and Zelenak (1988) found evidence to indicate that information furnished by parents concerning perceived symptomology could be regarded as reliable. Additionally, irrespective of a two- to six-month time span, the provision of this information by the parents of a deceased was still found to be reliable.

Conceptual Concerns

Psychological autopsy has been described as "a rather felicitous title for the amalgamation of a wide variety of information and conjecture pertaining to the dead subject" (Shaffer et al., 1972, p. 309). Although a somewhat rueful perspective, this statement justifiably highlights that simply because a recurring group of features can be identified within previously studied groups does not necessarily imply that these features can be used validly in some predictive capacity. Although studied samples of individuals who have committed suicide may have been found to commonly suffer from depression, for example, this in itself does not necessarily suggest that an individual who suffers from depression and is found dead in equivocal circumstances committed suicide. Thus, there are grounds to ponder the fundamental capacity of psychological autopsies in accurately explaining the intentions of a deceased person.

As previously mentioned, Canter (2005) challenges some of the traditional concepts in determining an equivocal death as a suicide. One example is that suicide will necessarily have many identifiable antecedents (e.g. Shneidman, 1969) and instead suggests that suicide may be committed in a seemingly spontaneous or surprise manner (Canter, 2005). Similarly, the concept that most individuals intending to commit suicide communicate their intentions in some capacity (e.g. Faberow & Shneidman, 1961; Shneidman, Faberow & Litman, 1976) or that suicide notes left by deceased persons will provide some coherent explanation for why they committed suicide are similarly questioned by Canter (2005).

Unfortunately, research into the ultimate validity of psychological autopsies in determining a deceased's intention in an equivocal death will always be hampered by the logistical factors of the circumstance. Whereas the effectiveness of a drug can be assessed by measuring the reduction in a particular disease, an analogous evaluation of psychological autopsy is not possible because the precise answer is lost with the deceased. Thus, the definitive reasoning and intentions of the deceased cannot ever be established because they are not alive to provide a definitive criterion on which accuracy and thus validity of the psychological autopsy can be measured.

Nonetheless, some promising research has been undertaken or proposed in an effort to remedy some of these concerns. In examining reported symptomology between suicide victims and attempted suicide inpatients, Brent and coworkers (1993) found encouraging results in terms of the validity of diagnosis obtained through psychological autopsy procedures. Similarly, Ogloff and Otto (1993) offer some useful suggestions wherein the validity of psychological autopsy procedures could, to some extent, be examined in the future. One suggestion is a quasi-experimental trial of subjects examining an equivocal death. The particular case under examination would involve a matter in which the *correct* mode of death had been previously determined. Consequently, subjects could evaluate the case concerning the equivocal death. The accuracy of their conclusions could be determined by their concordance with the previously ascertained correct mode of death, thus providing some tentative indications of validity through measurement.

PSYCHOLOGICAL AUTOPSY AND THE LEGAL SYSTEM

In comparison to other psychological techniques, psychological autopsy appears to occupy a somewhat paradoxical position in terms of the admission of its testimony within the U.S. legal system. Despite concerns surrounding a paucity of scientific evidence to support the merits of psychological autopsy (e.g. Ogloff & Otto, 1993), testimony derived from the technique has increasingly gained admission in U.S. legal proceedings, including precedent-setting appellate court decisions.

Judicial consideration of psychological autopsy in jurisdictions outside the United States, such as the United Kingdom or Canada, appear somewhat limited. In instances in which psychological autopsy, or concepts relative to the technique, have been considered (e.g. Chard, 1972; MacIntosh, 1997; *R. v. Valley*, 1986; *R. v. Weightman*, 1991), the judiciary appears to demonstrate a disinclination to admit such evidence. Possibly the most incisive decision in which the specific merits of psychological autopsy were considered within the jurisdiction of the United Kingdom was in the judgment of *R v. Guilfoyle* (2001) in which the proffered testimony based on the technique was rejected, with the court commenting that:

> Psychiatric evidence as to the state of mind of the defendant, witness or deceased falling short of mental illness may, of course, as we have said, be admissible in some cases when based, for example, on medical records and/or recognised criteria. . . . But the present academic status of psychological autopsies is not, in our judgment, such as to permit them to be admitted as a basis for expert opinion before a jury. (*R. v. Guilfoyle*, 2001, p. 68)

Irrespective of the legal position in the United Kingdom or Canada, within the U.S. legal system psychological autopsy as a concept appears to enjoy a rather well-established history, particularly in the context of civil litigation (e.g. Clark, 1988; Dregne, 1982; Lichter, 1981). Indeed, examples of the psychological autopsy concept can be found in U.S. case law dating back to the 1930s and the intention of a deceased in the context of a *"gift in contemplation of death"* (e.g. *United States v. Wells*, 1931; *Neal v. Commissioner*, 1931).

The scope of the present chapter unfortunately does not allow for a detailed discussion of U.S. case law pertaining to psychological autopsy. A good overview of the apparent judicial reasoning surrounding the admission of the technique in the U.S. legal system can be found in Ogloff and Otto (1993). As these authors note, there are numerous examples in which, in the context of civil proceedings, U.S. courts have admitted testimony derived from psychological autopsy. The context of these cases includes matters such as workers compensation, medical malpractice, and insurance claims (e.g. *Campbell v. Young Motor Company*, 1984; *Evans v. Provident Life & Accident Ins. Co.*, 1990). Interestingly however, U.S. civil jurisdictions appear not to have allowed evidence derived from psychological autopsy when the testimony relates to matters of testamentary capacity and intestate succession (e.g. *Estate of Skulina*, 1988).

The admission of testimony derived from psychological autopsy within criminal proceedings has not been as clear or as readily accepted as it has been in the civil arena. Indeed, a number of decisions concerning the admissibility of psychological autopsy testimony in criminal proceedings have seen this evidence rejected by the courts (*Arizona v. Montijo*, 1989). However, what has been suggested as a precedent setting decision arose in the case of *Jackson v. State of Florida* (1989) in which the Florida Appellate Court upheld an earlier decision to admit testimony derived from a psychological autopsy (Jacobs & Klein-Benheim, 1995). In this case, and in direct response to challenges concerning the admissibility of the testimony derived from psychological autopsy, the Florida Court held that:

> We perceive no distinction between the admission of the expert's opinion in this case and, for example, admitting psychiatric opinion evidence to establish a defendant's sanity at the time of committing an offense or to prove the competency of an individual at the time of executing a will. (*Jackson v. State of Florida* (1989)

Thus, within civil proceedings in the United States, and with some exceptions, there appears to be an acceptance of psychological autopsy as an admissible form of expert testimony. However, within criminal jurisdictions there appears to be some reluctance by the courts to admit testimony derived from the technique, with the exception of the decision of *Jackson v. Florida* (1989).

CONCLUSION

The concept of psychological autopsy is, arguably, a remarkably old technique (Isometsa, 2001). Contemporary conceptions of the technique generally see its use in varying, yet complementary, roles as both an operational mechanism to examine the mental status of a deceased party (particularly in circumstances of equivocal death) and as a method to study and understand epidemiological patterns in the perpetration of suicide. In both roles the technique generally appears to enjoy varying degrees of success (Isometsa, 2001). In addition to these functions, numerous authors have also noted the vicarious therapeutic benefits that often arise from the use of psychological autopsy with respect to interviewees such as grieving relatives of the deceased (e.g. Beskow, Runeson & Asgard, 1991; Diller, 1979; Sanborn & Sanborn, 1976).

Notwithstanding the apparent growth and success of the technique, there is a range of notable concerns about both the methodological reliability of the employed procedures and the validity of the conclusions drawn from psychological autopsies. Despite these reservations, the technique, with a few exceptions, appears to enjoy a good standing within the U.S. civil legal system in which expert testimony based on the technique has been admitted. However, the admissibility of psychological autopsy in U.S. criminal proceedings has not been as readily embraced despite a notable precedent that may clear a path for its further use in this jurisdiction in the future.

Appendix

PSYCHOLOGICAL AUTOPSY GUIDELINES

1. Alcohol History

   a. Collect family history
   b. Research amount ingested regularly
   c. Research evidence of binge drinking
   d. Research evidence of blackouts (known from friends, family, acquaintances)
   e. Research evidence of driving under the influence of alcohol
   f. Research evidence of alcohol-related offenses
   g. Research evidence of family problems (alcohol related)
   h. Research evidence of work difficulties connected to alcohol
   i. Research evidence of blood level (BAL) g/L at time of death

2. Suicide Notes

   a. Examine content
   b. Examine style
   c. Have handwriting expert review writing style

3. Writing

   a. Review any past writing by the deceased
   b. Peruse any diary of the deceased
   c. Examine school papers for topics of essays or term papers
   d. Read letters to friends, family, coworkers, acquaintances

4. Books

   a. Examine books of the deceased
      i. Look for books on the occult, life after death, death
      ii. Look for actual books on suicide
   b. Assess books checked out of local libraries

5. Relationship Assessments

   a. Interview people who knew the deceased, including
      i. Close friends
      ii. Close intimate heterosexual or homosexual companions
      iii. Acquaintances
      iv. Mother, father, siblings
      v. Coworkers and supervisors
      vi. Other relatives
      vii. Physicians and/or mental health professionals
      viii. Teachers
   b. Construct level of intimacy on the basis of discussions with "close" friends
   c. Assess people's reactions to the victim's death
   d. Secure a history of marriages and divorces
   e. Examine relationship with children
   f. Look for anger directed toward particular people

From: Ebert, B.W. (1987). Guide to conducting a psychological autopsy. *Professional Psychology: Research and Practice, 18*, 52–56.

6. Marital Relationship

    a. Note any significant problems that may have made the deceased person depressed
    b. Look for history of extramarital relationships
    c. Assess the overall quality of the relationship

7. Mood

    a. Identify mood fluctuations
    b. Look for symptoms of depressions
       i. Weight loss
       ii. References to depression
       iii. Problems with memory
       iv. Fatigue
       v. Sleep disturbances
       vi. Withdrawal
       vii. Decreased libido
       viii. Appetite and/or taste changes
       ix. Constipation and diarrhea
    c. Look for mood indicators during last few days
       i. Interview friends and family
       ii. Interview anyone surrounding the deceased

8. Psychosocial Stressors (note and chart importance on Holmes & Rahe Scale factors)

    a. Recent loss: death of people or pets
    b. Relationship separations: divorce, breakups of significant relationships
    c. Loss of job
    d. Legal and financial problems
    e. Demotion, promotion, and so on
    f. Reaction to stressors
    g. Move to a new location

9. Presuicidal Behavior

    a. Giving away important possessions
    b. Paying up insurance policies
    c. Payment of debts
    d. Arrangements for children and pets
    e. Sudden order in deceased's life
    f. Change or initial creation of a will

10. Language

    a. Identify any specific references to suicide (deceased may have stated, "Have a party in remembrance of me," or "You won't have to worry about me anymore")
    b. Note any changes in language before suicide
    c. Analyze language (tapes, recollections of conversations, writing) for morbid content

11. Drugs Used

    a. Identify all drugs used by deceased
    b. Assess interactional effects of legal and illegal drugs in use

12. Medical History

    a. Review complete medical history
    b. Note any unusual symptoms or diagnoses
    c. Note any terminal illnesses or diagnoses

13. Reflective Mental Status Exam of Deceased's Condition Before Death

    a. Orientation
    b. Memory
    c. Attention
    d. Concentration
    e. Mood and affect
    f. Hallucinations or delusions
    g. Cognition, IQ
    h. Language
    i. Judgment

14. Psychological History

    a. Look for previous suicide attempts (type, method)
    b. Assess reason for treatment if involved in therapy
    c. Research evidence of depression, manic depression (bipolar disorder)
    d. Research past psychiatric hospitalizations
    e. Examine diagnoses
    f. Examine evidence of impulsive behavior
    g. Examine any recent or past psychological tests (e.g. was the victim given the Rorschach and was the suicide constellation served via the Exner system?)

15. Laboratory Studies

    a. Examine ballistics
    b. Evaluate powder burns on hands and body

16. Coroner's Report

    a. Conduct complete drug screen
    b. Identify any poisons
    c. Read for detailed description of physical functioning/health of deceased at time of death

17. Motive Assessment

    a. Make a chart divided four ways: Murder, Suicide, Accident, and Natural, recording data to support each as it is uncovered
    b. Report the possible reasons for suicide
    c. Report the possible reasons why the subject could have been murdered (identify enemies, illicit activities)

18. Reconstruction of Events Occurring on the Day Before Deceased's Death

    a. Make a step-by-step chart of subject's movements and activities
    b. Form a chronological history of the victim that immediately precedes death

19. Assess Feelings Regarding Death as Well as Preoccupations and Fantasies

20. Military History

    a. Look for evidence of difficulty adjusting, such as letters of counseling (LOC), letters of reprimand (LOR), Article 15 action (A15), or court-martial proceedings (Note: A15 is a form of nonjudicial punishment for offenses not serious enough to warrant a court-martial and include repeated lateness, driving under the influence of alcohol, sleeping on duty, or negligence on duty. Punishment from an A15 can include reduction in rank, fines, or removal from duty.)

    b. Attempt to secure job ratings (airman promotion rating and officer effectiveness rating)

    c. Look for decorations or awards

    d. Notice whether deceased was in a combat zone at any time

    e. Look for evidence of posttraumatic stress disorder in Vietnam veterans

    f. Determine the number of assignments and which were at the request of the victim

21. Death History of Family

    a. Examine history for suicide by other family members

    b. List immediate deceased family members and their mode of death

22. Family History

    a. Identify family members and relationships with deceased

    b. Examine the socieconomic status of family

    c. Identify any conflicts that occurred before death of the victim

23. Employment History

    a. Identify number and types of jobs (high-risk work may indicate the existence of subintentional behavior for quite some time)

    b. Look for repetitive problems

    c. Assess whether any problems existed before death (e.g. coworker conflict, failure to progress as planned)

    d. Note any disciplinary action

24. Educational History

    a. Assess educational level

    b. Identify any problems with teachers or subjects

    c. Note special interests or topics (e.g. in particular, look for special interests in death)

25. Familiarity With Methods of Death

    a. Examine belongings for guns, knives (e.g. the deceased may have had five or six loaded weapons around his or her house regularly)

    b. Look for lethal drugs

    c. Note deceased's interest in and knowledge about weapons

26. Police Report

    a. Critical facts will be obtained by review of the police investigation

    b. Pay special attention to ballistics data

REFERENCES

Appleby, L., Cooper, J., Amos, T., and Faragher, B. (1999). Psychological autopsy of suicides by people under 35. *British Journal of Psychiatry, 175*, 168–174.

Aranto, M., Demeter, E., Rihmer, Z., and Somogyi, E. (1988). Retrospective psychiatric assessment of 200 suicides in Budapest. *Acta Psychiatrica Scandinavia, 77*, 454–460.

Arizona v. Montijo, 774 P.2d 1366, 1368-70 (Ariz. Ct. App. 1989)

Aumiller, G.S., Corey, D., Brewster, J., Allen, S., Gupton, H., Cuttler, M., and Honig, A. (2008). Defining the field of police psychology: Core domain & proficiencies. *Journal of Police and Criminal Psychology, 22*, 65–76.

Barraclough, B., Bunch, J., Nelson, B., and Sainsbury, P. (1974). A hundred cases of suicide: Clinical aspects. *British Journal of Psychiatry, 125*, 355–373.

Bendheim, O.L., (1979). The psychiatric autopsy: Its legal application. *Bulletin of the American Academy of Psychiatry and the Law, 7*, 400–410.

Beskow, J. (1979). Suicide and mental disorder in Swedish men. *Acta Psychiatrica Scandinavia, 277*, 1–138.

Beskow, J., Runeson, B., and Asgard, U. (1991). Ethical aspects of psychological autopsy. *Acta Psychiatrica Scandavia, 84*, 482–487.

Blau, T.H., and Alberts, F.L. (2004). *The Forensic Documentation Sourcebook* (2nd. ed.). Hobokin, NJ: Wiley.

Brent, D.A., Pepper, J.A., Kolko, D.J., and Zelenak, J.P. (1988). The psychological autopsy: Methodological considerations for the study of adolescent suicide. *Journal of the American Academy of Child and Adolescent Psychiatry, 27*, 362–366.

Brent, D.A., Perper, J.A., Moritz, G., Allman, C., Friend, A., Roth, C., Schweers, J., Balach, L., and Baugher, M. (1993). Psychiatric risk factors for adolescent suicide: A case control study. *Journal of the American Academy of Child and Adolescent Psychiatry, 32*, 521–529.

Campbell v. Young Motor Company 684 P.2d 1101, 1103 (Mont. 1984).

Canter, D.V. (2005). Suicide or murder? Implicit narratives in the Eddie Guilfoyle case. In L. Alison (Ed.), *The Forensic Psychologists Casebook* (pp. 315–333). London: Willan Publishing.

Carney, S.S., Rich, C.L., Burke, P.A., and Fowler, R.C. (1994). Suicide over 60: The San Diego study. *Journal of the American Geriatric Society, 42*, 174–180.

Cavanagh, J.T.O., Carson, A.J., Sharpe, M., and Lawrie, S.M. (2003). Psychological autopsy studies of suicide: A systematic review. *Psychological Medicine, 33*, 395–405.

Chard (1972) 56 Cr .App. R. 268

Cheng, A.T.A. (1995). Mental illness and suicide: A case control study in East Taiwan. *Archive of General Psychiatry, 52*, 594–603.

Clark, D.C. (1988). Psychological autopsy in the courtroom. *Suicide Research Digest, 2*, 3–4.

Clark, D.C., and Horton-Deutsch, S. (1992). Assessment in absentia: The value of the psychological autopsy method for studying antecedents of suicide and predicting future suicides. In R. Maris, J. Berman, J. Maltsberger, and R. Yufit (1992) *Assessment and Prediction of Suicide* (pp. 144–182). New York: Guilford.

Conwell, Y., Duberstein, P.R., Cox, C., Hermann, J.H., Forbes, N.T., and Caine, E.D. (1996). Relationships of age and Axis I diagnosis in victims of completed suicide: A psychological autopsy study. *American Journal of Psychiatry, 153*, 1001–1008.

Curphey, T. (1968). The psychological autopsy: the role of the forensic pathologist in the multidisciplinary approach to death. *Bulletin of Suicidology, 4*, 39–45.

Danto, B.L. (1979). New frontiers in the relationship between suicidology and law enforcement. *Suicide & Life Threatening Behavior, 9*, 195–204.

Diller, J. (1979). The psychological autopsy in equvocal deaths. *Perspectives in Psychiatric Care, 17*, 156–161.

Dregne, N.M. (1982). Psychological autopsy: A new tool for criminal defense attorneys? *Arizona Law Review, 24,* 421–439.

Ebert, B.W. (1987). Guide to conducting a psychological autopsy. *Professional Psychology: Research and Practice, 18,* 52–56.

Estate of Skulina 425 N.W. 2d 135 (Mich App. 1988)

Evans v. Provident Life & Accident Ins. Co., 803 P.2d 1033 (Kan. Ct. App. 1990)

Faberow, N. (1968). Suicide: Psychological Aspects. *International Encyclopedia of the Social Sciences, 15,* 390–394.

Faberow, N., and Shneidman, E.S. (1961). *The Cry for Help.* New York: McGraw-Hill.

Fisher, P., and Shaffer, D. (1984). Methods for investigating suicide in young children and adolescents: An overview. In H.S. Sudak, A.B. Ford, and N.B. Rushford (Eds.), *Suicide in the Young* (pp. 139–257). Littleton, MA: John Wright PSG.

Foster, T., Gillespie, K., and McClelland, R. (1997). Mental disorders and suicide in Northern Ireland. *British Journal of Psychiatry, 170,* 447–452.

Gavin, M., and Rogers, A. (2006). Narratives of suicide in psychological autopsy: Bringing lay knowledge back in. *Journal of Mental Health, 15,* 135144.

Gould, M.S., Fisher, P., Parides, M., Flory, M., and Shaffer, D. (1996). Psychosocial risk factors of child and adolescent completed suicide. *Archives of General Psychiatry, 53,* 1155–1162.

Hawton, K., Appleby, K., Platt, S., Foster, T., Cooper, J., Malmberg, A., and Simkin, S. (1998). The psychological autopsy approach to studying suicide: A review of methodological issues. *Journal of Affective Disorders, 50,* 269–276.

Hazelwood, R.R., Dietz, P.E., and Burgess, A.W. (1982). Sexual fatalities: Behavioral reconstruction in equivocal cases. *Journal of Forensic Sciences, 27,* 763-773.

Henriksson, M.M., Aro, H.M., Martunen, M.J., Heikkinen, M.E., Isometsa, E.T., Kuoppasalmi, K.I., and Lonnqvist, J.K. (1993). Mental disorders and comorbidity in suicide. *American Journal of Psychiatry, 150,* 935–940.

Henriksson, M.M., Martunen, M.J., Isometsa, E.T., Heikkinen, M.E., Aro, H.M., Kuoppasalmi, K.L., and Lonnqvist, J.K. (1995). Mental disorders in elderly suicide. *International Psychogeriatry, 7,* 275–286.

Isometsa, E.T. (2001). Psychological autopsy studies: A review. *European Psychiatry, 16,* 379–85.

Jackson v. Florida 553 So 2d 719 (Fla Dist Ct App 1989).

Jacobs, D., and Klein, M. (1993). The expanding role of psychological autopsies. In A.A. Leenaars (Ed.), *Suicidology: Essays in Honor of Edwin S. Shneidman* (pp. 209–247). Northvale, NJ: Aronson.

Jacobs, D., and Klein-Benheim, M. (1995). The psychological autopsy: A useful tool for determining proximate causation in suicide cases. *Bulletin of the American Academy of Psychiatry and Law, 23,* 165–182.

Jobes, D.A., Berman, A.L., and Josselson, A.R. (1986). The impact of psychological autopsies on medical examiners' determinations of manner of death. *Journal of Forensic Sciences, 31,* 177–189.

Jones, D.R. (1977). Suicide by aircraft: A case report. *Aviation, Space and Environmental Medicine, 48,* 454–459.

Lesage, A.D., Boyer, R., Grunberg, F., Vanier, C., Morissette, R., and Menard-Buteau, C. (1994). Suicide and mental disorders: A case control study of young men. *American Journal of Psychiatry, 151,* 1063–1068.

Lichter, D. (1981). Diagnosing the dead: The admissibility of the psychiatric autopsy. *American Criminal Law Review, 18,* 617–635.

Litman, R. (1984). Psychological autopsies in court. *Suicide and Life-threatening Behavior, 14,* 88–95.

Litman, R. (1989). 500 Psychological autopsies. *Journal of Forensic Sciences, 34,* 638–646.

Litman, R., Curphey, T., Shneidman, E. Farberow., N.L., and Tabachnick, N. (1963). Investigations of equivocal suicides. *Journal of the American Medical Association, 184*, 924–929.

Meloy, J.R. (2004). Indirect personality assessment of the violent true believer. *Journal of Personality Assessment, 82*, 138–146.

Neal v. Commissioner 53 F.2d 806 (8th Cir. 1931).

Neill, K., Benesohn, H.S. Farber, A.N., and Resnik, H. (1974). The psychological autopsy: A technique for investigating a hospital suicide. *Hospital and Community Psychiatry, 25*, 33–36.

Ogloff, J.R.P., and Otto, R.K. (1993). Psychological autopsy: Clinical and legal perspectives. *St. Lewis Law Journal, 37*, 607–646.

Poythress, N., Otto, R.K., Darkes, J., and Starr, L. (1993). APA's expert panel into the Congressional review of the USS Iowa incident. *American Psychologist, 48*, 8–15.

R. v. Guilfoyle [2001] 2 Cr. App. Rep. 57.

R. v. MacIntosh (1997) 117 C.C.C. (3d) 385 (Ont. C. A.).

R. v. Valley (1986) 26 C.C.C. (3d) 207

R. v. Weightman (1991) 92 Cr.App.R.291

Review of the Navy Investigation of USS IOWA Explosion: Joint hearings before the Investigations Subcommittee and the Defense Policy Panel of the Committee of Armed Services, House of Representatives, 101 Cong. Hearings held December 12, 13, and 21, 1989.

Roy, A. (1981). Suicide in chronic schizophrenia. *British Journal of Psychiatry, 141*, 171–177.

Rudestam, K.E. (1979). Some notes on conducting a psychological autopsy. *Suicide and Life Threatening Behavior, 9*, 141–144.

Ruderstam, K.E. (1971). Stockholm and Los Angeles: A cross-cultural study of the communication of suicidal intent. *Journal of Consulting and Clinical Psychology, 36*, 82–90.

Sanborn, D.E., and Sanborn, C.J. (1976). The psychological autopsy as a therapeutic tool. *Diseases of the Nervous System, 37*, 4–8.

Schlesinger, L.B., (2006). Celebrity stalking, homicide, suicide: A psychological autopsy. *International Journal of Offender Therapy and Comparative Criminology, 50*, 39–46.

Selkin, J. (1994). Psychological autopsy: Scientific psychohistory or clinical intuition? *American Psychologist, 49*, 74–75.

Selkin, J., and Loya, F. (1979). Issues in the psychological autopsy of a controversial public figure. *Professional Psychology, 10*, 87–83.

Shaffer, D., Gould, M.S., Fisher, P., Trautman, P., Moreau, D., Kleinman, M., and Flory, M. (1996). Psychiatric diagnosis in child and adolescent suicide. *Archives of General Psychiatry, 53*, 339–348.

Shaffer, J.W., Perlin, S., Schmidt, C.W., and Himmelfarb, M. (1972). Assessment in absentia: New directions in the psychological autopsy. *Johns Hopkins Medical Journal, 130*, 308–316.

Shneidman, E.S. (1969). Suicide, lethality and the psychological autopsy. *International Psychiatry Clinics, 6*, 225–250.

Shneidman, E.S. (1981). The psychological autopsy. *Suicide and Life-Threatening Behavior, 11*, 325–340.

Shneidman, E.S. (1994). The psychological autopsy [comment]. *American Psychologist, 49*, 75–76.

Shneidman, E.S., and Faberow, N.L. (1976). Sample psychological autopsies. In E.S. Shneidman, N.L. Farberow, and R.E. Litman, (Ed.) *The Psychology of Suicide* (pp. 497–510). New York: Jason Aronson.

Shneidman, E.S., Farberow, N.L., and Litman, R.E. (Ed.) (1976). *The Psychology of Suicide*. New York: Jason Aronson.

Snider, J.E., Hane, S., and Berman, A.L. (2006). Research Note: Standardizing the psychological autopsy: Addressing the Daubert standard. *Suicide and Life Threatening Behavior, 36*(5), 511-518.

United States v. Wells 283 U.S. 102 (1931).

Werlang, B.S.G., and Botega, N.J. (2003). A semistructured interview for psychological autopsy: An inter-rater reliability study. *Suicide and Life Threatening Behavior* 33(3), 326-330.

Yanowitch, R.E., Mohler, S.R., and Nichols, E.A. (1972). The psychosocial reconstructive inventory: A postdictal instrument in aircraft accident investigation. *Aerospace Medicine, 44,* 675–678.

Chapter Twelve

CRISIS NEGOTIATION

JAMES S. HERNDON

O ver the past forty years or so, the techniques and practice of negotiation
have been applied to crisis situations confronted by law enforcement
personnel. The early beginnings are generally traced back to the New York
Police Department (NYPD) in the 1970s, to events in the world that tended
to feature hostage taking as a key element of criminal and political behavior.
From infrequent use to standard practice, crisis negotiation has become com-
monplace in law enforcement. The context, content, and process of crisis
negotiation will be broadly considered in this chapter.

Because of the extensive literature on the topics of crisis/hostage negotiation and space limitations in a chapter such as this, the approach taken herein is to organize the material according to distinct subtopics. Each subtopic
will be briefly covered, paying particular attention to information that may
be useful for those interested in applied criminal psychology. Reference cita-
tions at the chapter's end should be helpful in further exploring the many
aspects of crisis/hostage negotiation.

Throughout the chapter, the terms crisis negotiation, hostage negotiation,
and crisis/hostage negotiation will be used interchangeably. This is often the
case in the literature cited. Crisis intervention is also a term that is frequently paired with negotiation. The use of these terms, which is reflective of
changes in philosophy and practice as the field evolved, should be clear
when taken in the context of article, chapter, or book cited. A barricade situation is one in which a subject refuses to come out, sometimes with or without hostages. Hostages (persons held against their will as a form of barter)
play a key role in negotiation considerations. Unless otherwise stated, negotiator refers to appropriately trained and duly authorized police personnel.

BACKGROUND, HISTORY, AND ICONS

The historical events that laid the foundation for the need for hostage negotiation as a police approach include the Munich massacre of Olympic athletes at the hands of terrorists in 1972, as well as the spate of airline jackings that seemed epidemic in the 1970s. McMains and Mullins (1996) provide a concise discussion of the events in the development of the NYPD hostage negotiation concept as well as the Federal Bureau of Investigation (FBI) initiatives that followed. Many of the classic articles on hostage negotiation were assembled in a compendium by Romano, Getz, and McCann (1998). Other authors have devoted some attention to the development of hostage negotiation techniques in law enforcement (e.g. Blau, 1994) and crisis situations (e.g. James, 2008).

What has been referred to as "first-generation" hostage negotiation (the police response to terrorist and political activities) has gradually evolved into "second-generation" crisis intervention (applying crisis intervention principles to criminal encounters and domestic disturbances). Many hostage negotiation teams (HNT) were renamed crisis negotiation teams (CNT) to reflect this refinement of philosophy and technique (e.g. OCSO, 1999, 2001). A good summary of the evolution of hostage negotiation in law enforcement is provided by Call (2003).

When one enters the literature on crisis/hostage negotiation, almost immediately two names come to the fore: Frank Bolz and Harvey Schlossberg. These two individuals share the credit for introducing and developing the techniques of crisis negotiation for law enforcement application. Each gave an account of his role in the process – Bolz in Hostage Cop (Bolz & Hershey, 1979) and Schlossberg in *Psychologist with a Gun* (Schlossberg & Freeman, 1974). In person, each can tell many tales of how things came to be. No doubt one person played off the other in a synergistic way that led to the refinement of a method that has found its way to almost all law enforcement agencies today. However, recognition must also go to the late Simon Eisdorfer, who is credited with developing the NYPD hostage negotiation team (*New York Times*, 2005).

EARLY TRAINING AND DEVELOPMENT OF BASIC MODELS

In the beginning, the application of negotiation in the law enforcement context simply meant talking to the suspect, rather than using a tactical approach to resolve a crisis situation. Talking was seen as a better alternative to force, especially when the lives of innocent hostages hung in the balance (Soskis & Van Zandt, 1986). So, the strategy to "isolate, contain, and negotiate" emerged. Training models emphasized the importance of time and containment to the effective resolution of potentially lethal encounters. Trainers instructed would-be negotiators in the history, development, philosophy, and techniques of negotiation that emerged from police trial and error applications. Anecdotes and "war stories" were plentiful in early training sessions (Bolz & Hershey, 1979; Schlossberg & Freeman, 1974). Not much emphasis was placed on communication techniques *per se*, other than the need to convince the barricaded suspect/hostage taker to give up and come out. Negotiators were generally selected for their ability to carry on a good conversation.

As negotiation began to take hold in the law enforcement arsenal, the process came under scrutiny in an effort to better understand the dynamics in typical situations (*see* Abbott, 1986; Wesselius & DeSarno, 1983; Whittle, 1988). In a study conducted by Holmes (1991), an attempt was made to formulate a developmental phase model of negotiation; however, the model seemed to fit training simulation situations better than it did actual hostage situations. Other models attempted to fit the elements of a crisis situation into negotiator training (Herndon, 1994) or to provide useful analogies that might facilitate training (Herndon, 1996), or both.

Abbott (1986) presented a time-phased model for hostage negotiation based on time-sequence relationships that occur during the negotiation process. This was intended to be used as a yardstick by which to measure the process of negotiations. Similarly, Strentz (1995) discussed the cyclic crisis negotiation time line that can help a negotiator determine that a situation is winding down toward a peaceful solution.

Figure 12-1. shows the major components in police crisis negotiation, around which this chapter is organized. The content (players) of negotiation includes the hostage taker, the hostages (victims), and the hostage negotiator. Issues surrounding each are presented in what follows. The context of negotiation, in terms of this chapter, is the law enforcement crisis team call out. The process of negotiation includes the dynamic interactions that occur between and among all players. External forces, such as organizational, social and political pressures, tend to impinge on the process. Mental health consultants often play a role in the outcome. In addition, time is always a factor.

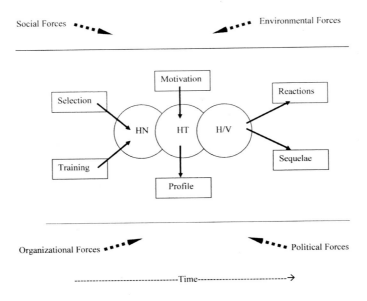

Figure 12-1. Organizing framework.

APPLICATION AND EXAMINATION OF THE PROCESS

From the very beginning of the application of negotiation techniques to law enforcement situations, there have been efforts to examine the process, not only to explicate and elucidate but also to educate. Schlossberg (1979) described in general terms the police response to hostage situations, and Fuselier (1981) provided a practical overview of hostage negotiations. Even the moral considerations involved in police responses to hostage takers have been explored (Betz, 1982).

Maksymchuk (1982) provided a very basic outline of the types of hostage takers, hostage situations, and offensive actions to be considered in most police calls for assistance. The anatomy of a hostage situation was presented by Wesselius and DeSarno (1983) as they exemplified the social psychological interplay between hostage and hostage taker. Friedland (1986) examined hostage negotiation types, processes, and outcomes. An empirical examination of the process of negotiation between a barricaded subject and police negotiators was detailed by Powell (1989) in his doctoral dissertation at the University of Iowa.

The high-risk factors associated with crisis/hostage situations were discussed by Fuselier, Van Zandt, and Lanceley (1991); these factors were identified as those that increase the possibility of the victim being killed or the hostage taker committing suicide. Among these factors were the subject being under multiple stressors prior to the incident, the subject's background of male dominance, prior similar incidents and problems with the hostage, and, the subject's lack of family or social support systems. Ramesh (1992) was critical of police negotiation by stating that strategies employed not only may fail to resolve certain hostage situations but may also continue to invest the police with power to define meanings and to characterize the service they render to the public.

Dolnik (2003) contrasted the dynamics of crisis negotiations in barricade versus kidnapping incidents. Because of the differences cited (location of victims and identity of perpetrators), the components of crisis negotiation that have been successful in resolving barricade situations may be inapplicable to kidnappings. Other important variables and distinctions occurring in crisis situations faced by negotiators are discussed in the edited work of Rogan, Hammer and Van Zandt (1997). A full range of psychological aspects of crisis negotiation is covered in the chapters put together by Strentz (2006).

COMMUNICATIONS AND SPECIALIZED TECHNIQUES

Negotiation is fundamentally communication. This statement may seem overly simplistic; however, it is important to realize that the emphasis on communication techniques did not come until many lessons had been learned through ineffective communications in hostage situations. Early negotiation was a strategy of containment and isolation, allowing time to work in favor of the release of hostages and using negotiation to stall and vent (defuse) the situation. Unfortunately, in law enforcement (as well as in other occupations), time is money, and overtime pay considerations often led to an action imperative to "go tactical." Better communication techniques were needed to resolve situations peacefully in a timely manner.

Early arguments were made for negotiation over tactical assaults (e.g. Bolz, 1982). Organizational resistance and inertia were hard to overcome in the early years of negotiation. Talk was tolerated, but only for so long. Communication strategies came under scrutiny. Richardson (1983) examined the communication strategies in barricade and hostage confrontations to include the rationale for the commitment to resolve such crises through communication rather than through tactical assault, the underlying theory and research, and the actual strategies recommended and practised by negotiators as taught by the FBI Academy. He proposed suggestions to refine communication response strategies, both short term and long term. Other communication analysis studies are reported by Fowler, Devivo and Fowler (1985) and Rogan (1990).

Mullins (1995) offered some advanced communication techniques for hostage negotiators, those designed to influence others and increase compliance. Other researchers examined the message affect in crisis negotiations (Rogan & Hammer, 1995), and Slatkin (1996) made the case for therapeutic communication.

Recognition of the importance of active listening became the focus of consideration among hostage negotiators (Noesner & Webster, 1997). Royce (2005) analyzed the critical role of active listening in the case of a police negotiator in New South Wales, Australia during the process of serving a high-risk warrant on an armed suspect. Royce concluded that active listening was a critical factor in the resolution of the crisis. Keenan (2007) encouraged the development of an empathetic response in police crisis negotiators, noting that trainees who were exposed to the FBI-CNT model showed no increase in the level of observed emotional empathy as demonstrated by pre- and post-training testing.

Some researchers have argued for the importance of roleplaying as a means to increase negotiator effectiveness (Van Hasselt & Romano, 2004; Van Hasselt, Romano & Vecchi, 2008). Certainly, roleplaying contributes to the development of better negotiation skills by adding situational realism. Research focusing directly on the communication process during crisis situations has shown that verbal communication has a direct impact on the outcome (McClain, 2004; McClain, Callaghan, Madrigal, Unwin & Castoreno, 2006). The value of words as disarming tools was noted by Charles (1999; 2007) and Slatkin (2005) who offered a general guide to some useful communication stratagems and strategies for law enforcement.

Taylor (2002) proposed a cylindrical model of communication behavior that posited the interrelationships among communication behaviors in crisis negotiation. By analyzing 189 dialogue spans transcribed from nine resolved cases and using forty-one coding variables, Taylor identified three dominant levels of suspect-negotiator interaction (avoidance, distributive, integrative) and three thematic styles of communication (identity, instrumental, relational). Such research contributes to a better understanding of communication dynamics, which are essential to crisis resolution.

Communication as negotiation, and vice versa, is essential to effective crisis resolution. Listening and understanding require disciplined practice, and true communication can be inhibited by world view differences between law enforcement and other categories of people (*see* Docherty, 1998). Intelligence gathering is a never-ending component of crisis negotiation.

HOSTAGE-TAKER ISSUES

Behind hostage-taking behavior can be found motive. Behavior tends to be purposeful; hostages are usually taken for a reason. An excellent discussion of the variations of motives found in different types of hostage takers can be found in Hacker (1976). Knowing that one is motivated by personal (emotional), criminal (instrumental), or social/political (ideological) issues certainly makes a difference with regard to the negotiation tactics and strategies employed. Why people take hostages is a paramount issue in resolving standoffs successfully. As a minimum, such knowledge can serve to facilitate communication.

There has been some consideration in the literature for the case of dealing with various personality types (disordered or otherwise), such as the antisocial personality or the paranoid schizophrenic. Lanceley (1981) discussed the former, describing features of this type of personality disorder and offering the negotiator tips on how to deal with such hostage takers. Strentz (1983) focused on the "inadequate personality" as a hostage taker. It is interesting that this carryover from the 1968 *Diagnostic and Statistical Manual of Mental Disorders (DSM-II)* still influences present-day negotiator thinking. This speaks to the danger of getting stuck on labels. Whereas mental health professionals may be able to ignore such archaic labels (i.e. no longer in *DSM*) and focus on the presenting symptoms, less knowledgeable negotiators may get stuck (the training literature still uses the term "inadequate personality" to this day) to the detriment of effective negotiation. A hostage taker is not merely a diagnostic label, and poor labeling clouds behavioral prediction. Perhaps, it would be better to focus on overt behavior during and immediately prior to a crisis, rather than off-the-cuff diagnoses or someone else's opinion of the suitable label.

No doubt, however, mental status of the negotiator is an issue to contend with. A common encounter during crisis situations tends to be the person suffering from paranoid schizophrenia. Strentz (1986a) discussed negotiating with the hostage taker who displays symptoms of paranoid schizophrenia. More recently, Mohandie and Duffy (1999) spoke to the symptoms of paranoid schizophrenia in greater detail, its prevalence in society, violence risk associated with the illness, and crisis management strategies. They provide negotiator/first responder guidelines. Taking a broader view, Miller (2007) presented an outline of guiding principles and techniques for negotiating with the most common forms of mentally disordered hostage takers.

Other complicating factors besides motivation and mental status include language and age. DiVasto (1996) considered the particular difficulties encountered when one attempts to negotiate with a hostage taker who does not speak English as a first language. It becomes imperative to have interpreters available if negotiation is to proceed effectively. When dealing with older persons in crisis, there may be a particular concern about suicide potential. Slatkin (2003) pointed out that "negotiators need to employ strategies designed to incorporate the effects of aging and the older individual's reaction to the aging process." Terhune-Bickler (2005) addressed the impact of subject suicide on the negotiator. She noted, "when the negotiators were unable to 'succeed' in the sometimes unrealistic task of preventing the suicide, they felt a myriad of emotions, including defeat and betrayal."

NEGOTIATOR ISSUES

What would crisis and hostage negotiation be without the negotiator? More than likely, it would become a police tactical engagement. Thus, the negotiator is the essential component in the process, the person in the middle between hostage takers and hostages. The negotiator is the wedge between peaceful surrender and dynamic confrontation. The negotiator is pivotal in ensuring a nonviolent resolution to situations that all too often escalate into chaos and tragedy. Given such a heavy responsibility, it is essential to consider the characteristics needed to be successful in the role of hostage negotiator.

Gelbart (1979) was among the first to address this issue. In his doctoral dissertation at the University of Southern California, he examined the psychological, personality, and biographical variables that seemed to be related to success as a negotiator. Strentz (2006) summarized the California study by pointing out that effective negotiators had highly adequate social skills, communications ability, self-assurance, and social presence. They were also intelligent, ambitious, forceful, insightful, resourceful, and versatile, according to measures on the California Psychological Inventory (CPI) and other instruments.

Other early research on the desirable qualities of hostage negotiators was conducted by Tatar (1982). He administered a standardized battery of personality and motivation measures to a group of experienced law enforcement officers who had volunteered for hostage negotiator training. He found that factor analysis produced four dimensions of high relevance to police work and hostage negotiation: emotional stability, extraversion, instinctual gratification, and liberal orientation.

Knowing something about what makes an effective hostage negotiator leads the way to the identification of optimal selection criteria and the delivery of relevant training. Gettys and Elam (1988) sought to do just that, to identify characteristics of negotiators and develop a selection model based on personality data. Survey data reflecting personality characteristics important to hostage negotiators were compared with personality test data obtained from a sample of hostage negotiators. Results indicated that hostage negotiators were above average in their ability to communicate effectively with others, self-confident, good at divergent thinking, and helpful and sympathetic in their dealings with other people. Going beyond test data and personality characteristics, Birge and Birge (1994) pointed to the importance of police employment history as a predictor of success as a negotiator, meaning that past success in resolving crises should predict future success in similar situations. Gruchacz (1997) and Slatkin (1996) also addressed selection and training issues, respectively. Strentz (1996) focused on the sociopsychological traits of successful negotiators. More recent attention to the negotiator selection process (balancing departmental policies while selecting the right personnel) was the focus of research conducted by Kisthardt (2000). This research questioned the assumption that there is a specific set of personality traits common to all negotiators across all law enforcement agencies. Rather, each job in each agency is unique; job analysis must be completed prior to selection to ensure the psychological dimensions are fully understood.

Regini (2002) addressed the selection of the CNT leader, as well as the rest of the team, and the assignment of team responsibilities. His discussion provided an assortment of general traits of the effective leader (e.g. experience and knowledge), as well as some mention of specific familiarity with behavioral sciences and psychological and sociological concepts. The best CNT members seem to come from the ranks of the best criminal investigators; they tend to be nonconfrontational and nonjudgmental in their approach to cases and have exceptional interview and interrogation skills. The roles of primary negotiator, secondary negotiator, and other team members figure heavily in team effectiveness.

Firsthand accounts of the job of a hostage negotiator are insightful and aid one's understanding of the nature of the work and what kind of person is successful and effective. A publicized conversation between current and former members of the NYPD hostage negotiation team and an FBI crisis negotiator is a case in point (Cambria, DeFilippo, Louden & McGowan, 2002). Most recently, retired FBI agent Cliff Van Zandt published an account of his "life on the edge as an FBI hostage negotiator" (Van Zandt & Paisner, 2006). Lanceley (1999) published a useful on-scene guide that provides a good insight into the nature of the work of a negotiator.

HOSTAGE ISSUES

The hostage is at the heart of hostage negotiation. Safety and survival of the hostage undergird the process of negotiation and dictate the dynamics thereof. The physical and psychological well-being of the hostage(s) is an ever-present concern for all parties involved. Hostages are the bargaining chips and become the focus of much attention, either directly or indirectly. The effects of being held hostage have received attention in the literature.

One of the earliest discussions of a well-recognized hostage reaction to being held captive, the Stockholm Syndrome, was provided by Strentz (1979). Identifying with the aggressor as an ego defense and developing negative feelings toward the police (who are seen as posing danger due to imminent tactical assault) form the basis for hostage survival strategy. Hillman (1981) described the psychopathology of being held hostage, and Solomon (1982) carried out an empirical study involving thirty-five former hostages using a forty-one-item questionnaire. The results supported the belief that the Stockholm Syndrome does develop in hostage situations and can be affected by negative hostage-taker treatment of hostages. On the other hand, Olin and Born (1983) argued that the Stockholm Syndrome is not inevitable and may depend on factors that are under police control to reduce the likelihood of violence being done to the hostages by the hostage-taker.

Fuselier (1988) considered, among other things, victim responses to being held hostage, the theoretical explanations for the Stockholm Syndrome, the psychological sequelae, and treatment suggestions after release from captivity. Suggestions for persons who may become hostages were provided by Bolz (1987) as a form of inoculation against negative effects and as tips to maximize survival. Giebels, Noelanders, and Vervaeke (2005) conducted eleven semi-structured and in-depth interviews with victims of two types of hostage taking (sieges and kidnapping); results showed that all hostages reported feelings of helplessness, but feelings of isolation and uncertainty were stronger among kidnap victims.

Attempts to put the Stockholm Syndrome in a balanced perspective are evident (*see* Fuselier, 1999). A recent article does a very good job of summarizing what is understood and misunderstood about the Stockholm Syndrome and victim responses to being held hostage (De Fabrique, Romano, Vecchi & Van Hasselt, 2007). An estimated prevalence rate of 27 percent (derived from data suggesting that 73 percent of captives show no evidence of the syndrome) is sufficient to warrant treatment approaches such as debriefings and posttraumatic stress disorder(PTSD) interventions.

The primary aim of hostage negotiation is to obtain the release of hostages. Their well-being and safety drives the need for sound theory and practical applications of the behavioral sciences.

ROLE OF MENTAL HEALTH PROFESSIONALS AND USE OF PSYCHOLOGICAL DATA

Central to the importance of this chapter is the role played by mental health professionals of various backgrounds in the process and outcome of crisis situations. Utilization of and reliance on these professionals has become more typical over the past few decades as law enforcement agencies have come to recognize the contributions that can be made by someone knowledgeable in applied behavioral science. Some of the relevant literature is highlighted in the following paragraphs.

As early as 1977, consideration was being given to the role of mental health professionals (i.e. non-law enforcement personnel) in police negotiations (*see* Pearce, 1977). Johnson (1978) expanded the discussion to a broader range of behavioral scientists. Powitsky (1979) considered the use and misuse of psychologists in a hostage situation. Hibler (1984) developed a consultation guide for mental health professionals who take part in hostage situations. Other early writings on this topic include Wardlaw (1984), Fuselier (1988), and McMains (1988). More recently, Feldman (2004) presented a general discussion of the role of the mental health consultant on hostage negotiation teams. Similarly, DeBarnardo (2004) considered the psychologist's role in his discussion targeting emergency mental health professionals.

An empirical study conducted by Butler, Leitenberg and Fuselier (1993) surveyed 300 law enforcement agencies in the United States that employed a negotiator in hostage incidents. Thirty-nine percent indicated that they used a mental health consultant for negotiation teams. The use of a mental health consultant contributed to an increase in the number of incidents ending in surrender and a decrease in the number of incidents ending in tactical assault. The use of a mental health consultant to assess the perpetrator reduced the number of incidents resulting in injury or death of a hostage. This study provided data-driven support for the use of mental health professionals in crisis negotiation. Updated statistics pertaining to utilization and effectiveness can be found in Delprino and Bahn (1988) and Fuselier (1988).

Havassy (1994) supported the use of a psychologist as part of the negotiating team. Taking it further, Hatcher, Mohandie, Turner, and Gelles (1998) discussed the four roles and related functions of psychologists on crisis/hostage negotiation teams. They prefaced this by noting that "the invitation to the psychologist to participate in the hostage/crisis negotiation team appears to depend upon three factors." Hatcher and colleagues (1998) identify these factors as mutual acceptance, professional credibility, and an ability to function in the field. The roles typically fulfilled by psychologists in crisis/hostage negotiation include the consultant/advisor, the integrated team member, the primary negotiator, and the primary controller. These roles are ordered from most frequent to least frequent.

When using a mental health consultant, there are a series of questions that may be asked during the incident phase that call upon the expertise of a psychologist. Slatkin (2000) suggested a number of questions that can aid the negotiation process during the beginning, middle, and terminal phases. These questions focus on the psychological profile of the hostagetaker; characterizations of the situation; and suggested negotiation strategies, approaches, and directions.

The use of psychological data was a consideration raised by Poythress (1980). This predated the widespread use of psychologists who are better able to interpret and apply psychological data. The point is noted, however; psychological data in the wrong hands can be a hindrance as well as an aid to understanding behavior in the hostage/barricade context. Personal accounts about the experiences of psychologists on crisis negotiation teams add to the appreciation for their roles and insights (Herndon, 2003, 2006; Strentz, 2006).

ORGANIZATIONAL AND SYSTEM RESPONSES

Law enforcement organizations that assemble crisis negotiation teams must consider a number of issues. Matters of individual negotiator selection and training were mentioned earlier, but, from an organizational perspective, it is important to consider the structure and readiness of the entire team (*see* Regini, 2002). Early discussions in the literature focused on organizing the team (Maher, 1976), team values (Schlossberg, 1980), team development (McMains, 1995), and team profiles (Hammer, Van Zandt & Rogan, 1994; Rogan, Hammer & Van Zandt, 1994). The team must function as a unit, and it is imperative that joint training be conducted with the tactical team to ensure coordination and cooperation during high-risk calls (*see* OCSO, 2001 for an example of a high-risk incident general order). The high-risk incident commander has to ensure that both teams work well together. Magers (2007) discusses the importance of leadership, especially the ethical issues involved in making the best decision: negotiation versus tactical assault. Wind (1995) clarified the role of the field commander in critical incidents while Noesner (1999) addressed negotiation concepts for commanders. Vecchi (2002) offered in-sight into the conflicts that can arise between tactical and negotiating teams and how the two teams can collaborate for a successful outcome. Birge (2002) noted that balance is the key when it comes to the use of negotiation versus tactical responses.

The value of situation boards for use by negotiation teams is the subject of an article by Duffy (1997). Position papers are a means whereby expert negotiators can provide advice to teams during incidents (Dalfonzo & Romano, 2003). These tools can facilitate the process and contribute to an effective outcome.

Crisis negotiation is not just the concern of law enforcement. As Turner (1989) noted, there is the necessity for other organizations, such as healthcare facilities, to have a written response plan in place for the eventuality of a hostage incident. In a world of ever-increasing workplace violence, corporations and private companies must do their part to protect employees and customers/clients from danger while developing contingency plans that facilitate working with law enforcement in the event of an incident.

PROCESS AND OUTCOME ASSESSMENT AND EVALUATION OF EFFECTIVENESS

With forty or so years of development and application, a fair question to ask, is how effective is crisis negotiation? Over the years, tracking incidents has been a hit or miss effort, with some agencies doing a better job than others of keeping accurate records of hostage/barricade situations that resulted in a team call out, and the resolution or outcome thereof. It was, and is, not uncommon in many agencies for negotiation teams to keep an after-action report; the challenge has been to build and maintain a centralized, nationwide database that is accurate and reliable. In the mid-1990s, the FBI began the hostage/barricade data system (HOBAS) in an attempt to rectify this problem. Only one reported study has been found in the peer-reviewed literature that reports an evaluation of the effectiveness of HOBAS. This study questioned whether HOBAS can be reasonably expected to render the representative, unbiased data that is expected from it (Lipetsker, 2004).

Prior to HOBAS, there were several noteworthy academic attempts at assessment and evaluation. For example, Leary (1980) focused his doctoral research at George Mason University on an evaluation of the FBI's hostage negotiation training program. Similarly, Strentz (1986b), in his doctoral research at Virginia Commonwealth University, conducted an evaluation of two training programs designed to enable hostages to cope more effectively with captivity stress. Head (1989) took a broader, systems perspective in his doctoral research at the State University of New York at Albany when he considered the specific characteristics of hostage incidents and the policies used by U.S. law enforcement agencies in handling them. For this research, Head created a database of U.S. hostage incidents occurring over a ten-year period by drawing upon a number of official and unofficial sources. Survey research conducted by Zatwarnitski (1998) at George Mason University looked at the interpersonal and situational dynamics of hostage negotiation situations. Responses indicated that 70 percent of hostage takings were of a domestic nature and most hostages were women and children. Hostage takers were predominately male and were typically known by or related to the hostages. Louden (1999) analyzed the hostage negotiation practices of 276 local, county, and state police agencies in the United States (with at least 100 sworn officers) that used some standard system of negotiation response to hostage and barricade situations. This was a comprehensive study examining nine specific hypotheses and gathering extensive descriptive data. The findings added to what is known about the structure and processes of hostage negotiation teams. McGowan (2004) focused on the NYPD to study whether hostage and barricade incidents (selected sample) that are resolved violently differ from incidents that are resolved without violence. Findings and conclusions from this nontraditional contextual model approach to evaluation (departing from research that used a motivational model) support the hypothesis that a phenomenological model based on context, containment, and conversation is superior to a motivational model for predicting incident resolution. As laudable as these doctoral research projects are, more systematic research along these lines is needed before firm conclusions can be reached.

There is ample anecdotal and testimonial evidence that argues for the utilization of crisis negotiation over a tactical response, and there are corresponding accounts of success in the overwhelming number of incidents. Tracking hostage/barricade calls and tabulating peaceful resolutions in one medium-sized law enforcement agency in the southeastern United States from September 1992 through March 2002 revealed that 90.6 percent of the incidents resulted in a peaceful surrender (Herndon, 2003). One atypical incident was the focus of national media and served as the basis for refined training in tactics (Herndon, 2001). Taken as a whole, review of ten years' experience as a psychologist on a hostage negotiation team pointed to several lessons learned: behavioral profiling is more effective than instant *DSM* diagnosis, criminal history is a good predictor of situation outcome, listening trumps talking, shrink talk can be nonsensical, and some situations are non-negotiable (Herndon, 2006). Lanceley (2004) addressed lessons learned from the vantage point of an FBI hostage negotiator; he compared the job of a salesman with being a negotiator. His lessons include recognizing a non-negotiable situation; realizing it is not about you; everyone on scene is a salesman/negotiator, so a consistent message is important; people believe in demonstrations far more than in words; keep it simple; and it is not over until it is over. In *Facing Down Evil*, retired FBI negotiator Clint Van Zandt recounted most of his memorable cases and gave the reader a glimpse of what it is like to be on the inside (Van Zandt & Paisner, 2006). Impressions about the effectiveness of hostage negotiations can be derived from such personal accounts.

The most-recent evaluation research that appears in the peer-reviewed literature is that of Van Hasselt and colleagues (2006) and Van Aelstyn (2007). Van Hasselt and co-workers (2006) report on an empirical investigation of crisis (hostage) negotiation training. Using forty-five FBI special agents, a pretest and posttest design found significant gains in scores as a result of the two-week training course. This, however, can in no way guarantee transfer of training success in the field. Van Aelstyn (2007) looked at perceived characteristics that facilitate the successful conclusion of crisis situations. He had difficulty discerning the degree to which negotiator education, experience, and training affected the outcome of negotiations.

The importance of crisis/hostage negotiation to police work in particular, and society in general, requires that evaluation research be an on-going effort. There should be formative as well as summative program evaluation, and attention needs to be paid to proximal as well as distal criteria. Content and process issues must be considered, as well as contextual variables. Only in this way will the technique be refined through systematic validation.

CINEMA AND FILM PORTRAYAL

As with many areas in police work, the movies can play an important role in informing the public about what goes on behind the badge. Some movies (documentary or fictional) may contribute to a better understanding of police procedure; some may obfuscate matters. A few popular examples of hostage negotiation are mentioned in the following.

An incident that was made famous by the movie *Dog Day Afternoon* (Warner Home Video, 1989) gave the NYPD much notoriety over hostage negotiation. This film is a fictionalized version of a bank robbery gone bad, in which police negotiators are called in to peacefully resolve the standoff. It is not an altogether unfamiliar theme in movies of this genre, but, being based on a true incident, *Dog Day Afternoon* can be considered a classic introduction to police hostage/crisis negotiation.

Scenes of hostage negotiation doubtless appear in numerous Hollywood produced movies; one attempt to glean some of these scenes for the benefit of self-reflection occurred at a hostage negotiator conference (Herndon, 2000). One movie that emphasized negotiators as individuals was *The Negotiator* (Warner Brothers, 1998). In this film a wrongfully accused negotiator (Samuel L. Jackson) takes hostages in the police department and will only negotiate with a fellow negotiator (Kevin Spacey). Techniques and tactics of negotiation are displayed with the intensity and drama of an action film. Of course, the best negotiator wins. In a similar vein, but with a different twist, a made-for-TV movie, *Hostage Negotiator* (USA Network, 2001), tells the story of an FBI negotiator who is set up by her spouse, also an FBI agent who has blown his career; she uses her skills to resolve a hostage standoff involving her own children. Again, superior skills in communication prevail. An older HBO movie, *Dead Silence* (HBO, 1997), that starred James Garner and Marlee Matlin, featured an FBI negotiator (Garner) tasked with resolving a standoff in an old slaughter house where a busload of deaf children were being held as hostages. Personal issues and past mistakes intruded in the negotiator's mission yet all ended well. Taken together, these three films depict negotiators as complex people who have their own personal crises to contend with whilst performing their duties effectively by drawing on experience and training in negotiation.

Two documentaries place hostage negotiation in a more realistic perspective. *A&E* released *Hostage Negotiators* in 1998; this episode of "Dangerous Missions" features pioneers in the field (e.g. Frank Bolz) and former hostages (e.g. Larry Haber) to provide a glimpse of what it is like from both the negotiator's perspective and that of the hostage. The Discovery Channel aired *On the Inside: Hostage Negotiators* in 2001; it "looked at the difficult jobs of hostage negotiators and their successes in the past 30 years." Actual incidents are examined and experts are interviewed. One of the incidents was the Waco, Texas, event involving David Koresh and the Branch Davidians. This example is one that has received much criticism because of the disastrous outcome. A recent ABC News (2007) presentation (*Death in Waco*), hosted by Ted Koppel, took a hard look at what went wrong and questioned the FBI's role.

The popular appetite for negotiator fare was fueled for a while by a short-lived TV series (September 5, 2006–July 20, 2007; 18 episodes) titled Standoff (Fox, 2006). The demise of this series may be due in part to poor acting and poor casting as much as it was due to an annoying subplot that involved sexual innuendo among star negotiators. The FBI took a hit when this series aired and failed, at least in terms of negotiator prestige.

A discussion of negotiator films would not be complete without mention of *Inside Man* (Universal, 2006). Starring Denzel Washington, Clive Owen, and Jody Foster, this thriller pits the wits of a detective/negotiator against a shrewd bank robber and his crew, leaving the viewer wondering who actually outwitted whom. It was exciting, but true to life?

The portrayal of hostage negotiation in movies and films, although entertaining and possibly informative, leaves much to be desired in terms of a balanced presentation of the complexities of the field, the intense training involved, the dedication of police personnel, and the importance of behavioral science knowledge to effective crisis resolution.

FOCUS ON THE FUTURE

As we consider the history and development of crisis negotiation, the past good and bad challenge us to look to the future with the thought of where the field is going and needs to go. Not much has been written from this point of view. Greenstone (1995) was among the first to lament the divide that has developed between tactical teams and negotiation teams, suggesting that the future should return to a past recognition of the importance of a synergistic effect derived from crosstrained personnel. It is important to remember that negotiation should be given every opportunity to succeed and that a tactical response should not be the police imperative. We only need to look at some recent famous examples to realize that a rush to storm the fortress has disastrous consequences (e.g. Agne, 2003). Take time to talk should be the mantra.

Hancerli (2005) examined the history and development of hostage negotiation on a worldwide scale and offered future recommendations to governments, police agencies, and researchers. Among his five recommendations for governments were that they should always allow negotiation with hostage takers (reversing the policy that "we never negotiate with terrorists") and trust their own police units to take responsibility and resolve the situation peacefully. For police agencies, he offered four recommendations, including the need for all agencies to establish negotiation teams, that negotiation teams not "compete" with tactical teams because neither is subordinate or superior to the other, and that agencies establish behavioral science units to assist with crisis calls. For researchers, Hancerli recommended that more empirical studies be conducted and that more academic contributions be made to the literature of hostage negotiation resolutions. Greater cooperation between police agencies and researchers will lead to more effective strategies in crisis negotiation.

What the next forty years hold is impossible to predict. By examining the past practices of crisis negotiation and by continuing to examine the process through research and evaluation, the future should be characterized by improvements and refinements in this aspect of police work.

CONCLUSION

Crisis negotiation is an important area of police work. Over the past forty years, the techniques of negotiation have been modified and refined, better selection and training methods have been utilized to build a cadre of highly skilled practitioners, lessons learned have been applied, and the role of behavioral science has been expanded as an adjunct to crisis/hostage negotiation. Research has been, and continues to be, carried out that examines the various aspects of the negotiation process. The future looks bright for crisis negotiation as an effective intervention to difficult situations.

REFERENCES

ABC News (2007). *ABC News Classics: Death in Waco.* Released May 24. Burbank, CA: The Walt Disney Company.

Abbott, T.E. (1986). Time-phase model for hostage negotiation. *The Police Chief, April,* 34–35.

A&E (1998). *Dangerous Mission: Hostage Negotiators.* New York: A&E Television Networks.

Agne, R.A. (2003). Interaction problems in crisis negotiation: A case study of the Waco stand-off. *Dissertation Abstracts International, 64,* 1131.

Betz, J. (1982). Moral considerations concerning the police response to hostage takers. In F. Elliston and N. Bowie (Eds.), *Ethics, Public Policy, and Criminal Justice.* Boston, MA: Oelgeschlager, Gunn and Hain, Pub.

Birge, R. (2002). Balance is key: Conducting successful hostage negotiations. *Law and Order, 50,* 102–106.

Birge, A.C., and Birge, R. (1994). Crisis negotiators: Personnel selection. *The U.S. Negotiator, Winter,* 5–7.

Blau, T.H. (1994). *Psychological Services for Law Enforcement.* New York: John Wiley & Sons.

Bolz, F., and Hershey, E. (1979). *Hostage Cop.* New York: Rawson, Wade.

Bolz, F.A. (1982). Hostage negotiations – When every word counts. In R.A. Scanlon (Ed.), *Law Enforcement Bible, No. 2.* South Hackensack, NJ: Stoeger Pub. Co.

Bolz, F.A. (1987). *How to be a Hostage and Live.* Secaucus, NJ: Lyle Stuart.

Butler, W.M., Leitenberg, H., and Fuselier, G.D. (1993). The use of mental health professional consultants to police hostage negotiation teams. *Behavioral Science & the Law, 11,* 213–221.

Call, J.A. (2003). Negotiating crises: The evolution of hostage/barricade crisis negotiation [Online]. Retrieved March 12, 2008. Available: http://www.crisisinc.com

Cambria, J., DeFilippo, R.J., Louden, R.J., and McGowan, H. (2002). Negotiation under extreme pressure: The "mouth marines" and the hostage takers. *Negotiation Journal, 18,* 331–343.

Charles, L.L. (1999). A disarming conversation: Creating critical incident change in a crisis negotiation. *Dissertation Abstracts International, 62* (10A), 3341.

Charles, L.L. (2007). Disarming people with words: Strategies of interactional communication that crisis (hostage) negotiators share with systemic clinicians. *Journal of Marital & Family Therapy, 33,* 51–68.

Dalfonzo, V.A., and Romano, S.J. (2003). Negotiation position papers: A tool for crisis negotiations. *FBI Law Enforcement Bulletin, October,* 27–31.

DeBarnardo, C.R. (2004). The psychologist's role in hostage negotiations. *International Journal of Emergency Mental Health, 6,* 39–42.

De Fabrique, N., Romano, S.J., and Van Hasselt, V.B. (2007). Understanding Stockholm syndrome. *FBI Law Enforcement Bulletin, July,* 10–15.

Delprino, R.P., and Bahn, C. (1988). National survey of the extent and nature of psychological services in police departments. *Professional Psychology: Research and Practice, 19,* 421–425.

Discovery Channel (2001). *On the Inside: Hostage Negotiations.* Silver Spring, MD: Discovery Communications, Inc.

DiVasto, P.A. (1996). Negotiating with foreign language-speaking subjects. *FBI Law Enforcement Bulletin, 65,* 11–15.

Docherty, J.S. (1998). When the parties bring their gods to the table: Learning lessons from Waco. *Dissertation Abstracts International, 59,* 6115.

Dolnik, A. (2003). Contrasting dynamics of crisis negotiations: Barricade versus kidnapping incidents. *International Negotiation, 8,* 495–526.

Duffy, J.E. (1997). Situation boards. *FBI Law Enforcement Bulletin, June,* 17–19.

Feldman, T.B. (2004). The role of mental health consultants on hostage negotiation teams [Online]. *Psychiatric Times, XXI.* Retrieved April 11, 2008. Available: http://www.psychiatrictimes.com/show/Article.jhtml?articleID=59100159.

Fowler, R., Devivo, R.P., and Fowler, D.J. (1985). Analyzing police hostage negotiations: The verbal interactional analysis technique. *Emotional First Aid: A Journal of Crisis Intervention, 2,* 16–28.

FOX (2006). *Standoff.* New York: News Corporation.

Friedland, N. (1986). Hostage negotiations: Types, processes, outcomes. *Negotiation Journal, 2.*

Fuselier, G. (1981). A practical overview of hostage situations. *FBI Law Enforcement Bulletin, 50,* 5–12; *50,* 10–15.

Fuselier, G.D. (1988). Hostage negotiation consultant: Emerging role for the clinical psychologist. *Professional Psychology: Research and Practice, 19,* 175–179.

Fuselier, G.D., Van Zandt, C.R., and Lanceley, F.J. (1991). Hostage/barricade incidents: High-risk factors and the action criteria. *FBI Law Enforcement Bulletin, 60,* 6–12.

Fuselier, G. (1999). Placing the Stockholm syndrome in perspective. *FBI Law Enforcement Bulletin, July,* 22–25.

Gelbart, M. (1979). Psychological, personality and biographical variables related to success as a negotiator. *Dissertation Abstracts International, 39,* 4558-B.

Gettys, V.S, and Elam, J.D. (1988). Identifying characteristics of hostage negotiators, and using personality data to develop a selection model. In J. Reese and J. Horn (Eds.), *Police Psychology: Operational Assistance.* Washington, DC: Federal Bureau of Investigation.

Giebels, E., Noelanders, S., and Vervaeke, G. (2005). The hostage experience: Implications for negotiation strategies. *Clinical psychology and Psychotherapy, 12,* 241–253.

Greenstone, J.L. (1995). Tactics and negotiating techniques (TNT): The way of the past and the way of the future. In M.I. Kurke and E.M. Scrivner (Eds.), *Police Psychology into the 21st Century.* Hillsdale, NJ: Lawrence Erlbaum Associates.

Gruchacz, J.A. (1997). Crisis negotiator selection. *The International Journal of Police Negotiations and Crisis Management, 1,* 55–59.

Hacker, F.J. (1976). *Crusaders, Criminals, Crazies: Terror and Terrorism in Our Time.* New York: W.W. Norton & Co.

Hammer, M.R., Van Zandt, C.R., and Rogan, R.G. (1994). A crisis/hostage negotiation team profile. *FBI Law Enforcement Bulletin, April,* 8–11.

Hancerli, S. (2005). Toward successful negotiation strategies in hostage situations: Case study approach and future recommendations. *Masters Abstracts International, 44,* 1216.

Hatcher, C., Mohandie, K., Turner, J., and Gelles, M. G. (1998). The role of the psychologist in crisis/hostage negotiations. *Behavioral Sciences & the Law, 16*, 455–472.

Havassy, V. (1994). *The Psychologist as Part of the Negotiating Team.* Unpublished manuscript. Los Angeles, CA: Psychological Resources.

HBO (1997). *Dead Silence.* New York: Home Box Office, Inc.

Head, W.B. (1989). The hostage response: An examination of U.S. law enforcement practices concerning hostage incidents. *Dissertation Abstracts International, 50*, 4111.

Herndon, J.S. (1994). *Crisis Theory for Crisis Negotiators.* Orlando, FL: Orange County Sheriff's Office.

Herndon, J.S. (1996). *The Runner's Guide to Negotiations.* Orlando, FL: Orange County Sheriff's Office.

Herndon, J.S. (2000). *Cinema Portrayal of the Hostage Negotiator: Part Shrink, Part Psychic, Part Sage.* Presentation at the Florida Association of Hostage Negotiators, Orlando, Florida, May 25, 2000.

Herndon, J.S. (2001). *The Meadow Woods Incident: Inside the Hostage Negotiation Van and the Hostage Taker's Mind.* Presentation at the Texas Association of Hostage Negotiators, San Marcos, Texas, January 9, 2001.

Herndon, J.S. (2003). *Shrink in the Van: The psychologist's View of Crisis Negotiation.* Invited presentation, University of Central Florida psychology honors program, November 23, 2003.

Herndon, J.S. (2006). *Ten Years on a Hostage Negotiation Team: Insights from a Sheriff's Psychologist.* Presentation at the annual conference, Society for Police and Criminal Psychology, Bethesda, Maryland, October.

Hibler, N.S. (1984). *Hostage Situations: A Consultation Guide for Mental Health Professionals.* Washington, DC: U.S. Air Force Office of Special Investigations.

Hillman, R. (1981). The psychopathology of being held hostage. *American Journal of Psychiatry, 138*, 1193–1197.

Holmes, M.E. (1991). An interaction analysis of developmental phases in authentic and simulated negotiations between police and hostage-takers and barricaded suspects. *Dissertation Abstracts International, 52*, 2756.

James, R.K. (2008). *Crisis Intervention Strategies* (6th ed.). Belmont, CA: Thomson.

Johnson, T.A. (1978). A role for the behavioral scientist in hostage negotiation incidents. *Journal of Forensic Sciences, 23*, 797–803.

Keenan, G.J. (2007). The development of the empathic response in police crisis negotiators. Unpublished manuscript.

Kisthardt, A.M. (2000). Selecting hostage negotiators for the Pennsylvania State Police Special Emergency Response Team: An examination of methods of personnel selection. *Masters Abstracts International, 45*, 2946.

Lanceley, F.J. (1981). Antisocial personality as a hostage-taker. *Journal of Police Science and Administration, 9*, 28–34.

Lanceley, F.J. (1999). *On-Scene Guide for Crisis Negotiators.* Boca Raton, FL: CRC Press.

Lanceley, F.J. (2004). Negotiation lessons learned by an FBI hostage negotiator [Online]. *The Negotiator Magazine.* Available: http://www.negotiatormagazine.com/article235_1.html

Leary, E.R. (1980). *An Evaluation of the FBI's Hostage Negotiation Training Program.* Unpublished doctoral dissertation, George Mason University.

Lipetsker, A. (2004). Evaluating the hostage barricade database system (HOBAS). *Journal of Police Crisis Negotiations, 4.*

Louden, R.J. (1999). The structure and procedures of hostage/crisis negotiation units in United States police organizations. *Dissertation Abstracts International, 60*, 1338.

Magers, J.S. (2007). Crisis negotiation leadership: Making ethical decisions. *Journal of Police Crisis Negotiation, 7*, 5–25.

Maher, G.F. (1976). Organizing a team for hostage negotiations. *The Police Chief, 43,* 61–62.

Maksymchuk, A.F. (1982). Strategies for hostage-taking incidents. *The Police Chief, 49,* 58–65.

McClain, B.U., Callaghan, G.M., Madrigal, D.O., Unwin, G.A., and Castoreno, M. (2006). Communication patterns in hostage negotiations. *Journal of Police Crisis Negotiation, 6,* 27–59.

McGowan, H.M. (2004). Context, containment and conversation model: A study of the New York City Police Department's hostage and barricade resolution strategies. *Dissertation Abstract International, 65,* 1129.

McMains, M.J. (1988). Expanding the psychologist's role as a consultant to police departments hostage negotiations. *Journal of Police and Criminal Psychology, 4,* 2–8.

McMains, M.J. (1995). Developing teams for crisis negotiation. *Journal of Crisis Negotiation, 1,* 17–25.

McMains, M.J., and Mullins, W.C. (1996). *Crisis Negotiation: Managing Critical Incidents and Hostage Situations in Law Enforcement and Corrections.* Cincinnati, OH: Anderson Pub. Co.

Miller, L. (2007). Negotiating with mentally disordered hostage takers: Guiding principles and practical strategies. *Journal of Police Crisis Negotiation, 7,* 68–83.

Mohandie, K., and Duffy, J.E. (1999). Understanding subjects with paranoid schizophrenia. *FBI Law Enforcement Bulletin, December,* 8–16.

Mullins, W.C. (1995). Advanced communication techniques for hostage negotiators. *Journal of Crisis Negotiation, 1,* 7–15.

New York Times (March 22, 2005). Simon Eisdorfer, 87, who began the hostage unit, dies [Online]. Available: http://www.nytimes.com/2005/03/22/obituaries/22eisdorfer.html

Noesner, G.W. (1999). Negotiation concepts for commanders. *FBI Law Enforcement Bulletin, January,* 6–14.

Noesner, G.W., and Webster, M. (1997). Crisis intervention: Using active listening skills in negotiation. *FBI Law Enforcement Bulletin, August,* 13–19.

OCSO (1999). Special Order 15.0: Crisis Negotiation Team. Orlando, FL: Orange County Sheriff's Office. Effective April 13.

OCSO (2001). General Order 280: High Risks Incidents. Orlando, FL: Orange County Sheriff's Office. Dated April 23.

Olin, W.R., and Born, D.G. (1983). Behavioral approach to hostage situations. *FBI Law Enforcement Bulletin, 52,* 18–24.

Pearce, K.I. (1977). Police negotiations: A new role for the community psychiatrist. *Journal of the Canadian Psychiatric Association, 22,* 171–175.

Powell, J.O. (1989). Negotiation processes in hostage and barricaded incidents. *Dissertation Abstracts International, 50,* 3747.

Powitsky, R.J. (1979). The use and misuse of psychologists in a hostage situation. *The Police Chief, 46,* 30, 32–33.

Poythress, N.G. (1980). Assessment and prediction in the hostage situation: Optimizing the use of psychological data. *The Police Chief, 47,* 34–36, 38.

Ramesh, C.N. (1992). The influence of power on hostage negotiation outcomes: A contextual, descriptive, and fantasy-theme analysis. *Dissertation Abstracts International, 53,* 2163.

Regini, C. (2002). Crisis negotiation teams: Selection and training. *FBI Law Enforcement Bulletin, November,* 1–5.

Richardson, L.K. (1983). Communication strategies in barricade-hostage confrontations: Theory, research, and police experience. *Dissertation Abstracts International, 44,* 0322.

Rogan, R.G. (1990). An interaction analysis of negotiator and hostage-taker identity, goal, relational goal, and language intensity message behavior within hostage negotiations: A descriptive investigation of three negotiations. *Dissertation Abstracts International, 51,* 3957.

Rogan, R.G., and Hammer, M.R. (1995). Assessing message affect in crisis negotiations: An exploratory study. *Human Communication Research, 21*, 553–574.

Rogan, R.G., Hammer, M.R., and Van Zandt, C.R. (1994). Profiling crisis negotiation teams. *The Police Chief, 61*, 14–18.

Rogan, R.G., Hammer, M.R., and Van Zandt, C.R. (1997). *Dynamic Processes of Crisis Negotiation: Theory, Research, and Practice.* Westport, CT: Praeger.

Romano, S.J., Getz, V.L., and McCann, M.F. (Eds.) (1998). *Crisis Negotiation: A Compendium.* Washington, DC: Federal Bureau of Investigation.

Royce, T. (2005). The negotiator and the bomber: Analyzing the critical role of active listening in crisis negotiations. *Negotiation Journal, 21*, 5–25.

Schlossberg, H. (1978). [Book review] Crusaders, criminals, crazies: Terror and terrorism in our time. *Crime & Delinquency, 24*, 102–104.

Schlossberg, H. (1979). Police response to hostage situations. In J.T. O'Brien and M. Marcus (Eds.), *Crime and Justice in America.* Elmsford, NY: Pergamon Press.

Schlossberg, H. (1980). Values and organization in hostage and crisis negotiation teams. *Annals of the New York Academy of Sciences, 347*, 113–116.

Schlossberg, H., and Freeman, L. (1974). *Psychologist with a Gun.* New York: Coward, McCann & Geoghegan, Inc.

Slatkin, A. (1996). Enhancing negotiator training: Therapeutic communication. *FBI Law Enforcement Bulletin, 65*, 1–6.

Slatkin, A.A. (1997). *The Stockholm Syndrome and Situational Factors Related to its Development.* Doctoral dissertation, University of Louisville.

Slatkin, A.A. (2000). The role of the mental health consultant in hostage negotiations: Questions to ask during the incident phase. *The Police Chief, July*, 64–66.

Slatkin, A.A. (2003). Suicide risk and hostage/barricade situations involving older persons. *FBI Law Enforcement Bulletin, April*, 26–31.

Slatkin, A.A. (2005). *Communication in Crisis and Hostage Negotiations: Practical Communication Techniques, Stratagems, and Strategies for Law Enforcement, Corrections, and Emergency Service Personnel in Managing Critical Incidents.* Springfield, IL: Charles C Thomas.

Solomon, V.M. (1982). Hostage psychology and the Stockholm Syndrome: Captor, captive and captivity. *Dissertation Abstracts International, 43*, 1269.

Soskis, D.A., and Van Zandt, C.R. (1986). Hostage negotiation: Law enforcement's most effective nonlethal weapon. *Behavioral Sciences & the Law, 4*, 423–435.

Strentz, T. (1979). Law enforcement policies and ego defenses of the hostage. *FBI Law Enforcement Bulletin, 48*, 2–12.

Strentz, T. (1983). Inadequate personality as a hostage taker. *Journal of Police Science and Administration, 11*, 363–368.

Strentz, T. (1986a). Negotiating with the hostage-taker exhibiting paranoid schizophrenic symptoms. *Journal of Police Science and Administration, 14*, 12–16.

Strentz, T. (1986b). *An Evaluation of Two Training Programs Designed to Enable Hostages to Cope More Effectively with Captivity Stress.* Doctoral dissertation, Virginia Commonwealth University.

Strentz, T. (1995). The cyclic crisis negotiation time line. *Law and Order, March*, 73–76.

Strentz, T. (1996). Hostage/crisis negotiation: The socio-psychological traits of successful negotiators. *Law and Order, June*, 70–73.

Strentz, T. (1997). Understanding Waco and other disasters. *Law and Order, April*, 86–92.

Strentz, T. (2006). *Psychological Aspects of Crisis Negotiation.* Boca Raton, FL: CRC Press.

Tatar, M.A. (1982). The police personality and desirable qualities of hostage negotiators: An investigation of psychological dimensions and approaches to the assessment of state policemen who volunteer for training as hostage negotiators. *Dissertation Abstracts International, 43*, 2396.

Taylor, P.J. (2002). A cylindrical model of communication behaviors in crisis negotiations. *Human Communication Research, 28*, 7–48.

Terhune-Bickler, S.D. (2005). That wasn't supposed to happen: …crisis negotiators' responses to incidents that resulted in suicide. *Dissertation Abstracts International, 66*, 351.

Turner, J.T. (1989). Hostage-taking incidents: An organizational response. *Journal of Police and Criminal Psychology, 5*, 25–29.

Universal (2006). *Inside Man.* Universal City, CA: Universal Studios.

USA Network (2001). *Hostage Negotiator.* Hollywood, CA: Paramount Pictures.

Van Aelstyn, M.A. (2007). Crisis negotiation: An evaluation of perceived characteristics that facilitate the successful conclusion of crisis situations. *Dissertation Abstracts International, 68*.

Van Hasselt, V.B., Baker, M.T., Romano, S.J., Schlessinger, K.M., Zucker, M. Dragone, R., and Perera, A.L. (2006). Crisis (hostage) negotiation training: A preliminary evaluation of program efficacy. *Criminal Justice and Behavior, 33*, 56–69.

Van Hasselt, V.B., and Romano, S.J. (2004). Role-playing: A vital tool in crisis negotiation skills training. *FBI Law Enforcement Bulletin, February*, 12–17.

Van Hasselt, V.B., Romano, S.J., and Vecchi, G.M. (2008). Role playing: Applications in hostage and crisis negotiation skills training. *Behavior Modification, 32*, 248–263.

Van Zandt, C., and Paisner, D. (2006). *Facing Down Evil: Life on the Edge as a FBI Hostage Negotiator.* New York: G.P. Putnam's Sons.

Vecchi, G.M. (2002). Hostage/barricade management: A hidden conflict within law enforcement. *FBI Law Enforcement Bulletin, May*, 1–7.

Wardlaw, G. (1984). The psychologist's role in hostage negotiations. *The Police Chief, 51*, 56–58.

Warner Brothers (1998). *The Negotiator.* Burbank, CA: Warner Brothers, Inc.

Warner Home Video (1989). *Dog Day Afternoon.* Burbank, CA: Warner Brothers, Inc.

Wesselius, C.L., and DeSarno, J.V. (1983). The anatomy of a hostage situation. *Behavioral Sciences & the Law, 1*, 33–45.

Whittle, R.A. (1988). Hostage negotiations: A situational/motivational approach for police response. In M.J. Palmiotto (Ed.), *Critical Issues in Criminal Investigations* (2nd ed.). Cincinnati, OH: Anderson Pub. Co.

Wind, B.A. (1995). A guide to crisis negotiation. *FBI Law Enforcement Bulletin, October*, 7–11.

Zatwarnitski, T.A. (1998). Hostage negotiations: A survey of police negotiators trained at the Canadian Police College. *Dissertation Abstracts International, 59*, 6115.

INDEX

281